Jesus in Our Wombs

ETHNOGRAPHIC STUDIES IN SUBJECTIVITY

Tanya Luhrmann and Steven Parish, Editors

1. *Forget Colonialism? Sacrifice and the Art of Memory in Madagascar*, by Jennifer Cole

2. *Sensory Biographies: Lives and Deaths among Nepal's Yolmo Buddhists*, by Robert Desjarlais

3. *Culture and the Senses: Bodily Ways of Knowing in an African Community*, by Kathryn Linn Geurts

4. *Becoming Sinners: Christianity and Moral Torment in a Papua New Guinea Society*, by Joel Robbins

5. *Jesus in Our Wombs: Embodying Modernity in a Mexican Convent*, by Rebecca J. Lester

Jesus in Our Wombs

*Embodying Modernity
in a Mexican Convent*

Rebecca J. Lester

UNIVERSITY OF CALIFORNIA PRESS
Berkeley • Los Angeles • London

Epigraph: Simone Weil, *The Need for Roots*, trans.
Arthur Willis (1952. Reprint, New York: Putnam,
1995), p. 41. Reprinted with permission.

University of California Press
Berkeley and Los Angeles, California

University of California Press, Ltd.
London, England

© 2005 by The Regents of the University of California

Library of Congress Cataloging-in-Publication Data

Lester, Rebecca J., 1969–.
  Jesus in our wombs : embodying modernity in a
Mexican convent / Rebecca J. Lester.
      p.   cm. — (Ethnographic studies in subjectivity : 5)
  Includes bibliographical references and index.
  ISBN 0-520-24266-1 (cloth : alk. paper) —
  ISBN 0-520-24268-8 (pbk. : alk. paper)
    1. Monastic and religious life of women—Mexico—
Psychology.   2. Postulancy—Psychology.   3.
Women—Mexico—Social conditions—Psychological
aspects.   I. Title. II. Series.
BX4220.M4L47   2005
255'.9'00972—dc22   2004007652

Manufactured in the United States of America

13   12   11   10   09   08   07   06   05
10   9   8   7   6   5   4   3   2   1

Printed on Ecobook 50 containing a minimum 50%
post-consumer waste, processed chlorine free. The
balance contains virgin pulp, including 25% Forest
Stewardship Council Certified for no old-growth tree
cutting, processed either TCF or ECF. The sheet is
acid-free and meets the minimum requirements of
ANSI/NISO Z39.48—1992 (R 1997)
(*Permanence of Paper*).

For my parents

and

for Daegan

To be rooted is perhaps the most important and least recognized need of the human soul.

Simone Weil, *The Need for Roots*

Contents

List of Illustrations   xi

Acknowledgments   xiii

Introduction   1

PART ONE · *Contexts*

1. Female Bodies and the Touch of God   33

2. The Siervas   48

3. Religious Formation   65

PART TWO · *Becoming Women in Christ*

4. Brokenness: Restless in My Own Skin   95

5. Belonging: Sisters in Arms   111

6. Containment: Producing the Interior   132

7. Regimentation: Making the Mindful Body   161

8. Self-Critique: Diagnosing the Soul   180

9. Surrender: Turning It Over to God   193

10. Re/Collection: The Temporal Contours of the Self   210

11. Changing the Subject: Transformations   229

PART THREE · *Articulations*

12. Mexican Modernities   265

13. Bodies and Selves: Theorizing Embodiment   303

    Appendix: Glossary of Catholic Terms and
    Selected Central Prayers   309

    References   315

    Index   331

Illustrations

FIGURES

1. Temporal self and eternal soul   84
2. Convent floor plan, first floor   135
3. Convent floor plan, second floor   140
4. Convent floor plan, third floor   143
5. The therapeutic process   249
6. The therapeutic process and the dynamics
    of religious formation   253

TABLES

1. Demographic averages and ranges   9
2. Demographic numbers and percentages   10
3. Levels of religious formation   15
4. The pillars of formation   89

Acknowledgments

This book emerges out of long process of personal discovery and transformation and owes as much to the sustaining energy of others as to my own intellectual toil. It is my great pleasure to thank, first and foremost, Tanya Luhrmann, advisor of the dissertation upon which this book is based, and treasured mentor and friend. Her incisive intellectual guidance, coupled with an enthusiasm and belief in this project that filled in when mine faltered, was a driving force and an inspiration to me throughout this process. Many thanks, also, to Roy D'Andrade, Eric Van Young, James Holston, Charles Briggs, and Michael Meeker, who made up the remainder of my dissertation committee, and whose guidance has been invaluable. I owe a special debt of gratitude to Bruce Knauft, whose assistance on this and other projects has gone light-years above and beyond the call of duty, and whose high standards always push me to want to go that extra mile. Many thanks also to Richard Shweder, John Lucy, and Richard Taub at the Committee for Human Development at the University of Chicago, where significant elements of this book were hammered out while I held the National Institute of Mental Health's Postdoctoral Training Fellowship in Culture and Mental Health from 1999 to 2002.

I am grateful as well to the faculty at the Center for Religion and Psychotherapy of Chicago, where I completed a two-year specialization course in self psychology and religion. The intellectual stimulation and nurturing environment of the CRPC significantly shaped the theoretical framework of this book. I am particularly indebted to Lallene Rector for her assistance in this project.

I would like to offer special thanks to Eleonora Bartoli, Heather Lindkvist, and Aarti Pyati, for offering me the most unusual mixture of true friendship and intellectual challenge. It was in the context of our writing group that this book took shape. Thank you also to the students of my "Gender, Culture, and Madness" seminars at the University of Chicago and Washington University, whose stimulating questions about early formulations of this manuscript were extremely helpful. Many thanks to the students in my "Argumentation through Ethnography" seminar at Washington University. Their critical insights helped me enormously in the revising of this manuscript. I am grateful to Glen Marker for his support throughout my fieldwork (particularly those 5:00 A.M. walks to the convent) and during the write-up of the dissertation.

I would like to thank Stan Holwitz, my editor at the University of California Press, for his enthusiastic support and expert advice in the revision of the manuscript and Jacqueline Volin, Elisabeth Magnus, and Randy Heyman (also at UC Press) for their help in preparing the manuscript for production. I am very grateful to the reviewers of the original draft for their extremely helpful and constructive suggestions.

It is my pleasure to acknowledge the generous research support of the following: the Jacob K. Javits Memorial Fellowship, the Wenner-Gren Foundation for Anthropological Research, the Center for Iberian and Latin American Studies (University of California, San Diego), the Department of Anthropology (University of California, San Diego), and the Charlotte W. Newcombe Memorial Fellowship Dissertation Award.

On a more personal note, I would like to express my deep and enduring gratitude to my parents, Arthur and Linda Lester, whose love and support have gone too much unacknowledged over the years but never unappreciated. I could never have written this book without their unfailing encouragement. To the light of my life, Daegan, whose impending birth precipitated the finishing of the dissertation and who fills my life with a very special joy: thank you for the immeasurable gift of being your mom. I hope I don't screw it up too badly.

And finally, my deepest and warmest thanks to the Mexican sisters who so generously welcomed me into their lives and entrusted me with their stories. I hope this book speaks to the profound respect and friendship I feel for them. I will be forever grateful.

Introduction

Does a theory of the self require a theory of the body? If so, why? How might the systematic theorizing of an embodied self alter our understanding of subjectivity and social processes? This book is an account of how eighteen young women in a Mexican convent engaged in certain bodily practices with the explicit aim of reshaping their subjective experiences along a particular line of development. As such, it is a grounded engagement with current debates regarding embodiment and experience. But it is also an exploration of the ways in which gendered subjectivities may become politically and socially charged as a means of articulating cultural conflicts about modernity and how these larger meanings take on significance for people on the most intimately personal levels. Fundamentally, then, this book addresses the question of how we create meaning in our lives through embodied practice. I approach these issues within the context of a Roman Catholic convent in Puebla de los Ángeles, Mexico, a highly elaborated domain for the production of embodied self-knowledge.

PUEBLA DE LOS ÁNGELES, SEPTEMBER 3, 1994

At 4:45 A.M. the Grand Silence is compromised as eighteen sleepy young nuns tumble from their beds to recite the rising prayer in the cold darkness of the convent dormitory: "I pray, Lord, that you accept all my works, my thoughts, my emotions, and my desires as reparation for the many sins that will be committed today in this world. . . ." In the echo-ing silence following the prayer, thirty-six bare feet pad across the cold stone floor toward the showers. Arms and legs are scrubbed, faces washed, and teeth brushed in preparation for morning prayers. Hospital-like curtains are pulled around the small beds, and shadows play behind them as the young women slip on the various layers of the blue postu-lant uniform over white cotton undergarments and arrange delicate black veils carefully over their still-damp hair. In the cool, predawn blackness the young women file out of the dormitory, down two flights of stairs, across the patio, through a hallway, and into the chapel, where they will remain in concentrated meditation for the next two hours.

Another day has begun for the postulants of "the Siervas," a short-hand for the congregation's official name.[1] Unlike cloistered orders, which are devoted to prayer and contemplation, active-life orders like the Siervas view it as their mission to labor tirelessly and selflessly in the service of others, particularly those on the margins of society: the poor, the forgotten, the fallen souls. Every moment of every day the nuns mor-tify their bodies and their souls, their sacrifice a powerful force in the sal-vation of the world. They strive to become living testimonies of Christ's immeasurable love, and they hope that as His[2] brides, each will serve as a humble exemplar of how to be a woman in a world gone mad.

For many in Mexico today the world seems, indeed, to have gone mad. It is a world where politicians funnel eighty-four million dollars from the national coffers into Swiss bank accounts, where protesters sew their mouths closed with black nylon string in politically motivated hunger strikes, where students take to the streets in angry riots, and where policemen slaughter dozens of campesinos and hide their bodies in shallow graves. Divorces and homicides are up, literacy rates and education are down, and many young people seem more engaged with what's happening on *Friends* than in their own backyards.

But something curious is happening at the margins of the political turmoil and social upheaval. Each year scores of young women—more and more each year—are leaving the warmth and protection of their homes, leaving their friends, their families, their high schools and uni-versities, to march through the convent doors, where they will surrender

---

1. I will use this appellation when referring to the congregation, as well as pseudo-nyms throughout the book, to respect the privacy of the sisters.

2. I use the capitalized masculine pronouns *He, His,* and *Him* when referring to God and to Jesus to be consistent with the sisters' own representations.

themselves body and soul to Christ for eternity. The estimates are staggering.[3] But despite a general increase, one congregation—the Siervas—stands out, boasting a tripling of new entrants over the last fifteen years.[4]

What might motivate a young Mexican woman to become a nun at a time when a modernizing Mexico offers her so many new and exciting opportunities not open to women only a generation ago? What might a young woman's feeling of religious vocation tell us about changing constructions of womanhood and femininity in the wake of these social transformations? And what might account for the startling revival of interest in this particular congregation?

I spent eighteen months with the entering class of new Siervas during 1994–95. When I first went to the field I was concerned with trying to understand young women's motivations for entering a nunnery. I wanted to get a feel for what goes on emotionally, psychologically, and spiritually with these women as they try to decide if they should pledge themselves eternally to Christ and the church. I soon found, however, that the question I should be asking was not so much what brought the women to the convent. Most of these young women decided to enter the nunnery, I discovered, with only a vague understanding of what the religious life was or what to expect once they got there. The more interesting question, I realized, was what kept these women there, day after day. The year of the postulancy is a kind of trial period. The door is open. The postulants have taken no vows and, as they are continually reminded, are free to leave at any time. So what keeps them there, waking up at 4:45 in the morning to bathe with cold water and sit in silent prayer for two hours before breakfast? What keeps them there, working and studying, unable to make even small purchases, write a

3. Exact numbers are difficult to come by because some congregations count postulants and novices in their yearly reports and others restrict their numbers to sisters who have already professed either their temporary or perpetual vows. The increase noted here is based on my review of records at the Centro Inter-religioso de México in Mexico City and numbers reported in the *Statistical Yearbook of the Church* (Office of Church Statistics, 1984–94) and the *Catholic Almanac* (Foy and Avato, 1986–94), as well as on interviews I conducted with the vocations coordinators of several congregations, the director of the Office of Vocations in Puebla, and the Vatican liaison for vocational development in Mexico City. While there was not a clear consensus on the actual degree of increase in female vocations in Mexico in the past fifteen to twenty years (estimates ranged from 40 percent to more than 100 percent), all were strong in their feeling that there had been a marked rise, an interpretation borne out by my interrogation of church documents.

4. Based on records in the congregation archives to which I was generously granted access by the sisters.

letter, or make a phone call without permission from a superior? What keeps a woman there, knowing she will never again lead an independent life, will never have a home and a family of her own, but must instead remain poor, chaste, and obedient in the service of Christ or risk the eternal damnation of her immortal soul? Clearly, something more is going on for these women than a superficial infatuation with the idea of the religious life or a desire to take advantage of the economic resources the convent might offer to a poor girl from a Mexican pueblo. Something is going on in the convent that claims these women—something that makes the force of "the call" so irresistible that they willingly, and even joyfully, give up everything to follow it. I became interested in how, over the course of their first year in the convent, these new nuns moved from initially feeling unsure about their own motivations for entering the nunnery to experiencing this decision as reflecting an intimate, personal calling from God that they were compelled to answer.

THE ARGUMENT

I want to be clear that I am not interested in psychoanalyzing these women or discovering what deep-seated conflicts might have prompted them to give up sex and comfort for a life of bleak austerity and sacrifice. Rather, I propose an answer in terms of a transformation of subjectivity. In line with the arguments of Bordo (1993), Probyn (1993), and Luhrmann (1989), I saw that, through the engagement of the specific daily practices of convent life, new entrants to this congregation underwent a shift in sensibilities, perceptions, interpretations, dispositions, and memory—a transformation of subjectivity that the sisters understood as the progressively acute discernment of their true vocation according to God's plan.

My argument is that joining this particular congregation seemed to help these young postulants deal with tensions about being a woman in contemporary Mexico by offering them an alternative to two conflicting cultural models of femininity: the modern, upwardly mobile, techno-savvy, independent woman and the traditional, domestic, morally solid homemaker. The sisters understood the process of religious formation as reclaiming a submerged authentic femininity and then mobilizing that femininity to heal a world ravaged by violence and injustice. Through their religious training the postulants learned to experience religious vocation not only as a personal calling but as an urgent social and political obligation. It was this aspect of the program that seemed to be the most compelling for the women involved.

The transformation to a more authentic, politically engaged femininity in the convent centered on the new nun's coming to experience her body as a site of interaction among different existential domains. She had to learn to understand her experience of who she was when she entered the convent as illusory, grounded in the persuasions of the mundane world. She had to question all the things she thought she knew about herself and the world and to come to see them as partial and often contorted reflections of the truth. At the same time, she had to recognize that she had been called to play an important role in God's larger plan of salvation: that is, she had to understand herself as existing not only in the here and now but as an eternal soul that could be saved or damned and could lead others to salvation or perdition. Each postulant was schooled in how to experience her body as the medium through which these different aspects of self—the embodied, temporal self and the nonbodied, eternal soul—interacted and were made manifest. As she progressed in her training, she learned how to read her body—its sensations, inclinations, energies, temptations, frustrations—as indicators of how successfully she was managing this relationship between worldly and spiritual demands. She learned to view her body as the domain of negotiation between these two existential frames, a negotiation that became manifest in the very inclinations of her flesh.

As the initiates became progressively more adept at experiencing their bodies as mediating worldly and spiritual aspects of self, they were guided to understand this process as one of inhabiting a new and authentic femininity. In a May retreat on the Virgin Mary, for example, one month before they were to enter the novitiate, the mistress of postulants observed to the group that the ten months of the postulancy were like the months of pregnancy—that the postulants were, in a spiritual sense, gestating Jesus in their own wombs. They had become, in other words, simultaneously the daughters, brides, *and* mothers of Christ, orienting toward a spiritual rather than a physical model of femininity and reproduction. Learning to construct a meaningful new experience of body/self/soul that embraced—rather than denied—such paradoxes as they developed and changed over time was at the heart of the transformation these women underwent in their first year.

I do not, however, want to suggest that the postulants' motivations for entering this congregation were purely intrapsychic. Rather, it became clear to me from spending time with them that this intimate,

personal process of regendering in the convent proceeded in direct dialogue with concerns about modernization, political power, and cultural
change that were highlighted in the Mexican cultural arena. Specifically,
the postulants learned to understand their conflicts about femininity as
emblematic of a larger discomfort with modernity. Their engagements
with gender, then, entailed engagements with political and social discourses as well. In this way, the postulants' experiences in the convent
interarticulated with religious commitments on the one hand and with
broader secular cultural issues on the other. These issues became personally meaningful for the postulants as they were guided toward an
altered understanding of gendered subjectivity and its relationship to
the lived experience of the body. Gradually, initiates came to understand
their experiences of the call, and their choices as women in answering it,
as politically relevant declarations of self.

In sum, my argument rests on five fundamental propositions:

1. The convent philosophy overlaps with broader cultural concerns
    in Mexico about modernity, social change, and cultural identity.

2. Gender is one of the principal tropes through which these
    concerns are articulated, both within the convent and outside it.

3. Selves are always embodied. Embodied selves are always gendered.

4. Gender, then, operates on several different levels simultaneously—
    from the psychological to the political—though not necessarily
    in a systematic or coherent way. Indeed, gendered articulations
    at different levels can and frequently do come into conflict. The
    congregation's ethos "gets inside" the postulants—shapes their
    subjectivities—by engaging them as gendered beings, persuading
    them to feel personally committed to the congregation's
    philosophy.

5. The mechanism for this transformation is the performance of
    bodily practices that reconfigure the relationships among body,
    self, and soul.

RELIGIOUS VOCATION

The core language for articulating the compelling relationships among
personal, spiritual, and political concerns in the convent was that of
religious vocation. One morning, as we were scrubbing the breakfast
dishes, I asked Marta, one of the postulants, if she ever wished she could

just stay in bed until noon. She laughed at first but then became quite serious. "People think we have such a hard life," she said. "And it can be difficult sometimes. It's not easy, that's true. But they don't see the other side of it. The religious life is the most *beautiful* thing in the world! It's so amazing—it's hard to explain. But we're all here because we *want* to be here. We're here because we're in love with Christ and want to be with Him. We're following our vocation—it's that simple."

But while it may seem simple when phrased this way, the process of discovering one's vocation is, in fact, intensely emotional and complicated. The sisters (in line with the teachings of the Catholic Church) believe that all humans have been given a vocation by God. This does not mean that our lives are predestined or that we will necessarily follow a preordained life path. Rather, it means that since before we were born—indeed, since the creation of the world—God conceived of us in His mind and chose for us a path that is most propitious, both for us as individuals and for the bringing about of the Kingdom of God on earth and the salvation of all humankind. A vocation, then, is somewhat like a potentiality—the kind of life we *could* lead, the service to God and humankind we *could* give, if we were to conquer our selfish ambitions and humbly surrender ourselves to God's plan for us. But God, the sisters say, does not force us to obey. He has given us free will. We can elect, then, to follow God's calling, or we can ignore this calling and, by implication, work against the realization of God's plan. The first step, however, is to discern what that calling is. When Marta and the other postulants talked about their vocations, then, they were positioning themselves within this larger theological and existential context from which they could create meaning for their lives.

Whether or not we as outsiders recognize the objective "truth" of religious vocation, it is, without a doubt, very real for the women involved. Immortal souls are at stake. These young women come to the convent searching for meaning, seeking to discover what God is asking of them and whether they are up to the task. The outcome of this process is far from certain. Not everyone makes it through. Some people drop out. Some are asked to leave. Others thrive and become enormously content. I found that the sisters felt themselves to be on an intensely challenging voyage of discovery—of themselves and of God— that had its own developmental trajectory. Newcomers saw themselves (and were seen by the other nuns) as being at the very beginning of an awesome transformational process that would—if their vocations were genuine and their resolve strong enough—slowly change them from "worldly women" into "brides of Christ." This ethnography is an account of how these young women came to experience themselves as divinely called to join the Siervas and of their personal and spiritual transformations during their first year in the convent.

THE CLASS OF 2003

The popular image of nuns is that they are depersonalized beings, women who have surrendered their individuality and been reduced to the lowest common denominator of self through uniformity in dress, speech, act, and belief. While this is not entirely untrue, it is only part of the story. In fact, the sisters embrace their individuality—from Mother Miriam's signature red scarf during the winter to the black leather jacket Mother Carmelita likes to sport over her habit whenever the temperature dips below sixty degrees. Excessive eccentricity, of course, is frowned upon, but the sisters are in every sense "individuals"—women with their own histories and dreams, likes and dislikes, personality quirks and special gifts.

Accordingly, the sisters describe the progressive discernment and then fulfillment of their vocations within the order not as whittling away parts of the self to fit into a preset form of "nunliness" but as blossoming into this form. The preconvent self is seen not as too "big" for the demands of the nunnery, but as too "small"—a seed of a self as yet unrealized, as yet unconsecrated, as yet unsacred. Each new sister is seen as bringing to the convent her entire self, faults and all, which will serve as the springboard for her realization of God's plan for her. God, the sisters believe, calls women to the religious life *because of who they are, including* their imperfections. They should not question His will but only to try with all their might to become what He asks them to become. As I describe this process of "becoming" in the following chapters, it will be helpful to know a bit about these women and what they brought with them to the convent gates.

The autumn I began fieldwork with the Siervas, twenty young women had decided to join. This was quite a large incoming class, but not completely out of synch with the trend the congregation had been seeing in the past several years. Though it was seen as a blessing to have so many vocations, Mother Veronica, the mistress of postulants, confided to me toward the end of the year that having such a large group posed some particular difficulties in terms of group dynamics. This was perhaps complicated by some of the personalities

TABLE 1. Demographic Characteristics of Postulants:
Averages and Ranges

Item	Average	Range
Age	21.6 years	18 to 31 years
Age when first felt vocation	13.1 years	4 to 22 years
Number of children in family	7.5 children	4 to 14

in the group as well. The group was made up of the following young women:

Magda, age 18	Thea, age 19	Amelia, age 22
Rosita, age 18	Alicia, age 20	Clara, age 22
Celeste, age 19	Carlota, age 20	Abby, age 24
Dulce, age 19	Pauline, age 20	Carmen, age 29
Evelyn, age 19	Surella, age 20	Iris, age 30
Haydee, age 19	Mina, age 21	Ruth, age 31
Marta, age 19	Pipa, age 21	

I gathered life history information from the postulants through countless conversations and interviews over a period of eighteen months. I was able to collect specific biographical data on eighteen of the twenty women. Two of the postulants (Pipa and Pauline) left the congregation before the first year was over. Here I will present information on the remaining eighteen postulants, with whom I was able to double-check my information throughout the entire fieldwork period and in exit interviews. Tables 1 and 2 illustrate the general demographic data I retrieved.

Though these numbers are too small to draw any definite conclusions, we can tease out what seem to be some central themes. The information suggests that, generally speaking, the postulants were young adult women who came from relatively large families with strong Catholic roots. There seemed to be no significant trend in terms of class background, and the group was fairly evenly split between those who came from cities and those who had grown up in villages or small towns, although the majority of them were from the city of Puebla or surrounding areas.

A few aspects of these data, however, are particularly interesting and deserve special attention. First, the average age at which these women reported consciously feeling that they had been called to the religious

TABLE 2. Demographic Characteristics of Postulants:
Numbers and Percentages

Item	Number	Percentage
Had sibling(s) die in childhood	8	44.4
Postulant's position in birth order:		
Oldest		11.1
Second oldest		38.9
Middle		38.9
Youngest		11.1
Youngest female		50.0
Postulant's education level:		
Middle school	7	38.9
Trade school	1	5.5
High school	5	27.8
College/professional	5	27.8
Parents officially married in the Catholic Church?		
Yes	14	77.8
No	4	22.2
Parents deceased?		
Father deceased	3	16.7
Mother deceased	1	5.5
Both deceased	0	0.0
Both living	14	77.8
Place of origin:		
From Puebla or other large city	10	55.6
From village or small town	8	44.4
From Puebla metropolitan area	12	66.6
From neighboring area	6	33.3
Family socioeconomic status:		
Upper middle class (professional)	6	33.3
Middle class (trade/service industry)	6	33.3
Lower class (farmer, factory worker)	6	33.3
Mother's work history:		
Informal sector	2	11.1
Formal sector	1	5.6
Homemaker	15	83.3

life was 13.1 years. This could be significant in that this is the age at which young girls are often entering puberty and beginning their transition into womanhood. Second, while there seemed to be no consistent trend with regard to position in the sibling order, a full 50 percent of the postulants were the youngest daughters in their families. This is notable when we consider that in Mexico traditionally the youngest daughter is expected to remain at home and care for her parents rather than pursue her own marriage and/or career. Third, over one-quarter of the postulants had an education level ranging from completion of at least some college to attainment of a professional degree before entering the convent. This is remarkable, considering that over 18 percent of women in the state of Puebla are illiterate and that 37.7 percent of Poblana women either have never completed elementary school or have received no formal education at all (Instituto Nacional de Estadística, Geografía e Informática 2000). Finally, it is notable that 83.3 percent of the postulants came from families in which the mothers did not engage in any kind of work outside the home but rather confined themselves to domestic duties. The postulants were all young, ambitious, passionate women who wanted to work actively to better conditions in their country and in the world. As I developed close relationships with them over eighteen months, it became clear to me that they found the traditional models of female domesticity most of them grew up with to be inadequate for helping them navigate the contemporary pressures and demands of womanhood in a rapidly changing Mexican society. This factor is, I believe, vital for understanding these women's experience of religious vocation.

THE POLITICS OF FAITH

I argue that postulants' changing experiences of religious vocation during their first year in the convent become a means of articulating personal and political concerns about the consequences of "modernity." The understanding of modernity in which the postulants are schooled during their formation, while emphasizing selective elements, is not idiosyncratic to this order. It is a view that references larger debates going on in contemporary Mexico, debates about what it means to be Mexican, to be a woman, to be a good person. What is interesting about what goes on in the convent is how the postulants engage this view of modernity from a decidedly religiopolitical perspective and link it to their notions of what it means for them to pledge themselves, body and soul, to Christ.

The most important part of the postulants' education in these matters comes from the study of the history of the Siervas and the vision of its founder. The mission of this congregation, which was founded by a Mexican priest in 1885, enfolds a complex and clearly articulated social and political philosophy in which femininity and the actions of women are central. When woven together with the theological strictures of the Catholic Church and engaged within the context of Mexico's current social and political tensions, the congregation's philosophy seems to provide new nuns with a powerful impetus for a process of unself-conscious transformation of political subjectivity. The recent success of this order in attracting and keeping new entrants may have something to do with the parallel between a larger nationalist discourse targeting modernity (and Americanization in particular) as an evil force slowly eroding a utopianized "traditional" Mexico and the particular critique of the modern subjectivity set forth by the congregation's founder. In both views, modernization is coded as a foreign, masculine entity that first sweetly romances and then dominates and cruelly rapes the traditional female values of Mexican society. The main perpetrator of this violation, in this understanding, is the United States, a bully of a nation bent on forcing its consumer-capitalist ethos on its weaker neighbor to the south.[5]

The specific experiences of convent life in this congregation were set up by the founder to be technologies for the cultivation of a particular sort of subjectivity that would, if all went according to plan, become the catalyst for the regeneration of Mexican society and the salvation of humankind. In the founder's understanding, this subjectivity—this particular way of knowing, experiencing, being in, and relating to the world—was purposefully and undeniably female, Mexican, and Catholic, as defined against the "masculine" and "Protestant" values perceived to be foundational to American-style modernity.

The postulants enthusiastically engaged this key aspect of the congregation's teachings, which they encountered daily in the classroom, in lectures, in videos, and in conversations with Mother Veronica and other older sisters. As the year wore on, I began to notice that more and more the postulants' comments about women and modern life revealed an unusual mixture of feminist and traditionally Catholic interpretations that seemed to echo their founder's teachings. Comments about

5. For an orientation to the emerging nationalist discourses in Mexico, see Bartra (1992, 1993, 1994), Bonfíl Batalla (1990), and Escobedo Delgado (1988). This issue will be taken up in more detail in chapters 2 and 12.

the "superior" abilities of women to keep financial accounts and run organized businesses were coupled with observations about how these were God-given duties so women could be effective housewives. Discussions about the acuity of women's intuition and their proclivity for taking extenuating circumstances into consideration before making moral judgments were followed by warnings of how women's imaginations could run wild if not kept in check, making them prone to flights of fancy and to mistaking their own self-made fictions for fact. Observations about women's concerns for social justice (eliciting, on one occasion, cheers of "Mujeres! Mujeres!" [Women! Women!] from Celeste) were followed by disclaimers about how this, of course, did not mean women should forfeit their femininity. "A woman should be 100 percent woman—always" was a favorite saying in the convent.

This view of women and femininity also took center stage in the postulants' discussions of their vocations. At a retreat held on December 14, 1994, at the novitiate the postulants were given worksheets to help them think through issues facing women today. We broke into groups of two to discuss the readings, and Evelyn and I strolled out to the gazebo in the back of the novitiate near the cow pens to do the assignment. As we read through the points on the worksheets, Evelyn began to talk about how difficult it was for women to "be true to their essences" as women today and how this had influenced her decision to become a nun. "Women in the twentieth century don't live like Mary," she told me. "They have too much liberty. I saw a debate about abortion on TV last summer. Those women who call themselves prochoice think they can do whatever they want with their bodies. But it's not true. What they think of as 'liberty' is really preventing them from being free because they're slaves to what society is telling them they have to be. They're not being true to themselves as women, and this makes it impossible to follow the will of God." I asked her where she thought this "false" perception of liberty comes from. "From the media," she said, without hesitation.

> What do you see on TV? You see shows like *Baywatch* and *Beverly Hills 90210* and things like that. It's true that in the United States you are much more liberal, and you have a different understanding of what women should be than what we have here. And all of this comes here. And we Mexicans are so enamored with everything that comes from there. We can't get enough of American things! So we think our women have to be like yours. But this doesn't work here in Mexico. It's like taking clothes that don't fit you and putting them on. You end up looking ridiculous.

I asked Evelyn how she saw herself figuring into this situation. "Well, it's hard, you know?" she mused.

> It was hard for me on the outside, because everyone wants to be accepted, right? Everyone wants to be in style, to be popular. So you go along with what your friends want, no? You copy what you see on TV, you try to be cool. You do what your friends do, even if you know it isn't really right. And that's what I did. I went out to clubs all the time, wore short skirts, the whole thing. But it didn't feel right. I tried to ignore it, but I couldn't. I kept feeling that I was missing something, that I wanted more. That's when I began to think maybe I had a vocation. It took a long time for me to come to terms with the whole idea, but I started going to retreats and things, and finally, when I started to get involved with the Siervas, I felt like I was on the right track.

In the convent, the postulants learn how to reinterpret these feelings of not really "fitting in" as women in the outside world as the call from God to pursue a different, more authentic femininity. They are aided in coming to see their vocations to the Siervas as part of this larger struggle on the political as well as the religious front. I saw that as the postulants proceeded through the religious formation process in this congregation, their subjective experiences of their vocation seemed to change as they learned what it meant to be a "good Sierva" as defined in the order. They worked consciously to become the prototype of the curative subjectivity outlined by the founder and came to experience themselves as such, with varying degrees of success and difficulty. As this reshaping proceeded, I saw that the postulants' understanding of what it meant to have a vocation was reoriented as well, bringing it in line with the specific philosophy of the congregation as a template for the production of an "antimodern" feminine subjectivity. Over time, the postulants were gradually persuaded to experience joining the Siervas as a proactive moral and national obligation to which they had been especially called.

CHANGING SUBJECTS

In accordance with Catholic norms, the sisters call the transformational process of becoming a Sierva religious formation. The entire formational process lasts nine years from postulancy to the profession of perpetual vows, though this process is often extended by a year or more of involvement with the community before entry as a postulant (women in this stage are called aspirants). The general outline of the formation process is presented in table 3.

TABLE 3. Levels of Religious Formation

Level	Characteristics	Duration	Program Year
Aspirant	Living at home, deciding if want to enter convent and which congregation to choose.	1–5 years	Year 0
Postulant	Living in convent, first intense encounter with the religious life. Goal is to test feelings of vocation to see if they are genuine.	1 year	Year 1
Novice	Time of intense retreat in preparation for professing first temporary vows. Take the habit at the beginning of this stage. Live a cloistered life at the novitiate, on the outskirts of town.	2 years	Years 2–3
Junior Sister	Begins with the profession of temporary vows. "Internship" period where sisters are sent all over the world to live and work alongside perpetually professed sisters. Renewal of temporary vows at increasing intervals (1 year, 2 years, 3 years).	5 years	Years 4–8
Third Probation	Return to Central House for 1 year of intense retreat in preparation for professing perpetual vows.	1 year	Year 9
Profession	At the end of the third probation year, those sisters who wish to continue profess their perpetual vows.	Indefinite	Indefinite

Religious formation is, I learned, a process that is both cyclical and directional: as the postulants move along a particular line of development, they also replicate a pattern of discovery and discernment. Although the core elements of each formation stage are similar, the intensity and depth of the explorations gradually increase as a woman moves along the path of formation. Certain recurring themes, then, appear at different points—and with different intensities—throughout the nine years of formation. This dual cyclical/progressive organization of the formation process reflects the organization of time within the church itself (see Williams 1975) and becomes, as we will see in chapter 10,

a key element of subjective reorientation for the postulants as they negotiate their new identities as Siervas. Specifically, formation is a developmental process designed to create in new entrants an altered experience of
self as simultaneously rooted in the world and spiritually transcendent
and eternal. These apparently contradictory constructions of self are
brought together in the domain of the physical body and manifested in its
desires, inclinations, vulnerabilities, and triumphs. The goal of formation
in the convent is to help newcomers develop a particular sensitivity to
these processes and to come to experience them as the voice of God.

From my experience with the sisters, I suggest that there are seven key
elements in each cycle of formation and that each element entails and
builds upon the preceding while at the same time laying the foundation
for the next. These seven elements are (1) a recognition of a sense of *brokenness* within the self; (2) the search for a feeling of *belonging* to a community of other similarly "broken" selves; (3) the accommodation to
containment through the structuring of boundaries around and within
this community; (4) the *regimentation* of the body according to the
values and goals of the community; (5) an intense, unforgiving *self-
critique* to identify the cause of the self's brokenness; (6) *surrender* of the
personal will in the pursuit of wholeness; and (7) the *recollection* and
reordering of one's life through the lens of this altered experience of self.

These processes are not entirely discrete and there is a considerable
degree of overlap among them. Indeed, their division into seven distinct
"stages" is somewhat arbitrary—the sisters themselves do not talk
about the process in this way, at least not explicitly. These are not, in
other words, local terms, and this is not a local model (though the sisters certainly do acknowledge and talk about a developmental arc to the
process of change over the first year). Rather, my organization of the
first year of formation into these seven categories reflects what I
observed to be the practical consequences of the formation program as
the new nuns learned the skills needed in the convent. As the postulants
progressed through their first year, I saw that their attentions were
guided toward these different aspects of their formation at different
times and that later processes were predicated on their mastering earlier
ones. The themes and practices were introduced in a certain order but
once introduced remained important and underpinned the acquisition
of new skills. Here I am concerned with detailing this cycle—and the
relationships among its elements—as it manifests in the postulants' first
year in the convent, and how this in turn relates to the transformation
of subjectivity these women experienced.

In the first stage—Brokenness—entrants to the convent learn a new language for articulating psychic and social discomfort as perhaps representing "the call" from God. In this process, they are led to see themselves not as isolated individuals but as members in a select group of people who, like them, have been hand-picked by God for special service. The goal of this stage is to promote a specialized form of self/other recognition that involves, somewhat ironically, a heightened awareness of misrecognition of both self and others (as well as God) before entering the convent. As a result, these women talk about a sense of genuinely being seen for the first time in their lives and of coming to truly see others with new eyes—"God's eyes," as they call it.

As the young women officially enter the convent and become postulants, this sense of similarity and common cause leads them to establish intense emotional ties to each other and to the mistress of postulants, who oversees their formation at this level. This is the second stage in the process, Belonging. As the year proceeds, the sense of cohesion and identification is intensified and lays the foundation for the more difficult tasks the postulants encounter in their formation.

The third stage—Containment—involves a process of accommodation to the convent's complex hierarchy of inside/outside distinctions, ranging from the architecture of the building to the social interactions between the sisters to the management of the boundaries of the body. These techniques of enclosure—distinctions between various "insides" and "outsides"—function to highlight not only the qualitative differences between domains (between the convent and the world, between levels of formation, between cloistered and communal areas of the building, between the sisters themselves) but also the boundaries between these two realms as particularly significant foci for the articulation of power. It is at the edge of such boundaries that the convent—as an ideological apparatus—generates its meanings. I suggest that one of the principal consequences of this system is a privileging of "the interior space" (whether inside the convent walls or in the spirit of the person) as holding sacred potential.

The fourth stage—Regimentation—involves the rearticulation of these concerns with boundaries and interiority through the management of the body. As the postulants become habituated to the rigorous life of the convent, their bodies come to mediate between the interior sacred space of the soul and the exterior world of physical demands and temptations. Rather than flee the body in pursuit of a "pure" spiritual experience, however, the postulants learn to manage their physicality in such a way that the tension between the "soul" and the "body" is experienced without being resolved, where the discomfort and concerns of the physical body become a means of spiritual transformation.

Once the body has been successfully domesticated and then effectively mobilized, the focus turns to the fifth stage in the process, Self-Critique. In psychodynamic terms, we might think of this stage as an encounter with the Ultimate Other (for the nuns, God) and the systematic dismantling and reconfiguring of one's relationship to this Other. During this stage the postulants enter a period of intense internal critique, where they are guided to confront their own personal and spiritual failings in a harsh and unrelenting light. They learn that what they took to be a satisfactory relationship with God is, in fact, a betrayal of Him, due to their foregrounding of their own agency (a worldly orientation), even within their spiritual lives. Only when they have fully experienced the depth of their failings in their relationship with God are they thought to be prepared for the next stage of this process.

The remedy to this fractured bond with God, the postulants learn, is to cultivate the subjective orientation of *entrega*—an attitude of surrender and sacrifice that involves willfully turning over the self to God. This is the task of stage six—Surrender. *Entrega* is not a complete relinquishing of personal agency but a nuanced renegotiation of this agency characterized by the progressive externalizing of control and internalizing of responsibility. If the postulants are successful in negotiating this part of their formation, they come to experience a sense of release and comfort that stands in sharp contrast to their earlier feelings of guilt and pain for betraying God.

The seventh and final stage of this process—Recollection—involves the narrative (re)integration of the transformations achieved in the previous six stages within an altered developmental perspective of self. In this stage the "official" meanings of formation are more explicitly integrated into each woman's own personal history and experiences, as she literally re-collects bits of her life and orders them in a new way. For the postulants I worked with, I saw that this stage involved recasting and retelling their life stories from the perspective that they have been called by God and that their joining the Siervas at this historical juncture was meant to happen. Postulants reorder past experiences and rearticulate their subjectivity in terms of the transformational process they have undergone, which imparts to these experiences a sense of determinacy and significance that the sisters take to be divinely ordained.

A NEW WAY OF KNOWING

At the end of this process, the postulants experienced themselves to be significantly changed from their former selves. They described to me a palpable sense of transformation, a feeling of becoming someone new, someone sacred. This did not mean, I learned, that the old self had been obliterated but rather that this self had become mobilized along a different trajectory and was viewed through a new developmental lens. Through these seven stages—Brokenness, Belonging, Containment, Regimentation, Self-Critique, Surrender, and Recollection—the postulants underwent what I came to understand as a bodily transformation of their selves, a reformulation of their subjectivities that hinged on an altered phenomenology of their physicality. Their bodies were enlisted in the development of an alternative way of knowing.

For a young woman to stay in the congregation, she must come to believe, without question, that God has chosen her for this specific life, in this specific place, at this specific time. The sisters' concept of vocation is both existential and practical. Knowing one's vocation not only reinforces key religious and spiritual beliefs but also has very real implications for one's day-to-day existence. After all, discerning one's vocation often determines what a young woman will do with the rest of her life.

Only rarely does the knowledge of vocation come in the sort of lightening strike of revelation described by some of the more colorful Christian mystics. Usually, this knowledge grows slowly, over time, and amid much doubt and questioning. And almost never is a vocation that has not been tested against the harsh realities of the daily toil of the religious life seen as genuine. The sisters say that the knowledge of vocation is a very different kind of knowledge than we are accustomed to in our daily lives and thus that one must go about gaining it in very different ways.

"Knowing you have a vocation for the religious life is like knowing you're in love," Sister Margarita explained to me.

> You may have a vague sense that something's happening to you, but then one day you're like, "Wow! I'm really in love!" And that realization changes the way the world looks to you. The colors are brighter, the sun is warmer, all that sort of thing. And it changes your life. But if someone asked you [indicating me] *why* you love your boyfriend, you could give some reasons, like he's generous or smart or whatever. But a lot of people fit that description. You can't really put into words what it is that makes you *love* him—and *know* that you love him—in the way

that makes you want to spend the rest of your life with him. It's the
same thing for us, except we fall in love with Jesus and want to spend
the rest of our lives with *Him*. Finding your vocation is like that moment when it first hits you that you're really in love, and that it's forever.

And as in the case of human love, the sisters say, you cannot force a
vocation that was not meant to be. If a young woman has truly been
called to the religious life, she must come to this knowledge slowly, and
it must be gleaned from the sensations she feels, the way she performs
her work, her physical experiences in prayer, and her emotional attunement to the people and the world around her.

But the relationship with God is not like human relationships, in
which we often let things take their course ("If it's meant to be, things
will work themselves out"). The sisters engage in a number of activities
and practices designed to draw out the feeling of being in love with
God, to test it, challenge it, undermine it, validate it, and finally (if the
feeling remains) nurture it. As they progress through the seven stages of
transformation, newcomers to the order approach an altered phenomenology of embodiment that fundamentally shifts their experience of
self. Through living and working side by side with other women, they
learn new methods of perception and imagination that tie them to a
community of others whom they come to recognize as significantly similar to themselves in God's eyes. By managing their physical bodies they
develop a heightened sensitivity to interiorization as a process of bounding sacred potential and harnessing it for radical transformation. By
physically placing themselves in the service of authority, they come to
inhabit bodily the ideal of *entrega*. And they learn to retell and reinterpret the stories of their fleshy selves—their struggles and temptations,
difficulties and triumphs—as reflections of their changing relationship
with God. In this way, new entrants achieve a bodily transformation of
self that draws its meaning from a particular cultural and moral
universe.

VIRTUAL SELVES AND THE PROCESS OF TRANSFORMATION

I propose an understanding of this process of transformation that draws
on and integrates specific theoretical claims from psychoanalytic self
psychology, gender studies, anthropology, and embodiment theory.
Specifically, I argue that formation in the convent involves a threefold
dynamic: (1) selectively "mirroring" new entrants in different ways at
different stages of the process, reflecting back to them both who they

are at any given moment (what I call their "experiential selves") as well as who they are striving to become as good Siervas (what I call their "virtual selves"); (2) enabling them to recognize with increasing precision the disconnects between their experiential and virtual selves and to engage in specific convent practices that gradually weave these selves together in a personalized understanding of their vocations; and (3) progressively incorporating (both psychologically and, literally, into the body) this new sense of being as fundamental to how they experience and live in the world. In this way, newcomers to the convent gradually learn not only to "read" themselves through praise or disapproval from the older nuns and their peers about their attitudes and behaviors but also (and more importantly) to develop strategies for making themselves authentically recognizable as "good Siervas" in the eyes of the congregation and, they hope, of God.

We might think of formation in the convent as something like walking through a carnival house of mirrors—as one walks along, turns corners, moves back, or moves forward, different perspectives of oneself are reflected in different ways and interact with each other in relatively predictable patterns, based on the positioning of the mirrors in relation to one another and to one's own body. While each person who walks through the same house of mirrors may meet a similar pattern of reflections, the reflections themselves are different for each person. They can also be manipulated by what one does—raising an arm, making a face, sitting down. In other words, the structure and patterns of reflection are objectively present but can be engaged differently on the basis of the characteristics, actions, and intentions of the person herself in relation to these structures.

This metaphor begins to capture something of how I think of religious formation in the convent. But it goes only so far in thinking about the formation process, and it is here that the work of theorists such as Kohut (Kohut 1971, 1977; Kohut, Goldberg, and Stepansky 1984) on self psychology and Benjamin (1988, 1995, 1998) on intersubjectivity become useful. Mirrors unproblematically reflect what is placed in front of them. Though images can be distorted or manipulated if the mirror is concave or convex, a mirror has no personal stake in the process of reflecting or in what the subject makes of his or her reflection, and the scientific principles involved (the reflection of light, etc.) remain unaffected by the subject's feelings about them. In the convent, however, the "mirrors" involved are human mirrors, subjects in their own right who have personal motives, specific intentions, blind spots, and powerful emotions. Thus the mirroring they provide for the new nuns is necessarily partial, subjective, and pointedly interested. Further, it is directly affected by the way the postulants themselves accept, reject, challenge, or elicit aspects of this mirroring. In other words, formation in the convent is an intersubjective process, unfolding within a highly structured institutional environment that shapes (but does not entirely dictate) the terms of these relationships.

In exploring this dynamic, my work differs from some of the more well-known accounts of institutional life and subject formation. Goffman (1961), for example, wrote about "total institutions" (such as prisons, hospitals, and mental asylums that dictate and control every aspect of inmates' lives), analyzing how such entities cultivate specific subject positions and moral orientations in their subjects. He proposed that the all-encompassing character of such settings forces inmates to accept a revised model of reality and, consequently, to learn new strategies for thinking about themselves as part of that reality. Foucault (1973, 1977, 1979), too, was concerned with the production of subjectivities in institutional settings. He argued that the point of leverage for institutional power is the nexus between desire and the body, and he suggested that by figuring and working on the body in particular ways (for example, via the panopticon), institutions come to hold a certain purchase over the domain of desire and hence subjectivity. Asad (1993) has written specifically on the production of subjects within religious settings. His primary concern is with the use of techniques of asceticism and bodily discipline as the avenue through which institutional priorities become individual ones, gradually producing willing subjects of transformation.

Each of these perspectives is compelling, and each contributes important tools for thinking about what I observed in the convent. But at the same time I find them to be limited in terms of understanding the process of formation for the Siervas. The women who come to the convent are young adults with their own unique subjectivities, which they must learn to alter in specific ways in order to continue successfully in the congregation. This subject (re)formation proceeds within a highly specialized context, with certain beliefs, practices, and values that are explicitly different from (yet are in constant dialogue with) those in the outside world and that each initiate must come to internalize as her own. Moreover, this process is facilitated by other women who are themselves distinctly interested participants in the process. Given this, I feel that a simple top-down account of how the convent program inculcates new initiates would provide only part of the story. What is needed is a model of subject formation that both recognizes and takes seriously the distinct subjective experiences of all the participants (the postulants themselves as well as others around them) while at the same time attending to the specific cultural and moral content of this process and how it positions the "new" subjects in relation to existing understandings and categories. In other words, I am interested in how people's lived subjectivities relate to the subject positions they occupy and how, through intersubjective processes like mirroring, these two elements can come to correspond, but always in ways marked by the idiosyncratic features people bring to them.

One of the principal aims of this book, then, is to explore the subtle and complex dynamic of subject formation within the convent as an intersubjective process rooted in particular cultural and moral understandings. This ethnographic argument, in turn, speaks to my main theoretical argument: we cannot adequately theorize about subject formation without simultaneously theorizing processes of gendering and dynamics of embodiment. And to talk about these three processes together, we need a model for thinking about the interarticulation of cultural and psychological processes in a multisubjective social context without falling into the theoretical vortex of extreme relativism. This book sketches the outlines of such a model.

INNER SPACE: FIELDWORK IN A CONVENT

I came to do fieldwork in a convent by a rather circuitous route. I began my graduate studies in 1991 fascinated by eating disorders—debilitating diseases where young women slowly, methodically, and sometimes successfully starve themselves to death. Anorexia is a notoriously intransigent illness, largely because the women who suffer from it cling passionately—desperately—to their disordered eating behaviors, claiming that only in denying themselves the most basic nurturance do they feel liberated and alive.

As an anthropologist, I became intrigued by the ritualistic aspects of anorexic food behaviors—meticulously chopping food before eating it; eating only at certain times, in certain places, at a certain pace; using special plates or utensils for meals. I wondered how these activities (which seem to revolve around issues of purity and pollution) might relate to the self-project many anorexic women themselves describe as spiritual or existential. In my first year of graduate school I began working in an eating disorders clinic, and the following year I wrote my master's thesis on anorexia nervosa as a contemporary ascetic practice.

During this time, I also pursued further training in psychiatric diagnosis and psychotherapeutic techniques. As part of the psychiatry and anthropology program at the University of California in San Diego, I attended classes with first-year psychiatry residents and learned about a whole range of issues, from conducting a mental status exam to differential diagnosis to the neurochemistry of different psychiatric medications. Following this year of instruction, I was permitted, along with the psychiatry residents, to begin psychotherapy training at the university's training clinic near downtown San Diego. I was supervised by a licensed therapist and saw patients part time for approximately sixteen months.

While researching anorexia, I became acquainted with the historical literature on medieval ascetic nuns. There is an active academic debate about whether these women were anorexic in the contemporary psychiatric sense. Describing what he terms "holy anorexia," Bell (1985) makes a psychological argument: he interprets life histories and hagiographical documents as clearly indicating that women such as Catherine of Siena and Teresa of Ávila did indeed suffer from the syndromes we now call anorexia and bulimia. Bynum (1987), on the other hand, makes an essentially cultural argument: she maintains that medieval ascetic women were *not* anorexics and bulimics because they expressed and experienced their behaviors through a religious medium and made union with Christ, not thinness, the goal of their food practices. I found this debate both riveting and inspiring. But despite the extensive literature on medieval women's mysticism, I found that there were no solid ethnographic accounts of how religious women themselves might understand their self-denying behaviors. I wanted to find out.

Taking my cue from the historical literature, I set out in 1994 to study the contemporary analogues of these medieval fasting nuns. I decided to locate the research in Mexico, an overwhelmingly Catholic country, and I settled on the city of Puebla de los Ángeles after learning that Puebla has traditionally been the country's center of female monastic life. I arranged to affiliate myself with an incoming group of nuns in an active-life congregation based in the city (the Siervas) and to accompany these postulants through their first year of religious formation.

I arrived in Puebla expecting to find frail, depleted nuns who wished to escape their bodies, disciplined women who saw their materiality as an impediment to saintliness. I didn't. Most of the sisters, in fact, were plump and were enthusiastic eaters. With a few notable exceptions, they seemed to have unremarkably normal relationships to food.

I found something else unexpected as well. As I have noted, I quickly learned that the sense of religious vocation was far from clear to these women when they first walked through the convent gates. Most of them came to the convent with not much more than a vague, undefined sense that they were somehow "supposed" to be there. During the first year this inkling was subject to constant scrutiny and testing, both from the women themselves and from the congregation as an institution. The postulants anxiously looked for any sign—no matter how small—that their vocations were genuine. At the same time, they were wary of their own senses of calling, and they relied on outside validation from their superiors as to whether their experiences were "real."

I did not, therefore, find the kind of focused, premeditated self-denial and body discipline I had anticipated. Rather, what I observed was something much more subtle. I did find a conflict around gender to be central for the nuns I worked with, and, as I will explore in the chapter 12, these concerns did seem to share some features with those expressed by women with eating disorders. But the nuns were concerned not with the thinness of their bodies but with the state of their souls. And their project of transformation was not only a personal quest for existential resolution or wholeness but a mission for the restoration of the Mexican nation. The salience of discourses of modernity and cultural identity in the convent and the centrality of these concepts to how the postulants understood their own religious and personal commitments were unexpected findings, requiring me to reconceptualize central aspects of the original research plan. I became somewhat less interested in what motivated these women to join the convent in the first place and more interested in how they were transformed once they got there.

During my fieldwork I had access to all members of the community and all areas of the convent (except the private sleeping quarters of the professed sisters), but I spent most of my time with the postulants, and my schedule was determined by theirs. The days in the convent are long and are packed with activities carefully orchestrated to ensure the proper formation of the sisters. A typical day for the postulants looked something like this:

A.M.

4:45	Wake up, shower, dress
5:30–6:30	Morning prayer
6:30–6:45	Lauds
6:45–7:30	Mass
7:30–8:00	Breakfast
8:00–8:15	Visit to the Eucharist
8:15–9:30	Morning chores
9:30–11:00	Class with the mistress of postulants
11:00–11:30	Adoration of the Eucharist
11:30–12:30	Class with the mistress of postulants

P.M.

12:30–12:40	Examination of conscience
12:40–1:15	The midday meal
1:15–1:30	Visit to the Eucharist
1:15–2:30	Afternoon chores
2:30–3:30	Recreation time
3:30–5:00	First afternoon class
5:00–5:45	Second afternoon class
5:45–6:10	Rosary
6:10–6:20	Vespers
6:20–6:30	Examination of conscience
6:30–7:00	Dinner
7:00–7:15	Visit to the Eucharist
7:15–8:00	Evening chores
8:00–8:30	Recreation
8:30–9:00	Compline
9:00–9:30	Silent reflection
9:30	Lights out

I did not live at the convent, though the sisters invited me to. I thought it important not to limit my experience of Mexico or of Mexican women to the Siervas but to become part of the larger community in Puebla. Along with my work in the convent, then, I became integrated into the local neighborhood, community, and university networks and built friendships with men and women from all walks of Mexican life. I lived with a Mexican family for a time, had my own apartment for several months, and lived with a single mother pursuing a college degree for another period of time. I usually arrived at the convent at 5:30 A.M. and stayed until 6:00 or so in the evening. On many occasions I stayed later.

As I was interested in studying the motivations for joining a convent and the experience of religious formation, attaching myself to an incoming class of postulants was ideal because it allowed me to be party to the intriguing transformation of these young women as they moved gradually from being "outsiders" like me to being "good nuns." I saw the unfolding of the mysteries of the religious life through their eyes and shared with them the exhilaration, fears, anxieties, joys, and frustrations of the sacrifices they were making. I moved fluidly among the roles of student, friend, naive buffoon, counselor, butt of jokes, and shoulder to cry on. These women were convinced that they were part of an awesome project of both social and spiritual regeneration, and I was able to share with them the beginning of their journey.

But the fieldwork posed particular difficulties not routinely encountered in other field contexts. Despite the hospitality and warmth of most of the sisters, my research proceeded in what was effectively their home, their private space, which was not normally opened to outsiders. There was no "public" place where I could inconspicuously hang out and watch the goings on of the convent. Unlike a bustling village square or a dynamic corporate headquarters, convents are characterized by structure, silence, and formality. Every second of the postulants' day was planned, structured, accounted for. "Your life belongs to God now," the mistress of postulants used to say. "If you waste time, it's God's time you're wasting." The days were filled with prayer, meditation, classes, study, meals, and brief periods of recreation. I was included in all. But my conversations with the women were limited, at least in the beginning, to stolen moments between activities, passed notes during classes, the rare meal where talking was permitted, and recreational periods.

I took scattered notes in a pocket-size notebook and wrote up my field notes in the evening or early the next morning. I did not tape-record any conversations with the postulants until the end of the research, when the mistress of novices (the remaining postulants had passed on to the next level of training by that time) kindly allowed me to disrupt their busy schedule for final interviews. I scheduled other taped interviews with various other individuals primarily in the last four months of my fieldwork. Fortunately, many lively and important discussions took place in the classroom, where I could inconspicuously record in my notebook, almost verbatim, what was being said. Many of the direct quotes in this book come from these exchanges.

Another difficulty was that I was, most definitely—in my dress, my speech, my beliefs, and my coloring—an outsider, an intruder in their cloistered halls. While this is a common situation for anthropologists in all kinds of field settings, the particular context of the convent made certain aspects of this difference particularly significant. I am not Catholic. I was raised Jewish. Initially, I was concerned that this might pose a problem for the research, but it proved to be an advantage. I am, of course, not baptized, and the nuns would have much preferred—for my own sake—that I had been so. But the sisters hold great affection for the Jewish people, whom they recognize as God's Chosen People to whom the Savior was born. They talked explicitly and often about the connections between Judaism and Catholicism. "Jesus was a Jew and Our Mother Mary was a Jew!" Mother Lynette told me one day. "The Jews and the Catholics are very close, and we respect and love the Jews as God's Chosen." In short, the sisters tend to view Jews as good, holy people who have gotten everything "right" aside from not accepting Jesus as the Messiah. This, they maintain, can be rectified.

This puts the Jews in a completely different category from the Protestants, who, in the sisters' view, have perverted the teachings of Jesus to meet their own ends. It is one thing to not accept Jesus as the Messiah. It is quite another, the sisters say, to profess this acceptance and yet to promote heretical understandings of what it means. This hostility toward Protestantism on theological grounds is exacerbated in Mexico by the fact that thousands of Protestant missionaries enter the country each year, evangelizing primarily in the rural areas. The sisters, like many other Mexican Catholics, view this as a direct and calculated assault on Catholicism and on traditional Mexican values. I seriously doubt that I would have been allowed to conduct the research had I been raised Protestant.

As a Jew, then, I was in something of a special category in the congregation. I was not expected to have much understanding of church doctrine or practice, so I could ask even the most basic questions without fear of embarrassment or disapproval. I was not expected to believe in the teachings of the church or to profess the Catholic faith. Nor was I seen as a threat in the sense of having any personal or religious interest in undermining the teachings of the church or misrepresenting what I learned in the convent. But though I came to be accepted by the sisters and integrated into the "family" of the congregation in many ways,

I was not, and never could be, an insider in the complete sense, particularly in this most intimate domain of faith.

The research was concentrated in the Central House of a particular congregation, but my contact with this world reached much wider. As news of my research interests spread, I was quickly adopted by the religious community of the city and came to know many of the priests, nuns, seminarians and missionaries in the area. I visited dozens of convents, seminaries, and churches all over the city and state. I attended perhaps three hundred masses, went on missions, sang in Christmas plays, joined vocational retreats, and participated in spiritual exercises. I sat through hundreds of classes in theology and meditation and prayer. Gradually, this world of crosses and candles, incense and whispered silences became more intelligible to me.

Slowly but surely, the sisters let me in, allowing me to experience with them all the highs and lows of the community life, from the intense emotionality of religious retreats and almost giddy excitement of holiday celebrations to the tensions of internal political wranglings and the anxiety and fear that come when a vocation seems shaky. As the research progressed, I, like the postulants, became more skillful at navigating this world populated by subtlety and innuendo, whispers and meaningful glances and the power of the unseen.

ORGANIZATION OF THE BOOK

The book is organized into three parts. Part 1 frames the ethnography by outlining the theoretical questions that shape the study and describing the historical and social context in which the postulants engaged in their process of religious formation. In chapter 1, I situate the ethnography within a larger literature on embodiment and experience and highlight some of the themes that will play a central role in the ethnography as it unfolds. In chapter 2, I sketch the history and political commitments of the congregation, its investment in a particular vision of Mexican national identity, and the location of the order in contemporary debates on social and religious fronts. Chapter 3 considers the structural process of religious formation as a transformational program designed to produce proper subjects who will carry on the work of the congregation in these domains.

Part 2 turns to the process of transformation itself, with one chapter dedicated to each of the seven stages discussed: Brokenness (chapter 4), Belonging (chapter 5); Containment (chapter 6); Regimentation (chapter 7), Self-Critique (chapter 8), Surrender (chapter 9), and Recollection (chapter 10). Chapter 11 is a theoretical consideration of the psychological and social mechanisms at play in this process.

Part 3 extends these analyses beyond the convent walls. Chapter 12 mobilizes the ethnographic specificity of part 2 in dialogue with the current literature on the elaborations of multiple modernities through discourses of religion. Here, I consider the postulants' experiences in the convent as part of a larger nationalist debate in Mexico that centers on concerns about gender and "progress." In chapter 13, I reconsider the fundamental problematic of theorizing an embodied self and offer a provisional model for approaching questions of embodiment and subjectivity.

PART ONE

Contexts

CHAPTER I

Female Bodies and the Touch of God

In medieval Europe, nunneries like the one I spent time in were believed to be special crucibles for the struggle between good and evil, a savage war waged in and through the medium of female flesh. From inside convent walls, religious women such as Catherine of Siena, Teresa of Ávila, Julian of Norwich, and Clare of Assisi reported startling bodily experiences, from levitation to stigmata to surviving on nothing but the Eucharist. The experiences of these women, though enchanting to laypeople, who sometimes traveled hundreds of miles on pilgrimage to pray outside the convents, posed a troubling conundrum for the church. These graphic bodily manifestations seemed to affirm the notion that women were more "material" in their natures than men, more closely attached to the body, and more susceptible to physical temptation (supernatural or otherwise). But these miraculous experiences also posed the dangerous possibility that such physicality might provide a more direct experience of God than the male-mediated sacraments. So while some in the church viewed these women's fasting, bleeding, levitating, and raptures as concrete signs of God's grace and favor, others decried them as spectacles sent by the devil to lure people away from the authority of the church. In both cases, the issue at hand was how to make sense of female bodies that did not behave as expected.

Even today, the question of what was really happening to these medieval women is the subject of heated academic and theological debate. One reason that these medieval female ascetics have so long intrigued scholars of religion and psychology is, perhaps, that their experiences seem to reference a complex theology of embodiment. Indeed, concerns about bodies are at the heart of Catholic doctrine and practice. Theologically, the physicality of the human body of Jesus is the cornerstone of the church's teachings. Jesus is believed to have been simultaneously 100 percent human and 100 percent divine, the paradox of this nature being itself evidence of God's omnipotence. Salvation came to humans, according to the faith, precisely in and through the intense physical suffering Jesus experienced in the passion and crucifixion. Graphic representations of this suffering are pervasive in Catholic iconography. Further proof of Christ's divine nature is sought in the doctrine of the resurrection, the belief that on the third day after His death, Jesus' body was reanimated and transported to heaven, later to appear in glorious (nonbodied) form to His disciples. These physical elements of the passion, crucifixion, and resurrection, known as the paschal mystery, are reenacted in the Mass, in which the church asserts that the wafer and wine literally become the body and blood of Christ, to be consumed by the faithful—incorporated into their own living bodies.

Other bodies are similarly central to Catholic theology. The doctrines of the perpetual virginity of Mary and her bodily assumption into heaven hold very special significance in Catholic teachings. Relics of saints—pieces of human bone, skin, or hair—are treated with reverence and are believed to hold special power, particularly if the saint died as a martyr, enduring excruciating physical suffering for the love of God. The faithful, it is believed, will be resurrected in their human forms at the Second Coming, so the cremation of corpses is strongly discouraged.

Taken together, these particular articles of faith set Catholicism apart from other forms of Christianity, and indeed conflicts over these sorts of beliefs frequently instigated the splitting of various Protestant religious movements from the Catholic Church. It would be reasonable to suggest that in many ways Catholicism is, at its core, a theology of bodies.

The body is also a central concern in Catholic practice, with the bodily dimensions of sin given particular importance. Catholicism, more than other forms of Christianity, is concerned with human sexuality as a potentially dangerous force to be carefully controlled. Premarital and extramarital sex are deemed mortal sins, as is masturbation. Birth control and abortion are prohibited. No one but God, the church contends, should decide when to create—or to destroy—a human life. The sanctity of this life is evident, according to Catholic teachings, in the integrity and purity of the human body as the perfect manifestation of God's image in the flesh. As specialists in the faith, Catholic priests and nuns must give particular attention to the maintenance of bodily purity by removing themselves physically from the world and remaining celibate in their service to the church.

The body, then, has multiple meanings in Catholicism. It is the jailer of the soul, the vehicle of sin. It attaches the soul to the world, placing it in constant peril of being led into damnation. The body is temptation, the flesh weak and easily corrupted. But the body can also be an instrument of purification of the soul. The desires and impulses of the body can be harnessed and redirected so that the experience of physical need can itself become a prayerful practice. "We make a ladder of our vices," Augustine (2002) wrote, "if we trample those same vices underfoot." The concern in Catholicism, then, is not merely with the physical body but also with the body as vehicle of the senses, as a link between our interior lives and the world around us. And because the body marks this boundary between the inside and the outside, it is elaborated as simultaneously a source of power and an arena of danger.

It was precisely because of this ambivalence about the body that the experiences of medieval female ascetics were so troubling to the church. Though issues of the body had been central to Catholic theology for centuries, the regulation and monitoring of bodily experience within the religious life became one of the church's principal concerns during the medieval period. Bodily experience was (and still is) considered to be of particular importance when dealing with young women, who are held by the church to be especially prone to somatization and imaginative exaggeration. Strictures regarding eating, sleeping, dress, comportment, styles of prayer, manual labor, and contact with the outside world took center stage in the management of female monastic communities during this period in ways not nearly so pronounced in male communities (Bynum 1987).

Though the church has undergone substantial changes in the past six centuries, teachings about the body still form the core of Catholic theology. And, as recent scandals within the Catholic Church make glaringly clear, understandings of sexuality and gender in particular continue to constitute a key part of these beliefs. A concern with experiencing—and then controlling—proper desires within the physical body remains paramount.

Control and regulation of the body—in the convent or elsewhere—is contingent upon a particular understanding of what the body is and what bodily practices can (and cannot) achieve. Foucault (1977, 1979, [1985] 1986, [1986] 1988) and Asad (1993), among others (for example, Mahmood 2001; Beduhn 2002; Hollywood 2002; Glucklich 2001), have described how body discipline can be mobilized in religious and other kinds of communities as technologies of control and the institutionalization of desire. Indeed, this view of body discipline first sparked my interest in doing an ethnography of a contemporary convent.

I did not find among the Siervas (or any of the other dozen or so congregations I had contact with) the kinds of extreme asceticism reported in medieval accounts. What I did find, though, was more interesting—a less overt but equally charged use of body discipline across domains of experience and practice. As an active-life order, the Siervas cannot live by a simple deny-the-body philosophy. Their work is physically strenuous, and it requires great reserves of energy and stamina. The sisters run day and boarding schools, geriatric care homes, and missionizing centers throughout Latin America and Africa. They work as teachers, nurses, and caregivers, in addition to staffing and maintaining all of the order's buildings and farmland. Blisters, calluses, scrapes and bruises, and sore muscles are par for the course as the sisters lift, carry, pour, wash, scrub, cook, milk the cows, and care for children and the elderly. New entrants to the order, then, quickly lose any romantic notions they may have had of escaping their physicality in pursuit of a loftier, ephemeral spiritual union with God. Rather, they must learn how to balance the care of the body with the care of the soul. They must understand that these two endeavors are not mutually exclusive but reciprocal and complementary.

The forms of body discipline I observed in the convent, then, were much subtler, much more nuanced than rigorous fasting, wearing of hair shirts, or painful flagellation. As micropractices of discipline and control they are arguably more effective in the alteration of internal experience than extreme (but less frequent) disciplinary tactics, functioning together in what we might call an aesthetics of embodiment. They focus not so much on radically depriving or punishing the physical as on developing new ways of experiencing physicality—the body's location and movement in space, bodily expressions of the attitude of self, manipulation of desires for spiritual ends. Cultivating this new relationship to one's own physicality—a relationship that involves the development of a new kind of intimacy with the body—is one of the primary tasks of the ten months of the postulancy.

BODIES AND SUBJECTS

As I returned from the field and began to pursue these issues in the literature, however, I found that the dominant approaches to understanding subjectivity and transformation did not seem to get at the heart of what was going on in the convent. Indeed, in trying to make sense of what I observed in the convent and what the nuns themselves told me about their experiences, I was compelled to grapple with several key problematics in the theorizing of bodies and selves. How, for example, do we think about the body as simultaneously material (flesh and bone) and constructed in and through social and political discourse? How do we think about the relationship between these contingent bodies and subjective experiences of self in various contexts? Specifically, I had to wrestle with how to think about the body as both a locus of experience and an object of analysis.

Theories of the self and subjectivity fall into two broad orientations in terms of how the self as a thing has been conceptualized and theorized (Csordas 1994a; Mansfield 2000; Chodorow 1999). For our purposes here, I have chosen to think of these as the "seat of being" (subjective) orientation and the "illusion of interiority" (antisubjective) orientation. Significantly, both these perspectives maintain that the phenomenology of the self—subjectivity—is constructed through social processes. They differ, however, in the ways these processes are construed to be grounded (or not) in an authentic, empirical domain of experience.

The Self as a Seat of Being

The "seat of being" perspective holds that the self as an authentic psychological phenomenon actually exists, is knowable to some extent (or to a great extent), and is subject to certain discernible rules of development and performance. The self in this understanding is the inalienable essence of an individual, a locus of independent initiative and action. It is a free and autonomous rational being, the origin of all knowledge. As such, this view maintains that we have not only the ability but also the *duty* to come to know our selves as intimately as possible and, through this self-knowledge, to know the world around us. The self in this view is the unique core of one's being, the arbiter of absolute truth.

This understanding of the subject has roots in Western philosophy as far back as the Greeks but became ascendant in theories of the person during the Enlightenment period as new methods for documenting and

analyzing the material world provoked a certainty that ultimately everything could be known and understood through scientific means. Enlightenment thinkers on the self (most notably Descartes and Kant) argued
that the only irreducible truth is the fact that the "I" is an experiencing
entity through which the exterior world is recognized, categorized, and
known.

This concern with discovering the "truth" about the self took an
affective turn in the romantic period, where there emerged a focus on
the phenomenology of feeling as means of discerning the ultimate
"truth" of nature and the universe. Unlike the Enlightenment thinkers,
who largely focused on the self as the origin of categories of perception
and reason, the romanticists (e.g., Poe, Emerson, Thoreau, Hawthorne,
Melville, Proust, Irving) argued that intuitions and feelings are revelatory of the self, which is in turn revelatory of the truth of being. Perception of the world through the self in this view, then, was not so much
a function of cognitive, rational processes as a sort of gestalt of feeling
requiring a searching self-knowledge to articulate.

In the late nineteenth and early twentieth centuries, the concern with
the self took yet another turn. Feelings themselves became subject to
rationalist rules as psychoanalysis became ascendant as the dominant
"scientific" approach to the self. Significantly, psychoanalysis (and its
later articulations in object relations theory and self psychology) holds
that one is not born with one's self or subjectivity intact and that the self
instead emerges through one's engagement with one's (gendered) body
in social context over time. The self of psychoanalysis, then, was
grounded in material reality in a way that the Enlightenment's abstracted
self and the romanticists' passionate self were not, and it provided something of a bridge between the two. As a consequence of psychoanalysis's
concern with both the material body and the social processes that
govern the development of the self, gender became a focus of interest,
emblematic of the notion of the self as constructed but undoubtedly
genuine.

Feminist critics of traditional psychoanalytic conceptualizations of
the self have engaged these theories in terms of how social relations
themselves constitute notions of health and dysfunction (cf. Chodorow
[1989] 1999, 1999; Dinnerstein 1976; Kristeva 1982; Irigaray 1985a,
1985b; Benjamin 1988, 1998; Flax 1990; Mitchell [1974] 2000;
Hughes 1999; Caplan 1993). Though their specific concerns and arguments differ, on the whole these scholars argue that received understandings of gender as an essential, timeless, and unchanging subjective

orientation to which a self does or does not properly adhere must be reconsidered as products of particular historical and social circumstances and that this then demands a reconsideration of rigid developmental trajectories and, consequently, of absolute standards of health and illness. But despite the feminist critique of the ways in which gender relations have been conceptualized, most of these theorists continue—either explicitly or implicitly—to endorse the notion that the self does indeed exist and that the experience of that self is grounded in some sort of material reality, while recognizing that this reality is itself a product of relationships of power.

Chodorow explores these dynamics in *The Power of Feelings* (1999), where she attempts to account for the construction of personal meaning in and through motivated interaction with cultural structures. Chodorow positions herself in direct opposition to theorists who, in her view, posit a deterministic relationship between cultural epistemologies and individual experience (e.g., Lutz, Rosaldo, Foucault, Bourdieu), thereby eliminating the psychological as a legitimate domain of study. She writes, "I argue against the view that subjectivity is shaped, determined, or constituted by language and culture, or that feelings, identities, and selves are culturally constructed. . . . [T]he inner world is not a direct reflection or a result of that which is given and exterior" (5). Instead, she maintains, we must concern ourselves with "the relations between inner and outer, individual and social, psyche and culture, that place where the psychological meets the cultural or the self meets the world" (6).

In response to those who would dismiss the psychological from consideration, Chodorow (1999) offers a theory incorporating the psychoanalytic notion of transference as the process by which past experiences and current understandings are mobilized in the perception and processing of current interactions and events. Her theory is, she contends, "an argument for the existence of an irreducible realm of psychological life in which we create unconscious personal meaning in the experiential immediacy of the present" (1). To illustrate this assertion, she reconsiders gendering as a process through which personal meaning and cultural discourses interarticulate within the context of such subjective processes as the sense of self, the tone of individual feelings, and emotionally imbued unconscious fantasy (72). Though she recognizes that human experience is a process of construction that unfolds within the context of various social and cultural "realities," she insists that "if cultural meanings matter, they matter personally" (170) and that the

workings of the inner, psychological world are at least as much at stake
in this process as is the external world of cultural discourse. The self, in
short, must be taken seriously.

The Self as an Illusion of Interiority

What I call the "illusion of interiority" perspective traces its genealogy
back to Nietzsche, who maintained that there is no such "thing" as a
self as a locus of independent will and control. This perception of the
self as a real thing, he argued, is a cultural production, a function of ideologies of power. When we are convinced that we are masters of our
own lives and responsible for our own circumstances, power can work
all the more effectively by keeping our gazes turned inward and away
from a critique of the circumstances that have produced our situations,
while at the same time compelling us to modify our internal experiences
to resonate with social expectations. In this way, we effectively become
agents of our own submission, while laboring under the illusion that we
are asserting our own free will and control over our lives. The "illusion
of interiority" perspective elaborates on these basic ideas and focuses
on the processes by which "illusions" of interiority are manufactured,
are maintained, and gain ascendancy at different historical moments.
To differentiate the culturally constructed experience of interiority from
the notion of the essential self espoused in the "seat of being" tradition,
scholars in this school often use the term *subjectivity* (as opposed to
self).

Perhaps the best-known representative of this approach is Foucault,
though he began to retreat from this position in his later works. In the
simplest terms, Foucault argued that the idea of the self as a space of
essential identity and private experience—as a locus of individual sovereignty and control and as the ultimate arbiter of the truth of one's
being—is ideology in the Marxist sense of the word. It is a myth, a construct through which power becomes inscribed on individual bodies.

Foucault (1973, 1977, 1979, [1985] 1986, [1986] 1988) was particularly interested in the apparatuses and institutions through which individuals become interpolated with the constructs and practices that mold
them into agents of their own submission—medicine, psychiatry, the
prison system, the church. He was especially concerned with how one
key domain of human experience—sexuality—became the conduit for
the impression of power structures on the internal life of individuals. At
the same time, however, he noted that he was "much more interested in

problems about techniques of the self and things like that rather than sex. . . . [S]ex is boring" (Foucault [1972] 1982: 229) and cautioned, "It would be wrong to say that the soul is an illusion or an ideological effect. On the contrary, it exists, it has a reality, it is produced permanently around, on, within, the body by the functioning of a power that is exercised on those who are punished" (Foucault 1979: 29). In other words, Foucault acknowledged that the experience of interiority is a powerful force that definitively shapes the lives of individual people, and he was interested in how this subjective experience of "the inside" is produced through engagements with cultural practice.

Foucault actually mirrors many of the thinkers in the "seat of being" orientation in his assertion that a certain kind of affective investment—a cathexis, if you will—of the material body becomes a grounding for the production of the self. He differs from them, however, in terms of the analytic direction his argument takes. The "seat of being" thinkers tend to view this cathexis of the body as originating first and foremost within the self, with the affect emanating from the lived experience of an authentic core housed in a material body. Foucault, however, comes at it from the other direction. The cathexis, he claims, comes not from personal affect but from the apparatuses of power, which depend upon bodies to perpetuate certain systems of truth. "The body is," he writes, ". . . directly invested in a political field; power relations have an immediate hold upon it; they invest it, mark it, train it, torture it, force it to carry out tasks, to perform ceremonies, to emit signs. The body becomes a useful force only if it is both a productive body and a subjected body" (Foucault 1977: 25–26). In Foucault's view, then, the cathexis of the body comes not from the inside but from the outside, making bodies (their shapes, habits, practices, locations, desires, etc.) of paramount importance to the workings of power. But because power works through concealing its aims, the structures also function to convince us that this body-cathexis is of our own making and desire—that there *is* an "inside" to which we are responding through our close attention to bodily concerns—when in fact this illusion of a core self is what enables the successful reproduction of systems of domination.

Antisubjective analyses like Foucault's push us to reinterrogate traditional understandings of the self and subjectivity. We have seen that two of the domains that have been particularly central to the "seat of being" understanding of self are the notion of the self as the locus of motivation and action and the idea of gender as the expression of the "true" self. Perhaps not surprisingly, then, some contemporary theorists—for example, Bourdieu and Butler—have taken these up as particularly promising areas for rethinking.

Bourdieu's theory of practice (1990, 1995, 1998) does not at first glance place him in the "illusion of interiority" camp. In many places, Bourdieu states that he is concerned with bridging objective and subjective conceptualizations of practice. But a closer reading of his work reveals, I suggest, a distinctly antisubjective epistemology. We can see this when we consider one of Bourdieu's best-known concepts—the *habitus.*

According to Bourdieu (1990: 53), "The conditionings associated with a particular class of conditions of existence produce the habitus, systems of durable, transposable dispositions, structured structures predisposed to function as structuring structures, that is, as principles which generate and organize practices and representation." The habitus ensures that individuals act according to the social rules of a given situation. As the players become more adept at the "game," they become virtuosi—experts at navigating the habitus according to the internal logic of its structure. In the process of becoming experts, individuals are inscribed with the values and logic of the habitus in the domain of bodily practices, which eventually come to assume the sense of being "natural." In this sense, then, Bourdieu is interested in how the repeated performance of certain cultural practices induces in people particular sets of dispositions that they then see as having originated within themselves (rather than as being functions of the practices they engaged in). Here he closely parallels Foucault's formulation of the workings of power, though Bourdieu's focus is much more on how the micropractices of everyday life are interconnected in webs of significance (to borrow a Geertzian term) that govern our experiential engagements with the world.

Butler (1993, [1990] 1999) takes the question of motivation and practice into the realm of gender, where she argues that what we once thought to be the ultimate essence of subjective experience is, in fact, an illusion produced through engagement in cultural practices. Butler questions "identity" as a real thing, suggesting that it is a normative ideal rather than a true descriptor of experience. Instead of looking "inside" for true identity, she says, we should direct our attention at external practices, how they are collected to imply a certain kind of core that we then take as genuine. This is particularly evident in the regulatory practices of gender. How, Butler asks, do the regulatory practices that govern gender also govern culturally intelligible notions of identity? If certain kinds of gender identities fail to conform to those norms of cultural intelligibility, they then appear only as developmental failures or logical impossibilities. And, she wonders, if identity is an effect of discursive practices, how much is gender identity an effect of the regulatory practice of compulsory heterosexuality?

Butler comes at these questions from a poststructuralist position, which (in its simplest form) holds that there are no real things "out there" in the world that are then subsequently represented in language. Rather, poststructural thought maintains that all things exist only in and through language and thus do not have any genuine preverbal, precultural essence. This is particularly true for notions of the self, which Butler (and others in this school) claim cannot and does not exist extralinguistically. As such, the self is always already a function of language. And since language and meaning are themselves produced through relationships of power (with gender being a primary axis along which these relations are articulated), the self as traditionally conceptualized (as a seat of being, a locus of independent action and control, a private domain of experience) not only is misconstrued but perpetuates the very systems of power that constrain its production. In other words, Butler's poststructuralist position denies the notion of the psychological person as a substantive entity in its own right and instead views this sense of interiority as an illusion of ideology.

SUBJECTIVITY AND THE BODY

Current theorizing of self and subjectivity tends to fall along these two lines, with subjectivity postulated either as an essential truth or as an illusion of discourse and practice. Though both the "seat of being" and "illusion of interiority" perspectives maintain that the self and its subjective phenomenology are culturally constructed and that the cultural processes at play can be discerned and examined, the problem is that these perspectives, at their cores, seem to negate one another, making any integration of them extraordinarily difficult. The "seat of being" perspective holds that the self—as an entity—does exist as something separable from (if not wholly independent of) social context. The "illusion of interiority" perspective, in contrast, maintains that the self is an illusion conjured out of collections of bodily practices and that it therefore cannot be mobilized as a source of knowledge outside the context in which this illusion is perpetuated. In terms of the body, this means we face the theoretical problem of dealing conceptually with either a disembodied self or a de-selfed body, neither of which fully captures the complexities of human experience.

Making sense of my experiences with the nuns—in terms of both the changes I observed and what they told me of their own feelings of transformation—required me to attempt to hold these two models of subjectivity simultaneously, despite their contradictory claims. The nuns certainly believe that there is an essential component of being—what they call the soul—and that this soul is manifested in particular ways contingent on our social and historical circumstances. At the same time, however, they maintain that we are persuaded by "the world" to adopt a false sense of self that is illusory and functions to serve the structures of earthly power. The process of transformation in the convent hinges not simply on the demystification of the illusion of the worldly self or on the reification of the essential, timeless soul but on a progressive and systematic integration of these two domains of existence within a new moral universe.

Making sense of this subjective transformation through either of the two dominant approaches to subjectivity and culture was for me a difficult intellectual enterprise. After grappling with these issues for some time, I returned to the issue that seemed so central to the sisters in the convent—the bodily transformation of the self—and decided to focus on embodiment as a common denominator of these two dominant approaches to self and subjectivity. While the relationship between the body and the self is theorized very differently in the two perspectives outlined above (and, indeed, what counts as "body" and "self" is contested as well), a focus on embodiment nevertheless seemed to open a domain for dialogue between these perspectives.

THEORIZING EMBODIMENT

The most ambitious scholarship on the subject of embodiment has largely come from feminist cultural studies, where the relations between the material body, the engagement with gendered practices, and the "truth" of the self remain central concerns. Probyn (1993: 2) voices the position of many feminist scholars by deconstructing the presumption of a disembodied self as not only impossible but dangerous: "As an object, the self has been variously claimed and normally left in a neutered 'natural' state, the sex of which is a barely concealed masculine one. And until very recently, when selves got spoken they were also taken as a-gendered although of course they were distinctly male."

De Lauretis (1987: 15) makes a similar point in her discussion of technologies of gender, noting that theories that propose to be "gender-blind" (in the sense that they are theories of the self that do not specify a particular gender) actually function as technologies of gender, in that they ignore the differential constitution of female versus male subjectivities: "Hence the paradox[:] . . . in order to combat the social technology that produces sexuality and sexual oppression, these theories (and their respective politics) will deny gender. But to deny gender, first of all, is to deny the social relations of gender that constitute and validate the sexual oppression of women; and second, to deny gender is to remain 'in ideology,' an ideology which (not coincidentally if, of course, not intentionally) is manifestly self-serving to the male-gendered subject."

In other words, theories of the self that claim to be gender-neutral are not—and cannot be. This makes them particularly dangerous: although they appear to counter traditional gender assumptions, they instead inadvertently reinscribe them in a more covert way. In keeping with the "illusion of interiority" orientation, then, these authors argue that we cannot take the "self" as a given but must instead deconstruct it as a cultural and social production. But unlike the "illusion of interiority" perspective, most feminist work on embodiment does not deny the existence of a self per se; rather, it objects to the theorizing of an abstract self, ungrounded in material reality. The aim here is not to dismiss the self as an illusion but to redirect our attention to the fact that selves are, first and foremost, *embodied* experiences of the world and therefore require a more nuanced engagement with the problematics of embodiment.

Scholarship along these lines has attended to such bodily questions as race and ethnicity (hooks 1981, 2000; Anzaldúa 1987; Moraga and Anzaldúa 1983), sexuality and sexual practice (Parker, Barbosa, and Aggleton 2000; Blackwood and Wieringa 1999; Ferree, Lorber, and Hess 1999), postcoloniality (Fanon 1967, [1963] 1968; Spivak 1987, 1999; Spivak and Harasym 1990), maternity and motherhood (Hanigsberg and Ruddick 1999; Fineman and Karpin 1995; Ginsberg and Rapp 1995), rationality (Natter, Schatzki, and Jones 1995; Walters 1994; Gould [1983] 1984; Bordo 1999; Jaggar and Bordo 1989), medicalization (Kaplan and Squier 1999; Treichler, Cartwright, and Penley 1998; Martin 1992, 1994; Komesaroff 1995), disability (Mitchell and Snyder 1997), and psychiatric "illness" (Bordo 1993; Burck and Speed 1995; Smith and Mahfouz 1994; Chesler [1972] 1997; Figert 1996; Thompson 1994; Ussher 1992), with the particular focus in these works being the articulation between cultural processes concerned with the body and the subjective experience of that body as a source of personal meaning.

ANTHROPOLOGY AND THE BODY

These issues seem, perhaps, a little abstract. It is here that engaged anthropology can make a significant contribution. We spend time with our subjects. We get to know them as individuals, with their own life histories and particular circumstances, while at the same time attending to the larger cultural processes at work. In recent years (and one might speculate as to the causes of this trend) anthropology seems to have returned to a concern with the body and the phenomenology of embodiment. Traditional analyses of the body as cultural artifact and template of meaning (e.g., Turner, Douglas) have been remobilized to look at contemporary issues such as postcoloniality, postmodern discourse, gender theory, and discourses of medicalization. Some of the recent anthropological studies that grapple with questions of embodiment address emotions (Lutz 1988; Wierzbicka 1999; Desjarlais 1992), cognition and memory (Lucy 1992; Cole 2001), physical illness and suffering (Kleinman 1988; Kleinman and Das 1997; Green and Sobo 2000; Martin [1987] 2001, 1995; Romanucci-Ross, Moerman, and Tancredi 1997), psychiatric distress (Kleinman and Good 1985; Hsu 1983; Bateson 1999), political resistance (Comaroff 1985; Comaroff and Comaroff 1993), religiosity (Asad 1993; Mahmood 2001), medical procedures (Downey and Dumit 1997; Lindenbaum and Lock 1993; Stein and Stein 1990), sexuality (Stoller 1985; Herdt 1997, 1999; Ortner and Whitehead 1982), and practices of gendering (Ortner 1996). For the most part, however, embodiment as conceptualized in these approaches tends to replicate the distinctions discussed above, with the body presented either as an essential source of meaning or as an object of cultural inscription. This is due, not to any particular shortcoming on the part of these theorists, but to the fact that the questions with which they were grappling suggested they turn to one perspective or the other as the most relevant theoretical orientation for their particular concerns.

A few anthropologists, however, have become interested in the way these two elements of embodiment—the body as both a source and an object of cultural meaning—are held together simultaneously in the experiences and practices of being, and how this is shaped by cultural context. In her work on the Zar cult, for example, Boddy (1989) explores the ways that women's bodies become sites where moral discourses about personhood, femininity, and social responsibility are both articulated and contested. She is concerned not so much with the structuring of individual subjectivity as with the ways bodies are enlisted into "service" from multiple directions at once (and with multiple and sometimes even contradictory results), and with how Sudanese women take up this multiplicity strategically as they reimagine themselves and the world. In examining illness and healing among the Yolmo Sherpa in the Himalayas, Desjarlais (2003) moves beyond the traditional meaning-centered approach to understanding ritual healing practices and argues instead for a more sensitive engagement with the aesthetics of illness and healing as, above all, embodied ways of knowing. By focusing on the tactile, sensual dimensions of healing, Desjarlais troubles our received notions of subjective change as first proceeding from a shift in belief or thinking and only secondarily manifesting in altered emotional or bodily sensibilities. Csordas (1994b) examines the healing practices of charismatic Catholics as a form of therapeutic self-process. In bringing together the phenomenology of Merleau-Ponty and the practice theory of Bourdieu, Csordas is, among other things, challenging us to think beyond the mind/body dichotomy toward a notion of what Burkitt (1999) calls a "thinking body" or a "body of thought."

I find all of these works conceptually creative, intellectually rigorous, and theoretically provocative. They have challenged us to interrogate some of our most fundamental assumptions about the nature of human experience and have opened up new ways of thinking about the human body as a process of meaning as well as an artifact of biology and culture. And, as is always the case when opening up new domains of inquiry, they have enabled us to see where there is work yet to be done. In my reading of this literature, one significant missing element seems to be a detailed, ethnographic account of the self-conscious, systematic use of bodily practices to reshape the (gendered) self within an elaborated system of meaning, coupled with a detailed model for understanding the psychological processes at work in this transformation. The present book is addressed to this task.

CHAPTER 2

The Siervas

It was early September, and the walk to the Central House of the congregation—its world headquarters—was a chilly one for my 7:30 A.M meeting with Mother Anabel, the mother general. I was there to get her formal permission to begin my research with the sisters. I sat down in the reception area waiting for our appointment, very nervous as always. But I had seen the mother general several times before in interaction with other nuns and "outsiders" like myself, and she'd always seemed pleasant. I comforted myself with this thought as I waited, stifling a sleepy yawn.

The Central House is located on a side street, just two blocks from a park famed for the nighttime escapades of Puebla's underground culture of transvestite prostitutes. Like most Mexican buildings, the convent reveals from the outside nothing more than an imposing concrete wall, the only identifying detail being a small plaque near the front gates bearing the congregation's name. When one looks directly upwards from outside, the iron bars on the windows (a common feature of all Mexican buildings) become a patchwork of metal that, if it weren't for the particular women living inside, one could almost imagine as a trellis upon which some young suitor might climb to serenade his beloved.

But the outward austerity of the cold, square building is deceiving. Just inside the towering, creaky, black iron gates is a spacious open-air courtyard with colorful flowers around a life-sized statue that portrays the congregation's founder embracing adoring children. The two cars of the convent—a Ford Taurus station wagon and a Dodge truck—are parked here when they are not shuttling the nuns about town on their business.

Bordering the courtyard to the south are a series of rooms, two of which belong to the remarkably ancient priest who has been the chaplain of the convent for over fifty years, and a small dormitory and bathroom that are primarily reserved for young women who wish to have an "experience" at the convent—a short stay of one to four weeks to see if they want to enter the congregation the following autumn. To the north of the courtyard are two tiny rooms with their own bathrooms, where Doña Luisa and her nineteen-year-old son, Paco, live free of charge in exchange for Doña Luisa's help in the kitchen and Paco's service as a general handyman.

Bordering the courtyard to the west is the convent library, a treasure trove of over five thousand books that has thick oak tables and leather-lined chairs for comfortable reflection or study. At any time of the day or night, provided it is not during the singing of the Hours, Mother Rosalita is here—indexing, cataloguing, reading. As the caretaker of the library for over thirty years, she is herself a living card catalog and knows the exact location of each item in the library, whether you give her the author, the title, or a few words about the subject. Her skin, looking as delicate and wrinkled as the pages of the old books she so lovingly cares for, leaves one totally unprepared for her sweetly toned and extraordinarily youthful voice—the only remnant of a vibrant youth that disappeared long ago in the embrace of the congregation.

To the east of the courtyard is the receiving area—a small anteroom attached to a larger living room with comfortable couches and chairs for meeting with visitors to the convent. In this anteroom, crammed with souvenirs and memorabilia from each house of the congregation from Kenya to Columbia, I first met Mother Anabel.

A very attractive woman of about fifty, Mother Anabel breezed into the room, smiled brightly, kissed me on the cheek, and welcomed me to the convent. She was originally from Italy, so her Spanish was crisp and had a singsong quality, making it easy to understand. But she was an imposing woman—she carried herself gracefully, but as if aware of her authority. She seemed a bit more restrained in her movements than the other nuns I later came to know, and every gesture seemed to be deliberate—for a certain purpose and nothing more. Otherwise, she would often sit or stand as still as a statue—on the outside, that is. One got the sense of an extraordinarily vibrant force inside the shell of nun, cross, and habit. She peeked out at me through strangely penetrating eyes, full of intelligence and irony, and seemed to evaluate my every word and movement from behind an expression of composed serenity.

As mother general of the congregation, Mother Anabel is the elected head of the community and all its houses throughout the world and is the supreme authority on all intercongregational matters. Elected for a term of six years, with a two-term limit, the mother general is not singularly permitted to make any radical changes in the basic structure of the institution without the vote and consent of the six members of the General Council (four general assistants including the vicaress (second-in command), plus the economist and the secretary of the congregation). But she can and does make decisions regarding, for example, the transfer of sisters between houses, minor changes in the daily schedule, whether a sister may be permitted to visit home or begin a course of study, and, on this particular occasion, whether an anthropologist will be welcomed within the convent walls.

I was extremely fortunate to have happened upon the congregation during one of the rare windows of time when the mother general was actually in residence at the Central House. Although the Central House is the mother general's designated home convent, her duties require her to travel to each house of the congregation (seventy-eight in all) at least once every two years, in addition to fulfilling the requests for her presence at fiestas and celebrations, dedications, and ceremonies. She is an extraordinarily busy woman, and her time and attention are always in demand.

Fortunately for my research, she is also a very educated woman, with a doctorate in theology and a keen understanding of the process of dissertation research. She immediately grasped the nature of my study and the kind of extended contact I was looking for, and she was pleased at the prospect of a non-church-sponsored academic study of the religious life. "You'll reach many more people with your work than the traditional kinds of studies that are done," she told me. "It's important for people to understand what we do here, that despite the crisis in vocations that the church suffered after Vatican II, there are still many, many young women entering the convent and doing the Lord's work."

But as sympathetic as she was, her acceptance of my research plan did not come without reservations. "We are a family here," she cautioned.

A *family*. And just as you wouldn't want someone coming into your living room, sitting on your couch and taking notes about everything you do, some of the sisters may not be particularly comfortable with you here at first. The most important thing is respect. If they feel you are respectful of them, they will accept you, and they will make you feel like part of our family as well. But if I get *any* sense that you are violating *any* of these conditions or interfering with the sense of family we have here, that will be the end of your project. I won't hesitate for a moment. Is that understood?

It was indeed. In the course of the research, I was to experience exactly what Mother Anabel meant about the "protectiveness" of the convent family as I moved back and forth between being an "insider" and being an "outsider"—and sometimes straddling these two categories in ways not wholly comfortable for the sisters or for myself.

Our negotiating out of the way and a date selected for my introduction to the convent, Mother Anabel patted my knee and held up her fingers in that "wait just a second" sign Mexicans use (which, I later learned, actually means "Stay put and entertain yourself— I'm in no rush.") She returned to the anteroom about ten minutes later clutching a blue and white book, which she handed me with pride—the *History of the Congregation*.[1] "You have a few days before you start here," she said. "Now you have some homework! Read about our founder, Rebe. Let him into your heart. He will guide you in your research. Learn about our history, who we are, what our mission is. It's as alive for us today as it was for our founder over a hundred years ago." I toted the book home in my backpack and spent the next several rainy, late-summer days curled up with a bottomless mug of manzanilla tea and what the sisters believe to be the story of a saint.[2]

ORIGINS: THE POLITICAL-RELIGIOUS HISTORY OF THE CONGREGATION

The divine mustard seed, which I do not know how it came into my
hands and was sown in such an appropriate time and place, was
born and grew, and today shelters in its branches a great number of
poor, who are the children and the preferred of God.
                                                            Father Muro, *Letters*[3]

As I turned the pages of the congregation's *History* I found myself immersed not simply in the story of one man who founded one religious order. The story of the congregation has unfolded within the context of

1. The exact title and full reference information for this book are withheld so as to keep the identity of the order confidential.

2. In 2000, the congregation's founder was indeed canonized by the church.

3. The author's real name and the book's exact title and full reference information are withheld so as to keep the identity of the order confidential.

an extraordinarily combustible sociopolitical situation. In fact, the congregation's entire philosophy and theory of practice emerged from this larger context as a direct response to it. The story of the congregation, then, is not simply a story about a man who felt called by God and the small group of young women who followed him. It is also a story of revolution and oppression and passionate resistance. It engages the nineteenth-century philosophical debates igniting the European and American intellectual scenes regarding the moral dimensions of in-the-world action in the face of rapid technological development. It reveals at its core the various articulations of race, religion, and gender central to constructions of Mexicanness as the nation moved from independence to revolution and embarked on the radical project of modernization—tensions that tore the new nation apart. In this way, the story of the congregation can be understood as a grounded articulation of the social, political, economic, and cultural struggles engulfing Mexico in the late nineteenth and early twentieth centuries. Specifically, the congregation was an active interlocutor with popular and intellectual debates regarding Mexican national identity and what constitutes "true" Mexicanness. This continues to the present day, shaping the postulants' understandings of their own religious experiences.

The congregation was founded in 1885 by Father Juan Miguel de Muro y Cuesta, a Mexican priest with a particular critique of modern society and an unusual vision for the redemption of humanity—a philosophy that continues to shape present-day life in the congregation. Unlike many orders that have lost contact with the vision of their founders or perhaps never even knew it, the Siervas have made it a priority of the community to nurture and actualize the spirit of the founder through careful adherence to his vision in every detail of convent life. Indeed, they cite this dedication to their roots as the principal strength that has carried them through the turbulence in Mexico's political history when so many other congregations closed or permanently fled the country. Beginning with the first day a woman enters the congregation as a postulant (or preferably even before), each prospective sister is encouraged and (eventually) required to read the founder's voluminous writings, meditations, spiritual exercises, and letters, as well as the many books written about the founder and his life. These materials are used extensively in classes in all the levels of formation, and by the time a sister professes her first temporary vows it is expected that she has mastered this vast literature and has adopted the founder's spirituality and vision of social regeneration as her own.

Born on November 10, 1851, Father Juan Miguel de Muro y Cuesta was the first and only son of wealthy Spanish (Creole) parents. His mother died only two weeks after his birth, and, following her death, Juan Miguel's father left the family's hacienda and moved with the boy to Mexico City to live with his sister, who became the child's primary caretaker.

Father Muro, like most young men of his class, was educated at home by private tutors, his father and aunt ensuring that he received a strictly traditional Christian education. At the age of thirteen he began studying Latin under the direction of a local priest in preparation for entering the religious life, as he did at the young age of fifteen.

In the early part of his priesthood, Father Muro distinguished himself by his exceptional oratorical skills, his enthusiasm, and his sensitive and careful guidance as a spiritual director; so much so that audiences at the church often overflowed into the street on the days he performed Mass. In addition to his regular demanding duties, he organized a catechism class for girls and wrote a series of letters concerning the education of children in the home. During these years Father Muro formulated some of the ideas that would later crystallize into a complex vision for the regeneration of society and the salvation of humankind.

THE MISSION OF THE CONGREGATION

Through a divine predilection, for which I will never be able to
show my gratitude enough, I am destined to continue the
redemptive mission of Christ Our Savior. Because of this, I am
obligated to imitate Him in His pains and joys, as much as is made
possible for me through His grace and under the protection of my
Most Holy Mother.

Father Muro, *Meditations*[4]

The late nineteenth century was a period of radical transformation in Mexico. The economic and social reforms implemented under the leadership of Porfirio Díaz (1876–1910) were explicitly aimed at making Mexico a "modern nation" on a par with the United States (González Díaz, 1988; Guerra Castellanos, 1988; Stavenhagen, 1990; Durante Espinoza 2001). Infrastructure was targeted as a key element of

4. The author's real name and the book's exact title and full reference information are withheld so as to keep the identity of the order confidential.

modernization, as was the opening of the Mexican economy to foreign investment. As a result, Mexican markets quickly became the playground of (mostly) American entrepreneurs. As the traditional Mexican small business owners and farmers were swallowed by international corporations, increasing numbers of peasants migrated to the cities for work. This created a new social class of poor urban peasants—dislocated from their families, uprooted from their traditional homelands, anonymous workers in the moneymaking enterprises of powerful foreign corporations. The relentless pursuit of economic security and success threatened to supplant traditional Mexican religious and cultural values as the lower classes assimilated the capitalist ethos of the big foreign corporations to survive in their rapidly changing world.

In direct response to such "evils" of modernization, Father Muro began to formulate his theological agenda. He did not take an explicitly political stance or directly confront the foreign-owned corporations or secular government he so despised. Rather, he directed his critique below the surface, to the ideological assumptions underlying and bolstering the secular rationalist philosophies that he saw as a disease eating away at Mexican society. "We find society unhinged and at the point of disappearing," he lamented. "Theology infected by the modern encyclopedia, denaturalized philosophy, politics segregated from God, and the prostituted arts are some of the other elements of decomposition that, like rot, slowly but surely erode the social edifice and in the end bring it crashing down. Raising up theology, reestablishing the sound principles of philosophy, restoring the kingdom of God in politics, and ennobling the arts through Christianity are the only means of salvation that remains in our society" (*Essays*).[5]

Secular rationalist philosophy and its "liberal" agenda had penetrated the nation through the holes punched in its borders by big business and the pulsing wires and cables of modernization. Like a cancer slowly working its way through the body to the heart, Father Muro argued, this new modernity had come to threaten the very soul of Mexico—its core, its identity: "Today more than ever evil has penetrated our society and all of the errors that overseas have caused so much evil. They have been transmitted to our land, tearing us away from our tradition and our religion, to later tear us from our beloved

5. The author's real name and the book's exact title and full reference information are withheld so as to keep the identity of the order confidential.

country" (*Essays*). Significantly, Father Muro elsewhere directed his attack at the state's propagation of this ideology and its legitimization on all levels of the "new modern society": "Society is enslaved by the power of the state absorbing the individual as in the pagan nations. . . . [N]ever has the world been such a slave as it is under the imperialism of modern liberalism" (*Essays*). Father Muro's position here was unambiguous. Further, he believed a larger political design to be at work, supported and tacitly directed from interests outside Mexico (specifically, the United States and, to a lesser degree, Europe) and designed to muscle out the traditional Catholic values that he saw (and his Siervas still see) as so central to Mexican society.

In line with other conservative thinkers of late-nineteenth-century Mexico, Father Muro linked this "liberalism" to the rampant materialism associated with capitalist production and introduced into the country through the liberal policies of Porfirio Díaz, who (not coincidentally) also happened to be widely criticized as an American sympathizer. Mexican society had turned, Father Muro believed, from being concerned with embodying the moral and ethical values at the heart of Catholicism to worshipping at the altar of the new pagan god of consumerism: "Society today marches toward the future without a clear path, and moral civilization, which has been almost completely lost, has ceded its place to a civilization which is purely material. . . . Paganism, even in its plastic form, has returned to the world. The universe misguided and obscured once again finds itself again about to succumb. The Word made man will not descend again to save this world, but only to judge it" (*Essays*). Both liberalism and capitalism, Father Muro claimed, fostered a particular interpretation of human life and human relationships that was based in the commodification and "dehumanization" of the individual, particularly the poor individual who labored in service of the rich.

The totality of Father Muro's vocation was revealed to him in startling clarity on a summer day in 1885. According to congregation legend, he was walking from León to Calvary one morning when he came upon a horrific scene that was to change his life forever: by the edge of a river he saw two tiny infants who had been abandoned by an "ingrate" mother (*History*) being ripped limb from limb and greedily devoured by snarling wild boars. From that day on, the story went, Father Muro knew that evangelizing was not enough—that he had to work actively to change the conditions of life for the poor in Mexico and to counter the "degeneration of society" that he believed to be not only symbolically but materially revealed in the bloody incident. That

very day he decided to build a shelter for poor children and orphans—
what was to become the first house of the congregation. Father Muro
founded the congregation with the specific mission of helping Mexico's
dislocated, disenfranchised peasants to reclaim their "traditional" Mexican values and dignifying them as human beings. His consuming passion was to elucidate the "dehumanizing" effects of the path Mexico
was following and to wrest clean, healthy souls from the clutches of
capitalist exploitation. A brilliantly colored oil painting graphically
depicting the gruesome baby-eating scene hangs in the hallway leading
to the chapel in the Central House.

RECLAIMING FEMININITY: A CRITIQUE OF
"MODERN" SUBJECTIVITY

We can see from his writings that Father Muro was a sophisticated
thinker who recognized the social significance of the philosophical shift
to scientific, liberal rationalism during this period—both globally and in
Mexico in particular—and then meticulously deconstructed it within
the framework of his personal theological orientation. Himself an avid
philosopher, Father Muro directed his critique at what he saw to be the
heart of the matter—what we might call the *subjectivity* produced and
cultivated through the forces of industrial capitalism and modernization and bolstered by the Protestant ethic. But this subjectivity—which
he identified as rational, liberal, secular, positivist, and, paradoxically,
both individualistic and dehumanizing—took on an added dimension
for Father Muro when viewed through his particular theological lens. It
assumed a gender.

Here, we come to the most important feature—the crux—of Father
Muro's vision and, consequently, of the charism of the congregation.
Through much thought and reflection, Father Muro came to locate the
decay of Mexican values and identity at the heart of society—with
mothers who had been "masculinized" by capitalist development. In
other words, the "modern" subjectivity produced through the forces of
industrial capitalism and modernization and seasoned with Protestant
ideology took, for Father Muro, a contaminating masculine cast, "masculinizing" both the culture and the individuals who adopted it and
depleting Mexico of its most precious and essential natural resource—
good Catholic mothers.

Convinced that the only way to eradicate the evils of "modernity"
was to go to the source, Father Muro concluded that the education and

formation of women were both essential and urgent for building a new society. In his view, young women were, by the grace of God, the only possible saviors of a world in crisis, and a concern for the "proper" formation of young women came to eclipse the other works of the congregation.

The cornerstone of this framework was that women had both the vocation and the duty to protect the world from men, restoring to men the souls they had lost in their obsessive pursuit of knowledge and power. The femininity of women was the only antidote against the dehumanization of society, brought by progressive modernization and secularization along what was constructed as a male model of development. This refeminization of women and rehumanization of men had to begin in the home and, above all, with the mother. Indeed, Father Muro came to see the congregation's primary mission as the production of mothers for future generations—mothers who, through their influence as the heart and soul of the family, could bring about a regeneration of Mexican society: "Comply with the obligations of your state," he wrote to young Mexican women, "and you will be working for the regeneration of society. . . . Only a world of saintly women can regenerate the current family and social situation. But women will never do this for society unless they can do it first in their families" (*Essays*).

Given Father Muro's belief that only the proper shaping of young children could produce change, we can understand why this model of the good Mexican mother became the focus of his concern. He acknowledged that the father's influence was important, but he firmly maintained that the mother was the center of the family and the primary caretaker of the children and therefore the one who held principal responsibility for inculcating the values necessary for the transformation of society. "The salvation and sanctification of your husbands, children, and servants depend on you," he wrote. "If you want them all to be good, you should first give them the will to be so through your good examples and your counsel." And more, "If you see a weak and decentered family, do not blame its members. Look at the wife or the mother of the family, and there you will find the seed of evil. I assure you that if the mother or wife is good, so will be the family" (*Essays*).

Father Muro repeatedly stressed that this was a glorious mission specifically assigned to women:

> Great is, I repeat, the mission that heaven has conferred on the Christian matron! If you comply with your duties you will be a heroine and you will reach a great perfection. . . . Just as the hand is as useful to man as

the neck and the head, in the same way, as useful to Christian society as a nun who busies herself in the cloister in praying to the Lord for the sins of the people is a Christian mother who raises and educates her children to be obedient to the law of the Lord. As much as the nun in a monastery can sanctify herself, so can the matron of a domestic home. Follow, girls, the vocation that God has given you, and you can arrive in heaven. Follow the road that providence has marked for you and you will be saints. (*Essays*)

According to Father Muro, all women, like Mary, were called to divine motherhood—to conceive Christ in their hearts, to incubate Him in their bodies, and to give birth to Him through their children. But more than this, theirs was a mission also specifically *directed at* women, or, more specifically, at the young girls who would soon themselves be wives and mothers:

> [A good moral and Christian formation] is most important for the girls who later, if they become wives and mothers, will have direct influence over their husbands and over their children. No one can deny the immense influence that the Christian woman exercises over men, and all of history shows that the Christian wife can change the pagan and evil husband, making him Christian, good and useful. Likewise . . . [e]ven if, in the age of the passions, a youth strays from the straight path, in the majority of the cases the first principles inculcated by the mother make him return to the correct path. (*Essays*)

But one could not give what one did not have. A woman could not properly educate her own daughters if she herself was not properly educated. Father Muro incessantly lamented the dismal education available to young women in Mexico at this time (late nineteenth and early twentieth centuries), especially for poor girls whose families could not afford private tutors. But women in general were hopelessly caught between what he called the "old" and "new" systems of education, and he saw in this a representative case of the traditional religious and secular humanist philosophies fighting their most heated battles over the access to the minds of Mexico's youth:

> In my view, both systems [of education] are defective. The old one formed women capable to carry out all of the work of the home, but at the margin of culture, ignorant of all of the knowledge necessary for whichever state they embraced. In marriage, the men, feeling the women to be inferior, treated them harshly. The women were submissive, incapable of intervening or sharing in conversation with their husbands, caring for and loving their children, but without knowing how to educate them. The modern system goes to the other extreme. Education is

reduced to teaching children the basic elements of various sciences, but of course without delving into any with any depth, and omitting completely anything that refers to domestic work or the labors of the home. This produces vain and pedantic girls who will be neither good wives nor good mothers. And if they aspire to the religious life and they are able to persevere, they will make useless members. (*Essays*)

In response, Father Muro worked to integrate these two perspectives, developing a philosophy that was to give rise to the largest work and the bread and butter of the congregation—boarding schools for poor young girls.

Father Muro's philosophy, then, was undeniably woman centered. But it did more than create real flesh-and-blood mothers who could subvert the totalizing influences of secular rationalism through the "proper" religious formation of their children. It proposed a social theology grounded in a particular understanding of gender. Father Muro equated femininity with "humanness," religiosity, faith, piety, tenderness, morality, humbleness, servitude in the face of God—in short, with a certain kind of subjectivity. He clearly believed that femininity and a certain feminine subjectivity were pivotal to God's plan of salvation. Femininity, in this view, entailed an attitude of servitude, which in turn was the linchpin of the plan of redemption. Although this was not in itself a markedly unusual interpretation of the gospel, it assumed a particular prominence in Father Muro's vision.

Father Muro's plan for social regeneration, then, like much of his other theological formulations, reflected a double concern with both interior tailoring and the exterior manifestations of certain ideological convictions. Explicitly, Father Muro promoted the formation of young women, with a special eye to vocational and job training and the reintroduction of women into "culture." But implicitly, and perhaps more importantly, he promoted the cultivation of a specific "feminine" subjectivity as the antidote to the "masculine" secular rationalist philosophies that he perceived to be eating away at Mexican cultural and religious values. His sophisticated philosophy brought together elements of gender, nationalism, cultural identity, and religion under one banner—the banner of salvation.

Again, while Father Muro's interpretations of modernity or of Catholic teachings may not seem particularly unusual in and of themselves, the articulation of this understanding of gendered subjectivity through the prism of the social, political, and economic conditions of late nineteenth and early-twentieth-century Mexico is particularly striking.

Further, the coupling of these associations with an emphasis on decisive social action brings this philosophy into active dialogue with the process of globalization, debates about the value of human life, and beliefs regarding social responsibility and the morality of political agendas. The question of how this particular female subjectivity becomes personally meaningful to postulants living nearly a century after Father Muro's death is central to this ethnography.

Father Muro died on September 20, 1904, in a house of the order that today squats on a congested boulevard in Puebla and is the city headquarters for the Red Cross. The building was appropriated by the Mexican government in 1930, and the sisters still fume over the loss of the convent where their beloved father breathed his last. But he is close to them still. In 1956 Father Muro's remains were brought to the Central House and placed in the wall of the nun's chapel. Convinced of his sanctity and believing him deserving of greater glory, the sisters have worked tirelessly since his death for Father Muro's canonization. In 1990, as a result of years of historical research by Mother Anabel and the authentication of the miraculous healing of Sister Marguerite's knee, Father Muro was beatified by the Roman Catholic Church. In May of 2000, following the spontaneous and complete recovery of a priest who had prayed to Father Muro for strength, the Siervas' founder was canonized by Pope John Paul II as a saint of the church. His bones now rest in a Snow White—like glass case under the altar in the nuns' chapel—the very altar from which they receive Holy Communion every morning.

The sisters are especially devoted to their beloved founder. They recite devotions to him throughout the day. They pray to him in time of need, ask for his guidance and his protection, and entrust their family members and friends to his care. They dream of him at night. The postulants, in particular, place their treasured religious vocations completely and without reserve in the loving hands of Father Muro, whom they believe guides and protects them as his spiritual daughters. Iris shared this dramatic example with me one afternoon as we were working in the convent pantry cleaning and chopping vegetables for the evening meal:

> Last night I was praying in the Holy Hour, meditating on the Holy Body of Our Lord displayed on the altar. And I just started crying. I couldn't stop. I was thinking about everything Christ has done for me, all of the graces He has bestowed on me. "I have so many miseries! I don't deserve to be before you!" I thought. "Why, with all my miseries, do you still love me? Why have you put up with me all this year and brought

me to this point?" Afterwards, I went up and kneeled by the remains of
Father Muro and I prayed for his help because, more than anything in
this world, I want to be a Sierva.

"I want to be a Sierva." This phrase is inseparable for the sisters from
the intimate knowledge of and communion with their founder. Wander-
ing into the chapel during an "off-hour" when official prayer time was
not scheduled, I was likely to see one of the sisters kneeling, like Iris, on
the altar, bent over in prayer, contemplating the remains of Father Muro
and the sacrifices he made so long ago so that today she could wear the
holy habit of the Siervas.

A full thirteen houses would be founded in Father Muro's lifetime,
and the sisters would number 138 before his death. In the nearly one
hundred years since then, the congregation has weathered terrible trials
and survived the political turbulence that caused many other congregations to leave Mexico permanently or simply to close their doors forever. "But not us," the vicaress general told me. "No, not the Siervas! I
don't know why. But by the grace of God and Father Muro, we have
always had vocations."

Vocations, indeed. Today, the sisters number well over 600 (at last
count, the congregation had 647 members in Mexico alone), and the
seventy-eight houses of the congregation span four continents and seven
countries. Vocations have nearly tripled in recent years, and at least two
new houses were founded in the eighteen months I was with the sisters.
Both were novitiates—houses of formation founded to accommodate
the dramatic increase in vocations the congregation is witnessing.

CONTEMPORARY INTERPRETATIONS OF
FATHER MURO'S MESSAGE

The postulants, through extensive study of and engagement with the
teachings of their founder, became intimately acquainted with all levels
of Father Muro's vision of the "modern world," particularly his views on
their importance as women in the plan of redemption. "Ah, yes!"
exclaimed Alicia one day in the pantry, when I asked her about this aspect
of Father Muro's philosophy. "This is absolutely central. We have to start
studying this from the very first day we say we want to be Siervas. We
have to learn everything about it. It's what makes us who we are."

But the postulants did more than merely study Muro's writings. They
employed his ideas about modern life, Protestantism, and women in

their daily conversations and used his ideas to evaluate the behavior of people on the "outside" and make political commentary on the day's news stories. Perhaps more importantly, they gave Father Muro's ideas a contemporary flavor, applying them to uniquely twentieth-century problems, such as California's Proposition 187, the expansion of evangelical sects to Mexico, and pornography on the Internet.

One day, for example, as a group of us were walking to a chapel in downtown Puebla for a special intercongregational Holy Hour, Marta and I ended up hanging back a bit from the group, chatting amiably as we made our way down the crowded sidewalks. As she often did when we had the chance to speak alone, Marta began asking me what it was like to live in the United States. "Are there poor people there like here?" she asked. "Yes," I answered. "And in some ways they're more visible. You see more people in the streets there than you do here." "I guess that's because you don't have the same family closeness we have here in Mexico," Marta mused. After a pause she added, "Do you think the U.S. is losing its moral values?" "It's hard to say," I answered evasively. "Some people say yes, some people say no. And you? What do you think? Or what do Mexicans say here about the United States? "Well," she said, "we hear things about the U.S., that there's a lot of drugs and crime and things. But it's hard to know because we only see what comes through the media, which is always manipulated." This led us to talk about violence on U.S. TV. She brought up *The Simpsons,* which she said she understood to be "caricatures of certain types of people in the U.S." She talked about *The Itchy and Scratchy Show,* the cartoon the Simpson kids watch. "It's like, the cat eats a bomb or something and then it explodes!" Marta exclaimed, unbelievingly. "It's horrible! How can anyone laugh at that? Who laughs at that?" (I quickly stifled a giggle.) She went on to say that she thought TV violence in the United States was partially there to prepare its citizens to fight if there was a war. "I never really thought about these things before," she said. "I mean I did, but not consciously. But we're learning so much here [in the congregation] about how these things can influence a culture and affect people's values, and you can really see it."

In terms of gender, the postulants learned to apply their founder's understandings to contemporary issues and to view these issues, as they put it, "with new eyes." Most often, this took the form of articulating what many young Mexican women, including the postulants, experienced as a tension between "traditional" and "modern" styles of femininity in terms of national and cultural differences. One day, for example, as we were weeding the rooftop garden just off the postulants' dormitory, Carmen and I were talking about the influence of the American media on Mexico (a topic she initiated). "I don't like the liberalism of over there [the United States]," she said.

For example, you know that show *Beverly Hills [90210]*? I don't like it, but many young people here love it. And more than anything, they want to take on the identity of the teenagers on the show, you know? But the truth is, we don't have anything like that here in Mexico. The kids on the show are high school students, right? And the liberalism they have, you see it in sex more than anything. Particularly with the girls on the show. And girls here want to imitate what they see the girls on the shows doing. The girls on the show are these white girls [*muchachas güeras*], so girls here want to be white also, to dress like them, act like them—and what's the result? Now you're seeing more and more teenagers in Mexico treating sex like a game. More and more girls are getting pregnant. But since they had sex for fun and not because they really loved the boy, they have abortions. And now you're starting to see a decline in marriages, an increase in divorce—our values here are really changing, and it has to do with the media and Mexicans trying to imitate what they see Americans doing. Instead of defending our values, defending our way of living, we just leave our traditions and values behind because we're so enamored of the United States.

Magda put it somewhat differently but expressed similar sentiments. "It's hard, you know, being a woman today," she told me in a typical conversation one day as we were sweeping the classroom.

It's like we're finding a new way. We can't go back to the way things were. Even Father Muro saw that, almost a hundred years ago. But feminism in the American sense isn't the answer either. You see what it's doing to your country! Once the family disintegrates, the whole society disintegrates. So it's hard, you know? There has to be a balance between the old and the new. And as Father Muro said, the woman is the heart of the family, and the family is the heart of the society. So it's important for us women to find our way.

This "finding their way" as women in contemporary Mexico was central to how the postulants talked about their vocations, about finding out where God wanted them to be and do. As they—and I—sat through months and months of classes, lectures, workshops, and informal conversations about Father Muro's understanding of these issues and how they applied to modern-day Mexico, it became apparent to me that the congregation's program of formation aided the postulants in coming to terms with the tension of being "caught" between two undesirable models of how to be a woman. It was reinforced to the postulants again and again, day after day, that the choice was not to play the role of either the traditional Mexican woman or the liberated American feminist. There was, they learned in the congregation, a third way.

This "third way" the postulants learned in the convent legitimated a different way of being a woman. It was a mixture of elements, a selective combination of the "old" and the "new," which was then tied to a particular interpretation of Catholic doctrine and a specific understanding of Mexican cultural history. But this third way of being women did more than merely relieve the tensions of changing gender roles; the postulants learned that in it lay the future of humankind.

TRIANGULATING DISCOURSES

The congregation, then, in its history, mission, and contemporary articulations, speaks to three principal themes: religiosity, gender, and national identity. But more than this, it triangulates these issues. Religiosity, for example—whether or not one is a "good Catholic"—is seen as both a function and a barometer of gender (the proper performance of gender roles, particularly femininity) and national identity (the preservation of a sense of Mexicanness in the face of external cultural influences). Similarly, gender in this model—being a "good woman"— entails the embodiment of traditional Catholic values in the family and the community, and (by implication) the fortification of Mexico's cultural identity. And being a "good Mexican" in this view, at least for women, requires certain kinds of family and social orientations, including the edification of Catholic spirituality. In other words, the congregation offers new entrants a lexicon of understandings through which they are encouraged to reevaluate their experiences of themselves and the world. In the next chapter, I will turn to the general contours of the process of religious formation proper in the convent—the program of training through which young women are incorporated into the congregation and, over time, learn to become the Siervas envisioned by their founder.

CHAPTER 3

Religious Formation

Do not attempt to destroy the self-character of each novice. True
formation helps to expunge the bad that she has in her character
and to strengthen the good without destroying it.

Father Muro, Letters

Religious formation in the Catholic tradition refers to the preparation
of individuals for the religious life. It is the mental, physical, intellectual, psychological, moral, spiritual, and emotional training to which
an initiate subjects herself in pursuit of the particular set of skills and
internal dispositions that characterize the charism—the particular spiritual character—of her religious order. It is a reworking of the self
within a localized articulation of Catholic teachings about the nature of
the person, the soul, and the body. In the case of the Siervas, I suggest it
is also a technology of embodiment that rests on cultural and religious
elaborations of femininity as a phenomenological and practical site of
being.

The specific techniques of formation in the congregation are numer-
ous and complicated and are detailed throughout this book. This chapter focuses on the main themes and propositions that shape the process
of formation and help postulants internalize the congregation's ethos.

RELIGIOUS FORMATION FOR THE SIERVAS

"Think of fulfilling your vocation as a marriage," advised Mother
Catherine in class today. "You don't get married to be happy but to
make the other person happy. It's the same with the religious life.
You don't enter this life to be happy but to make others happy
around you. But if I sacrifice and surrender myself enough for
others, I will be happy, because this is where my happiness resides."

"I read that God does not demand this surrender, but your love
for Him is what moves you to do this willingly," offered Thea. "Isn't
it true that God never asks you for anything—it all comes from you,
from your love for Him? And the more you love Him, the more you
give. This sacrifice should not come from fear but from love."

"That's right," affirmed Mother Catherine. "To perfect ourselves
in love—this is what we're here for."

Excerpted from field notes, April 26, 1995

The Levels of Formation

The Siervas' constitutions characterize formation as a reciprocal process
between the entrant and God, with the congregation serving a mediating and guiding role. The stages of formation are frequently likened to
a courtship, with the congregation acting as a sort of matchmaker
between a woman and God. The "courting" process of formation is
designed to be long enough for one to clearly discern if the religious life
is truly her way or not.

There are five basic levels of formation: aspirant, postulant, novice,
junior sister, and third probation.

Aspirant. This stage can last anywhere from one year to five or six
years or even more, depending on the individual. The aspirant is one
who thinks she may have a vocation to the religious life and who
wants to be a nun. During the period of her *aspirantado* the aspirant
may tour various congregations, spend weekends at some of the convents, and attend the special vocational workshops organized by the
diocese that I will describe in chapter 4. Once she has chosen the congregation she "aspires" to, the aspirant begins a relationship with the
vocational director of that congregation, a nun who has taken her perpetual vows and who acts as a sort of sponsor for the newcomer. In
the case of the Siervas, this sister (Mother Josephine) educates the aspirant in the mission and charism of the congregation, visits the aspirant's family to talk with them about the religious life and what will
happen with their daughter if she joins the congregation and, I was
told, to evaluate the family's stability and the relationship between the
aspirant and her family. The sisters are very cautious about women
joining the congregation as an escape from their families, and they are
particularly concerned about any psychological or emotional difficulties the aspirant may have. The sponsoring sister makes herself available to answer any questions the aspirant or her family may have and

to help the aspirant discover and nurture her vocation. If it turns out that the aspirant decides she doesn't want to become a nun, or that she wants to join another congregation, the sponsor nun helps her find the most appropriate avenues for pursuing this goal. If the aspirant elects to continue this process with the Siervas, she moves on to the next stage in formation.

Postulant. On the six-month anniversary of the day the group entered the congregation as postulants Magda said to me, "I can't believe it's been six months. Six months ago today [she looked at her watch]—at this very moment! I was half crazy with my suitcases packed, ready to leave for the convent. Somebody called from there to make sure we were coming. My mom was ironing my clothes—Ay! I remember!" (excerpted from field notes, February 28, 1995).

The postulant stage lasts for ten months, usually from August to June of a given year, and begins when a young woman officially leaves her home and comes to live at the convent full time, declaring her intention to become a sister of the order. Although the postulants wear a special uniform and cover their hair with a veil while in the chapel, they have not yet taken any vows, and they can leave the congregation easily if they so choose by simply declaring this wish to the mother general. The postulancy is a period of study, reflection, and work designed to deepen these women's understanding of the religious life and to further test their vocation. The young women learn the ins and outs of the religious life in the congregation and study both Catholic doctrine and the history and charism of the congregation, as well as learning about the "arts" of being a nun—prayer, sacrifice, humility, and the like. This is where the women get their first taste of the religious life and what will be expected of them if they become Siervas. At the end of this stage, postulants who want to continue in the congregation must apply to enter the novitiate. Not all apply, and not all who apply are accepted. Those who are move on to the next stage of formation, receiving for the first time the habit of the Siervas and their own treasured copies of the constitutions and directory of the congregation.

Novice. This stage lasts for two years and is considered to be the most intense and powerful stage of formation. The novices do not live in the Central House but in another house out on the edge of town. The two years of the novitiate are cloistered in the sense that visits from and contacts with family and other outsiders are strictly limited. The novices cannot leave the novitiate grounds except in case of extreme emergency. Their time is spent in intense study and meditation to continue the development of their vocations and to further test their commitment to the religious life. This is said to be a time of active "courting" between the novice and Christ, during which she must decide if she wishes to become His bride forever. For this reason, the novices are often referred to as "novias," the sweethearts or brides-to-be of Christ. In accordance with this image, a postulant, on entering the novitiate, dons a starched white veil, like a bride (at higher levels of formation she will wear a black veil). From now on, she must never let her head be uncovered in public. At the end of the second year of the novitiate the graduating novices profess their first temporary vows, becoming junior sisters.

Junior Sister. This stage lasts for five years, with the last year being considered a separate stage of formation. Upon the profession of their first temporary vows, the novices (now professed sisters) are given assignments in other houses of the congregation that may take them as far afield as Italy, Africa, or the United States. During this time, the they work alongside fully professed nuns (those who have professed perpetual vows) and are totally immersed in the life and work of the congregation. In each region, meetings are held once a month for the junior sisters and their regional supervisor, and they go on special retreats to continue their education and formation. At the end of the first year of the *juniorado,* if she chooses to continue, the junior sister renews her vows for two years. At the end of these two years, if all is well, she renews for another three. If a woman wishes to leave the congregation for any reason, she simply does not renew her vows the following year and incurs no penalty or punishment.

Third Probation. This is the final year of the *juniorado* before the profession of perpetual vows. It is a year of "retreat" in the Central House devoted to intense study and contemplation—a dramatic change from the hard work and busy days of the last five years.

Perpetual Vows. At the end of the third probation year, provided she wants to move forward, the junior sister takes her perpetual vows and receives her wedding band from Christ. This "receiving of the ring" is considered to be the focus of the profession ceremony, and the nuns use it as a time marker: "Such and such an event happened before

I received my ring," or "I had just received my ring when . . ." After taking the perpetual vows (all the nuns change levels in July with great ceremony), the junior sisters become full-fledged sisters and are quickly given their new "assignments," which may take them anywhere from Puebla to Honduras to Kenya, depending on their interests and abilities and where they are needed.

Continuing Formation. But formation does not end with the profession of perpetual vows, and the sisters are quick to stress that formation is never complete. To be "completely formed" is to be configured, without defect, like Christ. Since this perfect configuration with Christ is not truly attainable by sinful, imperfect humans, formation is always a process of becoming and of striving for perfection. "Formation lasts your *whole life,*" Mother Veronica, the mistress of postulants, told us in class one day. "Christ's process of consecration lasted His whole life. It's the same way with all people, and especially with us in the consecrated life. To be a good Sierva, you must continue to seek perfection until the end." To aid them in this journey to perfection, the sisters have what they call "continuing formation": lectures, workshops, retreats, and classes in which they are encouraged to participate for the rest of their lives, although the frequency with which they do so is not mandated and is left up to each sister to decide.

As noted above, the sisters frequently compare the stages of formation to a courtship in that the process is one of building of an intimate relationship between a woman and God and is designed to be long and challenging enough for each woman to clearly discern if the religious life is truly her way or not. Like a human relationship, the sisters say, the relationship with Christ takes work, and the period of formation is specifically geared toward giving a woman the time and flexibility to work through whatever issues may arise for her. By the time a woman takes her vows, she should be absolutely sure she has a vocation, just as a regular bride should (ideally) be sure she wants to spend the rest of her life with her husband before taking her marriage vows. Religious formation, then, is a process of self-discovery and transformation that culminates—if all goes well—in a willing and happy union with God.

THE DOMAINS OF RELIGIOUS FORMATION

The goals of religious formation for the Siervas are many, but we can tease out several explicit domains of concern that find increasingly sophisticated expression as one moves up through the ranks. The principles of formation one learns (and hopefully embodies) as a postulant are the same as those one learns later. The difference is that as a woman becomes progressively more formed *(más formada)*, her understanding and appreciation of the spiritual and mystical implications of the formation should become clearer, thereby proving more powerful and penetrating.

There are, as I read them, three principal pillars of religious formation: the vows (the explicit and formal requirements of the religious life), the dispositions (the subjective orientations believed to be essential for achieving these formal requirements), and what I will call the metaphysical problematics (specific beliefs about the nature of the body, the self, and the soul that conceptually link the dispositions and the vows). The information presented here is taken from over one hundred classes, lectures, and workshops I attended with the postulants, from extensive discussions about the material with the postulants and with sisters at all levels of formation, and from both formal and informal interviews over a period of approximately eighteen months.

The First Pillar: The Vows

My experiences with the sisters persuade me that at the heart of the process of religious formation is a reorientation of embodied experience. The key to this transformation, the sisters believe, lies in a rechanneling of the passions, a sculpting of the "natural" impulses according to the vision of the congregation. Once a woman can claim some sort of control over what were previously unconscious processes, she can learn to manipulate them in order to foster the relationship between herself and God desired by the congregation. The control comes from first making "natural" inclinations explicit and then countering them through daily practice. The vows of poverty, chastity, and obedience are meant to assist the sisters in concretizing these inclinations so that they may then be targeted for change.

Poverty: Poor in Body and Spirit. The concept of poverty holds a pivotal place in all forms of Catholic religious life and is particularly central for the Siervas, who understand their mission to be one of working with the poorest of the poor. Poverty means literal material poverty, the relinquishing of material comforts. But for those who practice it, this vow is meant to reach much deeper, into the realm of desire.

Depriving oneself of possessions or material comforts is seen as a means to an end, a technique for breaking the fundamental link between the self and "the world," whose evil is thought to spring directly from our tendencies toward acquisitiveness and covetousness. The practice of poverty, then, is meant to set the practitioner in direct opposition to the values of the outside world, thereby freeing her to explore alternative ways of experiencing herself, others, and God.

The habit is the most visible expression of this vow, signifying that the Sierva owns nothing of her own, not even the clothes on her back. The constitutions state that "[i]n the vow of poverty, the sisters give up the right to material things without permission of their mother superior." Because of this, Father Muro made clear in his writings that the mother superiors had to take good care of their charges so that the sisters would not be tempted to provide for themselves. "We must be poor like those outside," Mother Veronica explained to the postulants in class one day, "although in reality we have it better than the people outside. We can go to the doctor if we're sick, we have a place to sleep and plenty of food. Our congregation gives these things to our postulants. But *within* this, we must live the vow of poverty. We must achieve detachment from all material things. But the Siervas are sometimes criticized," she continued. "People say, 'How can you say you're poor if you live in such a big house?' But we don't have anything the poor don't have. They all have TVs and VCRs. The important thing is that each individual nun doesn't own anything. And the nice things we do have— classrooms and the library—are there so that we can give better service to the poor."

In the early days of the congregation, sisters were asked to give a dowry to the congregation to help pay for room and board. This is no longer required, as it is believed that a sister's labor in the service of the congregation is payment enough for her keep. Some families, however, do elect to settle some money on the congregation in the name of a family member who has become a Sierva. In these cases, the money is kept in a local bank under the individual sister's name. If she decides to leave the congregation at any point, she is given this money plus interest. If she remains in the congregation until she dies, the money then becomes the property of the congregation. Since the postulants are just beginning to test the waters of the religious life and it is understood that some may not stay to "repay" the order for their keep, their families are asked to contribute what they can to aid with the maintenance of their daughters during this first year. Sometimes the families give money.

Others give payment in beans or other crops if their cash flow is tight. And if a family is unable to provide anything, the congregation asks only that they lend spiritual support to their daughter.

Ideally a sister should own nothing of her own, but the congregation does allow each nun to have a few personal items, such as books, sewing kits, or religious statues. Each professed sister has her own small room where she may keep these things (although all personal items should be out of sight except for a cross or a rosary with which she may want to decorate her wall). The postulants, by contrast, sleep in a barrackslike dormitory, with their personal space reduced to two drawers in a small nightstand (see chapter 6). Professed sisters do have their own habits, undergarments, shoes, and hose, but it is understood that, ultimately, these have been purchased with money from the congregation and therefore belong to it. The arrangement is somewhat different for the postulants, who are expected to provide their own clothing and materials. If, however, a postulant's family cannot afford to buy these things for her, the congregation will do so.

The sisters view the vow of poverty as particularly significant in today's world, which they see as being overrun with materialism and greed. As products of this world, newcomers to the congregation must struggle to release their attachment to personal belongings. Postulants are required periodically to switch beds, exchange notebooks, or throw away mementos as reminders that they should never get too attached to material things.

But even more important than material poverty, the sisters believe, is learning to maintain a spiritual poverty, a recognition that one *is* nothing and can *do* nothing without God. This, the sisters emphasized, is by far more difficult than material poverty because it means that one must release all claims to self-sufficiency and self-determination. It means, in short, that one must learn to surrender oneself completely into the care of God, becoming absolutely dependent on Him for everything. Releasing material things, Mother Veronica explained to me in an interview, is difficult but becomes easier once you see that the congregation really will provide you with everything you need. Spiritual poverty is much less tangible and requires a great deal more faith. But more than this, the sisters say, whether you receive the fruits of spiritual poverty depends on you and on the completeness of your surrender. Whereas you can embrace material poverty within the safety of the congregation, your spiritual needs may not be met if you are not 100 percent committed to this ideal. "But sometimes," Mother Veronica told me, "it's these times, when you've reached the end, and feel that you can't do *anything,* that God comes to you the strongest and fixes everything!"

Chastity: Saving Yourself for God. Although chastity is often the most sensationalized vow in theatrical or literary portrayals of the religious life, the sisters told me that chastity is not as hard as people generally think it is (although, they often added parenthetically, men may have more trouble keeping this vow than women). Chastity does not mean virginity, and a woman does not necessarily have to be a virgin to enter the congregation, though she must certainly renounce sexual activity once she does join. The practice of chastity, at least for the Siervas, entails not so much a physical state as an emotional attitude about one's body and one's femininity and how one uses them in the world.

"We cover our hair so that it doesn't serve to please men," Mother Veronica explained to us in class one day. "The vanity of a woman is her hair. God wants your *soul* to be combed and styled! Some nuns still have bangs tucked up under their veils. But who are you trying to please? God doesn't care about this. We should remember the example of St. Rose of Lima," she continued. "She was a beautiful woman, and many men wanted her. So she cut off all her hair, and the men fled, and that was that."

Chastity, then, means giving the most intimate part of yourself to God. It is a renunciation, a sacrifice. But, as with all sacrifices the sisters are asked to make, they consider it a renunciation not simply for the sake of renunciation but for the love of Christ. "If someone asks you why you want to be a nun, it's not because you don't have anyone to *do it* with!" said Mother Veronica, to the embarrassed laughs of the group. "It's that all we have is given to Christ out of our love for Him—our hidden man."

For the Siervas, the vow of chastity serves two primary purposes, one spiritual and the other practical. On the spiritual side, remaining chaste is an emulation of divinity and particularly of Mary, who, in their understanding, achieved the most sublime state of motherhood and of marriage through her chastity. To them, purity of the body in this sense represents a willingness to preserve all of one's valuable "feminine" characteristics (such as servitude, humility, caring, and generosity) for the service of God alone. The preservation of the body in this way symbolizes the preservation of the soul as dedicated to the matters of the spirit.

On the practical side, chastity is meant to free a woman from intense emotional commitments to particular people so that she can direct all her love and care to the poor in the service of God. Chastity in this context is considered to be evidence of fraternity, of loving everyone in one's life equally, without special favor. "Chastity is the love and the fraternity that we have among ourselves, the accepting of our sisters for who they are as human beings," explained Mother Veronica. Chastity is in many ways another manifestation of the vow of poverty—in this case, a poverty of strong emotional attachment to any one person. The vow of chastity, then, like the vow of poverty, is meant to help the sisters reorient their feelings about relations to others and to the world and to imbue their actions with new meanings that may or may not be desirable in their lives as Siervas.

Mother Veronica noted that the practice of chastity is considered to be more difficult for men than for women (who tend, according to conventional wisdom, to have more difficulty with the issue of fraternity). "They say that when men leave the religious life it's because they want sex," she told us in class. "Women leave the religious life because they can't live in community." But this doesn't mean, she stressed, that chastity is a nonissue for women in the religious life. "It's the same with us—we're human, too" she cautioned the postulants. "You must never think you're so strong that temptation will never happen to you. You must keep yourself far away from these situations. There are cases where women leave the convent for a nice pair of pants. This will be harder for you than for nuns in the cloister because you have so much contact with people. You must be vigilant. The devil comes in many shapes and sizes."

Obedience. Class handouts on obedience read, "Oh beautiful obedience! Oh free subjection! O rich poverty! Oh incomparable happiness of the true deprivation, in which happiness resides!" The sisters almost uniformly cited obedience as the most difficult of the three vows. Poverty and chastity, they explained, have to do with giving up external things. But obedience requires a woman to give up her own will, her claim to her own life.

The Siervas are not an overly strict order when it comes to obedience, but they do maintain a hierarchy that is to be obeyed. Each house in the congregation is headed by a mother superior who is elected for terms of three years by the professed sisters at that convent. Each geographic region is overseen by a regional mother and her assistants (usually two), who are appointed by the mother general every six years. Elections for the mother general herself and her council are held every six years, with a two-term limit. Among the sisters themselves, the hierarchy is set in terms of levels of profession. Postulants defer to novices, who defer to junior sisters. Junior sisters defer to third probation sisters, who defer to fully professed sisters. Within the professed sisters there is general equality, although respect and due reverence are given to those who have spent many years in the congregation.

The Central House, where I was located, has a somewhat complicated authority structure because it is home to several levels of profession and is also the home base of the mother general and her council. But the basic structure looks like this: each community in the Central House (the postulants, the third probations, and the professed sisters) is headed by a superior (Mother Veronica, Mother Catherine, and Mother Clarissa, respectively). These superiors are the first recourse to authority for the sisters under their charge; only in extreme or serious cases are decisions referred to the mother general. To perform a penitence (an act of atonement for a specific transgression) or to leave the convent on an errand, for example, a nun must have the permission of her superior. In addition, Mother Clarissa is the mother superior for the Central House as a whole and has authority over all its inhabitants, excepting the general council. The other general and her council are higher ranking in the congregation than Mother Clarissa, and when they are in residence, decisions are deferred to them.

There are, furthermore, strict rules about communications between levels of formation. The sisters place a premium on preserving the integrity of each level, and the *formandas* are encouraged to keep relationships with those in other levels to a minimum. If a sister does wish to speak or interact with someone in another level (for example, to get help studying for a test or working on a song, or to accompany her to the optometrist), both are to obtain permission from their respective superiors. Part of the reasoning for this, I learned, is that the sisters do not want those in the lower levels of formation (i.e., the postulants) to be unduly influenced by those in upper levels. The decision to remain in or leave the congregation must be based on intense personal scrutiny and should not be influenced by the fact that someone else has "made it" and is happy or, conversely, has had a negative experience. But in reality, friendships were made across the levels of formation, although they were generally kept fairly well hidden from the eyes of the superiors.

The sisters are taught that obedience should always be prompt, cheerful, and generous and should be manifested in everything they do during the day, from completing their chores to showing up in the classroom promptly when the bell rings. "All of the things we do are to conquer our will," Sister Linette, a third probation sister, explained to me. Proper responses to a request from a higher-ranking nun include "Yes, Mother," "Of course, Mother," and "With pleasure, Mother." Requests are expected to be attended to immediately and expeditiously. Such obedience, the postulants learned, should be undertaken with full awareness that obedience involves a domination of one's natural inclinations.

Our natural inclination to disobedience, the postulants and I learned, is a function of original sin, the disobedience of Eve in the Garden of Eden. As a result of Eve's disobedience of God, we were taught, humans have been distanced from the grace of God, and this sin must be atoned for with obedience: Mary's obedience, the complete submission of the self to the will of God. To make amends for the will-fulness and egoism of humans, the sisters believe their obedience should be perfect not only externally but also internally. The practice of obedience in their daily activities, they believe, opens them up to the reception of grace.

Obedience, then, has its rewards. The sisters believe that from the moment they surrender themselves to blind obedience—totally renouncing their liberty, never more belonging to the world—they will be free. They will experience, as Mother Catherine described it to us in moral theology class, "a spiritual and supernatural effect in their souls," they will "encounter a hidden treasure." A "field of unending, practical perfection" will open up to them, they will be happy not having liberty, and their souls "will expand with an unknown happiness." Their hands will be empty, but their hearts will be full—the opposite, they believe, of what happens to people in the world. In true deprivation, the sisters believe, resides happiness, holy liberty, a divine and pure joy. In this deprivation they approach the state in which the human ends and God begins.

The Second Pillar: The Dispositions

The three central—and related—dispositions that the Siervas maintain—humility, purity, and *entrega*—support the realization of the vows.

Humility: Becoming the Handmaiden of the Lord. The sisters told me obedience is said to be the hardest vow because a woman has to learn to suppress her own will in service of a greater good. This orientation of the will is the essence of humility. As Mother Veronica explained it to us, "Humility means not making excuses." It means taking responsibility for yourself and your actions and owning up to your limitations and faults. Although officially (in the language of the church) humility means considering oneself inferior to others, the Siervas do not necessarily agree with this interpretation. This may be the case sometimes, Mother Veronica noted, but to be effective in her work, each woman needs to maintain an equilibrium. "You shouldn't feel that you're 'nothing,' and you shouldn't hide the qualities you have," she told the postulants. "They've been given to you by God." Rather, humility in the Siervas' view means offering whatever strengths or talents one may have back to their source—God.

Humility (in the sense of recognizing one's limitations and taking responsibility for one's actions) is considered by the sisters to be the most basic of all the virtues. It is the foundation of poverty and obedience and is central to the Siervas' mission "because you can't live your vows without it," Mother Veronica said. "Humility is truth."

"Humility is so hard because we know that we're *not* humble," offered Thea during a class discussion on the topic. "It takes a lot of work to overcome this." "There are also degrees of humility," said Ruth. "This makes it very hard to practice, because it's not just a clearcut thing you do. It extends to everything." "The way to go up to God is to go down by humbling yourself," interjected Marta, reciting from a book of meditations she had been reading during Adoration. Pipa agreed but was troubled. She had found this the hardest virtue to practice, she said, because, to her, humility equaled humiliation. "But Sister," chimed in Celeste, "what bigger humiliation than to be *eaten* by another, as Christ does in Communion. All *sorts* of people take Communion. It is the ultimate humiliation to share your self with others in this way. If He can do it, so can we."

Mother Veronica gave the postulants some practical examples to help them understand just how important humility is to all aspects of their lives in the congregation, from the far-reaching to the mundane interactions of daily life. "You may be each other's superiors one day," she explained. "You may be okay with obeying someone older, but there may be cases when you have to obey someone younger than you." Mother Veronica said that when she first entered the congregation it was hard for her to call other sisters in higher positions "Mother" even when they *were* older than her and to kiss the hand of the highest-ranking sister in the house as was required. "Learning to do this without resentment was an important lesson for me."

Abby noted that Mother Carmelita had been a postulant with Mother Anabel; now Mother Anabel was the mother general and Mother Carmelita had to defer to her. "Just think," she said. "One of us could be a mother superior one day. And what humility to give such respect to someone you know so well!" "This takes humility on the part of the superior, too," said Mother Veronica. "You must be just and honest, you must be able to tell the hard truth, because a superior is in charge of all the souls of the subordinate nuns in her convent. It's also hard to assume authority over others when you know that, in reality, you are no better than they are. It is humbling to accept this position as the will of God, even if you don't feel comfortable with it."

But the attitude of humility must extend to what every sister does every day, she continued. "The congregation gives you a certain sense of security, the feeling of a big family, food, a roof over your heads. But you must be careful not to become greedy for material things, like money. Sometimes you may think, 'What if I leave? I'll have nothing' and you start to save up some money, to hoard it to feel safer. But this is a sign that you've lost your humility." To nurture the virtue of humility, the postulants must practice it every day. "If you have a talent or skill, you should put it at the disposal of others," Mother Veronica instructed. "If you can't help them at a given moment, go back when you have a free moment and help them then." Most importantly, humility works to counter pride. It includes asking for forgiveness for one's transgressions and learning to accept favors from others. It means taking responsibility for one's faults but giving credit for one's strengths to God. "If you're given a compliment," Mother Veronica illustrated, "you should say, 'Thanks be to God' for the gift He gave you. It's okay to recognize your talents, abilities, and virtues. But you must also recognize your faults, that you don't always do these things perfectly."

Perfectionism, then, is a sign of pride, a sign that one needs to work on developing the virtue of humility. "If you cry and cry when you make a mistake, you are saying that you think you can do things perfectly. You need to accept that we *all* make mistakes, we're all human," said Mother Veronica. "You must always remember that the hour of strength and effort is yours; but the hour of the results is the Lord's."

"When you think of humility, think of Mother Anabel," Mother Veronica continued. "She spends the whole year traveling around, spending only a few days in each place, hearing all the complaints of all the sisters. But you will never hear one word of complaint from her. She does it all out of love for the congregation." But the postulants, she said, had as many opportunities to manifest humility in their lives as the mother general did. "There are many ways to humble yourself in the daily things you do."

As an example, Mother Veronica told us a story about when she was just beginning in the religious life and she found out she was going to be transferred from her home convent to another house of the congregation. She didn't want to go, but her superiors told her she was going to be moved anyway. She went to the prayer room and cried and cried and cried, asking God why He was doing this to her. An older nun came in and asked her what was wrong. Mother Veronica could barely talk because she was crying so hard. But she told the older nun what she was feeling. The nun sympathized with her and comforted her. In the end, she was moved to the other house, and things turned out fine. "This was a very powerful experience for me," she said. "It taught me the importance of humility in living the vow of obedience. Whenever I need a reminder, I think of this situation."

Humility has been a central concern of the congregation since the beginning. Mother Veronica told us about the "old" days when the congregation was just getting started. In one house, the superiors had silver dishes and silver crosses to set them apart from the other sisters, their plates were washed separately, and they were treated regally. Then one day Father Muro came to visit the house and saw what was going on. "No!" he said. "We all must be the same!" So they took off the silver crosses and laid them aside.

Soon thereafter, Father Muro made some important changes in the structure of the congregation. It was common practice in the nineteenth century for religious orders to have "lay sisters," women who did all the "menial chores" (like cooking, cleaning, and laundry) while the full-fledged sisters did the "important work." Father Muro was uncomfortable with this arrangement. First, he changed the name of these sisters from "lay sisters" to "little sisters" (hermanitas), but soon thereafter he did away with this distinction altogether, saying that they were all sisters in Christ and should be treated as such. He decreed that the Siervas should all be active participants in the community.

Since the Siervas are an active order and have extensive contact with the world, the practice of humility can sometimes be particularly trying. "Ours is often thankless work," Mother Veronica explained. "Sometimes the attitude of the poor makes us angry because we're human. Sometimes we think, 'How can they be so ungrateful?' But we need to keep up in front that we work for the love of God and to please Him, and not for any other reason."

Purity: Transparent Simplicity. To maintain the spirit Father Muro left the congregation, the Siervas must practice humility with purity. "Purity" is not just physical or sexual purity, Mother Veronica explained, but purity of thought and intention, too. It means you must come to humility through simplicity. "Mother, what's the difference between simplicity and humility?" asked Marta in class one day. "It seems that humility is more profound." "It is," said Mother Veronica, "but simplicity is a part of humility." Marta was still confused. "It's like this," offered Celeste. "If humility is the root of obedience, simplicity is the seed."

To further develop the importance of the notion of purity as central to humility, Mother Veronica told the following tale with striking imagery. There once was a house, she said, where bloodstains kept appearing mysteriously on the carpet. No matter how many times the people in the house cleaned the carpet, there would be seeping new stains. Finally, chemists were brought in to try to figure out how to clean the carpet for good, but they were unsuccessful. The stains kept appearing. Could the postulants figure out what they were missing? The problem, Mother Veronica explained, was that the people in the house didn't look deep enough. They kept cleaning the surface of the carpet without looking for the source of the problem. There was, she explained somberly, a dead body under the floor, and as it decomposed its fluids stained the carpet. "If we want to achieve this purity of intention that is the foundation of humility," she instructed, "we must extract the 'dead body' from within ourselves."

In other words, purity for the sisters is bound up with relentless, unapologetic honesty with oneself. The practice of purity demands a corresponding practice of unmitigated self-awareness coupled with an absolute commitment to excise those parts of the self that are impure or polluting. Again, though this principle does apply to the physical body, it is not only (or even mostly) about physical purity. Rather, it is about a quest for authenticity and integrity of body, mind, and spirit so that one may more fully engage with the divine.

Like obedience, the dispositions of humility and purity take on a feminine cast for the sisters, and they are encouraged to look directly to Mary for guidance on how to manifest this virtue in their daily lives. Mary, they say, was a poor but virtuous girl, living her life as a normal person, when the angel of God descended from heaven and asked her to become the mother of the Messiah. Mary felt completely unworthy of such a grace, the sisters note, but she unquestioningly accepted the will of God, proclaiming herself His handmaiden and inviting Him to do unto her what He would. After Jesus was born, Mary cared for Him as a loving mother, even though she knew that He would someday be taken from her. After Christ's crucifixion Mary's faith did not waver, despite her overwhelming grief at the loss of her son. She continued to pledge herself to God and was rewarded for her unwavering faith by being assumed bodily into heaven to be reunited with her son as the wife of the Holy Spirit.

This is the prototype the Siervas emulate—to become servants, wives, and mothers to Christ in humility, as did Mary. In fact, *Sierva, Esposa, Madre* (Servant, wife, mother) is the title of a book of spiritual exercises, written by Father Muro and edited by Mother Anabel, that outlines the centrality of these three incarnations of womanhood in the mission of the Siervas.

Entrega: *The Dialectic of Surrender and Sacrifice. Entrega* is by far the most significant concept in the formation of young women as Siervas and will be taken up in more detail in chapter 9. Here, I will just briefly indicate how it relates to the other dispositions central to formation.

The notion of *entrega* infuses every aspect of the Siervas' lives, from the way they work to the way they socialize with each other to the way they pray. There is no equivalent word in English, but its meaning lies somewhere between "surrender" and "sacrifice," which the sisters describe as the respective roles of Mary and Jesus in the work of salvation. In the process of surrender, one turns the self completely over to the Other, becoming an instrument of the Other's will. In the process of sacrifice, by contrast, one retains an element of agency. Sacrifice implies a propitiatory relationship to the Other, whom one wants to please, to pay back. There is a sense of reciprocity, an ongoing mutuality.

Entrega, then, is akin to the notion of "throwing oneself into" something, as we do when we through ourselves into our work or undertake training to run a marathon. It means the voluntary endurance of suffering in pursuit of a distant, yet rewarding, goal. It requires a continuing commitment to this goal over a long period of time during which the achievement of the end is not necessarily assured. There is, then, an element of agency, a sense of choice and self-determination, and an expectation of results, either for oneself or for others. There is also a recognition that the outcome depends on multiple factors, many of which are outside one's control.

The sisters believe that *entrega,* like humility and purity, is a characteristically feminine disposition. They believe that women, by their natures, possess a special aptitude for this sort of complete, selfless surrender out of love for others. By developing an orientation to the world that is characterized by *entrega,* the sisters understand themselves to be embodying one of the most fundamental essences of femininity.

Formation, then, is not only—or even primarily—about altering one's external behavior, although this is clearly important. Rather, it involves refining internal dispositions that are linked to behavior in specific ways. Somewhat paradoxically, outward behaviors are taken to both manifest and shape internal states—they can be both a sign of one's dispositions and a means toward altering those dispositions. This is often very confusing for the newcomer because it is not always clear if a practice indicates the presence or the absence of the desired disposition. For example, if a postulant rigorously observes the Grand Silence and refuses to whisper with the others before going to bed, does this mean that she has adequately internalized the disposition of obedience? Or could it be that she struggles with precisely this attitude and is using pointed adherence to the rule of silence as a way of altering her disposition? In fact, it is both and neither. That is, the associations the postulants learn to make between behaviors and dispositions are complex and mutable and are highly dependent on. context and circumstances. Observing silence might be in one instance the practice of obedience and in another instance, for the same woman, an act of deliberate self-modification. A later chapter will return to this issue in examining more closely the specific transformative practices of the congregation.

The Third Pillar: The Metaphysical Problematics

Religious formation rests on certain understandings of the relationship between the temporal self and the eternal soul, and the process of transformation hinges on persuading a new entrant to accept and internalize these understandings as her own. In general terms, the congregation holds that life "in the world" operates with priorities and values that distract individuals away from living as God intended, encouraging the development of selves focused on autonomy, individualism, and instrumentalism. "The world" encourages—and even requires—prioritizing temporal experiences of self over a concern with the transcendental (nonbodied) self or soul. As a result, young girls who wish to enter the convent are believed to lack specific skills necessary for living the religious life, which must be acquired through a rigorous disciplining of mind, body, and spirit. This training can only properly proceed, the congregation maintains, once the destructive orientations to the world are dismantled. Then, ideally, the initiate is freed to develop as God originally intended, unfettered by worldly concerns.

As shown in figure 1, the temporal embodied self and the eternal soul are believed to be inextricably linked, but one is not reducible to the other. They are concentric without being coterminous. And at the center, for the sisters, is God. Religious formation involves learning to rest the spirit, the mind, and the body in this calm and serene center, the eye of a hurricane.[1]

Formation, then, is a dual process of deconstruction and repair that involves reorienting the phenomenology of embodied experience. One way it accomplishes this is by posing a core set of what I will call *metaphysical problematics* that the religious trainee must continuously negotiate in the process of her training. At stake in each is the question of the nature and scope of human existence, agency and responsibility—the "meanings" of life, death, and the workings of the universe. In working through the intricacies of these problematics in her own daily life, each sister learns to confront and question her most basic understandings of who she is and how she fits in to the larger fabric of the universe. These metaphysical problematics are (1) the dilemma of free will, (2) the shared sin of humanity, (3) the ideology of the temporal world, (4) the bonds of physicality, (5) personal accountability, (6) submission to the will of God, and (7) the rearticulation of self and soul. Though the sisters themselves do not use the seven identifiers I have chosen here, I am confident that they would immediately recognize and endorse these

---

1. As indicated by the dual-directional arrows, this model of the person can also be read in the other direction. God is at the center of one's being but also inhabits the region beyond one's own boundaries. The more perfectly a postulant orchestrates her temporal and eternal selves, the more clearly God can see His undistorted reflection *through* her and *within* her, and the more completely she can come to see herself as an integral part of God's glorification. I detail the specifics of this dynamic in chapter 11.

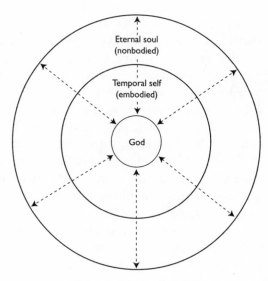

FIGURE 1. Temporal, embodied self and eternal,
nonbodied soul

problematics as I have described them as constituting, along with the
vows and the dispositions, core principles of religious formation.

The Dilemma of Free Will. God, the sisters believe, has a plan for each of
us, and this plan has been in place since the beginning of time, when all
souls were created. God has had intentions for us since "before we were
created in our mothers' wombs," as the sisters are fond of saying. But God
has also given us free will—we can choose not to listen or not to respond
to God's call or to actively work against His plan for us. Because of our
free will and our ability to choose either good or evil, we retain principal
responsibility for the state of our souls. Each initiate must grapple with the
degree to which she will voluntarily comply with what she believes to be
God's plan for her by turning over her body—her energies, activity, desires,
appetites, and inclinations—to the church.

The Shared Sin of Humanity. The postulants learn that they have fallen
prey to the temptations of worldly existence, attaching primary significance to their temporal selves to the neglect of their eternal souls.
This, they believe, is the state of the fall from grace that all humans
endure due to the disobedience of Eve and Adam in the Garden of
Eden—the result being a rupture between humans and God that is

characterized by a sense of great emptiness and longing. But unlike most people, the sisters maintain, their special vocation requires that they come to an immediate, visceral awareness of this rupture with God in a way that cannot be ignored and demands a response. In answering God's call, they work to reunite with God not only their own souls but the souls of others as well.

The postulants, then, must come to understand that they are inextricably one with the world, even as they elect to remove themselves *from* it by entering a nunnery. And they must learn to see their own private sins as having a direct impact on the state of others' souls, just as others' sins have on theirs. They must, in other words, develop an altered sense of their relationship to others as intensely intimate, while at the same time protecting themselves against the effects—spiritual or otherwise—such intimacy might bring.

The Ideology of the Temporal World. The choice between following God's plan and acceding to the temptations of the temporal world is complicated, the sisters say, by our living in a world that is only partially accessible to our daily awareness. The temporal world we walk around in is only a small part of all existence. We humans tend to focus on this temporal world—what we can see, touch, feel, smell—and to discount the reality of other dimensions of existence. This orientation toward the temporal world convinces us to strive for worldly goods and power. It promotes tendencies toward individualism, egotism, and seeing other people as merely means to desired ends. The focus on the material and temporal world serves the goals of Satan, the sisters maintain, and undermines the work of God. Conversely, an altered relation to the world and to others can facilitate the work of God and undermine that of Satan.

Newcomers to the congregation learn to understand "the world" as having induced in them an artificial perception and experience of who they are—in effect, a false self. They come to perceive this sense of self as just one aspect of their true, eternal beings. In the convent, the postulants must work to tease out which aspects of their worldly selves can (after concentrated training) be placed in the service of God and which aspects need to be relinquished altogether.

The Bonds of Physicality. Such a reorientation requires a transformed relationship to the material world, a new understanding of the material self. The sisters maintain that the soul and the body are united.

Acts of the body, then, are simultaneously acts of the soul. Evil is waged at the level of individual souls. Since the soul and body are united, this plays out at the level of individual bodies as well. The repetition of certain bodily acts is understood to transform the dispositions of the soul, whether toward virtue or vice.

New nuns must learn to understand and experience their bodies as articulating this relationship between temporal self and eternal soul. They must develop a particular sensitivity to their bodies' needs, desires, inclinations, and discomforts and learn how to interpret these bodily sensations as communicating something about the state of their souls. And they must develop a proficiency at *using* their bodies not only as barometers of the soul but as corrective instruments.

Personal Accountability. This close relationship between the body and the soul means that, by mastering the temporal self, individuals hold primary responsibility for whether they are living in grace (in accordance with God's will) or in sin (contrary to God's will). This is true for all people, but it takes on an added significance for the sisters, as they understand that they have consciously chosen to hold themselves to a higher standard of compliance than most other people "in the world." It is therefore the solemn responsibility of each sister to continually evaluate the degree to which she is living up to the standards set by God and the congregation, to identify areas that need improvement, and to strive to bring errant elements into line with God's will.

The postulants must develop both a keen self-awareness and a special kind of vigilance not only to external behaviors but also to internal states, inclinations, thoughts, feelings, and desires that may or may not be evident to others. This involves a level of self-scrutiny and evaluation that goes far beyond a mere adherence to accepted forms of behavior and reaches much deeper, necessitating a constant state of self-monitoring and correction that may be imperceptible to the outside observer. The fact that such self-critique is primarily internal and private heightens the personal accountability each woman has for her own process of self-correction. Ultimately, the truth of how well she is adhering to God's will is known only to herself and God. It is up to her, then, and no one else, to ensure that she is upholding her end of the bargain in that relationship.

Submission to the Will of God. The relationship between the nun and God is conceptualized as a dyad—a genuine relationship between two distinct (though metaphysically related) subjectivities. As such, it is often experienced by the sisters in ways that are similar to human relationships, complete with struggles, misunderstandings, disappointments, shared confidences, and new discoveries. And the sisters believe that the relationship with God, like human relationships, must be tended and nurtured in order to flourish. But because of original sin, the sisters believe that we reach to God (and He reaches to us) across a great distance. This distance is exacerbated by our mistaking our embodied selves as primary over our nonbodied souls.

An ideal relationship with God entails uniting our will with His. Just as our own actions can distance us from God, the sisters say, we also have the capacity to recognize our injured relationship with God and to repair this breach. We cannot, however, repair it through our own volition alone—repair can only come from God, who can choose to bestow this grace upon us (or not) depending on His will. We cannot direct the will of God, the sisters say, we can only submit to it. And only through this submission—this capitulation of personal will—can the relationship with God proceed.

Newcomers to the order must learn to manage this tension between the active and relentless pursuit of self-improvement and the more passive surrendering of ultimate control over the state of one's soul to God. A postulant must act in a practical sense as if her salvation were her responsibility alone, while at the same time developing a spiritual stance that maintains her ultimate powerlessness in the process.

The Rearticulation of Self and Soul. In the first weeks and months of formation, new sisters are guided in learning how to distinguish between their temporal (false, bodied) selves and their eternal (true, nonbodied) souls. As they become increasingly adept at experiencing and using their own bodies as the instrument through which they can explore and affect the relationship between these two dimensions of being, the overlaps and congruencies between the temporal self and the eternal soul become meaningful in new ways. The sisters believe that through our renewed relationship with God, we become able to recognize our authentic selves as God intended them to be—that is, as eternal souls temporally embodied in flawed human form. This new awareness, if embraced, can lead to an altered understanding of one's life.

In other words, the postulants must learn to understand their temporal selves and their eternal souls as distinct, yet metaphysically related. And they must come to understand the development—and later dismantling—of their false, worldly selves as part of a larger developmental process unfolding in the context of their vocation and, ultimately, of God's plan for salvation.

The seven metaphysical problematics of the formation process are interrelated in that each notion builds on the preceding one and serves as the foundation for the next. Table 4 summarizes this information.

The program of religious formation in the convent is designed to help young women achieve the subjectivity promoted by the congregation by walking them step by step through the internal transformation required of them as sisters in this order—by setting them on a "corrected" developmental trajectory based on a particular understanding of the relationships between their worldly selves and their eternal souls. And, indeed, the postulants themselves were absolutely convinced that they had undergone substantial transformation during the year, albeit in different areas and in different degrees. This was borne out by my observations as I watched the postulants change from eager but apprehensive newcomers to practiced, intense, mostly confident Siervas over the course of the first year. This transformation took time and was evidenced both in the postulants' actual performance of daily convent activities (showing up on time for class, doing a thorough job mopping the floor, staying awake during morning prayers) and in their general attitudes toward these practices. Some of the postulants improved dramatically. Some made progress in certain areas and continued to struggle in others. Two women in particular seemed resistant or unable to completely engage with these tools. Both women left the congregation before the research ended. While we cannot posit a direct cause-and-effect hypothesis, it seems clear that there is some correlation between engaging with these practices and "fitting into" and being contented with the particular style of life in this congregation.

Despite their drive for perfection, the sisters fully recognize their human limitations. Nevertheless, they remain passionately committed to the mission of their founder and understand their duty as Siervas to be particularly relevant in the modern world, where "masculine" greed, corruption, individualism, and secularism threaten to overrun the "feminine" values of charity, humility, community love, and religious devotion that they prize. The reshaping of their inner lives according to this philosophy, as the postulants were told again and again in a myriad of ways, was an essential prelude to the pursuit of a uniquely feminine humility and, perhaps ironically, sanctity. And the vehicle for this transformation, they learned, was their own female bodies.

TABLE 4. The Pillars of Formation

Pillars	Elements	Central Themes/Tensions
Vows	Poverty	Be poor of body and spirit
	Chastity	Save oneself for God
	Obedience	Become the handmaid of the Lord
Dispositions	Humility	"I am nothing without God"
	Purity	Transparent simplicity in act and intention
	Entrega	Dialectic of surrender and sacrifice
Metaphysical problematics	Dilemma of Free Will I can choose either to follow or to ignore God's plan	Free will vs. destiny
	Shared Sin of Humanity The sin of one compounds to the sins of all	Self vs. other
	Ideology of the Temporal World Attention must be focused away from the worldly/ temporal and toward the spiritual/eternal	"False" self vs. "true" self
	Bonds of Physicality The body and the soul are united and contingent	Body vs. soul
	Personal Accountability I am responsible for the management of my soul	Passivity vs. responsibility
	Submission to the Will of God Reunion with God comes only through complete surrender to Him	Control vs. surrender
	Rearticulating Self and Soul "True" and "false" selves become united within a new developmental perspective	Disorder vs. integration

BODY MANAGEMENT IN THE CONVENT

There are two broad domains of body management in the convent, the institutional and the individual. By the institutional management of the body, I mean the necessarily abstracted treatment of bodies in the congregation's philosophies and practices—as in, for example, the mandates that the sisters must rise at 4:45 in the morning and that certain forms of prayer must be executed while kneeling rather than sitting. The individual domain, by contrast, refers to individual women's selective modification of these concepts and practices by to address their own particular needs and goals. While these domains are closely linked and interdependent, they operate with somewhat different constructions of the body and understandings of the relationship between body and self. Institutional management is based on a universalizing view of human bodily experience and treats bodies as material entities that all have similar features, desires, and weaknesses. Individual management, in contrast, involves a more contingent phenomenology of the body, a recognition of the body as highly individualized through variable experiences.

These views of the body are not mutually exclusive, but they do have a particular relationship to each other. Through proper religious formation, the sisters believe, the institutional regimentation of bodies permits the emergence of effective management of one's own body in the pursuit of spiritual aims. One of the tasks of formation is to educate newcomers in the forms of body control employed in the convent and then to help them individualize these practices of discipline to confront their own obstacles. In other words, this aspect of formation makes institutional values about the body available for individual use.

From what I observed with the sisters, two things must be in place for this to happen. First, the postulants must develop a particular understanding of their bodies as bounding a sacred and potent interior space (chapter 6); second, they must habituate their bodies to the daily practices of the congregation (chapter 7). Through managing the experiences of the embodied self, the sisters hoped to reform the state of their eternal souls.

Thus the formation program in the convent functions as a developmental model of self-transformation that organizes interrelated core themes about the self in a particular sequential order while at the same time articulating them as tensions between embodied and transcendental experiences of self. The specific practices and strategies of the order assist new entrants in mediating these tensions through daily practice and an altered phenomenology of embodiment. As we will see, this program of self-transformation also functions as a technology of gender, persuading women to accept alternative understandings of their own femininity.

FULFILLING A RELIGIOUS VOCATION

The day I took my first Communion, I knew I wanted to marry God. I was only six years old, but as soon as I took Communion I knew. Then, when I was in sixth grade my grandmother died. She left me many of her things—her papers, some books. And she had some books on the life of Saint Theresa. I read this one small book, and I remember something St. Theresa said: "Jesus, I want to love you, in reparation for all those who don't love you." Oh imagine! To give everything for God! I knew then that I wanted to be an *enfermera* [nurse], a nun, and to serve the poor. And look at the congregation I'm in! I was thinking about all this when we had to do the self-analysis for the psychologist [a project they had to complete for their human relations class], and I remembered that's what I thought about when I was little. I thought, "That's how I want to be! [Referring to St. Theresa.] That's how I want to be—to be like, "God, I love you so much. And for all those who don't love you." Ahhhh—it's *bien padre* [way cool]!

Interview with Marta, April 12, 1995

According to the sisters, no amount of formation will make a good nun of the woman who does not truly have a vocation, a divine call. And, as Mother Veronica clarified, "God doesn't call us to human or temporal work but to *supernatural salvation*. And He calls us to work for the supernatural salvation of others."

This calling, the sisters emphasize, is strictly personal, with a particular end in mind, and is manifested directly to the persons of God's choosing. "As a nun," Mother Veronica instructed us, "you are going to configure yourself with the characteristics of Christ the Merciful Servant, as it states in our constitutions. But each of you also has her own special 'charism' that will be revealed to you by Christ throughout the course of your life in the congregation." Mother Veronica told the postulants that it was completely normal for them to wonder why they had been chosen over others to follow Christ in this special way. But, as she frequently cautioned them, they should never forget that it was a privilege to be called by God and that it was not their decision but His.

This calling, however, is not a one-way street. It takes the form of a dialogue between the person and God. In the sisters' understanding, there is one who calls (God) and one who listens and perhaps responds. We were told it was possible for someone to have a vocation and not to hear the call (and therefore not to respond), or to hear the call and not heed it. It is not enough for God to call one to the religious life, we learned. One must answer this call with decisive action. The next section will turn to how, precisely, new nuns learn to perceive, interpret, and respond to this call as they move through the seven stages of transformation.

PART TWO

Becoming Women in Christ

CHAPTER 4

Brokenness

Restless in My Own Skin

Would you give your life for the Kingdom of God?
The IDEAL is grand. . .
You should pray intensely to discover if God is truly calling you.
THEN, make a sacrifice in order to achieve this grace of predilection.
THEN, ask for guidance, first from God, and later from someone
   who can orient you.
OPEN YOUR HEART TO CHRIST!

From a brochure for a pre-religious-life vocational retreat

The first stage in the process of religious formation for future postulants is acknowledging a broken self and articulating that sense of brokenness within a religious framework. Specifically, postulants learn to interpret their experiences of *inquietud*—restlessness or discomfort with their present lives—as indicating the call from God to become a nun. Before entering the congregation, a young woman must develop the desire and motivation to dedicate her life to God and must come to see joining a nunnery as the natural and necessary outgrowth of this desire.

Many of the postulants told me that, until shortly before entering the convent, they had never seriously considered the religious life as an option. They had boyfriends and social lives, kept busy with school and sports and work and family. Some planned to or did attend college. But despite living normal, relatively happy lives, each recounted to me the experience of a creeping, then gnawing, sense that something was very, very wrong. As Marta explained it to me, "I just felt empty. It was like, I had all these things in my life, and I was happy enough, but *no me llenaba*—it didn't satisfy me." Each of the postulants described similar feelings: "I felt lost." "There was a hole in my heart." "Something wasn't right." "My life didn't fit right, like when clothes are too big or too small." "Something was broken inside me and I didn't know what."

There were different approaches to dealing with this feeling of emptiness. Some girls changed jobs, others left or started college. Still others
broke up with boyfriends or started spending late nights out at wild
parties. "I just wanted to find what I was missing," Abby explained.
"I was looking for something, but I didn't know what it was or where
to go to find it." Participating in some form of religious activity usually began as part of this searching process. Marta started teaching
catechism. Celeste began daily meditations at home. Dulce found she
enjoyed attending morning Mass. "It was like religion was a place
where I could find peace," Magda told me. "I went to church, and
afterwards I felt filled, complete. I was calm. It was a totally different
feeling from what I felt the rest of the day." Gradually, these women
began to wonder if perhaps they were being called to the religious
life.

Most of the young nuns I knew responded to this feeling first by ignoring it and hoping it would go away. But they reported that, try as they
might to get away from it, the sense that they were being called to the
religious life "followed" them, manifesting itself in small daily occur-
rences that, over time, started to seem too "weird" to be mere accidents
of circumstance. "I had this dream," Marta told me. She continued:

> Actually, I was at one of the retreats for aspirants [women who want to
> enter the convent the following year]. It was one of the first retreats, and
> I still wasn't used to all that long, silent prayer. So I kept falling asleep—
> it was kind of embarrassing, actually. But I was so tired! Anyway, at
> first, I had some silly dreams, like about going to the store to buy chick-
> en, things like that. But then I had a more vivid dream. In my dream, I
> was in a strange place with Mother Josephine, the director of vocations
> for the Siervas. She was standing to my right, and we were in front of a
> wall with bars—like a gate—to our left. We were looking at a painting
> of Jesus knocking at a door. In my dream, I heard a voice, speaking to
> me so that only I could hear it. "The door is there if you want to find
> it," the voice said. "And Jesus is knocking." This jolted me out of my
> sleep for good, and I apologized to God for being so lazy.
> Then, just two weeks ago, we [the postulants] were at the novitiate
> practicing for the profession ceremony where we're going to sing. And
> you know, just inside the gate there, there's a painting of Jesus knocking
> on a door. Mother Josephine was to my right, and the gate was to my
> left. I asked Mother Josephine what she thought of the painting, and she
> said something like, "Jesus is knocking. All you have to do is let Him
> in"—almost exactly like in my dream. It didn't register at first what had
> happened, but Rosita [another postulant, and one of Marta's best
> friends] said, "Just like in your dream!" I was stunned. I couldn't believe
> it. I was so shocked I could barely speak. I immediately apologized to

God for having such little faith and for not realizing on my own the significance of the incident. (Interview, July 4, 1995.)

Amelia, too, recounted to me one of the "signs" she received that
God was calling her to the religious life:

> I remember once, when I was about twelve, my friends and I were play-
> ing. I mostly played with boys back then. I have three brothers and me—
> I'm the only girl. I didn't have many girlfriends. Anyway, we were sup-
> posed to meet to play and I waited for them for an hour. I was there
> waiting and they didn't come. So I got very angry, and I went home. Later
> they came to see me in my house. And they said to me, "Why didn't you
> wait for us?" and I said, "I waited for you, but then I came home." "But
> why?" they asked. And I said, "Because I shouldn't spend too much time
> outside and away from home, because *I'm going to enter a convent!*" I
> don't know why I said that—it just came out. It wasn't something I had
> been thinking about or anything. But since then was when I feel that—
> how can I explain it? It was during this time that I started to say this a
> lot, that I was going to enter a convent. And since then, the idea never
> left me. Always, in different occasions, in different situations, this idea
> would come to me. It was constant. (Interview, August 3, 1995.)

After a while, many began to read these little incidents as signs that God
was actively steering them toward convent life.

When these "coincidences" became too frequent or too telling to
ignore, most women forced themselves to overcome their shyness and
anxiety and begin searching for answers. Do others feel this way? Could
it be true that I've been called by God? Am I fooling myself? Inventing
things? Could God really want *me*? What does this mean? What does
He expect of me? As Surella described it to me:

> When I first felt that God was calling me to the religious life, I couldn't
> believe it. I thought, "Why me, God? Why me? I love you, but me—a
> *nun?* No way!" I remember thinking, "My parents only have one
> daughter. Why not call my cousin? My aunt and uncle have four daugh-
> ters! Take one of them!" I just didn't understand what God wanted
> from me. Why would He want *me*, anyway? I have to tell you, I was
> scared. But I was also excited. The prospect of being chosen for some-
> thing so glorious was, well, thrilling. But at the same time, I was terri-
> fied. What if I was wrong, or I made the wrong choice? What if I'm not
> up to the task God has assigned me?

This quest for answers generally leads a young woman first to seek
out a spiritual advisor, someone she can talk to about what she's feeling.
This person is usually a priest, a nun, a youth group leader, or someone
else she feels comfortable with and trusts. The reaction to her curiosity

about the convent varies. Some, like Amelia, are told that they are not "nun material." Others, like Thea, are told that they need more experience with boys or should get out to more parties. But generally, the response is positive, if cautious. The girl is usually counseled to take her time in understanding her vocation—to look for answers and get information but to realize that the process of entering the convent is long and arduous and demands deep, searching introspection. It requires confronting parts of ourselves, they are told, that cause us pain or guilt or discomfort. It is a serious business, becoming a bride of Christ.

SEEKING THE WAY: THE PROCESS OF DISCERNMENT

Ayyyy! Well, I felt pretty bad when I finally told my parents I
wanted to become a nun. There I was, half crying and half laughing
and everything. My papa, um—he did accept it, but not all the way.·
So he's never come to visit me. Just my mother and my brothers and
sisters come. Yes, yes, it's very difficult, but, well, as long as you
have your ideals it doesn't matter so much. That is, in spite of
everything, you continue forward.
                                        Interview with Clara, August 7, 1995

The next step for young women considering the religious life is to attend a series of retreats put on by the diocese, where they begin to learn how to name the emptiness they have been feeling in the outside world, to put words to their discontent. They learn in the retreats that what they are experiencing may be the *inquietud,* the restlessness, of a soul called by God to the religious life.

These weeklong, biannual retreats are organized and run jointly by sisters from various congregations throughout the diocese. The retreats are held just before Christmas and during Holy Week (leading up to Easter) and are designed both to educate young women about the Catholic faith and the experiences of the religious life and to help them to discern their true specific vocation, whether it be the convent, matrimony, or the single life. The seven days of the retreats are packed with classes, group activities, recreation, chores, prayer, and self-reflection. There are two different levels of classes, and a young woman who is thinking of entering the convent—in any congregation—is expected to participate in both levels, at least once. As part of the research, I, too, participated in these retreats and completed both levels of preparation for the convent life.

To initiate this process of vocational retreats, a young woman must complete an autobiographical questionnaire designed, as it says on top, to "help you with your reflection about important aspects of your personal life" and "to allow you *to know yourself with more precision, to discover the presence of the Lord* throughout your life," as well as "to help those who will accompany you in your Christian and vocational maturation *to know you* more profoundly" (emphasis in the original). The questionnaire solicits basic information, such as educational background, birth date, home address, medical history, and names of family members. But it also gets at more personal issues, such as the relationship a young woman has with her parents and siblings, the qualities she most admires in the people around her, where she sees herself in the future, how she believes she is perceived by others, and what her feelings are about her vocation.

In addition to presenting this questionnaire, the requirements for participating in the retreats are that a young woman must, according to the brochure, "demonstrate a clear desire to know and understand the religious vocation, desire to truly engage with Christ (not in order to evade personal, family, or work problems), be between sixteen and thirty years of age, and submit a letter of presentation from her parochial school or from a nun who knows her." The cost of the first retreat I participated in (in December 1994) was N$70 or, at that time, about US$20. The second retreat, which was given after the devastating crash of the peso, cost N$100, or about US$15. This fee covered room (military-style barracks sleeping about thirty women in two large rooms with mattresses on the floor), board, and activities for the week. Participants were asked to bring sheets, a blanket, a pillow, a Bible, a notebook and pen, personal clothing, clothes for playing sports, a towel, personal items (such as shampoo and toothpaste), and a guitar or any other musical instruments they might play.

THE VOCATIONAL RETREAT:
A TRANSFORMATIVE EXPERIENCE

The retreats are held in a building called the Youth House, which is located on the grounds of the diocesan seminary on the outskirts of town—a cold and drafty old concrete structure filled with spiders and wasps and other wonders of nature. I arrived for the first retreat on time, not yet accustomed to the Mexican penchant for temporal flexibility. I lugged my suitcase, my pillow, and my sheets and blanket up the stairs and walked into the sleeping quarters to which I had been assigned. I stood there for a moment, taking it in—the smell of mildew rose from the tattered and stained mattresses, and I shivered at the tomblike aspect of the concrete walls and floor. I picked a bed in the sunniest spot I could find and sat down to write in my journal.

About a half an hour later I began to hear laughing and loud voices echoing up the stairwell from below. Soon, groups of young women began flooding in, talking and laughing excitedly and rushing to claim the choicest beds for themselves and their friends. Sheets flew and beds were made. Stuffed animals and candy and bookmarks and prayer cards (with pictures of Jesus, Mary, or a saint on one side and a novena or other meditation on the other) emerged from suitcases and backpacks. Deals were struck and places switched so best friends could giggle together late into the night. The place was transformed as the enthusiasm and energy of the young women seemed to scare away the gloom. The decibel level escalated and the chaos endemic to Mexican social situations found its whirlwind groove.

Once all the retreat participants were settled (relatively speaking), the sisters from the city's various congregations began the orientation interviews. Each young woman at the retreat was called by one of the sisters, who would assess her motivations for attending the retreat, ask her about her vocation, and assign her to one of the two levels of classes. Participants in the two levels would come together for meals, group activities, recreation, and some presentations but would be separated for the periods of direct instruction. Mother Josephine, the vocational director of the Siervas, who had invited me to participate in the retreats, told me that I was free to attend either level, since I was there more for research than for personal religious reflection. I decided to begin at the beginning and to join Level One.

Identifying the Call

The first level of classes is designed to give the women a general orientation to the doctrines of the Catholic faith and to introduce the concept of vocation as a specific calling from God that should not be ignored. As Sister Mary Margaret (of the Benedictines) told us on the second day of the retreat, the objective of Level One is "to give to the young women participants the fundamental elements of the Christian vocation to carry them to a process of conversion and progressive growth of faith, so they can come to commit themselves personally to Christ." To this end, the week is packed with classes covering various topics, including the different examples of vocation related in the Old and New Testaments; the responsibility of humans to participate fully in God's plan of redemption; the threat of Protestant expansion, especially in Latin America; the Catholic doctrines of baptism, confirmation, confession, salvation, and resurrection; the mystery of the Trinity and how the Holy Spirit works in our lives; sin and its consequences; accepting Jesus as our personal Lord and Savior; and the discernment of our specific vocation (layperson, nun, or priest).

Saying Yes to Christ: The Model of the Virgin Mary

Mary, the simple woman
Mary the woman listening
Mary, the chosen one since the beginning of time
Mary, the woman who believed, full of FAITH
Mary, woman of prayer
Mary, humble, simple, and authentic woman
Mary, who lived in poverty—her only treasure was her SON
Mary, mother with the spirit of SERVICE
Mary, mirror of hope
> *Poem written on the blackboard at the vocational retreat*

The core model presented to help these young women grasp the concept of vocation was the Virgin Mary, handpicked by God to be the mother of the Messiah. In the evening Mass led by Father Luís, the diocese's director of vocations, on the fourth night of the retreat, Mary was hailed as the "ark of God" who carried Christ—the word of God—within her. Just as the Ark of the Covenant carried the broken tablets of Moses— the Old Law—Mary was the vessel bringing the New Law (Christ's Law) to God's people. The next morning we continued with our study of Mary, her role in salvation and the example she provided for every facet of life. Mary was, we were told, the "model of the ideal woman"— the model mother, the model girlfriend, the model wife. Mary was the "symbol of the integral woman—woman without masks." She was the epitome of feminine intuition and compassion and sacrifice and suffering. "To whatever vocation God has called you," Mother Martita (of the Servants of Mary) explained, "Mary is your model." But more than this, we learned, Mary's story articulated the very essence of "vocation." "When the angel came to Mary," Mother Martita continued, "she was overwhelmed, confused, and awed by the fact that the Lord had chosen her. She was afraid that she was not worthy of the extraordinary grace that was being offered to her. But never once did she doubt the veracity of the vision or that God had indeed called her to something glorious. God, for His part, left the decision up to Mary—he did not force her (although, as the Supreme Deity He certainly could have). The angel told Mary that God wanted her to be the mother of the Messiah but that she could refuse if she so wished. But, it was emphasized, she surrendered herself completely to the will of God. 'I am the handmaid of the Lord,' she responded. 'Do unto me according to Thy word.' This is the essence of vocation."

Like Mary, many of the young women at this retreat felt that they had been called to serve God in a radical way—as Father Luís put it, to "incubate Christ within them just as Mary incubated the baby Jesus in her womb." And their response, the sisters stressed to them, should be no less dramatic and selfless than was Mary's. In a sense, we were told, the inkling of vocation—the *inquietud* manifested in the sense of emptiness or brokenness in our worldly lives—was like an angel God had sent to us to ask us to participate in the plan of redemption. Like Mary, we had been chosen by God for specific reasons. The reasons might not always be clear to us, the sisters explained, but it was not for us to question God. Our job was to nurture this feeling of vocation, to clarify what God wanted of us, and then to give our answer—to say "Yes" to God as Mary did and to give over our lives to His will.

This naming of a girl's *inquietud* or sense of brokenness as a communication from God seems to be strikingly powerful on a number of levels. Not only does it give these young women a vocabulary for talking about their feelings, but it ties them instantly to a community of others. As one teenager told me at the winter retreats, "I thought it was just me. I thought maybe I was doing something wrong. But now I understand that it could be that God is calling me. Me! Just like he's called so many others. So maybe this feeling I thought was so bad is really God's voice, asking me to join in." This naming also seems to offer the promise of healing. At this point, a girl can choose either to live with her *inquietud* a while longer or to take decisive action to discover if God really is calling her to the religious life. The second level of these retreats focuses on helping participants to deepen their awareness of their *inquietud* and, if it persists, to select a religious congregation to join.

Narrowing the Focus

The second level of the vocational retreat (which I completed the following year) is much like the first level in terms of the topics of instruction, but it encourages a deeper engagement of the themes presented and a more searching self-reflection on the part of the participants. The second level also features a series of presentations by sisters from the various congregations sponsoring the retreat so that a young woman in this level can begin to narrow her focus and select a specific order to join. Representatives of each order present their congregation's charism (the underlying ethos of the congregation, the "flavor" of the congregation, or, as one sister described it, the "color" of a particular order as part of the rainbow of religious organizations), history (when, where, why, how, and by whom the order was founded), and mission (the principal work of the order—health care, education, missionary work, administrative work, etc.—or, as in the case of the contemplative orders, the identification with a particular aspect of Christ's passion and death).

In addition to these presentations, the young women are counseled on the procedures for entering the religious life and the demands they will face if they elect this path, and they are given the opportunity to direct specific questions to a panel of the sisters. One of the greatest concerns expressed by the women at the retreats I attended was the demands of the vows of poverty, chastity, and obedience and whether they would be able to forgo material comforts, sex, and independence for the rest of their lives. The sisters on the panel acknowledged the challenge the vows presented, and many admitted actively struggling with temptations over the years. "But however daunting these sacrifices may seem," we were assured by Mother Tere of the Franciscans, "God never presents us with challenges we are ill equipped to meet." If God has called a woman to the religious life, the sisters believe that He will give her the strength to overcome all obstacles in her way.

The Final Step: Selecting a Congregation

In this pre-religious-life retreat, the Lord has led you to delve deep into your Christian life, and He has advanced you in your vocational process. But is that enough? . . . We want to help you clarify the path God has chosen for you so that you may follow Jesus more closely.

"Proyecto de Vida" (Life Project), worksheet distributed at the end of the retreat

Toward the end of the retreat week each participant in the second level is asked to designate one of the attending sisters as her spiritual advisor for the process of discerning her vocation, and it is expected (though not required) that a young woman will join the congregation of the sister she has selected. Together with this advisor, each participant completes a "Life Project"—a worksheet designed to help her reflect on her experiences during the retreat and to plan specific steps she will take in refining her vocation.

By the time most women completed both levels of the retreats, they were ready and eager to enlist in an order. I noticed that the elements that tipped the scale in favor of one congregation over the other could be something as central as whether the order was contemplative (cloistered) or active (working), the charism and mission of the congregation, or the particular philosophy of the founder. It could also be as seemingly insignificant as the color of the habits or the design of the ring received when the perpetual vows were taken.

The sense in the retreats as they neared their close was one of nervous anticipation and almost giddy excitement as different women chose different congregations and future sisters congregated on each other's beds in the dormitory to exchange addresses and phone numbers, to pour over the brochures of "their" congregation, and to fantasize about what their new life would be like. They toyed with calling each other *monjita* (little nun), *madrecita* (little mother), and *hermana* (sister) and sighed wistfully over bookmarks and prayer cards showing images of Jesus, much as their "worldly" counterparts might swoon over glossies of Luís Miguel.

As bags were packed and sheets folded, Bibles put away, and candy wrappers disposed of, many of the young women expressed a mixture of excitement and sadness. Almost uniformly, they talked about having been radically transformed by the retreat experience and felt certain they would never look at their lives in the same way again. Last-minute impromptu conferences were held on the now bare mattresses as ideas were brainstormed for how to break the news about joining a convent to family and friends.

At the closing ceremony of the retreat, we recited the following meditation, designed to help us persevere in the newfound knowledge of our vocations:

> Here I am, Jesus, like the blind man in the road. You pass by my side and I do not see you. I have my eyes closed to the light. . . . On feeling your steps, on hearing your voice, I feel in me as if a spring is brought forth, like a bird that escapes flying, like a life that cries for you. I am searching for you, I desire you, I need you to help me traverse so many paths in my life.
>
> Jesus, I am blind to so many things. It is life, with its lights and colors. It is pleasure with its irresistible force. It is money, with its chains that imprison us. I am commencing to live, Jesus, and everyone wants

my life. It comes toward me every day, this propagandizing world, cal-
culating and without piety. It comes at me every day, this world of the
easy, the comfortable, and the luxurious. And I allow myself to be
caught and held, like a fly that becomes trapped in the spider web. . . .

Jesus, open my eyes to your life. I want to fix my eyes on yours and
read in them your friendship. I want to see your face with my eyes puri-
fied. I want to open my eyes to the light of your gospel. I want to look
at life head on and with feeling. I want faith to light my way. I want to
see you and I want to learn that life, pain, and death, without your light,
are chaos. I want to see in each and every man a brother. I want to open
my eyes to myself and to look deep into my life. I want to fix my eyes on
things and seek in them your likeness.

. . . Touch my eyes with your fingers and open them to the light.
Then the way—my way, Lord—will be clear.

Amid hugs and tearful good-byes, the young women spilled out of
the building. The parents who had come to retrieve their daughters
seemed relieved to have them back again but searched their faces for
signs of change. As the posters were removed and the soccer balls and
basketballs were packed into closets, as the desks were straightened in
the classroom, the lights turned off, and the creaky metal doors bolted,
the old, concrete building settled back into silence.

BECOMING A SIERVA: THE JOURNEY BEGINS

When I saw the brochure of the Siervas it caught my attention—it
was bright yellow and really stood out. So I said, "Maybe this is the
one—I wonder what these sisters are like." So I set it apart from the
rest of the brochures. The others just didn't grab my attention. So I
read it, and I really liked their charism, particularly the part about
the Merciful Christ. Later, I told Father Miguel that I wanted to join
the Siervas and he said, "Good! They're the best in Puebla!"

Interview with Surella, August 5, 1995

Each of the postulants I worked with completed this vocational program, or one very similar to it in another diocese, as a prelude to sign-
ing up with the Siervas. Once a young woman decides she wants to join
the Siervas, she must submit a letter to the General Council explaining
why she feels she has been called to the religious life and why she desires
to enter the Siervas in particular. She must also present a letter of recommendation from her religious advisor and/or Mother Josephine; provide proof of baptism, confirmation, and completion of at least a
secondary school education; and pass a physical. Once this documenta-
tion has been submitted, the General Council of the Siervas meets to

consider the applications. The most important criterion for admission, the Mother General told me, is that a young woman must genuinely believe she might have a vocation to the religious life, as opposed, for example, to seeking refuge from a bad relationship, looking for an escape from home, or wanting to please (or vex) her parents. The private motives of applicants are, of course, difficult for the council to discern with any certainty, but the vocational retreats, recommendations from religious advisors, and period of exploration before seeking admission do give the council a good deal of information about a young woman's decision process. If a woman is thought to be requesting entrance for motives significantly other than truly feeling the call, she is often advised to wait a year (or more) to discern more clearly why she wants to become a nun and whether the religious life is really where God wants her. Sometimes women who are asked to wait reapply the following year and are accepted. Sometimes they reapply and are not. And sometimes they decide not to reapply at all. When final admissions selections have been made (generally in mid- to late April), Mother Josephine personally contacts each applicant to notify her of the council's decision.

"I remember when I got the call," Magda told me.

> I remember it like it was yesterday. I had turned in all my materials, but then I had forgotten about it. Well, not really *forgotten,* but I tried to push it out of my mind, because it was out of my hands. It was like, "It's in God's hands now," you know? So I was home one day, cleaning the house because it was my brother's birthday the next day and we were going to have a party. So the phone rang, and it was Mother Josephine. "Magda," she said. "They've accepted you! Congratulations!" "They accepted me?" I said. I think she was expecting me to be more excited. But to be honest, I was scared to death. I just said, "Thank you," and hung up the phone and went into my room and lay down on my bed. "They accepted me," I thought. "It's really happening." I had a hard time concentrating on my chores for the rest of the day because all I could think about was how I was going to tell my parents I was becoming a nun.

As the final cuts are made, the entering class is advised of the supplies they will need to purchase in preparation for joining the order: the postulant's uniform, long-sleeved white shirts, kneesocks, black shoes, underclothes, nightgowns, slippers, a watch, a Bible, a Liturgy, notebooks and pens, and personal items such as shampoo, lotion, and feminine napkins. These materials can cost several hundreds of pesos, well beyond the means of some Mexican families. Although, officially, the congregation is not obligated to support a woman financially and materially until she has professed her first set of temporary vows following the year of postulancy and two years of the novitiate, if the mother general and the General Council are convinced of the sincerity of a young woman's desire to enter the religious life and believe it probable that she has a genuine vocation, the congregation will provide these items to her free of charge.

As the time for the entering ceremony nears, Mother Josephine makes the rounds to the homes of the entering postulants, speaking with the parents and helping to break the news to them if the young woman has had difficulty finding the courage to do so herself. "Mostly, the parents just need reassurance that their daughter will be well taken care of," Mother Josephine told me. "They also need to realize that she's joining the congregation because she *wants* to—no one is forcing her, and she is free to leave at any time. The most important thing is to help the parents feel involved, to show them that they're not losing their daughter forever. She's just pursuing the path God has chosen for her, and this is a very honorable thing."

In the months leading up to the entering ceremony (held in late August—August 28 for the group I worked with), special retreats are held for the entering class so that they can begin to feel comfortable in the convent and can become more accustomed to the rhythm of the religious life. They may stay in the convent for up to a week at a time, sleeping in the small dormitory just south of the library. During the day they assist the sisters in routine chores and attend workshops on prayer, vocation, and the history of the congregation with Mother Josephine. They remain, however, "outsiders," and do not eat with the sisters or attend classes with the postulants or participate in the singing of the morning office.

Finally, the big day arrives. The soon-to-be postulants arrive with their parents in the early afternoon, and all file up the stairs to the postulants' apartments. Mother Josephine and Mother Anabel, the mother general, greet the new entrants and their family members in the postulants' classroom. Emotions run high. The young women have difficulty sitting still in the small desks in the classroom, and their nervous energy is contagious. Finally, the mother general finishes her introduction, and the women are sent upstairs to the dormitory to change into their uniforms.

The families are led into the central chapel, where candles and incense are burning. They are asked to pray that the Lord guide their daughters and help them to discover if this is truly the place they should be to best serve Him. They pray for the strength to let go of their daughters, to turn them over to Christ if that is indeed their calling.

Then the double doors at the back of the chapel open, and the entrants come filing in. No longer in their street clothes, they have been transformed. No more jeans and tennis shoes. No more flowered skirts and frilly blouses. No more makeup. No more earrings. Instead, they are dressed in identical blue jumpers, white shirts, beige kneesocks, black shoes, and black veils. There are muffled gasps—and some stifled sobs—from family members as the women walk quickly to the front of the chapel and file into the pews that have been reserved for them on the left side of the aisle. They are silent, but their faces reveal the complexities of the emotions going on inside them. They kneel down and wait for the Mass to begin.

"I remember kneeling there," Surella told me,

and I remember thinking, "I can't believe this is really happening! I can't believe this is really happening!" I was trying so hard not to cry. And the funny thing is that I didn't even know if I was crying because I was sad or because I was happy. Both, I guess. Anyway, we had the Mass, and it was *so beautiful*—I can't even describe it. I really felt like the Lord was right there with me. Right there, by my side. I think we all felt it. And when I took Communion, I knew that He was telling me that He would give me strength, that I was where He wanted me to be.

As part of the Mass, the mother general officially welcomes the new entrants into the congregation. From that moment forward, they are postulants of the Siervas.

When the Mass is over, it is time for the families to leave. The new postulants are given a few minutes to say their goodbyes. Amid much crying and hugging and, in some cases, last-minute attempts to get the young women to change their minds, the families finally start to leave. "That was the most painful thing for me," Magda said. "Watching my mother cry. I'd never seen her cry like that. But you know what? My father put his arm around her and comforted her. That's the first time I've ever seen him do something like that. So, as bad as I felt about leaving them, and the pain it was causing them, seeing that affection left me with a good feeling, knowing that maybe it brought them closer somehow. I felt like the Lord was telling me that everything would be all right."

As the last family members head outside, the big iron doors are swung shut. "I remember that sound," Magda continued. "That awful *clang* when they shut the big doors and then the sound of the key turning in the lock. And I thought, 'Oh no! I'm locked in! What am I doing here!' I was terrified. I cried for three days, I was so homesick. Actually, we all cried. No one really got much sleep those first few days. But, as Mother Veronica keeps telling us, the period of the postulancy is to help you see if you really have a vocation. You're free to leave anytime you want. That's very important. Knowing that helped me get through that first difficult period."

THE DILEMMA OF FREE WILL: NEGOTIATING WITH DESTINY

Most of the postulants told me that no matter how convinced (or not) they were of the veracity of their vocation, they entered the convent with a tentative, "try it and see" attitude. The ten months of the postulancy are meant to be a kind of dress rehearsal for the religious life, a trial period in which a young woman is challenged to confront her feelings of vocation and to determine if she is really being called by Christ or if she has mistakenly interpreted her feelings and should instead consider marriage and a family. Most of these women, then, are somewhat uneasy with the idea of becoming a bride of Christ and are insecure, scared, and completely overwhelmed by the notion that they may have been singled out by God for special service. Their vocation, they believe, comes to them from outside themselves and is a force completely beyond their control. They play no part, they say, in whether they have been called to be a nun; they can only decide whether they will submit to God's will. If this is truly their vocation, it is something that they are powerless to fight. "Sometimes you feel like a little boat, drifting here and there, and you almost capsize in the storm," Amelia told me. "But, from somewhere way outside, the Lord guides you and tells you, 'Over here. Come this way.' And everything you go through helps you to reaffirm this." During this stage future postulants learn to interpret a sense of discontent in their lives as perhaps—though not necessarily—indicating "the call," and they begin to grapple with a tension between their own desires and what they believe God is asking of them. They also learn that this tension can be eased by following a particular model of femininity, patterning themselves on the humble receptivity and servitude of Mary.

As they enter the convent, then, these women are desperate for meaning, desperate to know what is happening to them and how to make sense of what they are feeling. "I just wanted someone to tell me, 'Yes, you have a real vocation,' or 'No you don't,'" recounted Carlota. "But it's not that easy. No one can tell you for sure if you have a vocation or not. This is between you and Christ. You have to look deep inside yourself and listen to His voice and His spirit working within you. But it's so hard in the beginning because you don't know what it is you're feeling. You don't know why you feel that way or what to do about it. You don't know how to make sense of what's happening to you. It all seems so frightening and so overwhelming."

As the young women come together within the convent walls, they begin to learn strategies for making sense of these experiences.

CHAPTER 5

Belonging

Sisters in Arms

We want to please Jesus just like you want to please your husband. With a boyfriend, you want to please him and make him happy so he'll give his special affection only to you. But of course, it's different for nuns, because we have to share our boyfriend with so many other women!

Interview with Magda, December 28, 1994

Once a young woman has identified the Siervas as her congregation of choice and has completed the entering ceremony, she begins the process of becoming integrated into the congregation as one of their own. The sisters maintain that it is absolutely imperative for the successful formation of a postulant that she feel embedded in a solid, supportive community of peers and mentors who will see her through the challenges she will face in the coming years. She must come to feel not only that she lives within a particular religious group but that she herself *se lo pertenece*—is an organic part of that group, a natural and necessary component to its functioning. During this period, the new postulant comes to feel an intense desire and longing to become a Sierva in this more fundamental, integral way.

INTEGRATING THE GROUP:
THE CHALLENGES OF SOLIDARITY

Integrating twenty young women into a cohesive unit poses something of a challenge. The postulants must come to experience a special kind of bond with each other and with the congregation as a whole, to believe without question that they have been called together by God. This is a lengthy, difficulty, and often bumpy process.

In the convent, as with other kinds of groups—sports teams, sorori-
ties, men's lodges, universities, community organizations, nations—the
description of a classificatory position (I was born in the South) is not
the same as an actual identification with the group (I am a Southerner).
The movement between these two positions, when it happens, is usually
gradual and is dependent on the investment of emotional capital—the
cathexis, if you will—of some aspect of the group identity. Some people
quit drinking, for example, while others identify as "recovering alcoholics." Some people live in Indiana, while others are "Hoosiers." Inside
the convent, the postulants are guided in a similar shifting of their
understandings of why they joined the Siervas from "This is the group I
decided to join" to "God called me to the Siervas, here and now." It is
a naturalization of their decision to enter this order as something
ordained for them since before they were born. Their ability to experience this decision as both right and natural on a fundamental, visceral
level becomes for them an index of how well they have interpreted God's
will. We saw in the last stage—Brokenness—that in preparation for
entering the convent, they had each learned to interpret their sense of
inquietud as an indication that God wanted them to lead a different sort
of life, that they did not "belong" in the outside world. Now, within the
embrace of the community, they learn they must examine even more
closely the sense of belonging—or not—to the Siervas.

"At first it's kind of like a shock to your system," Evelyn told me.

> I mean, your whole world has been turned upside down. One day
> you're home in your house, living like you always do, and the next you
> have to get accustomed to a new schedule, new ways of doing things.
> But it's also so exciting! It's something you've been preparing for for a
> long time, and when you finally enter it's just so amazing. And all the
> postulants are excited—it's contagious. You realize that these women
> are going to be your sisters! So everyone really wants to share things
> about their families, their experiences. That helps carry you through the
> first few days.

And these first few days can be grueling. For most of the postulants,
this is the first time they have been away from home for any length of
time. In Mexico, it is customary for a woman to live with her family
until she is married, so coming to the convent is not just about entering
a new life; it also requires leaving the relative safety and comfort of the
family home, leaving behind one's childhood in a very real way. "I literally cried every day for a week," Rosita told me. "Not because I didn't
like it here but because I missed my family so much! I mean, I had never

lived away from my house before, and here I was! It was very, very hard for me at first." Joining the convent, then, is more than just a logistical decision. It represents for these girls a process of maturation, moving beyond themselves and becoming something more and different than they were before.

In many ways, leaving home for the convent is akin to American teens' going off to college for the first time, with a similar mixture of excitement, fear, anxiety, and hopefulness. Newfound independence is often coupled with a nostalgia for the comforts of home and childhood. This tension was worked out by the postulants in a number of ways, the most notable of which was what I came to think of as a pervasive performative childishness. This seemed strikingly incongruent with the increasing seriousness of their pursuit of God. As the year progressed, the postulants seemed to become more and more enamored with the trappings of young adolescent girlhood—stickers, cartoons, unicorns, rainbows, Disney films, using several different colored pens to take notes (red for headings, blue for descriptions, etc.). Even given the cultural differences regarding "maturity" between the United States and Mexico, these behaviors and attitudes were striking and were significantly more pronounced in the postulants than in other young Mexican women I knew.

I refer to this as a "performative" childishness not because I think it was disingenuous but because the intensities of such behaviors seemed to move in an arc—present but not dominant in the beginning; crescendoing in the middle of the year; and then slowly decreasing as the time to enter the novitiate neared. This suggested to me that perhaps something about these behaviors and attitudes articulated certain dimensions of the formation process itself. Over time, I came to understand this childishness as one arena through which the postulants were working out the tensions in the convent between surrendering control to external sources and assuming increasing internal responsibility for things in the outside world—subjective stances that seem to run headlong into each other in thinking about individual agency. I will return to these issues in more detail in chapter 9. I raise the issue of performative childishness at this point as an indication of the multilayered anxiety most of these young women feel when leaving home for the first time. Despite their enthusiasm to answer what they feel is God's call, this is a frightening change for them, and most have no prior experience of dislocation from their families to help guide them.

The postulants manage these stresses and adjust to their new circumstances in different ways, depending on their personalities and previous experiences. To get a sense of the diversity of the group I worked with, and their various strategies for managing life in the convent, let us consider two of the postulants, Rosita and Magda. These women came to the convent through different routes, and each confronted the challenges of the convent in different ways. But in their negotiating of the demands of convent life, they, along with the other postulants, came to discover some important commonalities—shared feelings and experiences that would become the basis for their sense of belonging.

Rosita: The Romantic

Rosita was an attractive, tall, dark-skinned eighteen-year-old from a small pueblo outside the city. She came from a very traditional family and had four brothers and three sisters. As the youngest daughter, Rosita was expected to stay home and care for her parents and not marry. Although she had never had a boyfriend and didn't particularly relish the idea of marriage, she told me she felt claustrophobic at home, as if she were being held back. Rosita was exceptionally bright and creative and had a particular talent for writing poetry and short stories. But she received very little encouragement for her academic interests at home. She was only permitted to complete *secondaria* (junior high school)—after the ninth grade, she was expected to stay home and help her mother with the care of the house. Rosita loved her family dearly but had long felt rejected and ignored by them—partly because of the number of siblings she had and partly because she was the youngest daughter. She expressed both resentment toward her family and guilt for feeling this resentment.

Rosita first began to hear the call when she was eleven years old. At the age of fifteen, against her parents' wishes, she entered a congregation in Mexico City (the Misioneras), where she remained for almost three months. But she soon grew homesick and depressed. She stopped eating and lost a considerable amount of weight. She became withdrawn and despondent and physically ill. Finally, she returned home, much to her parents' delight. But she still felt that her place was in the religious life, that it was where God wanted her. Through the vocational retreats of the diocese, she came to believe that her disappointing experience with the Misioneras did not necessarily mean that she lacked a vocation. On the contrary, she began to think it was meant to show her that her vocation was in another congregation—with the Siervas. Against the strong objection of her parents (threats of disowning by her father and impassioned crying and pleading by her mother), Rosita entered the congregation.

Through my own interactions with Rosita and observing how she interacted with the other postulants, I quickly came to see her as a sensitive, open, and exceptionally caring young woman. She was sweet, empathetic, and well liked. She was also very insecure. She very much wanted others to like her and shied away from any kind of confrontation or show of anger. I noticed that tension and conflict made her extremely uncomfortable and that she preferred to be quiet and let others discuss problems. She had a quick mind and a quick wit and had strong opinions on things but did not give them freely or easily. She would express her position only if asked and only if she felt comfortable with the person she was speaking with.

Rosita was also a relentless perfectionist. In the convent, she drove herself in her academics, art projects, and chores as well as in her prayer and meditations until she was physically and emotionally spent. In fact, she had to leave the congregation for a month early in the year because she had lost an excessive amount of weight and was evidencing inexplicable and frighteningly heavy nosebleeds. When she returned after her illness, she showed pronounced devotion in prayer, kneeling all through the morning meditation and Adoration (instead of sitting comfortably like the rest of the postulants). Although I am not sure if this was out of a desire for penitence or because she wanted to make a good impression to convince the sisters that she really did belong with the Siervas, I did notice that after a few weeks Rosita was, like the rest of the postulants, falling asleep in the morning meditation and in Adoration.

Despite her struggles, Rosita very rarely complained. She confronted pressures and problems with a smile or a joke to laugh off the tension. She went about her daily business—saying her prayers, doing her chores, studying for classes, learning how to sew. But she did each of these things—or tried to, at least—with all her attention and all her being, so that she did each thing to her fullest potential, "for the glory of God," she told me. Deep inside, she confided to me one day, she wanted with all her soul to become a saint and prayed every day for God to bestow this ultimate grace on her.

Magda: The Class Clown

Magda was the first member of the group I got to know in any depth. When I first arrived, she and I were assigned the chore of cleaning the classroom every morning and afternoon. By the time our month's chore rotation was up, we had begun a close, if complicated, friendship. Magda seemed to be a very conflicted young woman. Eighteen years old at the time of the research, she was the fourth of five children and had grown up in the city of Puebla. Her family life was a great source of tension for her. Particularly difficult was the situation with her parents. Magda's father and mother had been together for almost twenty years, but they were not officially married according to the Catholic Church. Her father had been married in the church to another woman long before Magda was born. When that relationship turned sour, he met Magda's mother, twelve years his junior. Against the objections of Magda's maternal grandparents, her mother and father began a life together. Bust since the church forbids remarriage, they could not be married in the church. Magda's parents were, then, officially "living in sin" and could not receive the sacraments of the church, including confession/reconciliation and Communion. This was extremely painful for Magda, who worried for their souls. This was compounded by the fact that, in the past year, her father had been spending an increasing amount of time with his former wife, who lived in the neighborhood where Magda had grown up. Magda felt, in some ways, that her becoming a nun would help bring her parents back to God. At least this was her hope.

Magda was generally viewed by the group and by her superiors as "difficult." She was frequently disobedient, sarcastic, or surly and often used inappropriate—and sometimes even cruel—humor to mask stronger emotions. Deep down, she seemed to generally mean well, but this side of her was usually buried under the layers of an abrasive, angry personality, which led her to fight with others and to tease them unmercifully to get a rise out of them. She angered easily and held grudges. She claimed to see herself as "very happy" and counted this as an asset, but over time I began to suspect that her joviality (at times seemingly affected and/or grossly inappropriate) was more of a cover for her deep pain and anger.

This anger made more sense to me as I learned about her family life. After many months of giving me idealized descriptions of her home life, Magda eventually admitted that she and her siblings endured severe beatings at the hands of her father (sometimes wielding equipment from his mechanic's shop) and that there continued to be many bitter fights and resentments within the family. Magda described her mother as a "traditional housewife—submissive and frightened of her husband." Magda told me she had long felt abandoned and ignored by her family.

Her father was too angry to communicate effectively with his children, and her mother was emotionally absent. Magda, it seemed, tried to compensate for this lack of affection by surrounding herself with older friends. In her mid-teens she was what she called "a club girl," going out to dance clubs and bars several nights a week. She had a few boyfriends, but only one serious one, who broke her heart.

Magda was, in short, the class clown—the one who acted out, made noise, and generally irritated people to get attention. She made fun of others in mean ways (for example, making fat jokes about Ruth), but she herself became very angry and defensive at any hint that *she* was being made fun of. A favorite phrase of the others toward her was "Don't be a clown!" which Magda once told me deeply hurt her feelings (although she seldom showed it at the time). She was good friends with Surella, but they got in tiffs quite often and would go through periods of not speaking. Magda was particularly resentful and envious of the five postulants in the "group of five" I will discuss below (Rosita, Carmen, Thea, Celeste, and Marta) and liked to gossip about whichever of the sisters she was currently having problems with.

Given all this, it is perhaps not surprising that Magda seemed to have trouble forming healthy friendships. She was often too intense for people, disrespectful of boundaries, and possessive. She tended to get very attached to people very quickly and had swings of intense love and intense hate. This was particularly evident in her tempestuous relationship with a junior nun, Sister Teresita. For several months Magda filled her days anxiously awaiting secret rendezvous with Sister Teresita where they could exchange notes (or, if they were especially lucky, a few words) or, alternately, fuming about how Sister Teresita was ignoring her, not responding with the same enthusiasm for their friendship as did Magda.

This relationship sparked a serious vocational crisis for Magda. Everyone in the Central House knew what was going on. The mother superior of the house, Mother Clarissa, finally intervened, forbidding Magda and Teresita to have any contact other than saying hello as they passed each other in the hall. Mother Veronica, the mistress of postulants, was slightly more understanding but urged Magda, for the sake of her own vocation as well as Teresita's, to put a damper on things. A nun's life is one of moving from house to house, wherever the congregation needs you, Mother Veronica told her. It is a bad idea to get too attached to specific people because that makes it all that much harder when you are separated.

Magda and I had many long conversations about her friendship with Sister Teresita and what it might mean in terms of the validity of Magda's vocation. I accompanied Magda on her biweekly trips to the orthodontist (she wore braces), so we were able to talk candidly, away from the other sisters. She never once suggested that her feelings for Teresita were other than platonic, but she nevertheless wondered if her attachment to Teresita was somehow a sign to her that she didn't have a vocation. Again and again she would ask me what I thought. "You're the researcher," she would say. "You're here to learn about what it's like to have a religious vocation. You've been with us for months. You must have some sort of opinion about whether or not I have a vocation." I would generally get around answering this question directly by asking her what *she* thought, what signs *she* thought God was giving her. She would hesitate at first but would eventually say that she believed deep down that Christ had called her to be a Sierva and that the congregation was where she should be. This would seem to make her feel better and renew her sense of purpose, at least until the next incident with Teresita would arise.

Some have suggested that the religious life may be a haven for those who have difficulty acknowledging or accepting their (homo)sexual feelings (cf. Curb and Manahan 1985; Thomas 1986). This may be the case with some people. It may even have been the case with Magda. But this interpretation runs the risk of underestimating the depth of the relationships heterosexual women can form with each other in a place like a convent. The sisters see themselves as united in a common cause, a glorious mission in which every one of them plays a vital part. They have come together, they believe, to sacrifice themselves to Christ, to love each other and all of humankind with boundless affection, and to appreciate each living thing as a manifestation of God's love. For someone like Magda, who seems to have difficulty maintaining personal boundaries, this might understandably be somewhat overwhelming and take forms not exactly embraced by the church, sexual or not.

Because of all these difficulties, Magda had periods of real struggle with her vocation. At first I doubted she would make it through her first year in the congregation, but as the year progressed she seemed to settle into the religious life. I particularly saw a change in her after we went on the missions, as I will discuss in chapter 9. I was with her, Rosita, Marta, and Mother Veronica for this experience, and it was interesting to see Magda begin to try on the role of Sierva. She found the whole experience remarkably moving and upon our return seemed to make a more concerted effort to get along with the other postulants and to take her formation more seriously.

Although the picture I have painted of Magda here may not seem to be particularly flattering, at least part of her behavior, I believe, may be seen as symptomatic of the natural process a person goes through when she undertakes a transformation as radical as that demanded by the Siervas. Despite good intentions and genuine commitment, some individuals are likely to encounter things in the religious life that elicit defensive reactions or unusual ways of managing stress. The process of formation seemed to be somewhat more arduous and challenging for Magda than for most of the other postulants. By the time I left, she seemed content in her black habit and white veil of the novitiate, and she spoke to me of how hard she was trying to live up to the ideal of the congregation. Nevertheless, the mother general wrote to me some months later that Magda had left the order.

COMMONALITIES

As the differences between Magda and Rosita suggest, the postulant group was diverse. But despite their differences, some important commonalities emerge among the postulants, commonalities that were elaborated in the process of helping each one believe that she belonged with the Siervas and nowhere else. I consider these in more detail in chapter 10 but mention a few general points here.

Almost uniformly, the postulants recounted feeling "the call" when they were quite young, pushing it to the backs of their minds, and then feeling it resurface in their teens. All of them followed circuitous routes to the Siervas, and only after several months in the convent did they come to understand the series of "accidents" that had led them to the Siervas to be divinely orchestrated.

In terms of family relationships, many, like Surella, Magda, Haydee, Amelia, and Alicia, reported experiences of being outsiders or the "black sheep" of their families. Several, particularly Celeste, Magda, Evelyn, Surella, Carmen, and Pipa, reported feeling a duty to atone for the sins of relatives, usually parents, who had either disregarded or rejected the teachings of the church. Socially, almost all of the postulants recounted that, as children and young adults, they preferred to hang out with adults or people older than themselves. Most had boyfriends before coming to the convent, and some were on the verge of marriage.

Perhaps most significantly, all the postulants expressed an *uneasiness with the expectations placed on them as women* and a sense that they were somehow "different" from other girls their age. Some, like Rosita and Carlota, told me they had never felt interested in having a boyfriend and had been teased about this by friends. Rosita even went so far as to make up a phantom boyfriend so her friends would stop pushing her to date. Others, like Amelia, Thea, and Marta, were tomboys who preferred to run around in jeans, keep their hair short, and play basketball with the guys. While Marta and Thea both had boyfriends, they both told me they could never quite see themselves as married women. Some of the postulants, like Carmen, Surella, Celeste, and Magda, seemed to approximate more mainstream notions of Mexican adolescent femininity in that they dated, had boyfriends, went to parties, and did other "girly" things. But they talked about how they had never felt completely comfortable in these roles. Coincidentally or not, each also had tales to tell me of boyfriends who were exceedingly jealous, unfaithful, and even violent. In any event, all of the postulants expressed to me, both individually in our interviews and in group discussions, the uneasiness they felt in trying to find a balance between fulfilling certain expectations of being a young Mexican woman (particularly having a romantic relationship that would lead to marriage) and having the freedom they wanted to play sports, go to college, and pursue a career. I will take a closer look at the way the postulants talked about this notion of "femininity" and the tensions surrounding it in chapter 12.

Over time, these commonalities came to override the differences the postulants brought with them from their own personal histories. Differences were not ignored, nor were they discouraged. Rather, the points of convergence—the shared experiences of young women coming of age in a time of change and confusion—became the glue that bonded the postulants to each other and to the other sisters in the congregation.

FORGING BONDS

Such bonding, however, is not left to chance. It is explicitly encouraged by the congregations in specific ways. During their first year, postulants are mentored through developing three primary levels of relatedness: with the congregation as a whole; with their cohort, and with the mistress of postulants.

Empathy and Support: A New Developmental Trajectory

The congregation as a whole greets the postulants as long-lost daughters returned home after a lengthy absence, or as one might rejoice in the arrival of a new baby. The sisters recognize the first few months of the postulancy as a highly emotional time for the young women, and they deploy a number of tactics to help the new postulants through this period. "The postulants have a difficult year ahead," Mother Wilhelmina, the vicaress general, explained to me early in the research. "It's very hard for them to leave their homes and their families and to live a new life here with us. We have to help them get over this separation, to feel at home here. Otherwise, they won't be able to get on with the work of formation because their hearts will still be at home." The attitude is one of empathy. The postulants are not told to "buck up" but instead are encouraged to explore their feelings of loss and loneliness as entirely natural. The older sisters help them by sharing stories of their own tearful entries into the congregation, often exaggerated and satirized to the point of being comical. The postulants learn, then, not to take themselves too seriously, to recognize that their feelings are part of a natural, developmental step in the process of becoming a nun, and to see their distress in larger perspective.

At the same time, they are reminded of Jesus' call to His followers, repeating on an almost daily basis Jesus' saying that "everyone who has left houses, brothers or sisters, father or mother, children, or fields because of My name will receive 100 times more and will inherit eternal life" (Matthew 19:29). They are told that Jesus recognizes the depth of the sacrifice they are making for Him and that He accepts this as an act of extraordinary devotion toward establishing the Kingdom of God. Again, then, the postulants are aided in developing a reflective stance toward their own emotional experiences that sets these experiences within larger developmental frameworks.

While the postulants are guided to accept their emotional struggles as part of a natural process of development in the religious life, the congregation at the same time offers alternatives. They are celebrated and embraced (both literally and figuratively) by the sisters as precious gifts to the church and to the order. "We have so many vocations this year!" exclaimed Mother Maria. "God is certainly blessing us!" The postulants are welcomed with a special Mass, and special prayers are offered up to help them persevere through the initial adjustment period. The officers of the congregation make visits to the postulants' dormitory to chat with them and welcome them personally to the order.

Getting Down to (God's) Business

As the newness of the convent begins to wear off and they start to settle into their new life, the postulants must contend with the requirements of the religious life. After the first few weeks, the special attention and delicate treatment are phased out and the postulants are increasingly expected to conform to the rules and schedule of the convent. The sisters recognize the difficulty of this transition out of the spotlight. The postulants go from being celebrated newcomers, the focus of excitement and care, to being the lowest-status group in the House. This is not to say that affection for them is withdrawn. Far from it. The sisters continue to be warm and encouraging to their newest members throughout the year. But once they have settled in and feel at least moderately comfortable in the community, the postulants must get down to the serious business of their religious formation. As Mother Veronica explained it to me, "It's like with children. You spoil them in the beginning because they can't do anything for themselves. But if you keep spoiling them as they get older, it just makes things more difficult in the long run because they won't be able to take care of themselves."

At this point networks of individual relationships become increasingly important. When they first arrive, the postulants—as a group—are welcomed by the sisters—as a group. Once the postulants have had more of an opportunity to get acquainted with each other and with their superiors, more individually significant relationships can be forged. Just as it is important for a new entrant to feel she is part of the congregation of "the Siervas," it is also imperative that she form relationships with specific individuals within the congregation who can, in a sense, personify this connection to the group as a whole. This occurs primarily on two levels: within the postulant group itself, and with the mistress of postulants.

Peer Relationships: Camaraderie and Competition

The bond with the cohort, the group with which one professes temporary and perpetual vows, becomes intense. But it doesn't begin that way. Though a few of the postulants in the group I worked with had met each other prior to entering the congregation at pre–religious life retreats or through mission experiences, the majority of them knew no one in the congregation aside from Mother Josefina (the vocations director). In other words, the entering group was made up of twenty young women who didn't know each other, many of whom had just left home for the first time and who found themselves new members of perhaps the largest and most powerful institution on the planet—the Catholic Church. Not surprisingly, then, postulant group solidarity becomes an important focus in the early stages of formation.

This bonding was facilitated in both active and permissive ways. The postulants were encouraged in the early weeks to spend time visiting and chatting with each other, getting to know their new classmates. They were not yet held entirely to the strict schedule of the congregation and were permitted a certain amount of "free time" for socializing with each other. Often, this kind of bonding happened while the postulants were assigned tasks related to getting settled—folding and storing their clothes, setting up their nightstands, learning how to do the laundry.

The postulants also participated in several team-building activities meant to help them learn more about each other and to build trust in the group. Sometimes these were anonymous, "secret friend" sorts of exercises, as when each postulant was assigned the task of writing a prayer about another postulant, incorporating into it specific details about that postulant's personality, strengths, and weaknesses. The prayers were then turned in to Mother Veronica, who read them aloud during recreation. The postulants blushed and giggled when they heard descriptions of themselves read aloud, and everyone tried to guess who the secret friend was who had written that prayer. When a secret friend was revealed, she and her sister postulant would embrace and often move their chairs around to sit next to each other.

On other occasions group activities were employed, such as standing with one's back to a group of three postulants and falling backwards into their arms as an exercise in trust. On another day, we cleared a space in the postulants' classroom and arranged some chairs in a circle. As we sat in the circle, Mother Veronica handed a large ball of string to Marta and asked her to throw it to another person in the group, saying aloud as she did so some particular positive attribute of that person. As she threw it, she was to hold onto the end of the string, so that there was a visible connection between the two women. Marta chose to throw the string to Amelia, announcing that she appreciated Amelia's talent in playing the piano. Amelia then threw the ball of string to another person in the group (keeping hold of a piece herself), articulating something she valued about that person as she did so, and so on. When the string had made the round of the whole group, with each of us holding onto part of it before throwing it to someone else, the center of the circle resembled a large spider web. Mother Veronica then instructed Surella to pull tightly on her part of the string. As she did so, Magda (to whom Surella had thrown the ball) was yanked almost out of her chair. The postulants giggled as Magda regained her composure and sat back down. Next, Mother Veronica instructed Rosita to drop her section of the string. As she did so, the connections among the rest of the group became loosened. "You see?" asked Mother Veronica.

> We are a community. What one of us does affects the others. You cannot be *exigera* (strict/demanding) without it throwing someone else off balance. And you can't neglect your responsibilities without it having repercussions for the rest of the group. We are all responsible for facilitating or hindering the formation of our sisters. You must remember that a nun cannot go around thinking that everything is about her, that she is isolated and that her actions don't affect others. Living in community is a very difficult thing, and it requires us to be mindful of how we affect others around us.

Despite the spirit of cooperation and support fostered in the group, competition did exist. Not surprisingly, perhaps, throwing together a group of young women from various walks of life to live as a "family" under stressful circumstances produces some tensions. The fact that these women are in a convent makes no great difference here—they are, after all, human beings, with needs for privacy and companionship and potentials for jealousies and resentments. As the newness of being in the convent wore off, these issues rose to the surface, and the cohesion of the group became a central topic of concern to the postulants. In our exit interviews, almost all of them referenced the changes in group dynamics over the year as indicative of the degree to which they—and others—were "living their formation."

For most of the year, gossip and factionalism was a constant problem in the group and was of great concern to Mother Veronica. There were two principal cliques and a third, more amorphous group of women who seemed to associate with each other by default. The most obvious clique was that of Marta, Rosita, Carmen, Alma, and Celeste, called the "group of five" by some of the other postulants. This group tended to be better educated (with the exception of Rosita, who had only completed junior high), more intellectual, more serious about academics, more mindful of following rules, and more outwardly passionate about their religious practices than the others, as well as being more physically attractive and generally more talented (intellectually and otherwise) than the others. Although none of the postulants came from exceptionally wealthy families, those in this group also seemed to have come from families slightly better off than the others.

This group was also somewhat unusual in the sense that their parents maintained what at least appeared to be committed and happy marriages. Many (though certainly not all) of the other postulants were dealing with fathers who had second families on the side. Surella, for example, had a particularly hard time with this in her family. She made several trips home to try to help out as best she could, but it took its toll on her. On many days she would be distracted and tearful and obviously distressed. The situation was made more difficult for her by the fact that her father felt responsible for Surella's decision to become a nun. He believed that she had entered the convent because she was taking on the guilt of his deception, trying to save him and her family by sacrificing herself. She adamantly denied this, protesting that she had wanted to become a nun because she honestly felt called to the religious life, but her father could not accept this and was tormented by the fear that he had forced her into the convent by his sin. He constantly pressured her to leave the congregation and come home. Although Carmen's father disapproved of her becoming a nun, none of the "group of five" seemed to deal with the same magnitude of family strife as Surella, Clara, or some of the others regarding their decision to join the congregation.

Interestingly, the "group of five" were also, on average, taller, more athletic, and lighter skinned than the others. Thea, Marta, and Rosita were all between five feet, six inches, and five feet, seven inches tall. Celeste was shorter, but still taller than most of the others, at about five feet, five inches. Carmen was the shortest of the clique (though not of the group in general), at about five feet, three inches. Although Carmen and Rosita were of a darker complexion, Celeste, Thea, and Marta were very light skinned and were teasingly called *güeras* by the others. There were no light-skinned women who were not part of this group.

I mention this because skin color seemed to be an important concern for the postulants (as it is for Mexicans in general) in a number of ways and in a number of contexts. Unquestionably, in Mexico (as in many cultures with a legacy of colonialism), it is considered "better" to be light skinned or white than dark skinned. It is "better" to have light hair and light eyes. It is "better" to have more delicate features and a longer, leaner build. Mexicans—men in particular—are counseled to "marry

light," in the hope that their children will be light skinned. It is prestigious to have a light-skinned woman on your arm. Such women are in
very high demand, especially if they have light eyes as well. The colonialist origins of these attitudes are obvious. The Spanish colonizers
brought their European looks to New Spain, and many noble or wealthy
families maintained the illusion, at least, of preserving the purity of
their race and their class by not marrying "beneath" them. Even today,
there are people of very light skin, light eyes, and light hair in Puebla.
Most of them belong to wealthy or prestigious families. So "lightness,"
I learned, represents many things—beauty, wealth, prestige, breeding,
culture, opportunity. And these things can easily become targets of jealousy for those who don't have the good fortune to be light or to have
the things lightness represents. I saw this again and again among the
postulants. Obviously, skin color was not the only distinguishing factor
of the "group of five," but it was a striking one.

The tensions surrounding this clique simmered for months, periodically manifesting in arguments or disagreements—sometimes petty,
sometimes not. The situation finally came to a head as the postulants
were preparing to leave for the novitiate, culminating in a dramatic
afternoon of tearful group confrontation mediated by Mother Veronica
and for which I was present. Apparently, the experience was productive,
and it seemed to bring about some healing for the group. As they moved
to the novitiate to face new challenges under the notoriously harsh
direction of the mistress of novices, the postulants seemed to reach to
each other for support. Abby described it to me this way: "We've really
united here [in the novitiate]. It's been a huge transformation. Now we
admire each other so much. It's like someone does something and you
say, 'But you weren't that way before!' But it's because of the grace of
God. It's like Mother Veronica used to tell us: 'You'll see,' she said. 'In
the novitiate there are so many graces, *so many* graces you will receive!'
And it's true. Here you *feel* it. You *feel* the presence of God" (interview,
August 9, 1995).

This change in the group dynamics, Abby explained, was evidence of
the hard, interior work in which each of the postulants was engaged.
Amelia agreed. "You look at where we were just four months ago, and
then you see where we are today," she mused.

> The difference is amazing. Look at what happened last week with Magda.
> She wanted to go to her brother's wedding, and Mother Veronica said
> she couldn't go. So Magda went to Mother Anabel to ask permission.
> When Mother Anabel told her she could go (not knowing that Mother

Veronica had denied permission), Magda was thrilled, like she had won a contest or something. But then when Mother Anabel found out what had happened and told her she *couldn't* go, she was very upset and angry. But *then*, when the decision was finally left up to Magda, she really struggled with it. Before, she would've just gone to the wedding without a second thought, happy that she had gotten her way. But she decided in the end not to go because Mother Veronica was against it. This is a *major* change for her. And that's just one example. That's why it's so important to really seize hold of your formation and follow the practices of the congregation. They may not make a lot of sense to you in the beginning, but they really do work. They really transform you. (Interview, March 3, 1995)[1]

This progressive forging of solidarity among the postulants does not proceed willy-nilly. Nor is it, as we have seen, necessarily a smooth process. It is a challenging task that is carefully guided and monitored by the mistress of postulants, a woman who wields substantial emotional, spiritual, and practical power in the postulants' lives during their first year.

The Mistress of Postulants

I beg the mothers in charge of forming future religious that they do so with efficacy, care, and charity and that for this they pray to Our Lord with great faith that He will light the way for them to form [their charges] in the true spirit of this institution.

Father Muro, *Letters*

During the first year, the postulants are expected to develop a particular sort of relationship with the mistress of postulants in which she should become, both functionally and symbolically, their mother away from home. Each stage of the formation process is managed by a *hermana formadora* (formation sister), who is responsible for the training of the initiates in that stage. In addition to formal instruction, the *hermana formadora* is charged with "creating a propitious atmosphere" for the formation of her "daughters." She is directly responsible for the day-to-day

---

1. I found the similarities between this and the conversations I have had with individuals engaged in twelve-step programs to be remarkable (see Lester 1999). In the twelve-step ideology, newcomers are encouraged to act "as if" there were an unseen power at work in the program, even if they don't understand it or particularly believe it to be true. Again and again I was told by twelve-step members that, regardless of whether one understands what is happening, if one has faith in the transformative potential of the program, it will change one's life.

business of formation, from deciding who will do what chores, to grant-
ing (or denying) permission to make phone calls, to dispensing shampoo. While the congregation outlines specific techniques and objectives
of the formation program, the *formadora* is given a good deal of liberty
in terms of how to implement them. She is free, for example, to develop
whatever rules or customs for the group she deems useful (e.g., how
towels are to be folded, how recreation times will be structured, who
must not sit next to each other in class because they pass notes), so long
as they do not run counter to the goals of formation or the charism of
the congregation. She is also the primary disciplinarian for her charges
and is expected to mete out appropriate punishment (in the form of
penitences or mortifications, to be discussed in chapter 8) when needed.
The development of the appropriate relationship with the *madre formadora* becomes an indicator, then, of a *formante*'s appropriate (or not)
engagement with the program of formation itself.

But this is not merely a relationship of authority and obedience. It is
a relationship between real people in the context of heightened emotional transformation. The congregation's founder, Father Muro, was
concerned that the role of the *formadoras* be nurturing and supportive
as well as regulatory and disciplinary. Consequently, the constitutions
mandate that the *formadoras* must maintain an attitude of receptivity,
discretion, respect for the person of the *formante,* and an openness to
dialogue. Their treatment of the *formantes* should be transparent and is
under scrutiny by superiors. If a dispute does arise between a postulant
and her mistress, either of the two can appeal to the mother superior of
the house or the officers of the congregation to assist in its resolution. I
only saw one instance of this, when Magda appealed to the mother general to override Mother Veronica's denial of her request to attend her
brother's wedding, the event Amelia referred to in the above quote.

The mistress of one's level of formation also has a strong voice in the
decision of whether to permit a candidate to proceed to the next level.
In the case of the postulants, Mother Veronica kept notes on their
progress (in files locked in her office) and submitted periodic progress
reports on each of them to the General Council. When the time arrived
for the postulants to apply for advancement to the novitiate, Mother
Veronica compiled these reports into a longer evaluation of each postulant's progress during the year, pointing to specific issues, conflicts, concerns, triumphs, struggles, and strengths she thought impinged on the
candidate's prospects for continuing in the congregation. The postulants were permitted to read these reports and were encouraged to use

their letters of application to the novitiate to respond to or illuminate anything in the report they found troubling. The postulants were on pins and needles for days before Mother Veronica distributed her reports to them. "After all, you can't lie in your letter about how great you are if Mother Veronica is going to tell them the real story!" said Thea, only half-jokingly.

The very nature and structure of the relationship between *formadora* and *formante* make it intense. The mistress of one's level of formation is the first in the chain of command and is due deferential obedience from her *formantes*. Though she is herself subject to the rules and regulations of the order, the *formadora* controls the basic elements of life in the convent for those under her direction. But more than this, the *formantes* are urged (and at the later stages, required) to cultivate close emotional and spiritual relationships with their *formadoras*. The postulants, for example, were encouraged to sit down with Mother Veronica at least once a month to talk about their vocations, how they were feeling in the congregation, what problems were brewing with their families that might be distracting them from prayer, and so forth. In this sense, the *madre formadora* functions as guidance counselor and therapist, helping her *formantes* confront and work through any situation or emotional conflict that impinges on their experience of God and vocation.

This can be a terrifying prospect for some *formantes*. Magda, for example, told me she didn't like the idea of someone knowing so much about her, from how much she ate at lunch to how she felt about her parents to her doubts about her vocation. She was very uncomfortable with the notion of sitting down with Mother Veronica and telling her about her most inner feelings and fears. "I'm just not that kind of person," she told me. "It's really hard for me. I don't like that feeling of being exposed." But, Magda acknowledged, if she really wanted to "make it" as a sister, she would have to get over her discomfort. "I guess this is one of those 'sacrifices' we have to make. For some people it's easy—they just sit down and everything comes pouring out. But for me, it's a real struggle. But I know it's something I just have to do. I don't know . . . maybe it'll get easier with time." These interactions with the *madre formadora* are not confessional in the sacramental sense, but they are most definitely confessional in nature, and they require the establishments of sincere bonds of trust. The postulants are expected to confide in their mistress more fully than they may have ever done with any one person before. The building of trust within the *formadora-formante* relationship is understood by the sisters as the first step in surrendering oneself completely to the service of God. If a young woman is unable to place her trust in her immediate superior, who is present with her in the flesh every day, how, the sisters say, can she possible turn herself over to an invisible and sometimes elusive God?

In addition to the spiritual aspects of this relationship as a sort of exercise in surrender and trust to God (as sequentially embodied in the church, the Siervas, and the mistress of postulants), these intense relationships with one's *madres formadoras* across the process of formation are meant to anchor the *formante* and to give her a sense of stability and support as she undergoes her transformation. Not surprisingly, perhaps, *madres formadoras* often become a permanent part of one's emotional and spiritual life. In times of crisis or difficulty, even sisters who have taken their perpetual vows frequently turn back to their own *madres formadoras* for guidance and comfort.

Not all of the postulants achieved this sort of bond with Mother Veronica, and even those who did did so in varying degrees. But the ideal to strive for was to turn to the mistress of postulants with an attitude of trust and humility. In return, she worked to guide each postulant in her proper formation, providing an example of responsibility and how to respond to the trust of others with kindness and grace.

Given this, I saw that one index of how these women changed over time was the ways in which peer relationships within the postulant group were juxtaposed to the relationship with the mistress of postulants. Toward the beginning of the year, for example, peer relationships often functioned as alliances against those in authority (as, for example, when Surella connived with Magda to buy stickers with their extra bus fare on one of their excursions to Magda's orthodontist). The older sisters, all of whom had been postulants themselves at one time, were not oblivious to these maneuverings and would sanction the postulants if they were caught outright. For the most part, however, they viewed this as a relatively normal part of the adjustment process. "We know more than they think we do about what they're doing," Mother Veronica told me. "We keep an eye on it. As long as it seems to subside over time, we don't worry about it. Only if a girl persists in trying to manipulate the rules after several months do we become concerned." Mother Veronica's instincts seemed to be right. By the end of the year, most of this sort of thing had stopped, and one was considered to be a true friend if she *reinforced* the voice of authority and helped a sister to comply with the rules, rather than to subvert them.

MUTUAL SUPPORT AND THE BONDS OF SISTERHOOD

The slow but deliberate building of relationships with the larger community, within the class itself, and with the mistress of postulants enables a young woman to feel as if she "belongs" with the Siervas and creates the foundation of the formation process. Religious formation is about radical transformation of a person's sense of herself and her purpose in the world. This is dramatic, difficult, and often scary work. It is, as Sister Leona described it to me,

> sort of like jumping out of an airplane without a parachute and going into a free fall. Or more like you have a part of the parachute but not the whole thing. The other people—your sisters—each have a part of the parachute, too. But it won't work without all the parts together, without the support of your sisters. So you all jump out of the plane. It's like the bottom falls out, and the things you once thought defined who you are evaporate. And the only thing that prevents you from being flattened on the ground is the fact that you know that everyone else is scared too and that you want to help each other make it down safely. You have to have that trust there. Without a sense of cohesion and trust, it's very hard to persevere. You can do it, because ultimately it's about you and God, no? But it's much, much more difficult.

During this stage, the postulants must come to understand themselves not simply as isolated individuals on their own spiritual journey but as intimately, inextricably connected to others. Transcending personal differences and relational difficulties to forge bonds with her sisters becomes a sort of template for how a postulant should understand and develop her relationship to humanity in general. Specifically, she begins to learn how to perceive herself and others within two simultaneous frames of reference—as fallible, human selves and as pure, eternal souls. And in getting to know her sisters, she learns that when these eternal souls are housed in female bodies, common experiences often arise, regardless of socioeconomic class, education, or other differences. These experiences become central in helping her connect with the other postulants, with her superiors, and with the vision of the congregation. The sense of community and solidarity created during these first few weeks in the convent functions as a source of strength and support— and sometimes distraction—as the postulants move to the next phase of their formation, learning strategies of containment.

CHAPTER 6

Containment

Producing the Interior

I now imagine I see the Imperial Heavens where the angels were
created by the Lord our God. . . . The beautiful . . . earthly paradise
where God created our first parents Adam and Eve and where they
were surrounded by every class of goodness. Then I see my soul
that, created by God, was destined to praise, make reference to, and
serve Him in this life, to later go and rejoice in Him in Heaven; but I
see my soul, by cause of sin, incarcerated in my body, and that
incarcerated like this, the first that was taken from it was its will,
and it was stranded here among the brute animals that are my passions. And my soul and body, that is to say, all of my being, is subject to the yoke of these brutal passions.

From *Sierva, Esposa, Madre,* the congregation's book
of spiritual exercises

As the group becomes progressively integrated, the postulants turn their
attention to learning to identify and to experience strategies of self-
containment in a variety of spheres. This, the sisters maintain, is the first
step in mastering the regulation of the physical self as well as the internal
dispositions, both of which must be retrained to adhere to the will of God.

TECHNOLOGIES OF ENCLOSURE

The ethnographic record is replete with concerns about boundaries:
boundaries of nations, of ethnic groups or clans, of social classes or sub-
groups, of sacred spaces, of ritual processes, of the body. Anthropological investigation has dealt not only with these boundaries themselves as
cultural artifacts but with their generative power in the production of
cultural categories. Psychological anthropology, in particular, has taken
up the question of how such culturally defined distinctions generate

appropriate "selves" within a given context, what Appadurai (1996: 179), using a somewhat different theoretical lexicon, calls the production of "local subjects." Scholars have been especially intrigued by what happens when these boundaries are transgressed, either through sanctioned *rites de passage* in which one moves from one status to another or through practices of resistance or subversion (Mattingly 1998; Omari-Tunkara 2003; Crapanzano 1986; Obeyesekere [1981] 1984; Boddy 1989; Comaroff 1985; Bloch 1992; Turner 1995).

Douglas ([1966] 1984), for example, demonstrated that the cultural elaboration of boundaries at varying levels of generality (e.g., the community) and locality (e.g., the body) imbues these spaces with a cultural potency that can be sacred or dangerous (or both) in relation to another categorical position. Van Gennep (1961) argued persuasively that ritual has an "inside" and an "outside" and that these boundaries are clearly marked in the elaboration of "thresholds"—both literal and symbolic—in the ritual process. But more than this, he suggested that subjects can sometimes traverse these culturally designated boundaries. Turner was concerned with precisely this process of transition in his examination of initiation rituals. Boundaries between genders, social groups, and objects and spaces (sacred versus profane) Turner suggested, produce particular sorts of subject positions in relation to the larger group. And a manipulation of these boundaries can affect a transformation in this subject position.

In other words, anthropologists have long recognized that making distinctions between categories—whether spatial, social, material, ritual, or anatomical—also necessarily involves the cultural elaboration of what lies within the boundaries of these categories versus what lies outside of them. It also requires the positioning of this inside and outside in relation to each other. Almost always, this involves the mobilization of cultural discourses of morality, with the relationship between the two categories embedded in larger systems of value. This is particularly evident in the various ways subject positions may be articulated, depending on what one wants to communicate. In an "us" versus "them" conflict, for example, the person articulating the situation is invariably part of "us," and "we" are in the right, as set against "them," who are clearly misguided. On the other hand, labeling someone as a Washington "insider" carries a different sort of implication—in this case, being outside is usually held to be the morally superior position. Thus, at least in terms of social relationships, the articulation of boundaries between an inside and an outside necessarily implies subject positions that reference a particular moral universe.

Social relationships, however, are not simply ephemeral abstractions. They are often materially (re)created through the positioning of actual bodies in space: in ghettos, bedroom communities, ethnic enclaves, prisons, mental wards. Indeed, as scholars such as Foucault (1977), Goffman (1961), and Hall (1990) have suggested, the material creation of certain sorts of spaces not only articulates and reinforces social distinctions among classes of individuals but can induce within these individuals the development of certain dispositions and behaviors— culturally appropriate selves—that carry the moral force of seeming "natural."

The convent I worked in is a material space designed to produce such an effect. More than a building, it is a complex social space elaborated within the institutional mandates of the Catholic Church. It contains a series of nested hierarchies of inside/outside distinctions demarcating various levels of interiority set in relationship to various sorts of exteriors. This serves to produce certain spaces (both literal and symbolic), each with its own rules and its own possibilities, which may or may not be consistent with each other. Some of these distinctions are obvious (such as the concrete walls that enclose the convent), but others are more subtle. This configuring of inner and outer worlds proceeds in three principal domains: the delimitation of space, the clothing of the body, and the control of body boundaries.

ARCHITECTURE: MAKING SPACE

The architecture of the convent produces various levels of enclosure through five principal inside/outside distinctions: the main gate, which marks the transition from the outside world to the interior of the convent; semipublic spaces where outsiders are permitted; community spaces accessible to all sisters; cloistered areas restricted by level of formation (e.g., the nuns' dormitories); and personal spaces. Figure 2 shows the first floor.

The Main Gate

The convent building is immense, taking up approximately half a city block in length and the entire block in width, and reaching four stories high at its tallest. There are few windows along the street, and those that do face the street have black iron bars (to keep others out, I was told, as opposed to keeping the women in). Two enormous and imposing black iron gates seal the main entrance to the building and are

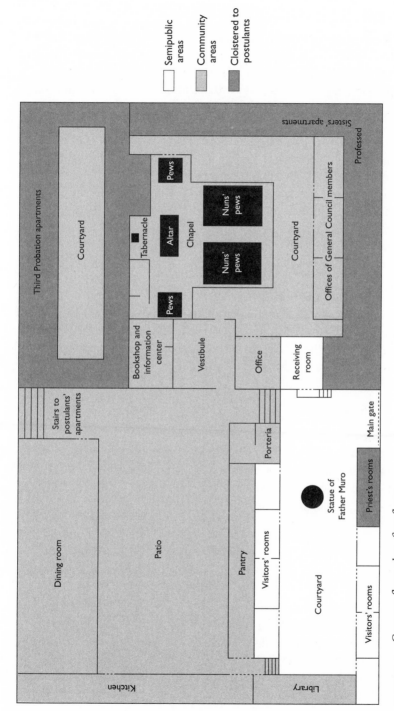

FIGURE 2. Convent floor plan, first floor

Semipublic areas

Community areas

Cloistered to postulants

Third Probation apartments

Courtyard

Stairs to postulants' apartments

Dining room

Patio

Kitchen

Bookshop and information center

Vestibule

Office

Pews

Tabernacle

Altar

Chapel

Pews

Nuns' pews

Nuns' pews

Courtyard

Offices of General Council members

Sisters' apartments

Professed

Receiving room

Porteria

Pantry

Visitors' rooms

Statue of Father Muro

Courtyard

Priest's rooms

Visitors' rooms

Library

Main gate

enclosed in sheets of black iron so that curious passersby cannot peer in. The gates (which can swing open to allow a vehicle through and into the courtyard) are kept closed most of the time, and access is gained through a narrow door set in one of the gates. This door itself has a small rectangle cut from the top with a sliding cover that acts as a peephole. The entrance *(la portería)* to the convent is staffed by a professed sister, as appointed by the mother superior of the convent, and this assignment rotates on a monthly basis. The sister in charge of the door sits in a glass-fronted room directly in front of the door but set back on the other side of the courtyard. She is responsible for determining who may or may not enter the convent and for notifying the appropriate sister that she has a visitor. She is also responsible for answering the phones and for distributing incoming mail.

The main entrance is a substantial physical barrier between the world inside the convent and *afuera* (the world outside), and passage between these two domains is carefully controlled. To enter from the street, one must ring a bell and wait for the sister in charge of the *portería* to ask one's business and decide if one should be permitted entry. Similarly, sisters are forbidden to leave the convent to go *afuera* without express permission of their direct superior (the mistress of postulants or mistress of third probations for those in formation, the mother superior of the house for the professed sisters). Ventures outside must be for a stated purpose, and the sisters always travel in pairs of two or more. *El mundo*—the world outside the convent gates—is viewed as hostile and dangerous for young women, and particularly for young women religious. Traveling in pairs is meant to reduce the risk of harassment or assault. The convent gates, then, mark the boundary between the convent—a space that is considered safe, nurturing, and validating for women—and the outside world.

Semipublic Areas

Just inside the main entrance is an open courtyard, bordered by guest rooms, the library, and the small reception room where I sat waiting for my first meeting with Mother Anabel. This courtyard and the waiting area are considered to be semipublic areas, and it is not uncommon to see people from the "outside" in these spaces from time to time. Visitors to the convent may wait in the courtyard or in the reception room for an appointment, and young women who wish to have "experiences" with the Siervas are permitted to live in the visitors' rooms for a week or so at a time. The elderly priest who performs the sacraments for the congregation lives in a series of small rooms on the courtyard's west side. And every other Friday, the sisters prepare sacks of food to be given away to the poor. These sacks are lined up in the patio, each one labeled with an individual's name. At 3:00, the gates are opened and people are allowed in to claim their sacks, exchanging their empty bags from the last distribution for the new ones laden with food. So while these areas are within the main gates of the convent, they function as transitional spaces between the inside domain of the convent and the world outside.

Communal Areas

Beyond these transitional areas, however, one needs very special permission to go. When walking up the steps past the *portería,* one has a palpable sense of entering a different sort of space. As one passes through the doorway at the top of the stairs (heading east), the area opens into a large patio. On the north side of the patio are two entrances, one to the pantry and one to the kitchen. To the right of the steps leading from the courtyard to the patio is a medium-sized room that serves as a hallway between the patio and the chapel area. Directly in front of the patio entrance is another large doorway, leading to a vestibule with entrances to the *comedór* (dining room) to the left, the postulants' apartments directly ahead, and the apartments of the third probation sisters to the right. Access to the patio and surrounding areas is restricted to people who are well known by the community or who have specific business that cannot be carried out in the visiting area, such as maintenance people and delivery people. These are the communal spaces of the convent, to which sisters in any level of formation are equally permitted access.

The Chapel and Tabernacle

By far the most important communal space in the convent is the chapel, situated spatially in the heart of the convent. The chapel is laid out in the shape of a cross, with the altar at the nexus, the tabernacle (a small, gold-gilt cabinet that holds the Eucharist) at the top, and pews extending to the sides and bottom (see figure 2). Above the tabernacle on the back wall of the chapel is a large, elaborately painted statue of Jesus, who looks down on the congregation while pointing to the sacred heart—encased in thorns—emblazoned on His chest. Arching above the head of this statue in large gold letters are the words DUEÑO Y SEÑOR—Lord and Master. Mother Wilhelmina explained to me that the Chapel's design is meant to represent the mystic body of Christ, with Christ (in the form of His statue) as the head, the tabernacle as the heart, and the sisters in their pews as the body. The altar sits at the center, connecting the sisters to Christ—and to all humankind—through the eucharistic celebration.

In its architecture and representations, then, the chapel holds and manifests the key symbols of the sisters' faith and devotion. Because of this, it is specially demarcated as a space different from the other areas of the convent. Accordingly, passage into and out of this special space is marked by ritual activity. Upon entering, the sisters dip their fingers in the font of holy water on the door and mark a cross on their foreheads as an act of purification. They then kneel and genuflect at the entrance to their pews as a show of reverence to the eucharistic presence housed in the sacristy. As they leave, they again dip their fingers in the font of holy water by the door and mark a cross on their foreheads "so that you can take the feeling of the presence of God with you," Amelia told me. "It's to remind you that God isn't only in the chapel, though we often feel Him most intensely here. But in reality, He's everywhere."

Cloistering by Levels of Formation

Last week Magda had Amelia draw her a Snoopy with the caption "Although we're far apart, we'll always be united in prayer." Amelia insisted on knowing who it was for first (which Magda tried to avoid divulging) but then drew it for her anyway. Magda persuaded Surella to pass the note to Sister Teresita [a junior sister] during afternoon chores. Magda saw Teresita a few days later, and they contrived a way to have a few moments to talk. Teresita thanked her for the Snoopy. Magda played innocent, claiming that she hadn't sent it, and said things like "Oh . . . pues que bueno que ya tienes otra amiga" (Well, how *nice* that you have another friend) with affected jealousy. This game was upsetting to Teresita, who did begin to doubt that Magda had sent the note. Magda eventually 'fessed up but asked Teresita why she acted like she didn't like her anymore. Teresita said that it had nothing to do with that but that the junior sisters are doing their *informes* now [self-evaluations as part of the request to renew their temporary vows] so she's trying to be extra careful. Magda said she understood—she just wished Teresita had told her this earlier so Magda didn't think the wrong thing.

Excerpted from field notes, April 5, 1995

Deeper within the convent, beyond the communal areas, are the apartments of the sisters, separated by levels of formation: the postulants, the third probation sisters, and the professed sisters. Each apartment area has its own dormitory or sleeping space, a recreation area, restrooms and showers, and areas for washing and drying clothes (see figure 3). These apartments are considered to be cloistered to outsiders, as well as to sisters in lower levels of formation, who cannot enter them without the express permission of the superior of that group. The postulants are forbidden to enter the apartments of the third probation or professed sisters without specific permission granted by Mother Myrna, the mistress of third probations. On the other hand, professed and third probation sisters are authorized to enter the postulants' apartments, since the postulants are at a lower level of formation. Normally, however, the third probation sisters do ask permission of the mistress of postulants before entering. This is done primarily to avoid interrupting any classwork or other activities in which the postulants may be engaged. Professed sisters seem to enter the postulants' apartments at will.

This separation by levels of formation is not merely a matter of building design; it is strictly maintained in the performance of chores, in the dining room, and in the chapel. The congregation's philosophy mandates restricting all the interactions among women from different levels of formation. Formation is viewed by the sisters as a delicate developmental process that can be easily disrupted if great care is not taken to maintain its integrity. Therefore, great pains are taken to articulate and enforce the boundaries—physical and social—between these groups. As Mother Veronica explained it to me, "If a postulant spends a lot of time with the third probations, she is likely to start comparing herself to them in terms of her level of formation, her proficiency in prayer and that sort of thing. But they have been in the religious life for years longer than she has, and she will always find herself lacking. The result would be that she feels inferior, and she might get frustrated and disillusioned and start to doubt her vocation, when in reality she may be proceeding along just fine in her own formation. It's just that she's at the very beginning of the process, and the third probations are well on their way down the path." Interactions among levels of formation can also be detrimental for those at the higher stages. "Likewise," Mother Veronica continued,

> if a junior sister or a third probation sister spends a lot of time with those at a lower level of formation, well—it can be difficult to maintain what one has learned, no? It is easy to be swayed by the behaviors of others. The professed sisters [including the junior and third probation sisters] should be an example to the younger ones, they should embody

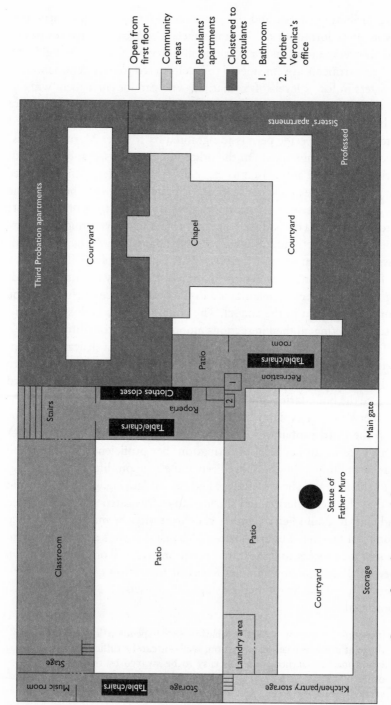

FIGURE 3. Convent floor plan, second floor

Open from first floor

Community areas

Postulants' apartments

Cloistered to postulants

1. Bathroom
2. Mother Veronica's office

Third Probation apartments

Courtyard

Chapel

Courtyard

Professed Sisters' apartments

Stairs

Clothes closet

Ropería

Table/chairs

Patio

Recreation room

Table/chairs

2

1

Classroom

Patio

Patio

Courtyard

Statue of Father Muro

Main gate

Stage

Music room

Table/chairs

Storage

Laundry area

Storage

Kitchen/pantry storage

the philosophy and charism of the congregation. This is hard to do if there is too much interaction among the levels. It's much better for the postulants to see the third probations carrying out their daily duties and truly *living* the example our founder set out for us.

Often, rules and regulations become most clear in their transgression, as I described in the case of Magda and her relationship with the junior nun Sister Teresita. As this situation demonstrates, the separation of sisters by level of formation is meant to further demarcate structural and social distinctions within the congregation, focusing each woman's attention on those in her group and away from those at other stages of their training. The purpose of this is to assist each sister in minimizing any distractions to her internal work—the intensification of her relationship with God.

Personal Space and Privacy

In an institution such as a convent, where personal possessions are forbidden and individualist ambitions discouraged, reeducating newcomers about the nature and character of privacy and personal space becomes a central focus. New entrants must learn to reposition the boundaries of the "private" self in relation to the institution. This does not necessarily mean a complete dissolution of the self or identity—in fact, the sisters would view this as counter to the aims of the congregation. Rather, new sisters must develop a different way of experiencing themselves as individuals in relation to other individuals and to the institutions of the congregation and the Catholic Church. We saw some ways this is played out in the chapters on Brokenness and Belonging. Here I will focus on the central architectural arena in which this reeducation proceeds: the postulants' dormitory.

The dormitory is a long, drafty rectangular room on the third floor of the postulants' section of the building. One of the long walls is punctuated by a series of curtainless windows reaching from about six feet off the ground to just below the dormitory's fifteen-foot-high ceiling. The walls of the dormitory are painted the same hummus-beige as the rest of the convent. The floor is covered in blue tile, giving the place an institutional feel. White, hospital-like curtains pull along tracks hanging from the ceiling to separate the postulants' beds, which form two lines along the length of the dormitory. The single-sized beds consist of a white metal frame and a thin mattress resembling a futon cushion. There are no box springs or mattress pads. White cotton sheets cover the mattresses and are in turn covered with a blue and white seersucker bedspread. Each postulant has one pillow and one heavy blanket to use in case she gets cold. Beds are assigned according to age, with the youngest of the postulants (in this group, Rosita) beginning the year closest to Mother Veronica's own room at the back of the dormitory (see figure 4). There are enough beds in the dormitory for twenty-four postulants, though there have never been that many in a single class. The extra beds remain unused, except for one that was assigned to me for the rare occasions when the postulants and I were permitted decadent afternoon naps.

The Nightstands: Letting Go of the World Outside

In addition to her bed, each postulant is allocated a small white nightstand with two drawers, which is enclosed along with her bed when the curtains are drawn. These apparently insignificant pieces of furniture actually come to figure prominently in the way the postulants experience their progress in the tasks of formation.

The nightstand is used to keep the postulants' toiletries (shampoo, soap, lotions, razors, toothbrush and toothpaste, sanitary pads, etc.), as well as books, letters, photographs of family members or friends, or anything else they want to keep close at hand. The nightstand is, perhaps, the most private place allowed the postulants, and as far as I could see, escapes any kind of official scrutiny. Consequently, the postulants often kept things here that they knew would meet with official disapproval. Surella, for example, kept a number of letters in her top drawer from the boyfriend she left behind, pledging his undying love for her and asking her to leave the convent and run off with him. Magda kept her mementos and notes from Sister Teresita in her nightstand. Carmen had a particularly luxuriant scented hand cream in her top drawer, and when they were feeling particularly decadent, some of the postulants would put it on and prance around, claiming to be like "modern" women going out for a night on the town. And almost all the postulants kept a hearty stash of chocolate in their nightstands. Given the nightstands' function as a special domain of personal privacy, it was something of a privilege to be permitted to look through another's nightstand, and opportunities for this sort of exploration arose on those occasional afternoons when the postulants were given some time to simply "hang out." Being permitted access to another's nightstand was a sign of camaraderie and trust—depending on whose nightstand was

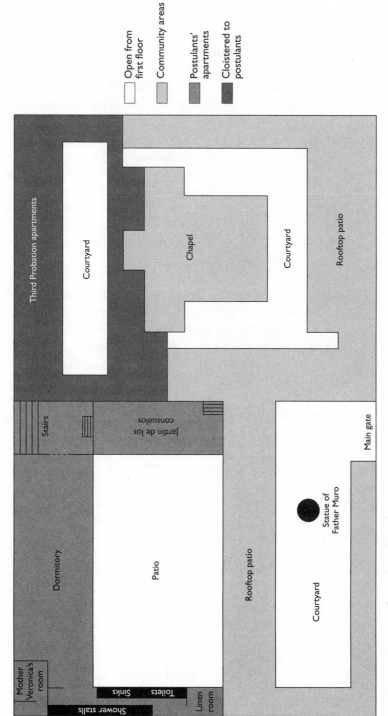

FIGURE 4. Convent floor plan, third floor

Open from
first floor

Community areas

Postulants'
apartments

Cloistered to
postulants

Third Probation apartments

Courtyard

Chapel

Courtyard

Rooftop patio

Stairs

Jardín de los consuelos

Main gate

Statue of
Father Muro

Courtyard

Rooftop patio

Dormitory

Patio

Mother
Veronica's
room

Shower stalls

Sinks

Toilets

Linen
room

the subject of interest, some were included in the activity and others weren't (fortunately for me, I often was).

Early on in the year, this nightstand exploration was a way of getting to know each other, of learning about each other's lives before coming to the convent, learning about each other's emotional commitments, struggles, and aspirations. But as the year went on, it seemed that the nightstands became a sort of space to hold onto the world outside the convent walls, and the postulants' management of this space and their possessions became progressively more ambivalent. Items that before had been mere curiosities, like Carmen's hand cream, took on the status of almost guilty pleasures. As they progressed in their formation, the postulants seemed less concerned about Mother Veronica catching them playing "dress-up" with the perfumed lotion than with what the desire to do so revealed (to themselves and the other postulants) about the genuineness of their vocations. In the same way, by the middle of the year, Carlota's love letters were no longer something to giggle over with the other postulants—her hanging on to them took on a different cast, becoming a more serious indicator for her and the others of the seriousness (or not) of her commitment to the religious life.

Mother Veronica periodically set the postulants the task of cleaning out and organizing their nightstands. They were given no specific instructions about what they could or could not keep, and Mother Veronica often used this time to catch up on her paperwork, so they were not supervised in this task. As the year progressed, I noticed that this activity took on the sense of being not merely a housekeeping chore but an indicator to the postulants themselves and the others of the degree to which they were letting go of the world "outside." Much as the postulants used to peek into each other's lives by rummaging through each other's nightstand drawers, they now shared with each other the items they were throwing away. Some of the postulants were much more private in general and simply went about cleaning and organizing their nightstands without spectacle. But most shared their struggles about letting go of various items with others, who would often remind them (sometimes jokingly, sometimes not) that it was a mortification and a manifestation of the vow of poverty to dispense with such worldly attachments.

Those who were more willing or able to let go of the physical remnants of their worldly lives were admired by others (sometimes grudgingly) as evidencing a strong commitment to the religious life and, by implication, a strong religious vocation. Those who had more difficulty with this became progressively more and more private about it, and it became something of an embarrassment to be found holding onto such items. Haydee, for example, kept a tube of lip gloss in her top drawer. Early in the year, she had often joked about how "worldly" she was for having it, had sometimes tried it on, and had shared it with others. By April, she had stopped talking about the lip gloss and it disappeared from sight. In late May, she dug it out of the back of her nightstand drawer and threw it away, calling a small group of us over to witness the event. She thought briefly about trying it on one last time before tossing it in the garbage but decided against it.

Within the great expanse of the convent building, then, the postulants maintained two small drawers as their private space. And as the year progressed, they were encouraged—subtly, but persuasively—to relinquish their hold on this space and to open it to the scrutiny of others.

Constant Companions

The postulants (who are at the lowest level of formation in the convent) eat, sleep, study, pray, play, and work in the company of others. They are never wholly alone unless they are sick and are sent to bed by the mistress of postulants. For the entire ten months of the postulancy, they are never physically isolated, never out of earshot of someone else. One effect of this lack of privacy is that the postulants discover that isolation or solitude come only in private prayer and internal experiences of God. And this, they are told, is precisely the point. As they move up in the process of formation and become more adept at the internal dimensions of prayer and meditation, they are given progressively more control over their own space. Novices (who live in a different building on the outskirts of town), for example, have rooms with walls on three sides, with the fourth covered by a heavy curtain, instead of the flimsy white curtains that separate the postulants' beds. Professed sisters have their own rooms, equipped with a bed, desk, nightstand, and small bathroom. As a sister becomes *más formada* (more formed), then, it is expected that she has internalized this new understanding of self and no longer needs such stark architectural reminders of how different the religious life is from *el mundo afuera*—the world outside. In part, this is because she learns to literally *embody* her personal space, maintaining it as an interior attitude rather than as a feature of the material world. Thus the sense of being alone changes from a material fact (no one else is around) to a purely internal experience. One of the most important tools helping the postulants to develop this disposition is the second domain of the demarcation of space, the clothing of the body.

THE POSTULANTS' UNIFORM

The uniforms and habits used by the congregation continue the process of enclosure in four principal ways. First, they testify to the separation of the sisters from the outside world, physically representing that they belong to a different domain. Second, these garments distinguish between levels of formation (postulant, novice, professed sister). Third, the habit or uniform literally encloses one's body in the material (actual and symbolic) of the congregation. And fourth, the garment itself has an inside and an outside. No adornment is permitted on top of the habit or uniform, but personal jewelry or trinkets may be worn if they are kept *inside*—tucked into the shirt, pinned to the inside of the garment— and out of view. The habit or uniform, then, functions as a tangible boundary marker separating two distinctly different spaces: just as the main gate marks "the convent" off from "the world," these garments further mark the boundary between the institutional self and the private person.

The postulants wear a specific uniform in the convent and are not permitted to don the habit of the congregation until and unless they are admitted to the novitiate. The postulant uniform is meant to mark these women as being in the first stage of formation in the convent and to help them to begin to internalize the significance of the habit in the religious life as a sign of poverty and humility. For underclothes, they wear regular white or beige cotton bras and underwear covered by a full (mid-calf) slip. Over this they wear white button-down long-sleeve shirts or loose-fitting turtlenecks. There is no specified style of shirt they must wear, but all clothes must be modest and free of decoration. Over the white shirt the postulants wear an aqua polyester jumper dress, which they must have made before coming to the convent (they may also purchase them from previous postulants who have graduated to the next level and have taken the habit of the congregation). The jumper is V-neck and sleeveless and comes in slightly at the waist before flaring out in an A-line to mid-calf. It zips on one side from just under the sleeve to mid-hip. On their legs the postulants wear beige kneesocks that are provided by the congregation. All sisters are permitted to continue shaving their legs if they so choose, and as far as I could tell, all of

the postulants (and most of the professed sisters) did this. On their feet
the postulants wear black shoes of their own purchase. The choice of
style of shoe is left up to each postulant, though excessive stylishness is
forbidden (Carmen, for example, asked Mother Veronica if she could
get some shoes like the ones I wore—black penny-loafer style, but with
a two-inch heel. Mother Veronica said no, that they were *demasiado
mundial*—too worldly—for a postulant). As the postulants soon learn,
life in the convent is hard work, and many soon opt for function over
form, with most of them purchasing nursing shoes by the end of the
year.

The postulants are not required to wear a veil at all times as the professed sisters do, though they are required to wear them in the chapel.
Each postulant is given a flimsy, black nylon veil that is placed over the
hair and fastened with a simple snap at the nape of the neck. The veil
hangs down just past the shoulders. The nylon material is slippery, and
I observed that the postulants' veils were often askew or would fall off
altogether, so that they took to using bobby pins or barrettes to hold
them in place. The sisters are permitted to keep their hair any length
they like, and most of the postulants kept theirs long for the bulk of the
year, pulling it back from their faces with barrettes, ponytail holders,
and plastic headbands. As the time for entering the novitiate and taking
the habit neared, however, many cut their hair short. "Once we have to
wear the habit and veil every day," Abby said, "we're not going to want
all this hair. You have to jump out of the shower, get dressed, and get to
the chapel. If you have long hair, it's going to be wet under your veil.
And besides," she continued, "they say that a woman's hair is her glory.
But Christ doesn't care about that! He cares about what's in our hearts."
Abby's words were a comfort to Marta, who had just returned from the
hairdresser. Marta's curly hair had been cut very short on the sides and
styled on top, becoming poofy and frizzy. She looked, we all agreed, like
a Q-Tip. As the year progressed, getting one's hair cut short (even, and
perhaps especially, when the outcome was unattractive) became an
important sign of commitment to the congregation, even before the
postulants submitted their applications to continue to the next level of
formation.

Aside from their hair accessories, postulants are not permitted any
kind of personal ornamentation. They cannot wear makeup, earrings,
bracelets, or anything else that is purely decorative and does not have a
functional purpose. They are required to wear a watch (which they are
to bring with them upon entering) and are permitted, if they choose, to

wear modest necklaces that can be hidden inside their shirts (many wear small crucifixes or saints' medals they received at their first Communions or other important events). They are also permitted to attach a large safety pin to the inside chest area of their jumpers, from which they can hang other small trinkets or charms they wish to keep close.

The general rules about personal adornment pertain to the professed sisters as well. The official habit of the congregation is made of black polyester and is similar in style to the postulants' uniform, save that the sleeves on the habit reach down to the wrist and the sisters wear white mock-turtleneck dickeys under the habit that peek out at the neckline.[1] The veil of the order is black, with a white ribbing 2 mm in diameter, as spelled out in the congregation's directory. It fits on the top of the head, just behind the hairline, and covers the ears before fastening at the nape of the neck. It hangs down to just below shoulder level. Each sister wears a cross specific to the congregation that hangs from a thin black cord around the neck. Those who have professed their perpetual vows also wear a wedding ring on the third finger of the left hand.

Sisters receive the habit of the congregation upon entry to the novitiate, though the novices wear veils of pure white rather than black—"because they're Christ's brides," Celeste explained. The black veil and cross are bestowed on the novices when they make their first temporary profession, and the wedding ring is received at the profession of perpetual vows. Instead of the kneesocks the postulants use, the novices and professed sisters wear *medias* (knee-high nylons). I was told they use these as opposed to full-length pantyhose for comfort and ease of movement, given the strenuous work they do.

The postulants learn in class that the uniform or habit has three main functions, according to the congregation's constitutions and directory. First, it is a sign of poverty and a reminder that one has relinquished ownership of material goods in pursuit of the kingdom of heaven. Each postulant, novice, and sister is permitted only two uniforms or habits, and each is identical to that of her counterparts.

Second, wearing the uniform or habit is meant to be an expression of humility and the fact that one has eschewed concerns about physical attractiveness. These garments are unflattering and can be uncomfortable, and any sort of physical adornment is absolutely prohibited. The purpose of this, Mother Veronica told us, is that the postulants must

---

1. Sisters who work in the heat of Africa wear habits made of beige or white cotton instead of black polyester.

learn to think of themselves in functional terms. "The point of the religious life is to ask yourself, 'How can I best function in the service of God?' The uniform and habit are to remind you that you have a particular role of service here, kind of like nurses in a hospital. What's important in the hospital is that role, what the nurses do. Not so much the person herself."

Third, the uniforms and habits are meant to reinforce in the sisters a disposition of modesty, of the appropriate dress and comportment of virtuous women. In addition to the actual cut of the uniforms and habits, which draws attention away from the curves of the female form and leaves nothing but the hands, face, and part of the neck exposed, these garments restrict the sorts of movements one can make. The postulants discovered this in sometimes amusing ways: if they turned their heads too fast when wearing their veils, they sent the veils veering off to one side or sailing off their heads altogether. Moving too quickly, bounding down the stairs, and bending over from the waist (as opposed to at the knees) were likely to bring the same result. Early in the year, the postulants would use bobby pins or barrettes to keep the veils in place when wearing them in the chapel. Toward the end of the year, though, most of the postulants had specifically decided *not* to use these fasteners and instead took it as a challenge to learn to carry themselves so that their veils did not fall off. They also increasingly wore their veils throughout the day (instead of just inside the chapel), and learning to keep one's veil in place through controlling the movements of their bodies became for them an important preparation for moving to the novitiate, the next level of formation. "Pretty soon, we're going to have our veils on all the time!" Evelyn told me. "The novices tell me that this is one of the hardest things to get used to, having something over your head all the time. The habits are similar to our uniforms, except for the dickey (which I hear can also be kind of uncomfortable). So that shouldn't be too much of an adjustment. But the veil is something else. You have to learn how to carry yourself correctly, like a *religiosa* [a nun]."

In my exit interviews with the postulants four months after they had entered the novitiate, almost every one of them independently mentioned donning the habit and veil as profoundly significant for them. "It's something really different," Surella told me. "It's kind of hard to explain. With our postulant uniforms we could move around pretty easily. We can still move fast in our habits if we need to, but it *does* feel different to be covered up to your wrists and to have this white part come up on your neck. And the veil! It definitely takes getting used to.

But you know what, Rebe?" Surella continued, "I love wearing my habit and veil. Every morning when we get up and get dressed, we meditate on how our habit is a sign of consecration to God. As we put on each part, we meditate on why we're here, why we've chosen to answer God's call. I never thought clothes could be so meaningful, but it's true. It's something very special to wear the habit of the Siervas."

The uniforms and habits of the congregation, then, elaborate the architectural elements of containment by further marking boundaries between different insides and outsides. They set the wearer apart as a person who belongs, not to the outside world, but to the world of the church—as the special property of God. Within the convent itself, these garments mark off the different levels of formation, enclose the body in the material of the congregation, and delimit each sister's personal space (the domain of trinkets and jewelry inside her uniform) from her social performance of the role of nun. This progressive closing in of the boundaries of the self continues in the third domain of containment, the enfolding of the body.

THE SENSING/SENSUAL BODY

In the convent, even the body is closed unto itself as the physical boundaries of the body become strictly managed. This management can be rather crudely described as monitoring what comes out of the body and what goes into the body. With regard to the former, the postulants learn they must take care in three key areas: gaze, speech, and comportment. With regard to the latter, they learn to control the appetite and practice chastity. In both, I observed that the central project seemed to be a reshaping of *desire*—for self-expression, for attention, for food, for sex—and the internalization of a particular set of dispositions of the self. I will examine this interior process of transformation in chapter 8. Here I will consider the *physicality* of the (en)closed body in the convent.

Gaze

The sisters practice what is called "a custody of the eyes," meaning that they must control their gazes and carefully monitor their visual landscape. This applies to looking at people as well as things like movies, magazines, or books that are considered inappropriate. Learning to maintain this custody of the eyes is an important part of the postulants' training during their first year.

In terms of interpersonal interactions, postulants learn that they must take care not to direct too much attention to others. The postulants are rarely alone and spend the vast majority of their hours in the company of their companions. Precisely because of the intensity of communal life in the convent, the sisters say, one must learn a particular sort of respect for the privacy of others, especially when this privacy is not facilitated by the context itself. This means, for example, not staring at others or observing their activities too closely or with too much interest.

This control of the gaze has two purposes. First, undue visual scrutiny of another is thought to be an invasion of privacy, an imposition of one-self into the space (physical, psychological, spiritual) of one's companion. Keeping custody of the eyes, then, is meant to establish interpersonal boundaries between individuals who live in extraordinary close circumstances, protecting both sisters—the viewer and the viewed—from the compromising of this personal space. Second, custody of the eyes is an important element in the practice of chastity. Various desires may be aroused through visual means, the sisters say, whether by inappropriate attention to another sister or by reading or viewing material that might stimulate such desires. The postulants' access to any kind of media was carefully controlled for this purpose—they were permitted no magazines (except for religious journals or missionary circulars), no books that did not directly pertain to the religious life, no newspapers (though they received reports of important news stories through the professed sisters when this was deemed necessary), and no television. The postulants did have a TV and VCR in their classroom and did watch videos with some frequency—mostly Disney films or religious productions. But these were selected by Mother Veronica and watched in her presence. If she deemed any part of the film to be inappropriate, she would stop the tape and fast-forward past the offending scene. The one striking deviation from the norm of cartoons and musicals came in April, when we watched *Schindler's List*. Most of the postulants found this film to be extraordinarily disturbing, but Mother Veronica insisted that we watch the entire thing (despite pleas for her to put on *The Lion King* instead) because, she said, it was important for the postulants to learn about the kinds of evil social injustice can bring about.

This practice of custody of the eyes is in stark contrast to the extreme scrutiny to which the postulants submit themselves in the process of formation. Every moment of every day is regulated. The postulants cannot eat, sleep, study, play, work, shower, dress, make a phone call, write a letter, or go to the doctor without the permission of the mistress of postulants and the knowledge of at least a handful of others. The postulants in the class I worked with were acutely aware of the scrutiny of their superiors and became progressively more nervous about this as the year progressed. The experience of this scrutiny became manifest one day in early May during lunch. The postulants were particularly animated that day and were talking and laughing loudly. Then, suddenly, Magda whispered, "*Hermanas! Hermanas!*" with such urgency that the postulants around her immediately quieted down to hear what she had to say. "*Hermanas!* The *Profesas* are watching us! No, no! Don't look over there! They look *bien enojadas* [really mad]!" "Ah, *con razón* [with reason]," remarked Carlota, who herself had been an active participant in the noise-making. "We're almost at the end of our postulancy. We should be *bien formadas* [well formed] by now. *Con razón, con razón.*" The postulants went back to their meals in silence, except for Magda's periodic updates of "They're still watching! They're still watching!" The elaboration of "the gaze," then, has two dimensions that are in tension with each other—the gaze is something one should not exercise toward others but is something to which one should willingly submit oneself with humility.

Speech

Silence at all times and all places is considered essential for the proper reorientation of the self in the religious life. Mother Veronica explained to us that this does not necessarily mean the absolute absence of speech, although sometimes it does (such as during meditation and during the Grand Silence, stretching from the completion of evening prayers until the beginning of morning prayers the following day). More, she said, silence means keeping all movements and interactions controlled, discreet, and modest. Silence means not letting the dormitory door slam and not plopping your books down on the desk or laughing too loudly during recreation, as well as observing the Grand Silence from evening to morning and maintaining silence during meals. As a rule, the postulants learn, communication should involve as little discussion as possible. It should be simple, straightforward, and plain. "Noise" in this context is not only verbal. The "noise" to be avoided is letting one's person be loud enough in any way to stand out or to be a distraction to others.

The concept of silence was the topic of special instruction for two weeks in early May as preparation for the spiritual exercises the postulants would attend before going to novitiate. To help them internalize the importance of silence, Mother Veronica divided the postulants into three teams corresponding to different types of silence—internal, external, and spiritual.[2] Each team was to post sayings related to their topic around the postulants' apartments and was to come up with various *prácticas*, exercises the group could do to help them achieve silence in these areas. The most effective *práctica* was that devised by the external silence group. Each postulant was given ten red tokens. Whenever she made excessive noise, either verbally or with other actions (like slamming the door), another postulant could call her on it, and the offending postulant would have to give the other postulant one token. The idea was that the postulant with the most tokens at the end of the week (meaning that she had both observed silence and called out others when they did not) would receive a special prayer offering. Clara was the winner. Magda lost all her tokens by the end of the second day.

The postulants claimed they learned a lot through this *práctica* about how difficult the practice of silence really was. But the exercise also produced some unexpected effects. On several occasions, there were angry exchanges between postulants when one was called out for making noise but refused to give up a token or when personal animosities crept into the whole procedure (so that some postulants were asked to give up tokens and others were not depending on friendship loyalties). In the end, though, the *práctica* seemed to have the desired effect. The usually high decibel level of the group was brought down a few notches and stayed that way for the rest of the year.

Physical Comportment

The sisters recognize that one can be "loud" with one's body as well as one's voice. But the noisiness of the body does not come only from carelessly slamming doors or thundering down the stairs. The body can be loud—or silent—in the orchestration of its movements, in the intensity of its expression. As part of their formation, then, the postulants learn

---

2. Internal silence, we learned, consists of the following points: evangelical (pure) thoughts of the presence of God, admiration of nature, meditative prayer, pardon of others (brings internal peace), seeing your sisters as manifestations of Christ, and remote preparation for communion with Christ. External silence refers to noise, action, and postures (which can reflect one's state of inner peace); the volume of one's voice; verbal messages; fraternity; and things around us (such as making noise while cleaning the pots in the kitchen). Spiritual silence, by far the most profound, has as its aim the immediate preparation for special communion with Christ; communion with one's sisters as communion with Christ and with the world; and concentration in meditation, the Eucharist, Adoration, the rosary, and the Liturgy of the Hours.

more than how not to laugh too loudly in the dining room—they also develop an aesthetics of comportment, an economy of action, and a deliberateness of movement noticeably different from the behavior of people on "the outside."

The sisters work hard and long and submit their bodies to difficult and at times backbreaking labor. Managing the comportment of the body, then, does not in any way mean that these women are not fully, physically active. Rather, the postulants learn that the movements and expressions of the body must be deliberately channeled into the service of the congregation and, by extension, of God Himself. The sisters, for example, do not stroll in a leisurely way—they walk with a purpose, toward a particular destination or task. They do not carry out their chores absentmindedly but give concentrated attention to the job at hand. They learn to develop a hyperawareness of the body's movements and actions—a *mindfulness* of their physical location in and through space—and it is this bodily attitude that postulants must learn to inhabit.

The Self Contained

The control of one's gaze, speech, and comportment, then, turns the body in on itself. The body becomes the container of the inner world, enclosing (but ideally not revealing to others) one's desires, difficulties, impulses, and emotions. When properly trained, it serves as a barrier against inappropriate self-expression or the undue intrusion of one's person into the role of sister. And, as I will take up in chapter 7, when coupled with the aesthetics of modesty, silence, and reserve, this management of expression encourages the development of a particular experience of the body as the regulator, stabilizer, and moderator of one's internal life.

The body, however, is not simply a material container of impulses and desires—it can (and frequently does) become the vehicle of them as well. The bodily desires of most concern in the convent are the appetite for food and the appetite for sex.

Food and Eating

We spent the afternoon chore time sorting through crates and crates of ice cream which were donated to us from somewhere—Aurrera, I think, because also in the car were several boxes from there of feminine napkins. We were given chocolate bars in the morning after Adoration and ice cream in the afternoon in recreation. I've OD'd on junk food lately, so I abstained. Thea was lamenting the fact that they put the tray of ice cream sticks right in front of her and she had to resist the temptation. She's *still* on her diet and has to lose more weight. She said she didn't lose much when she was home recovering from her knee surgery because of her immobility. I told her that if she's not careful, soon she'll look just like her cane.

Excerpted from field notes, April 26, 1995

The postulants were given strict instructions about the management of the appetite. As I will discuss in more detail in chapter 7, food was definitely viewed by the sisters as a potential temptation, and mealtimes were highly structured events. The sisters eat together in two shifts, with the postulants assigned to the first, beginning at about 12:30. All sisters are instructed by the congregation's directory to take care to observe temperance, prudence, and moderation in eating. The postulants, in particular, are instructed that as part of their formation they must learn to regulate their food intake so that they are eating enough to sustain them in their work but not so much that it impedes their abilities to concentrate fully on their duties, studies, and prayer.

Most of the postulants seemed to manage their intake of food with little difficulty (aside from a perpetual concern about gaining too much weight). I was surprised to see, though, that food and eating seemed to become more of a focus of concern as the year wore on. Rather than gaining greater mastery over their appetites, the postulants seemed to become significantly more anxious about food and eating as the time for entering the novitiate approached. And I learned that the postulants increasingly interpreted difficulty in controlling their appetites as communicating something negative about the genuineness of their vocations.

It is perhaps understandable that, since these women are permitted so few physical pleasures in the convent, the temptations of food and eating might become highly charged for them. The postulants showed a rather startling penchant for chocolate and sweets, one that was enthusiastically shared by Mother Veronica and many of the other sisters as well. Candy was without a doubt the treat of choice, after a hard day or simply (it seemed to me) as a reward for breathing. Mother Veronica would sometimes distribute lollipops or hard candies during class, and a huge bowl of candies and chocolates would make its rounds almost every recreation period. The arrival of a new shipment of ice cream or the baking of a cake inspired such excitement that Mother Veronica would sometimes cancel class so that the postulants could go watch the activities. When the postulants relinquished sweets during Lent, this was, then, an extraordinary sacrifice—but one that was rewarded with a doubling of sugar intake for a week or so after Easter.

While the postulants and other sisters took a playful view of this sort of *antoja* (craving) for sweets, other difficulties in controlling the appetite were taken much more seriously. Ruth, for example, seemed to struggle more than the others with controlling her food intake, and Mother Veronica would often bring up Ruth's weight and appetite in class when discussing the importance of learning self-control and moderation. One day, for example, Ruth complained to Mother Veronica that her stomach would growl so loudly in the morning before breakfast that she couldn't concentrate during morning prayers. Mother Veronica told her that if she ate less in general her stomach would shrink and she wouldn't get so hungry. The other postulants chuckled.

Ruth's weight and appetite also became fodder for jokes and teasing by the other postulants. Magda, for example, particularly enjoyed giving Ruth a hard time about her weight and took every opportunity she could to joke about it. She would complain that she couldn't sleep the night before because Ruth's bedsprings would squeak under her weight every time she rolled over. Or she would remark that she could always tell when Ruth was coming down the stairs because the floor would shake (which was untrue). Though they were somewhat shocked by Magda's comments, the other postulants would usually laugh at her jokes. This sort of teasing was mostly good-natured and not really meant to injure Ruth's feelings, though Ruth did confide in me during our exit interview that she sometimes found it very hurtful. "It's true that I struggle with my appetite and my eating," she said.

> I'm not happy about it, and it's something I try to work on because I know gluttony is a sin. Usually it doesn't really bother me when Magda or the others make a joke about it, because that's part of humility, no? To be able to laugh at yourself and not take yourself too seriously. But if I'm feeling like I haven't been attending to that part of me as carefully as I should, then the jokes do make me feel bad. Not because my sisters mean to hurt me but because it reminds me that I'm not doing what I should be doing. I'm not being vigilant. I'm being neglectful.

An even more striking example of the way appetite is configured in the convent is the saga of Thea's diet. On her doctor's recommendation, Thea embarked on an extraordinarily strict diet of approximately six hundred to seven hundred calories a day, coupled with injections of "vitamins." In the space of two months, she lost over twenty pounds. But Thea's startling transformation was more than physical. During the course of those two months, I observed her closely out of concern for her health. I was struck by the dramatic changes in her personality and her behaviors around food, and she and I had several conversations about her experiences of being on the diet. Particularly interesting to me was the evolution of interpretations she employed to talk about her feelings of hunger and deprivation, gradually moving from the physical realm ("my stomach is growling") to the spiritual ("I'm offering my hunger up to God").

Management of the appetite and control of food intake, then, complement the other forms of bodily enclosure in the convent by regulating the relationship between desires and the satisfaction of those desires through the body. As opposed to the domains of gaze, speech, and comportment, however, this satisfaction is found not through the expressions of the body itself but through incorporating something into the body from outside.

Chastity

The concern over protecting the body from undue outside intrusion is also evident in the practice of chastity. Though chastity includes many elements and is much more than simply the prohibition of sexual intercourse, I will discuss it here as a technique of bodily enclosure with the role of preserving a sense of bodily integrity and inviolability.

Women are not asked if they are virgins when they apply to the congregation, nor are they required to undergo a physical examination to determine whether this is the case. "We're not so concerned with what someone has done in the past," Mother Josephia, the vocations director, explained to me. "Just look at Saint Augustine! He certainly had his share of experiences. Just because someone may have had a sexual experience does not in and of itself preclude her from living a very successful life in the congregation, provided that she has confessed this sin and found reconciliation. God loves sinners and reaches out to them and welcomes them to Him. We are all sinners in some way or another. If a woman pledges herself bodily to Christ from day X onward, and fulfills this promise, God will be glorified. But," she added, "having such an experience might may make things more difficult for a sister in terms of living the vow of chastity. God made our bodies to enjoy sex so that we'll want to get married and have children. We can learn to channel this desire into other things, but it's probably easier to do that when you don't know precisely what the alternative is."

To assist them in channeling their desires, the directory of the congregation states that sisters who encounter people of the opposite sex in their work must "maintain appropriate reserve" and avoid "any familiarity or imprudence" (Article 145). They must be sure to remain in view of other people, declining to engage in anything that can give a false impression of their intentions or actions. At all times, they should be conscious that "on them depends the good name of the congregation and the appreciation of others for the consecrated life" (Article 146). In addition, sisters should avoid sexually suggestive readings, events, and conversations and should beware of those who might enjoy the challenge of seducing a woman consecrated to God. "Some men might come to you under the guise of wanting spiritual direction, but they really want something else," cautioned Mother Veronica. "Of course, you want to think that everyone has good intentions, but it's simply not so, so you have to be aware and vigilant. This is how the enemy [the devil] gets to us. He's sly and a liar. And the devil particularly wants to corrupt nuns because they are consecrated to God. So be careful, *mis hijas,* be careful."

In the course of their nine years of formation the postulants learn how, precisely, to channel their sexual impulses into other domains, such as care for children in the congregation's schools or tending of the elderly in the congregation's hospices. During this first year, however, the postulants are gently introduced to the issues of chastity and sexuality as permissible topics of discussion and are progressively encouraged to express their concerns and questions about this practice. They learn that by remaining chaste they are preserving their bodies as pure offerings to Christ and that chastity ensures that all the affective energy associated with sexuality becomes directed toward establishing God's kingdom.

Like the control of the appetite, then, the practice of chastity is meant to aid the sisters in regulating desire by establishing clear boundaries of the body. Though the body itself is seen to be the locus of desires for food and sex, the postulants learn that proper training and management of these desires can be achieved in and through the very body that produces them.

THE PRODUCTION OF INTERIORITY
THROUGH CONTAINMENT

The cumulative effect of accommodating to the elements of containment in the convent—the architectural specificity, the use of the uniform, the control of expressiveness and desire—is one of learning to mark off the internal self as the irreducible "interior" and therefore as the domain of essential transformation. Containment, as a process, does not simply mark the boundaries between an "inside" and an "outside." It productively creates these spaces and sets them in specific relationship to each other. But it also does so with a particular directional movement. The marking off of a specifically determined "inside" from a more generalized "outside" suggests a heightened concern with the character and quality of the interior as fundamentally different from the world beyond its borders. In this way, the process of enclosure is simultaneously a process of interiority—the production of one space *within* another, which then becomes a domain pregnant with its own unique potentialities.

This is certainly the case in the convent. There is a progressive internalizing of space, from the building's architecture to the structure of social relationships, to the management of the body. Many observers of the religious life have interpreted this turning inward as a homogenizing process, a denial of individual differences through the uniformity of practice, dress, and comportment. While there is an element of truth to this understanding, I saw something more complex in the convent than a simple denial of self in service of a larger institution. Rather, through these techniques of enclosure the sisters endeavor to prune away any external differences that might distract them from a genuine, unencumbered examination and correction of the interior self. The form and process of this interior critique are the subject of chapter 8.

THE IDEOLOGY OF THE TEMPORAL WORLD:
MAKING DISTINCTIONS

During this third stage, then, the postulants become more adept at distinguishing the spiritual from the mundane and marking the boundary between the two. Specifically, they learn that "the world" and its distractions promote an artificial manifestation of self that runs directly counter to the purity of being needed to encounter God. These distractions—inside the convent as well as outside—must be managed through the establishment and enforcement of different kinds of boundaries, and the postulants are introduced to strategies of how to achieve this. They learn that, as women and as nuns, they are particularly vulnerable to external temptation and violation and so must be specially attentive to these issues. They are encouraged to take Mary—inviolate and chaste, yet supremely receptive to God—as their model. If they are successful, they, like Mary, will come to experience—in their deepest interior—the kiss of God.

Before they are thought to be "ready" to approach and engage this interior, however, the postulants must learn to master the practical activities of the body. They must become experts in the management of the body so that the body can be properly enlisted in the project of transformation. We turn now to these practices of corporeal conditioning.

CHAPTER 7

Regimentation

Making the Mindful Body

The previous chapter on technologies of interiority dealt with the strategies in the convent for producing a particular phenomenology of containment through hierarchies of enclosure, with the desired result of this process being to highlight the internal/eternal self and the ultimate sacred, interior space. By early December—four months into their training—that experience of interiority becomes redefined as a tension between what we might call the embodied and the transcendental selves—the rebellious, desiring human, and her pure immortal soul. In this chapter I will examine how bodily discipline within the convent makes manifest tensions between embodied and transcendental selves while at the same time providing specific strategies for managing this tension.

As a total institution (Goffman 1961), the convent not only regulates the placement of individual bodies in space and time as a way of producing a certain experience of interiority but also works on the internal orientations of members by requiring them to relinquish control over all activities, including even the most basic elements of personal care and maintenance. Through the strict compartmentalizing and management of such practices, the institutional ethos becomes part of the participants' lived daily experience. Practices that center on the control of the physical body are particularly potent arenas for this "education." From many months of participating in the daily life of the convent, I came to discern six principal arenas of bodily experience the postulants must learn to master to get through the day: (1) the rhythm of daily life; (2) personal hygiene; (3) food and eating; (4) manual labor; (5) sociability; and (6) physical practices of piety.

RHYTHMS OF LIFE: THE DAILY GRIND

The first and most basic body discipline the postulants must learn is habituating to a new sleep/wake schedule in the convent. Without exception, the postulants told me they found waking up at 4:45 A.M.— and then staying awake throughout the day—to be the most challenging part of their adjustment to convent life. It was not uncommon in the early weeks for postulants to fall asleep during the morning prayer or at their desks during study time. In the beginning, Mother Veronica dealt with such interruptions with gentle encouragement or perhaps even by sending the depleted postulant upstairs for a nap. As time went on, however, the postulants were expected to have built up their stamina, to able to pace themselves, to maintain their stores of energy evenly so that they could make it through the day. By the end of the year, falling asleep in prayer—or at any other nondesignated sleep time—would bring the imposition of a penitence.

In addition to sleeping and waking on a radically different schedule than most people in the outside world, postulants have to master the sequence of activities that would fill their day. The convent schedule requires a radical reorientation of their sense of time and agency—they are no longer in control of what they do and when they do it—and effort is required in the beginning for the postulants to learn where they are supposed to be, doing what activity, at what time. Once a woman enters the convent, she is no longer control of when and where she will be doing any particular thing, from sleeping to eating to using the bathroom. While the rigid schedule does allow for some flexibility, a postulant much obtain special permission from a superior to alter her routine.

To assist the postulants of the group I followed in habituating to this new rhythm of life, a handwritten poster detailing the prayer, meal, chore, and recreation times common to all levels of formation (made for the postulants by the third probation sisters) was tacked up outside the classroom door in the postulants' apartments. An additional poster listing postulant-specific events (class and study times, times of special prayer or group activities) was taped up beside the other. A third poster detailing who was assigned to what chores for that month, who was assigned to shower when, and so forth was posted in the postulants' dormitory. These posters were in place for approximately one month. After that, the postulants were expected to know the schedule of the convent well enough to not need them.

Although the convent day proceeds along a clearly demarcated schedule, the rhythm of convent life is based in the practice of obedience. This means not only that one's superiors design the schedule and determine who will be doing which activity at what time but that the schedule itself is subject to modification at the superior's discretion. For example, though the schedule may indicate that the afternoon chores are to begin at 1:00 P.M. or that music class starts at 3:00 P.M., the mistress of postulants directs her charges at every turn. A postulant must never initiate an activity simply because the schedule indicates it is time for that activity to begin. She owes her obedience to her superiors and must wait for direction from them.

The strict regulation of periods of activity and rest, then, functions to remind and reinforce for postulants that they are now operating with a different temporal orientation than people in the outside world, which has implications for their daily lived experience on even the most basic levels. Different things are at stake in the convent, where recrimination involves not simply being reprimanded by the boss but endangering the state of one's immortal soul. The postulants learn that their energies should no longer be directed toward their own freely chosen activities; instead, they must be channeled in the service of God's will as manifested through their superiors. Thus the postulants must learn to submit their very bodily energies to an outside authority. Successfully practicing this different sort of life requires an experience of the body that is simultaneously personal and institutional—both a center of one's own independent initiative and responsibility and an object subject to the will of external authority.

CLEAN BODIES, CLEAN SOULS: PERSONAL HYGIENE

Good personal hygiene is mandatory in the convent, and maintaining a clean and tidy body is seen by the sisters as a prerequisite for maintaining a clean and tidy soul. "Your body is the temple of the Holy Spirit," Mother Veronica told the postulants. "You must respect it, care for it, keep it clean and pure, just as you would the chapel. Because your body is where the Spirit resides with you." This emphasis on cleanliness, however, is balanced against the sin of vanity. "God doesn't care how beautiful we are on the outside," Mother Veronica explained. "He looks for our inner beauty, our purity of heart. Caring for your bodies shows respect for the Lord. Adorning yourself or focusing on exterior appearance shows *disrespect* for Him and a lack of trust in His love for you."

Each morning, immediately following the rising prayer, those who were assigned shower time for that day scuttled off to the showers, carrying with them a towel, soap, shampoo, and anything else they might want to use in the shower (a razor for shaving legs, a shower cap, a loofa sponge, etc.), much as in a college dormitory.

The postulants were instructed to bring these items with them when they entered the convent, and all were marked with their names. As they ran out of shampoo and the like, their families brought them more (or brought them money to buy more) during their monthly visits. Those who had no family nearby or who could not afford new purchases were given these items by the congregation, which bought them in bulk and stored them in a room above the pantry.

As time went on, it became implicitly less desirable to request such things from the "outside." Those who, instead, chose to make do with the congregation's generic supplies were seen as evidencing "good formation"—not only were they willingly dispensing with worldly items, but the postulants seemed to take as very significant participating in the communal life of the order on such an intimate level as bodily cleanliness and feminine hygiene. "It's an issue of humility," Carlota told me. "I mean, it's embarrassing to have to ask Mother Veronica for feminine napkins or deodorant, you know? But our embarrassment comes from a false sense of pride. I mean, we're all humans, and our bodies have certain functions. That's the way God made us. To be embarrassed implies that we feel there's something special about us. But we're all the same. Getting over this is part of recognizing that our bodies are God's creation and belong to Him, just like everything else. When you think about it this way, there's no reason to be ashamed." The postulants learn that embarrassment or guilt about one's body or physicality indicates a worldly disposition, something they should work actively against inside the convent. Modesty, of course, is crucial to the sisters but should be born out of a healthy respect for one's body and the bodies of others, not out of fear, shame, or embarrassment.

Each postulant has enough undergarments and socks for a fresh change every day, four white shirts (one to be reserved only for Sundays), and two jumpers. The postulants embroider each item of clothing, from jumpers to underwear, with their initials to prevent mix-ups. Clothes are washed every third day, pressed and folded, and placed by

name in a communal clothing area (with separate bins for each postulant), ensuring that the postulants always look clean and neat.

This care of the body is meant to evoke in the postulants an attitude
of respect toward their bodies as marvels of nature, crafted by the hand
of God. This is decidedly distinct from concupiscence, the enjoyment of
pleasures of the flesh. The latter, the sisters say, involves an objectifica-
tion of the body as a vehicle of temporal, earthly desire. This leads to
the misperception that the body and the soul are equivalent or coterminous, reinforcing the worldly illusion that one *is* one's body. By contrast, the sisters must learn to cultivate an experience of the body not as
coterminous but as *concentric* with the experience of the soul—of different material form but fashioned from the same metaphysical substance in the image of God. They learn, in other words, that their bodies
are material articulations of their souls in the natural (vs. supernatural)
world. Just as God shows preference for pure, unadorned, clean souls,
they say, so too does He prefer pure, unadorned, clean bodies.

FEEDING THE SPIRIT: THE MANAGEMENT
OF FOOD AND EATING

Food for the sisters is both sustenance and temptation, both a necessity
and a luxury. Because of their heavy workload, the sisters must eat
enough to retain their stamina and strength—"A Sierva should eat like
a horse and work like a mule!" as Mother Maria frequently told the
postulants. At the same time, however, the sisters must maintain constant vigilance to ensure that this heartiness does not tip over into glut-
tony. "After all," Mother Wilhelmina explained to us,

> we work with the poor—people who sometimes go a year at a time with
> no meat to eat, just beans and tortillas. How would it look if we're out
> there working with starving people and we're all plump and jolly? No,
> Father Muro said we should become one with the poor, that we should
> live like them. Thanks be to God that the congregation can provide us
> with so much food so we can keep our strength. But we must always do
> so with the intention of giving our energies back to the poor whom God
> has called us to serve.

So while concerns about food and eating in the convent were not as pronounced as I had expected when I first went to the field, food was most
definitely viewed by the sisters as a special sort of substance—both a
means to increase their energies for service and a potential temptation.
Mealtimes, accordingly, were highly structured events.

Meals in the congregation are of central importance because they are almost the only times during the day (aside from prayer) when the entire community is in one place at one time doing the same activity, although the levels of formation are divided by tables. The dining room is a long room with the kitchen at one end. The tables are arranged so that the two long tables for the professed sisters are parallel to each other and are closest to the kitchen, with the General Council sitting at the table to the left of the kitchen opening. The table of the third probation sisters is further down the dining room, on the left side, and the postulants' table is parallel to theirs on the right. The table where the General Council sits is served first, followed by the table of the other professed sisters, that of the third probation sisters, and, finally, that of the postulants.

The meal ritual begins with the ringing of the handbell, which calls the sisters from their activities. As they file into the dining room, each sister goes to her appropriate table and stands behind her chair (particular seats are not assigned, aside from the custom of allowing the highest-ranking sister at a table to sit at the end closest to the kitchen). The tables are preset with plates, bowls, silverware, and glasses. Once the community is assembled, the sister who has been designated to lead the prayer begins, with the community responding.

"Deign, Lord, to bless us and these gifts that we have received of your generosity, to renew our strengths. In the name of the Father and of the Son and of the Holy Spirit."

"Amen."

Usually, the meals are taken in silence, while one of the sisters reads from the works of Father Muro, the encyclicals of the pope, or some other appropriate work. On these days, communications are to be whispered or, preferably, achieved through pointing, facial expressions, and nods of the head. Readings are chosen to correspond with the liturgical year. Sometimes a tape of calming "New Age" music is played. I personally found it difficult to concentrate on the readings at meals, but the postulants became very proficient at it. By mid-January, I started noticing that they would sometimes bring up these readings in recreation or make reference to them in class. Sometimes during meals someone would whip out a pen and jot down some notes on a napkin.

Not infrequently, however, the sisters are permitted to talk at meals. If talking is permitted on a given day, this is indicated by the ringing of a small bell. But this does not mean that anything goes. Ideally, one keeps one's voice low and avoids loud discussions or laughter (a constant struggle for the postulants, who, particularly early on, tended to get pretty rowdy). During meals, the sisters are not to talk about illness or sad things or to tell jokes, because such things are believed to interfere with eating and digestion.

The meals are served family style, with large platters of different food brought out from the kitchen by the sisters designated to serve that day (usually, this task fell to the third probation sisters, although the postulants would fill in if they needed an extra hand or if the third probation sisters were off on a retreat or an outing). Pitchers of water (or, sometimes, lemonade) are placed on the tables for each to serve herself, as are containers of tortillas.

The postulants are instructed that they should learn to eat "equally" each day and with temperance, meaning that they shouldn't be picky, eating only a little if they don't like the food and eating a lot when they do. Above all, food is to be seen practically, as fuel for the body in the service of God. "What if you tend to get fat or get pimples from certain foods, so this is why you don't eat them?" asked Pipa. "This is vanity," said Mother Veronica. "Do you really think God cares if you have pimples?"

I was reminded of the injunction to eat equally of everything from time to time when something particularly unpalatable to my American tastes went around (like the chicken's feet in the rice or soup made from pigs' heads). One day, for example, I was shocked to see that the main course was actually jiggly slabs of pig fat (no meat, just the fat) with the skin still on and little piggy hairs sticking out of it. I simply could not bring myself to eat it, or even to have it on my plate. The postulants jokingly used this opportunity to tell me that if I *really* wanted to know what they went through as nuns, I should eat a piece "as a mortification."

Some of the postulants had more trouble with the rules about meals than others. Carlota and Ruth, for example, were notorious for their big appetites. Haydee and Alicia were both very picky eaters and would often go without eating one thing or another, while making sure Mother Veronica didn't notice. Magda and Surella both had trouble with the idea of keeping silent during meals and would often position themselves so that they were facing the table of the third probations. They would then make faces and joke around with the third probation sisters—often including Magda's friend Sister Teresita—who were facing their way.

As the year went on, however, these incidents grew fewer and farther between. The cliques who used to make sure they sat together at meals dispersed. The postulants became aware, beginning in February, that

they were being subtly observed by the older nuns to see who seemed to
be proceeding well in her formation and who wasn't. As the time for
application to the novitiate drew nearer, the postulants made more concerted efforts to act appropriately, particularly in prayer or at meals,
when they would be seen by the older nuns.

Food and eating in the convent, then, is one specific arena in which
desire and obligation are negotiated through bodily experience. The
needs of the physical body must be constantly checked and balanced
against its desires, and the postulants must learn to monitor their eating
behaviors—not so much in terms of how much they eat as in terms of
their intentions in eating. If, for example, a sister has been laboring hard
all day and sits down to a hearty meal to replenish her strength, this is
endorsed by the congregation. If, however, the sister sitting next to her
eats the same amount out of boredom or inattention, this indicates a
behavior and an internal attitude that must be corrected. As with the
regulation of activity and rest, the management of eating in the convent
requires participants to submit what most of us consider to be intimate
bodily needs to an external regulatory system, while at the same time
highlighting the need for internal monitoring (Was I really hungry? Or
was I being gluttonous?), since it is the internal orientation of the sister
(as opposed to the act of eating itself) that is the crucial element in
determining the propriety of the behavior in question.

LABORS OF LOVE: MANUAL WORK

As a working (vs. contemplative) order, the Siervas maintain that service to God comes at least as much through in-the-world action as
through silent contemplation and prayer.[1] "As Jesus told Mary and

---

1. The diversification of the monastic groups into cloistered and working orders can
be traced to broader changes in church organization in the early thirteenth century. Before that time, monastic communities had served primarily as centers of prayer and
learning around which the church was organized, providing islands of stability in otherwise tumultuous political and social contexts. But as the influence of external religious
and cultural groups (e.g., the Moors) increased, a more sustained and proactive engagement with the world outside the monastery walls became an urgent concern. Increasingly,
the church recognized the need for a more concentrated engagement with the lay population both to counter the conspicuous presence of other religious groups and to provide
much-needed services to people ravaged by disease, poverty, and war. Francis of Assisi's
dramatic engagement with the poor in the thirteenth century (he is reported to have literally given the clothes off his back to a poor man and to have kissed a leper passing on
the road, among other things) is emblematic of the church's opening to "the world,"
though elements of these changes can actually be traced back to the innovations implemented by Benedict in the sixth century.

Martha," Mother Veronica explained it to us, "there are many ways of serving the Lord. Mary served Him by sitting at His feet and listening quietly to His teachings. Martha served Him by making the food and cleaning the house and bringing Him something to drink. And Jesus Himself said that Martha was just as respectable in her service to Him as was Mary. Contemplative orders follow the style of listening of Mary in this story. But active-life orders follow the style of Martha, serving Jesus through working hard with our hands and our backs, by caring for the poor of the world." Accordingly, the sisters are self-sufficient. They do not, as was customary in centuries past, have "lay sisters" to do the menial work in order to free the sisters up for "more important" tasks. "Father Muro was very against the idea of lay sisters," Mother Wilhelmina explained to me. "As he said—and rightly so—no work is too humble for a Sierva to perform. If *all* our work and *all* our energy is offered up to God, this pleases God as much as if we were in the chapel on our knees all day long. If we really want to serve the poor and to bring them to God, we have to unite with them. You can't do this if you are afraid of doing hard work."

And hard work, indeed, is what is required to keep the convent running. Each sister is assigned specific chores or duties. These are called the "occupations," and in the case of the postulants, these consisted of cleaning the postulants' dormitory and bathroom, cleaning the classroom, working in the kitchen, working in the pantry, doing the laundry, and cleaning the professed sisters' apartments. The postulants performed their occupations three times a day: after breakfast, after lunch, and after dinner.

The postulants were assigned to these occupations (in groups of two to four, depending on the amount of work the job demanded) each month by Mother Veronica in a process somewhat smilingly called "giving out the Will of God." The postulants were given some say in these assignments, but Mother Veronica made the final decisions. One of the criteria was that each had to do something she hadn't done before and/or work with at least one person they hadn't worked with before. When I first arrived at the convent, I worked with Magda cleaning the classroom. It was here, actually, that we had some of our most interesting discussions (although that work is supposed to be done in silence). Beginning in January, however, I began to alternate between the kitchen and the pantry. Not only could the sisters use an extra hand there, but this gave me the opportunity to interact with many sisters other than the postulants and to get a sense of the hustle and bustle of the daily life of the convent. Since both the kitchen and pantry are off the central courtyard, this also gave me a good view of who was coming and going, who spoke to whom, and what visitors came to the convent.

Work, for the Siervas, is not only necessary to the successful functioning of this convent. It is also an expression of one's servility and humility before the Lord and one's sisters. Thus we learned that the chores should be well done, with rectitude of intention. They should be done with as little talking as possible, quickly, and efficiently. "You should remember that everything we do we do for the Lord, not only to please our superiors," Mother Veronica told us.

In reality, however, the chores rarely went like this, at least in the kitchen or the pantry. More often than not, this time was used not only for scrubbing pots or chopping papaya but also for discussion, storytelling, and studying for exams. The older nuns who supervised this work generally did not seem to mind the chatting as long as things didn't get out of hand and the work was getting done. Sometimes they didn't mind even if things did get out of hand, as they did the day a group of us was charged with plucking still-warm, recently dead chickens, chopping off their feet (to be used to flavor rice), and cleaning out their insides. I found this almost impossible to bear, but Celeste, in particular, found it fascinating. She tried to make me laugh by making the chicken carcasses dance around on the counter and later by coming up to me, speaking through a finger puppet she had made out of a hollowed-out chicken's head.

Chore time sometimes seemed to provide an outlet, a release of "silliness" that was necessarily more restrained during other times of the day. But even so, the sisters worked very hard. Not everyone participated in the joking or talking every day, and some days were spent working in complete silence. Generally, however, I found the occupations to be an excellent opportunity to get to know the postulants and some of the other sisters in the convent and to participate in lively and interesting discussions on anything from family relationships to childhood nightmares to theology and even sex.

As they become more proficient at their chores, the postulants were told that increased attention should be directed to their internal states in the performance of their duties. "It's easy to get so used to doing something that it becomes routine," Mother Veronica told the postulants in class one day in early January. "And this is good. Because it frees your mind up for other things. But be careful, *hijas,* not to let your mind wander to just anything. If you do it right, even sweeping the floor or washing the pots and pans can become a form of meditation, freeing your mind for reflection on your day, on how you are living up to your commitments, on whether you are right with God. This is not a time for thinking about your family or what dessert you hope will be served at dinner." Mother Veronica gave specific advice on how to do this. "One thing I used to do," she told us, "was that every time I would sweep the floor, I would say, 'Thanks be to God' when the broom bristles touched down on the floor and 'I love you Lord,' when the bristles left the floor at the end of each stroke. You can use whatever little phrases you like, but something like this helps to orient you to God and away from other things." By working hard with their hands and their bodies, then, the postulants learn yet another strategy for submitting themselves bodily to an outside authority while at the same time retaining a sense of responsibility over their internal orientations to this labor.

SOCIABILITY IN THE NAME OF CHRIST: CRAFTING PLAYFULNESS

A strong sense of community is absolutely essential to the religious life. Living in community, the sisters told me, is at least as challenging as it is rewarding, and the general "vibe" among the sisters is of utmost concern. "You should love God through your sisters," Mother Veronica told us. "If things aren't right with your sisters, then they can't be right with God, either." Two daily "recreation" hours are set apart in the busy convent schedule for socializing and/or relaxing in the company of one's sisters. Recreation, however, is not simply "free time" in which sisters may do whatever they please (though, certainly, more flexibility is afforded professed sisters than postulants in this area). Rather, it is a structured time event. While sisters may generally choose how to amuse themselves during this time (by sewing, chatting, joking, playing, reading, etc.), they must do so communally, not sequestered off somewhere by themselves unless given explicit permission. The function of recreation, then, is not only to provide the sisters with some "down time" away from the demands of work but to carve out a space specifically for building and strengthening bonds among the group.

The postulants had recreation for an hour twice a day: after the afternoon chores and before afternoon classes, and after the evening chores and before Compline. Often Mother Veronica generated projects for the group that were to be worked on during recreation. In November and December we made Christmas cards to be sent out by the congregation.

In May, the postulants were told to sew pot holders for their mothers for Mother's Day. In June, the postulants were set to add their contributions to a photo album chronicling each class of postulants who came through the Central House.

By far the biggest and most arduous tasks for the postulants were learning to cross-stitch and then marking their clothes with their initials before moving to the novitiate. Each postulant was required to turn to Mother Veronica for inspection a completed alphabet and set of numbers, cross-stitched on a single piece of fabric without any major mistakes, before she was allowed to apply for the novitiate. Once the notices of acceptance had been conveyed, the postulants set about madly marking each and every piece of clothing they would take with them to their new home: six pairs of underwear, six pairs of knee-high hose, six undershirts, three bras, three slips, three pairs of pajamas, two habits, two dickeys, and two veils. This took the better part of two months.

Fortunately, although "recreation" generally consisted of such tedious work, it was made entertaining by the fact that, most days, the group could talk about whatever was on their minds. Sometimes this turned us to serious subjects (for example, the postulants took turns in June recounting their vocations to the group), but mostly this was a loud, raucous, laughter-filled hour. Some of the postulants (Magda, Lupita, Lidia, Marta, Abby, Evelyn, and Carlota, for example) engaged in the mayhem enthusiastically almost without fail. Others (like Celeste, Mina, Rosita, and Clara) usually preferred intimate conversation with those around them. Sometimes Mother Veronica would read (or would have one of the postulants read) from the letters of Father Muro or the story of a saint the postulants had expressed interest in. We would also sometimes listen to "educational" tapes, one of the most startling being one that claimed it was standard Protestant teaching that the pope was, in fact, a servant of Lucifer. This did not do much for endearing Protestantism to the postulants.

Recreation was also one of the rare instances when I was able to speak freely with the postulants (and them with me) for any continuous length of time. I took advantage of this situation whenever I could to ask for clarification on theological points, to bring up issues of Mexican cultural tradition, to become acquainted with some of the more reserved postulants, and to stimulate discussion on vocation. But I was not the only one who took advantage of recreation in this way. The postulants were extraordinarily curious about *my* opinion on things, how I viewed them and the congregation as a whole, what I felt about the Catholic religion, what my political views were, and what life was "really" like in the United States. I found myself discussing anything from Proposition 187 to why Americans bother to stand in line in public restrooms instead of simply rushing for the first open door.

As the year wore on, I noticed that the interactions between the postulants during recreation seemed much more measured—still jovial and silly at times, but in a much more controlled sort of way. Postulants who used to fill their free time with doodling or chatting began to find more constructive outlets for their energies without having to be asked by Mother Veronica. Marta and Rosita, for example, took it upon themselves in the last weeks before moving to the novitiate to reorder and catalog all the books in the recreation room, carefully labeling each according to subject, author, and year. Ruth and Surella offered to clean out and reorganize the medicine cabinet in the recreation room. Celeste and Amelia took the initiative to clean out the cabinets that stored the sewing supplies. Mother Veronica would silently nod her assent to such requests (for her permission was needed), but she did not show either surprise or particular pleasure at these self-directed chores. When I later asked her about this in an interview, Mother Veronica explained to me that there were two reasons she didn't make a fuss over the postulants' offering to do extra work during recreation time. "First of all," she said, "they should be offering to do those things because they want to be of service, not because they want praise or recognition from me or their sisters. If they are doing it simply to get praise, this is for the wrong reasons. Second," she continued, "doing extra work like that is a natural development of a woman's vocation. If she is truly engaging in her formation and is offering up all her energies to God, she should naturally come to a place where serving God through serving others makes her feel good. So this is to be supported in the postulants, of course, but not something that we should make a big deal about. After all, that's why they're here."

Recreation, then, is considered by the sisters to be an indispensable component of a very busy day. It is a time to recharge one's batteries and to make real contact with one's sisters. It is a time to question things, or to share experiences, or to discuss what is going on in the world. It is a chance for sisters to come together as a community, take a brief respite from the day's work, and remind themselves that their tasks are not individual burdens to be borne but part of a larger plan in which they play an important part.

THE PRAYERFUL BODY: PHYSICAL PRACTICES OF PIETY

The postulants must also habituate their bodies to the physical demands of prayer. They must learn how to sit in silent stillness for two hours in the morning without falling asleep. They must learn how to kneel in worship, ignoring the pain in their joints to focus all their attention on the glory of God. They must master the elaborate routines of the Liturgy of Hours, standing, sitting, kneeling, speaking, and responding at precisely the correct moments. They must develop a sense of tactile meditation as they concentrate on the sensation of the rosary beads slipping through their fingers during the afternoon recitation. They must learn to walk gingerly back to their pews after receiving Holy Communion and to kneel in intense adoration as the body of Christ slowly dissolves in their mouths and becomes one with their own. And in all of these areas, they must learn to be excruciatingly sensitive to their bodies—the pains, sensations, discomforts, and strains of their mortal flesh, as these, too, are thought to be avenues of communication with God. We bring all of ourselves into the convent, the sisters say. And we should be present—body and soul—with Christ, just as He was for us on the cross.

We might say that practices of piety in the convent involve not simply the abstracted soul but the organized semiotic relationships of the bodied self to other bodied selves and to the divine. Repeated engagement in these activities not only educates the new nun in the formalized relationships postulated among the components of self, other, and God but also (if she fully engages her formation program) encourages in her the core dispositional attitudes of humility, purity, and *entrega*. It does this by proposing to offer a technique for a visceral sort of bodily remembering of the soul's primordial union with God that strikes emotional chords via the experience of physicality. Two of the most central bodily components of prayer are posture and vocalization.

Posture

The posture or attitude of the body is a fundamental component of the proper practice of piety. While it is true, the sisters say, that one can pray at any time of the day while engaged in any activity from washing the dishes to riding the bus, prayer is best facilitated by the careful orchestration of body and soul in a state of heightened attention to the task at hand. Just as they learn that their bodies should be kept pure and clean as temples of the Holy Spirit made manifest in flesh, so, too, the postulants learn that the seemingly simple act of positioning their bodies in space can itself be a form of communication with God. The attitude of the body, they learn, tells God much about the attitude of the soul. In a course on prayer taught by Mother Veronica, the postulants learned how to take advantage of this fact to enhance their prayer experiences. There are four principal bodily postures used in prayer: sitting, standing, kneeling, and prostration.

Sitting, we learned, communicates rest, relaxation, receptivity, and readiness to listen. This is why, Mother Veronica explained, the sisters sit when listening to readings and performing the responsorial during prayer times. "The parallel," the mistress of postulants explained, "is with the biblical story of Jesus sitting down by Jacob's well to hear the word of God. We drink from God's well when we listen in prayer."

Standing, on the other hand, communicates an inner attitude of reverence and awe. In the Mass and other forms of prayer, one stands for the Glory ("Glory to the Father, to the Son, and to the Holy Spirit"), the reading of the Gospels, and the recitation of psalms. Standing is meant to express readiness and vigilance, reverence and respect.

Kneeling communicates an attitude of intense prayer. It is used for times of silent prayer, as, for example, in the morning, in Adoration, following Communion. "Kneeling is an expression of humility and sacrifice, a recognition of the majesty of God as King of the universe," Mother Veronica explained. "It's an affirmation that we recognize Him as our Lord and Master and that we are His humble subjects."

Prostration, the most extreme bodily position assumed in prayer, is used by the sisters only on rare occasions, such as the profession of perpetual vows or during the Chapter of Faults, a monthly exercise where the community of sisters sanctions its members for offenses, both minor and major. Prostration (lying face down on the ground with the arms out in the shape of a cross) is meant to convey an attitude of intense repentance or humble adoration. It expresses humility when one has offended others and is a posture of complete and total submission. The postulants learned that some sisters choose to use this position for their private prayer in their rooms but that it is not a recommended posture to assume in a public venue "because you can become a spectacle," Mother Veronica explained, "and this is directly contrary to the attitude of humility you are supposed to be experiencing."

The sisters maintain that body posture—in prayer and elsewhere—is linked to the dispositions of heart and reinforces them. They view the body as both expressing and constituting the internal attitude of self. In prayer, newcomers to the order must learn to inhabit a phenomenology of the body that, as in the other arenas of bodily discipline (the rhythm of daily life, personal hygiene, food and eating, manual work, sociability), elaborates the temporal self as concentric (though not coterminous) with the experiences of the soul. The body becomes the fundamental and essential link between the self and the soul without reducing one to the other. As the postulants position and reposition their bodies in prayer throughout the day—every day—the association of certain postures with certain dispositions ideally becomes habitual and moves from the realm of the intellectual (I should kneel when they consecrate the Host to indicate reverence) to something that is remembered in and through the senses of the body as a physical object in space and time (I feel reverence when they consecrate the Host, so I should kneel). This is undoubtedly a personal experience, but the aim of this habituation of the body is to produce a certain kind of link between the physical and the emotional.

Vocalization

It might be argued that, along with its focus on bodies, Catholicism is particularly concerned with the power of language. The world was created, the Bible teaches, when God spoke the words "Let there be light." Adam was given a soul by the breath of God. Jesus is "the Word made flesh." The transubstantiation of the Eucharist comes with the oral repetition of the words Jesus reportedly spoke at the Last Supper. The act of confession and forgiveness entails the verbalization of sin to a particular sort of listener, the recitation of the rosary enlists the voice in the meditation on the glories of God.

To critics of the Catholic faith, this concern with the oral pronouncement of particular phrases might appear to be tantamount to a sort of word magic, with the expert—the priest—essentially performing as a cloaked sorcerer chanting incantations. But regardless of one's perspective on these matters, the fact remains that practices of vocalization are central to the experiential dimensions of prayer as an intersubjective enterprise in the convent.

The sisters, following the teachings of the Catholic Church, designate specific periods of vocal prayer throughout the day that should be done in concert with—or at least in the presence of—others. The sisters maintain that vocal prayers are a spiritual obligation of the congregation. Ideally, the constitutions direct, they should be recited with fervor, in a loud voice, and with the words clearly pronounced. Vocal prayer complements mental prayer by helping to elevate the spirit and is one of the most effective ways of preparing the self for meditation and union with God. In other words, the proper communication between the soul and God is predicated on the externalization of this desire in the company of others.

Some forms of vocal prayer—such as the morning community prayer and the Offices of the Hours—must be recited in community with other sisters. Other forms—such as the Novena of Trust and the rosary—may be done solitarily, though they must still be vocalized, even if only in a whisper. This, in the sisters' view, makes internal states manifest in words that carry real power.

As the year progressed, the postulants talked more frequently about their enjoyment of communal prayer times. "I thought it was kind of boring at first," Evelyn told me.

> I mean, you say the same prayers every day. It's pretty easy to memorize them because we say them over and over and over again. But once you get the words down, something else starts to come into it. Each time you say the Novena of Trust, for example, you can start to really *think* about what it is you're saying and what you're offering up to God. And there's something really powerful about saying such things in front of your sisters: "I offer to you all my being—my thoughts, my desires, my aspirations." Imagine it! Here you are opening yourself completely to God, and you're right there with everyone else. But that's just it. Everyone is doing the same thing. We're all daughters of God putting ourselves in His service, all of our voices joining together in one voice. It's a really beautiful thing.

Mina told me that her most powerful prayer experiences came not so much when receiving the Eucharist but while singing hymns during the Mass. "I just love to sing!" she told me. "It's as if God's voice is resonating inside me, and when it comes out, it's my voice, but it's filled with the love of God. Sometimes I feel tears coming out of my eyes because it's so beautiful and I'm so thankful to be able to offer up my voice to Him."

Such acts of *proclamation in prayer* seemed to resonate particularly deeply for the postulants. "Vocal prayer for me is like the martyrs who died proclaiming their faith in Christ," Celeste told me.

> They were burned and tortured for their beliefs, but they still proclaimed their faith in a loud voice, even until the moment of their deaths. Now we are free to pronounce our faith without being afraid of being sent to the lions or something like that. Besides, if you feel this

faith, if you have the voice of God within you, you can't help but shout it out! You want to tell everyone about this wonderful love you've found! Just like when you have a new boyfriend, you can't stop talking about it with your friends, and you talk to him on the phone ten times a day. It's the same thing with us. The love of God fills you up so much that you *have* to proclaim it to the world!

Vocalization in prayer, then, seems to function in at least two ways in terms of bodily experience. First, the words of prayer literally emerge from and resonate in the physical body—from the vocal cords, through the throat, over the tongue, through the teeth, past the lips. Speaking requires coordination of breath, muscles, and mouth in a conscious shaping of sound.

At the same time, these words are reincorporated to the body through the act of listening. The sentiments of prayer are made manifest and externalized through speech and then received back into the body. But something else happens in the process. What is received back through listening is not the same thing as what was produced through speech. In the process of externalization, one's speech is united with the speech of one's sisters. The intimate sentiments of prayer, then, are made inter-subjective by their communal recitation. What one hears is an amalgam of voices, including—but hardly limited to—one's own. The meaning of prayer becomes more than an intimate personal communication with God; it rests in the bonds it enables one to forge with other struggling souls.

THE BONDS OF PHYSICALITY: LINKING BODY AND SOUL

In all the domains of body management—regimenting daily life, ensuring personal hygiene, regulating food and eating, showing dedication in manual labor, relaxing in sociability, and mastering the physical practices of piety—the goal of the regimentation is to train the body to be obedient to external elements rather than internal instincts and desires, while at the same time heightening awareness of these inner states. The postulants learn to discipline their bodies to meet various requirements (such as rising at 4:45, eating food one dislikes, scrubbing pots and pans, kneeling for hours in prayer) and to become extraordinarily sensitive to the sensations this discipline produces (exhaustion, nausea, resentment, physical pain). Tracking the intensity of these sensations over time gives a new nun a sort of barometer for measuring her progress. As Carmen told me one day, "When we first came to the congregation I could only kneel for something like twenty minutes without my knees and my back starting to ache. I've been praying to God to give me the strength to adore Him in this way because it's one of those things one should be able to do, no? And you know what, Rebe? This morning I knelt for a whole hour! My goal is to be able to kneel the entire two hours of the morning prayer. I'm getting there. With God's help, I'm getting there." Stamina and ability in the domain of physical discipline are directly linked to the quality of one's relationship to God.

This process happens more or less simultaneously with the progressive internalization of space discussed in chapter 6, producing an interesting tension between what we might call experiences of interiority and experiences of exteriority. The production of this tension seems to involves three steps: first, clearly recognizing and acknowledging the needs of the body (e.g., I'm hungry); second, determining how and to what degree these needs should be met, with the understanding that a sense of frustration or discomfort will naturally arise when worldly desires are starved (it's not mealtime, so I have to wait. I don't want to ask special permission for a snack because this would indicate a lack of discipline); and third, sitting with this experience of controlled deprivation or discomfort and internalizing it as prayer, a way of relating to the divine (I will offer up my hunger to God as a sacrifice and as a reminder of how much He suffered for me on the cross).

The concern, then, is with creating not a conquered or disciplined body but a *mindful body* (Scheper-Hughes and Lock 1987)—cultivating an aesthetics of embodiment that explicitly aims to continually produce tensions between eternal and embodied experiences of self, which then become themselves spiritually and psychologically meaningful. In the realm of prayer, for example, one should move from just trying to stay awake to focusing on posture and the attitude of the body in prayer as itself a form of connection to God. Pains and discomfort should be recapitulated into the prayer experience, offered up as empathic suffering with Christ. A successful trainee learns not to ignore her body but to productively use bodily sensations *as* prayer. This use of the experience of deprivation—or, to use more psychological language, optimal frustration—to transform the self is the subject of the next chapter.

CHAPTER 8

Self-Critique

Diagnosing the Soul

By February—six months into their formation program—the postulants begin to move beyond mere physical endurance to an intense internal critique. Once one's daily rhythm of physical activity is well established, a relentless introspection into the disquiet and anguish of the soul should begin. This is considered to be the most intense phase of the first level of formation.

At this point, the mistress of postulants and the peer group begin to guide the postulant through a difficult and delicate process of self-exploration that can at times be extraordinarily painful and demoralizing and at other times liberating and healing. She is reminded that she willingly entered into this process because something in her life felt broken or missing, and she had come to understand that this feeling might be the call from God. Now the postulants turn their energy more directly to exploring these feelings of loss and brokenness. They learn that the only way out of despair is through the cultivation of an intensely intimate relationship between God and the individual soul, a relationship that exists—that becomes real—only through a stark and fearless accounting of one's faults.

During the first half of the year, the postulants were primarily concerned with meeting the explicit requirements of convent life—getting up on time, following orders from superiors, making adequate progress in their studies—and these seemed to be the things the superiors attended to in their mentoring of the newcomers. Around February, however, there was a subtle shift in focus, a lessening of emphasis on the specifics of external performance (the postulants, it was assumed, should have mastered these details by then) and an increasing concern with the *internal* dimensions of compliance, what went on inside one's mind and heart and spirit, regardless of what the physical body was or was not doing. Beginning around this time, for example, superiors rarely sanctioned the postulants for not showing up to class on time but would instead chastise them for not demonstrating appropriate obedience in stopping what they were doing and coming to class when the bell rang. Instead of simply instructing the postulants to be less rowdy during recreation time, Mother Veronica would stress this as an exercise in practicing charity—keeping their voices low so that the sisters in the chapel would not be disturbed. Marta, who had been praised during the first six months for giving the right answers in class, began to be cautioned against evidencing a lack of humility by not letting others have a chance to show their knowledge.

There was, then, a subtle but tangible shift at this stage toward a reevaluation of the intentions and internal states behind external behaviors. The postulants learned that simply talking the talk and walking the walk of the convent was not enough—a more fundamental transformation of their internal orientations was necessary for religious formation to "work." And this transformation could come, they learned, only if they were willing to ferret out all the ugliness, sin, and decay that resided within them. "For a festering wound to heal, we must first clean it out, sanitize it," Mother Veronica explained to us. "This is what we must do during our formations—clean out the old to make way for the new. It will be painful, to be sure. But it's the only way."

THE EXAMINATIONS OF CONSCIENCE

To aid them in this "cleaning out" of their selves, the postulants were introduced to the examination of conscience—a thrice-daily evaluation tool used by the sisters for self-monitoring and reflection in all areas of the religious life. "Ándele, Madre!" said Marta, when Mother Veronica opened the discussion in class one day, and all the postulants opened their notebooks, eager to get started. We had known this was to be the topic for that day's class. The postulants (especially Marta, Thea,

Celeste, and Rosita) were excited about learning this technique, considered one of the most essential practices of the religious life in the congregation. We had all seen the older sisters at the morning prayer or in the meditation just before lunch scribbling in their little notebooks they kept in their pockets, and the postulants had remarked that it always seemed so mysterious, so official, so *nunlike*. Once we knew that they were doing their examinations and that there was a formula to the practice, the postulants became very eager to be let in on this trade secret.

The examinations are held in such reverence by the sisters because they are, from the very early stages of the formation process, one of the most essential tools for discerning one's vocation and, later, for nurturing and preserving that vocation while in the congregation. It is not just the act of doing the examinations that is so powerful, Mother Veronica explained to me in a separate conversation; the examinations represent an attitude, a way of living, in which one's thoughts, feelings, and actions are under continuous scrutiny and are held up against a model of divine perfection: Jesus Christ. The examinations are an external tool—a visible, tangible practice—that represents a continuing internal process of coming to know oneself and then remaking that self in the image of the "good Sierva." The postulants, still anxious (desperate, even) after six months to know "for sure" if they had a vocation to the religious life—to have proof of this one way or another—were more than ready to begin this process.

"Discerning your vocation is like sifting flour for a cake," Mother Veronica explained, as an introduction to the examination practice. "You take out what doesn't belong and leave the good stuff." The postulants nodded and um-hummed their understanding and began scribbling vigorously in their notebooks, trying to capture as much of what Mother Veronica said as they could. The postulants should look at their vocations not as a choice between a "good" life path (poverty, chastity, and obedience inside the convent) and a "bad" one (marriage, home, and children), Mother Veronica continued, but as a choice between two "good" ones. "Everyone is given a vocation, and becoming a nun can be a 'bad' thing for someone who doesn't belong there, just as marriage can be a 'bad' thing for someone who truly has a religious vocation," she explained. "The point, then, is to find out for sure where God wants you. And wherever that is, it is the right place for you and you will be happy." Placing married life and the religious life on equal footing in terms of "goodness" (at least in theory) makes the discernment of vocation more difficult, Mother Veronica observed, because "this requires much more careful attention to what the Lord is telling you and where He is steering you." The examinations that the sisters do throughout the day are designed to help them look inward, to take spiritual stock of their interior worlds and their relationship to Christ, to help them understand God's will more clearly and to follow this will, no matter where it leads.

The sisters do this stock taking three times each day—morning (in the morning meditation, to orient one's mind and spirit to the Lord and to begin the day in full consciousness of one's faults and how one will work to overcome them during the day), midday (the *examen particular,* an examination of one's spiritual attitudes, a moment of silence and reflection in the midst of a busy day to evaluate whether one is living up to God's will in one's interactions with others and fidelity to Him), and evening (the *examen general,* where one takes stock of one's attitudes in the latter half of the day and reviews all the activities, actions, and decisions of the day). This is a very personal exercise, and its exact form and content will differ from sister to sister. But some general guidelines encapsulate the central principles of religious formation within the congregation. They are the main tools the sisters use in shaping themselves into "good Siervas" and achieving consecration. It was these guidelines the postulants were so anxious to receive.

Mother Veronica began by listing the points of the examinations on the blackboard, copying them carefully from her own little notebook and referring once in a while to some xeroxed sheets on the table. She explained that these points were to be listed in chart form (with boxes next to each for every day of the week) in a small notebook, to be carried in one's uniform or habit at all times. The postulants were to place marks—checkmarks, x's, smiley faces, whatever they wanted—next to each item as they performed it adequately during a given day. From this point forward, until they left the congregation or died, Mother Veronica told us, the postulants would be expected to maintain a current version of this list, keeping track of their performance on the different points. They could keep past charts for their own reference or destroy them. As Mother Veronica continued writing, the postulants craned their necks to see and tapped one another, asking for words here and there and whispering excitedly to each other. The points of the examination are:

1. Arise Promptly and with Fervor
2. Quality of Meditation
3. Prayer
4. Liturgy of the Hours
5. Holy Mass and Communion
6. Adoration with the Spirit of Reparation
7. Particular Exam
8. Rosary
9. Occupations
10. Dining Room
11. Recreation
12. Attitude of Poverty
13. Chastity
14. Obedience
15. Humility
16. Charity
17. Mortification
18. Silence
19. Punctuality
20. Spirit of Faith
21. Equality of Enthusiasm
22. Order in All My Things
23. Avoid Criticisms and Gossip

While many of these items do, indeed, appear to refer to external behaviors, the point of the examinations, as Mother Veronica explained, is not so much to track whether one did or did not do something but *how* one did things, with what kind of spirit of intention. "For example, you might say the rosary every afternoon," she clarified.

> And you could mark this down in your chart. But let's say you were simply going through the motions, thinking all the time about other things you had to do, chores that were pending. So you *could* mark down that you said the rosary, but did you really? Was your heart and soul in it? No. The examinations are between you and God. You won't get a gold star for having checkmarks in the boxes next to "Rosary" all week. The other sisters won't be looking at your examinations. But *God* will know you weren't really spiritually present. You can't fool God by making a checkmark in a box. So use the examination as a tool for

being *honest* with yourself, for truly discovering where you might be having difficulties, and for attending to them.

One of the most difficult things about the examinations, Mother Veronica stressed, is that they force you to see just how pitiful you are in living up to God's—and even your own—expectations. "Do the examinations for just three days," she told the postulants. "Then you'll know what I'm talking about."

The next Monday, when class reconvened, the postulants were despondent. "I had no idea I was doing such a bad job of things," Rosita remarked. "I thought I was coming along pretty well, but once I started looking at it—*really* looking at it and being honest about things—I realized how much more work I need to do." "I had the same experience," offered Carlota. "I didn't realize I was having so much trouble with the practice of humility until we started doing the examinations. But yesterday I realized I get really annoyed sometimes when Mother Fatima always assigns me to take out the garbage and that even though I do it, I'm acting against the principle of humility because of my attitude." Several of the other postulants spoke of similar experiences, and the feeling in the room was one of both amazement and grave concern on the part of the postulants about their own levels of commitment.

"Yes, my daughters, now you see," said Mother Veronica.

What you are experiencing now is very normal, a sort of disillusionment in yourselves. Of course, we all like to think that we are good people, and generally we are. But are we good enough for *God*? This is a completely separate matter. Of course, God loves us for who we are, no matter what. But if *we* love *Him* and truly want to please Him, this requires an extraordinary amount of courage and humility to recognize our faults and to overcome them. You are only at the very beginning of this process, but it is why God called you here—He knows you are ready. The fact that you were not satisfied in the outside world, that you felt the *inquietud* to become a Sierva, means you are ready to face the truth of what God has to say to you.

THE BETRAYAL OF GOD

And this truth, for the postulants, is brutal. Over the next several weeks, they are slowly, lovingly, but firmly guided toward identifying the source of their discomfort in the world, their anguish and *inquietud*. Their prior difficulties were caused, they learn, by a deep rupture with God, which they themselves have perpetrated.

This realization comes as a shock for most of the postulants. These women tended to consider themselves good Catholic girls—human, to be sure, with faults and weaknesses, but essentially good, moral, religious women. But in the convent they learn that what they took to be a satisfactory relationship with God is actually a brutal betrayal of Him. God has done so much for us humans, they learn. He suffered excruciating pain and devastating humiliation in the person of Jesus, all so that we could be reconciled with Him. Again and again, they are taught, He has reached out to each one of them, gently and lovingly calling them—by name—to His embrace. And again and again, they have rejected Him, coldly turning their backs on Him, injuring Him with their ingratitude. But like a loving parent, they learn, He goes on trying to reach them, wishing only for their growth, wholeness, and love.

"I can't believe how miserable I am," Abby confided in me one day during this time.

> It's so painful. It is only by the grace of God that I'm even here, alive, breathing. And what have I done? Lived my life in the way that was most convenient for *me*, instead of for Him. I wish I could go back and redo my life so I could show Him how grateful I am for everything He's given me. There is so much to repay. But it has to be done out of love, not guilt. Sometimes it's hard to separate those out, though. But God doesn't want our guilt, He wants our love. So we have to get past our own bad feelings and offer everything up to Him.

During this stage, the postulants, with the guidance of Mother Veronica, confront the specific ways they personally have injured and betrayed God. They talk of this process as a fearless examination of their souls, a stark evaluation of every aspect of themselves. Specifically, they learn that their betrayal comes from their having fallen prey to the temptations of worldly existence, attaching primary significance to their temporal selves to the neglect of their eternal souls. Though this is the state of the fall from grace all humans endure, the sisters feel that, unlike most people, they must come to an immediate, visceral awareness of their rupture with God in a way that cannot be ignored and that demands a response. Following close on the heels of the concept of the examination of conscience, then, comes a second fundamental element in the process of self-critique—techniques of correction.

PENITENCE, MORTIFICATION, AND SUFFERING: RIGHTING THE WRONGS OF THE SELF

Magda stopped talking to Teresita last Friday at the urging of the mother superior of the convent. Magda said she now understands the issue of fraternity, whereas before she didn't. She's also

concerned for Teresita, that she might get kicked out. She's
concerned for herself, too. Yesterday, both she and Teresita
happened to come up on the roof at the same time during their
chores. Magda didn't talk to her, although they were working side
by side, alone. This was exceptionally hard for Magda, but she said
she knows now that Teresita "carries their friendship in her heart."
Nevertheless, she said she could tell that Teresita was upset by the
fact that Magda didn't speak to her. Teresita left the roof, then
returned shortly later and initiated some small talk with Magda.
She asked Magda why she didn't talk to her before. Magda
explained that she'd been getting in trouble with the mother
superior and that she was trying hard to understand how to live
fraternity.

Just then, the mother superior came up to the roof. "What's
going on? What are you two doing?" Magda and Teresita gave
moderately convincing answers. I asked Magda why the superiors
don't want them to talk to each other. "Because if you have special
friends and one of you is moved to another house, it could be very
hard for you," said Magda. "Your love and affection is supposed to
be for the entire world, not concentrated on a few people." Magda
said that when she went home for her Christmas visit, Teresita was
away on spiritual exercises. Magda thought about her the whole
time, and it was very hard for her, even through it was only three
days. She feels she must forget about Teresita and concentrate on
living in fraternity among the postulants. She knows she's guilty of
not doing this. She's been thinking only of herself and Teresita. She
said that even though they've been together several months, she
doesn't know many of the postulants very well. But she's trying to
open up more. "I really need to change," she said. "Do you have
any friends among the postulants?" I asked. "No. Not really," she
said. "I've kept myself pretty isolated." She said that in the
beginning, she, Surella, Haydee, Evelyn, and Carmen were a kind of
group, but Mother Veronica told them this wasn't proper and they
couldn't live that way in the convent. So Magda broke off with
them. She's still friends with them and talks to them, but she's not as
"preoccupied" with their lives and their problems as before.
"Sounds like it's a hard thing to learn," I said. "It seems inevitable
that you're going to make friends, or at least like some people better
than others." "Absolutely," said Magda. "But you have to actively
work against this."

After the encounter with the mother superior on the roof, Magda
headed downstairs and saw Mother Josephine, the congregation's
director of vocations. Mother Josephine had chastised Magda for
her relationship with Teresita, and now she threw Magda a warning
look. "Why is she always butting into my life?" asked Magda
rhetorically when telling me what happened. "Why doesn't she just
take care of her aspirants and leave me alone?"

This situation happened last Friday, and since then Magda hasn't
come downstairs during chores to see Teresita as usual (one of the
few times the different levels are in contact for any length of time).
Magda said she doesn't want Teresita and her to be seen together.
She still *wants* to go downstairs, but she's been asking some of the
other postulants to help her not to. She told Teresita that she
(Magda) is treating it as a mortification that they can't talk, and
Teresita should treat it that way too.

Excerpted from field notes, January 23, 1994

The process of religious formation in the congregation involves a
realignment of experiences of bodied and nonbodied selves within a
particular moral and social perspective. The key to this transformation
lies in rechanneling the passions, sculpting the "natural" impulses
according to the vision of the congregation. Once the postulants are
able to claim some sort of control over what were previously unconscious (or, at least, unselfconscious) processes, the focus of their training turns to learning how to manipulate these processes for specific
ends. This control comes from first making these inclinations conscious
and then countering them through daily practice.

Although penitence and mortification are related in the sense that
both are techniques for molding the self, these practices have very different meanings and applications in Catholic religious practice. A penitence, we learned, is an act performed as a way of righting a wrong, a
way of making amends for an action already committed (for example,
kneeling for the entirety of morning prayers as a penitence for falling
asleep in one's pew the previous morning). A mortification, on the other
hand, is a practice performed to alter one's internal dispositions so that
they do not manifest themselves in inappropriate actions (for example,
neglecting to take a serving of one's favorite dessert as an exercise in
humility and restraint). Mortification, then, is an integral part of the
daily fabric of the convent life, whereas penitence is engaged in only
when preventative mortification is not practiced effectively.

Penitence

Because a penitence is practiced as a corrective for inappropriate deeds
already done (as opposed to a more fundamental and diffuse attitude
addressed by mortification), the congregation maintains specific,
explicit rules about how and when penitences should be used and with
what goals in mind. We learned that the Siervas acknowledge two kinds

of penitence: public penitence (e.g., prostrating oneself in the chapel during morning prayers or atoning for an offense committed against one's sisters), which requires permission of one's superior in the convent, and private penitence (e.g., fasting), which requires permission of one's spiritual advisor (usually one's confessor).

Penitence is considered to be a powerful tool for self-transformation—so powerful, in fact, that the postulants were educated in the dangers of overzealous penitential practice. As Mother Veronica cautioned us, "Penitence is never an end in itself. It must be used as a means of elevating or bettering the self." Because of this, she said, the congregation places a premium on spiritual penitence over physical penitence. This is considered to be much more difficult than a simple physical penitence such as fasting. "Spiritual penitences, like asking forgiveness for bad behavior, are often harder than corporeal ones, like whippings or sleeping on the floor," Mother Veronica explained to the group. The postulants giggled at the extremity of such practices, and a few made comments about how they could never imagine doing such things. "It's true," Mother Veronica insisted. "Penitences, whether spiritual or physical, are a serious business. You must be very careful with them. You can do small things, like eating three tortillas at lunch instead of four, but for anything else you must get permission. And you must stop immediately if it's affecting your health."

The following two examples describe typical scenarios of how a penitence might be earned. One afternoon during afternoon chores, Carlota was assigned the task of washing out some large plastic bottles at the spigot on the patio. At one point, she ducked into the kitchen to talk to Ruth and left the water running in the bottle. She was gone too long, and the bottle filled and was overflowing a little. Sister Teresita, who was supervising chores in the pantry area that day, came up and realized Carlota wasn't there. When Carlota arrived, Sister Teresita told her she had to ask a penitence of Mother Veronica for her carelessness. A few moments later, after Sister Teresita had left, I asked Carlota if she was really going to have to do a penitence. "Yes," she said, her face screwed up with displeasure. "I have to go to Mother Veronica and tell her that I lacked the value of poverty, and then she'll give me a penitence." "And what are the penitences like?" I asked. "Well," she said, "it could be to go without bathing, or to recite some Our Fathers *en cruz* [kneeling, with the arms stretched out in a crucified position], or to say an extra rosary. Something like that." "Sounds pretty hard," I said. "Actually, the harder thing is to *ask* for the penitence," Carlota answered. "*Doing* it isn't that bad, but going up to Mother Veronica and saying, 'You know what Mother, I did this thing.' It's horribly embarrassing."

Sometimes, though, the impetus for imposing a penitence came from the postulants themselves. One day at lunch, Rosita asked Mother Veronica—on behalf of those postulants working in the pantry—for permission to do a penitence because they were having trouble refraining from munching while working around all the food. "Here's what we're thinking, Mother," said Rosita. "If you eat something during the morning chores, you can't have dessert at lunch. If you eat something during the afternoon chores, you don't get to eat dinner—you can only have a glass of milk." Mother Veronica said she thought the second proposition was too harsh and told them that it would be okay to say that if you eat during afternoon chores you can't have dessert with dinner and you also have to tell Mother Veronica what you ate in the pantry. Later that afternoon, Rosita was telling *everyone*, whether they worked in the pantry or not, about the penitence, and they all seemed very interested. "I guess I shouldn't have dessert tonight, then," said Amelia, "because yesterday I ate something in the afternoon." "But you're not working in the pantry!" said Evelyn. "Not officially," said Amelia, "but yesterday I was because I was covering for Marta while she practiced the violin, and today I worked for her there because she had to go to the doctor. So it still counts."

Most importantly, we learned that penitence should be viewed as a positive technique for bringing one closer to God rather than as a punitive exercise. Penitence, Mother Veronica instructed us, comes out of *love,* and God forgives out of love. So penitence should never be harsh or demanded. God doesn't want us to be miserable, we learned. Rather, He wants us to repent for our transgressions and live our lives in imitation of Him. Like the father in the story of the prodigal son, Mother Veronica taught us, God waits for us to come home, not so that He can chastise us, but to embrace us, to welcome us home.

Mortification

Yesterday the postulants went to the convent museum of St. Monica with the aspirants (there are thirteen this year) who had their monthly retreat. The postulants expressed shock and wonder at the harsh forms of body discipline employed in the past (many of the flagellation tools, etc., are on display at the museum). "Why did the manner of mortification change?" I asked. "You guys still do mortifications, but not like that." "That sort of mortification of the body used to be very important," said Pipa. "But the church decided that the relationship with God should be one of *love*, not *fear*. So the focus shifted from mortifying the body to mortifying the *soul*. It's like, 'Fast, sisters, fast, but not from food—from defects of charity, from egotism'—that sort of thing. Good thing, huh? [laughter] But those sorts of practices, the physical mortifications, are still done today. The difference is that now you need permission from a spiritual guide or confessor first. If he says yes, then you can do it. But if he says no, you can't. So these kinds of mortifications are still done, it's just that almost no one asks permission! [laughter from all the postulants]."

Excerpted from field notes, March 20, 1995

Mortifications are somewhat different from penitences, although they are related. Mortifications are considered to be a very personal matter, a way of transforming one's internal dispositions so that they more closely resemble the ideals of the congregation and of the church. As Mother Anabel explained it to me, each sister performs whatever mortifications she feels called to do, depending on her personal assessment of her internal dispositions. Some do, indeed, feel called to perform severe physical mortifications, but this number is small, Mother Anabel said, especially since the rules were changed in many congregations after Vatican II. As far as devices for physical mortifications go, Mother Anabel told me they still exist, and they're still used sometimes, but again, this is a very personal thing for each sister, and permission for such physical treatment must be granted by a superior to make sure it's really a calling from God and not a psychic imbalance. For example, Mother Anabel said, a sister might come to the mother superior and say, "I want to get up at 1:00 every morning and do penitence and mortifications." But the mother superior might say, "But sister, you're so grumpy with the other sisters!" and refuse the permission.

Mortifications, we learned, are meant to be a kind of preemptive strike against the manifestation of ill-formed dispositions in behaviors that are considered to be counter to the goals of the congregation and the church. So, for example, if a sister notices that she has difficulty feeling charitable toward a particular sister, she may decide to "mortify" herself by going out of her way to be nice to that sister in order to prevent her negative feelings toward that sister from becoming manifest in actions.

Through penitence and mortification, then, the postulants learned tangible responses to the knowledge gained through the inner scrutiny of the examinations of conscience. Learning about these practices did seem to provide the postulants with some reassurance that there were things they could proactively do to mend their relationships with God. But Mother Veronica was quick to caution them against falling into the trap of thinking they could manipulate God. "Some sisters perform excessive penitences or mortifications," she explained. "But this does not guarantee your closeness to God. *God* is the one who decides if He will be available to you or not, if He will be intimate with you or not. To think otherwise, to think that *you* control the closeness of the relationship, is to believe as the *indígenas* used to, that certain rituals can force the deity to do your bidding. This is not only arrogant but sacrilegious." The postulants learned that penitences and mortifications could be useful tools in reshaping the internal dispositions but did not ensure any particular sort of connection with God.

PERSONAL ACCOUNTABILITY: CRITIQUING THE SOUL

In reflecting on the process of looking inwards, of taking stock of the ways one has disappointed and betrayed God, the postulants talked about the pain this self-critique inevitably brings. "I feel so lost right now," Carlota shared with me one day. "I thought I would feel closer to God in the convent, but I feel farther away from Him than ever. But I know it's my own fault. We're learning in here how lazy we've been in tending to our relationship with God. So no wonder I feel so lonely for Him. I'm trying to work on my faults, but it's a long process. And it's so hard when I don't feel that confidence I used to—not confidence in God, but in myself. God is always constant. It's we who fail."

The postulants described their experience during this time as an intense, unremitting thirst for God, an overwhelming, constant, agonizing awareness of lack and yearning. And they all repeatedly asserted that the harder they tried to mend the breach between themselves and God—by doubling their enthusiasm in prayer, by adopting penitences, by employing mortifications—the more distant they felt from Him. Once they had reached this point, they were considered to be ready for the next stage: Surrender.

CHAPTER 9

Surrender

Turning It Over to God

Around March, the postulants began to turn from a concern with the cause of their broken relationship with God to the process of its healing. They were told that God would find them if they genuinely made themselves available to Him, if they made themselves "ripe" for Him to heal the rupture they were experiencing.

The postulants had to make a spiritual transition at this point. I saw that if they were successful they came to describe a palpable sense of release, a sort of resignation. Religious practice up to this point had been active and primarily discursive (even when internal). Now, after weeks of recognizing their faults through the examinations of conscience, profound introspection, and consultation with Mother Veronica, and employing the techniques of penitence and mortification to right the wrongs of their selves, the postulants were led to see this self-scrutiny as just one component needed to truly mend the ruptured relationship with God. At this point, they learned that intimacy with the divine should become more passive, a move from what one *does* for God to what one *is* for God.

This is what the sisters call the attitude of *entrega*. *Entrega* has a meaning somewhere between "surrender" and "sacrifice" and is believed by the sisters to be a quintessentially feminine quality. It signifies throwing oneself into something in an active way. It is, in a sense, an active passivity or an agentic surrender.

Entrega, we learned, is the most fundamental goal of the religious life in the congregation and enfolds all the concepts of obedience, humility, simplicity, and charity held to be so important for the Siervas. *Entrega* adds to this a sense of *suffering* as a noble, transformative experience. But suffering is valued only in so far as it is a component of *entrega.* "If we do not suffer, we will never transcend," Mother Veronica explained to us.

Suffering, we learned, is such an integral component of the Siervas' mission because it is believed to unite them with the people they feel called to help—the poorest of the poor, the lowest of the low. "Suffering leads us to be more sensitive to the experiences of others," Mother Veronica instructed the postulants. "Suffering is a value. Sometimes we are afraid of suffering, but it is suffering that makes us understand and helps us to value the suffering of others. We should seize it, even though we will feel pain."

The Siervas believe that suffering in this way makes them better servants, better able to identify with Christ's sacrifice on the cross and to connect with those whom they serve. Because of this, the postulants are taught that suffering (but again, suffering with an *intention* behind it, not simply suffering for the sake of suffering) is a path to sanctification. It is also a way of giving thanks for one's relationship with Christ. Mother Veronica told us that many sisters, for example, increase their mortifications before their twenty-fifth or fiftieth "wedding" anniversaries (anniversaries of taking the perpetual vows) or tend to see their illnesses and pains as "purifications" for their anniversaries.

But lest they see their lives as bleak and full of despair, the postulants were frequently reminded that suffering and *entrega* were not without their rewards. "Matthew 19:29 says that whoever leaves his family will be rewarded one hundred to one," Mother Veronica observed one day in class. "Don't you see it? Let's say that you have six brothers and sisters. Now you have six hundred! You just need to see all of your sisters here as your true sisters. And instead of only having one house, now you have seventy-eight! And besides all of this, you get eternal life!" "We already have it, Mother! We already have it!" interjected Marta, giddy with enthusiasm. "Ah, but be careful not to lose it," cautioned Mother Veronica. "It's your responsibility. You must follow Father Muro's example, despoiling yourself of everything, even of your own person. Think about the suffering Our Father suffered and the other saints suffered," she continued. "You should think, 'If they were as miserable as I am and they became saints, I can, too!'"

THE DUAL MOVEMENT OF EMPATHY

Psychologically speaking, *entrega* involves empathic identification in two directions: with Jesus and with humankind. On the one hand, the postulants should learn to suffer with Jesus, to reexperience the sacrifices He made for them in every fiber of their bodies and souls, and thereby to draw closer to Him. At the same time, they should understand their own pain at their distance from God as indicative of the state of humankind in general and the urgent need for reparation with the divine. The postulants learn that through cultivating the state of *entrega*—considered by the sisters to be a particularly feminine aptitude—they can perform the core work of the Siervas: as *reparadoras*, repairers of the rift between humans and God.

Reparation is not a specific practice of piety, as Mother Veronica repeatedly stressed to the postulants in class. Rather, it is the *spirit* in which one performs each act of the day. Reparation, she instructed us, means that the underlying aim of all a Sierva's acts, thoughts, and feelings should be to reunite estranged souls with Jesus. If a Sierva acts with this spirit of reparation, Mother Veronica told us, her life will change because she will be acting in conformity with the Spirit of Jesus. Reparation in this context implies conversion to the light and the way of Christ—conversion of oneself and, through this, conversion of other distressed souls. Although the Siervas take it as their priority to work toward this conversion for *all* souls, they are reminded that Jesus is the only one who can truly bring souls back to the fold. The Siervas can act as intermediaries, imploring Jesus to welcome back estranged sinners and offering up their own sacrifices for the freedom of these souls from sin, but in the end, they believe, it is Jesus who decides. The sisters cannot manipulate Him through their acts, no matter how faithful they may be. But just in case, this spirit of reparation or atonement should never fail. "The Siervas at all times should be *reparadoras*," Father Muro insisted again and again in his writings.

The sisters are called to live the spirit of reparation every moment of the day, beginning with the morning prayer:

> My God, I consecrate to You all of my thoughts, words, and actions of this day and everything good I do in it, with the special end of atoning and making amends to you for the sins of all the world, and principally as reparation for the offenses that you receive in the Sacrament of the Eucharist.
>
> Deign, Lord, to bless everything that I do and suffer in this day, so that in all things I do not look for anything except your love and your glory in my compliance with your Most Holy Will.

At the heart of this pledge is the sisters' promise that they will do every-thing in their power to counter, both in themselves and in their sur-roundings, the tendencies of the "modern" world. By turning themselves completely over to God—body and spirit—they strive to become vehicles for His work on earth.

To illustrate the notion of *entrega,* Mother Veronica recounted the following tale to the postulants. Just after Jesus' death, the Christians were persecuted throughout the land. One day, the Romans murdered a group of Christians by making them walk into freezing water. The pris-oners had been told that if they were to renounce Christ, they could avoid this horrible death. But the martyrs marched singing into the icy water. One soldier who was watching the spectacle was amazed when he saw the heavens open up and angels come down with golden crowns of martyrs to place on the souls of the dying. Just then one Christian said, "I renounce Christ! Let me out of the water!" The angel that was descending to crown him stopped and retreated. The soldier seeing this said, "I'll take your place!" and marched into the water and received his crown. (This was met by applause and cheers from the postulants.)

"This is exactly what we do here," Mother Veronica explained to the class. "We are like that soldier. We take the place of those who don't want to be faithful to Christ. But the difference is that we help reunite those people with God, we hand our crowns over to them. And we can go back into that water a thousand times to save a thousand souls."

"But we're not really 'martyrs' on that scale, are we, Mother?" asked Iris dubiously. "Well, virginity is considered a type of martyring of the self when there aren't these kind of persecutions," Mother Veronica answered. "So all of us are martyrs, although we may have some prob-lems thinking of ourselves this way because the usual sense of the word implies a physical death. A martyr who dies becomes sanctified by his or her own blood. We are sanctified by our sacrifice for others."

The postulants took the issue of reparation extremely seriously. Over time, they came to understand it as their ultimate purpose as part of God's plan of salvation, even if they had never heard the term before coming to the convent. "I never really thought about it until I came here," Rosita told me.

> But looking back now, I see that I always had this spirit of reparation. I was always very sensitive to the fact that there's so much sin in the world, so much greed, corruption, egotism. And much of that was in me! But even so, I remember that I was always praying for God to

forgive my family and my friends. I never prayed for myself. I see now that that was one of the first seeds of my vocation, and why God called me to the Siervas. We can truly help save others by becoming what God wants us to become.

Toward the end of my research, each of the postulants, like Rosita, expressed to me the centrality of reparation in their understandings of their vocations. Echoing their founder's teachings, each also explained this spirit of reparation as a counteractive force against the evils of modern society, principally greed, corruption, and individualism. "This is where we as Siervas can really make a difference," Surella told me. "Our charism is specifically to help reconcile people with God through our dedication and our sacrifice. It's a huge task because the world is in such chaos these days. There are so many forces luring people away from God. The very things that are idealized and rewarded in the modern world—egotism, materialism, greed—are the things that break people away from God. Our role is to be a sort of bridge, to help people return to God. Of course, it's not really *us* who's doing it. God works through us. But we can become His instruments."

The sisters, however, are well aware that sometimes people sacrifice and suffer for reasons other than love, and the postulants were repeatedly cautioned against getting drawn into confusing *entrega* with the simple performance of penitences and mortifications while losing sight of the ultimate goal to which they are (ideally) directed. They must strive to develop a healthy conscience, we learned, one that accurately discerns sin, or disposition to sin, and corrects it without going overboard. This is not, we were warned, an easy task, particularly in a context in which one is continuously and consciously striving for perfection. Sometimes one can get caught up in the ideal of perfection to the detriment of one's true advancement toward Christ. "Perfectionist people suffer much in the religious life because there are many details and rules to follow," Mother Veronica told us in class. "There's also the problem of comparing yourself with others. Sometimes small details, like a towel not being hung straight or the bed not being perfect, can take away from your inner peace. It's true that external order helps one with internal order, but there must be a balance." The cultivation of *entrega,* then, surrendering oneself to God *in toto,* is for the Siervas primarily an exercise in humility—reaching for the ultimate ideal, while at the same time recognizing that one will never achieve it.

TENDING THE SOUL: PRAYER AND WORSHIP

Marta and I talked today about her affinity for the Passion of Jesus.
She told me that when she first came into the convent, this is all she
thought about, and she somehow made *everything* relate to this—
Bible readings, class discussions, meditations, prayers, Holy Hours,
etc. The Passion has very special significance for her, she said,
because she feels she's been called very directly and specifically to
help share the cross of Christ. She feels this is why He's called
her—she feels He wants her for something special.

Excerpted from field notes, July 4, 1995

Cultivating an attitude of *entrega* and placing oneself in the role of
reparadora requires, the postulants learn, a particularly developed interior life built on contemplative prayer. From their very first day in the
convent, the postulants are taught that prayer is the beating heart of the
congregation, the core of the Siervas' spiritual life. Prayer is the most
vital, most important, and most precious aspect of the sisters' lives as
Siervas. It forms the foundation for all the other acts they perform
during the day.

Although they are an active-life order, meaning that they work "in
the world," the Siervas prefer to think of themselves as "contemplatives
in action." Though they work in schools and hospitals and orphanages
and nursing homes, the sisters still consider prayer—and particularly the reparation of souls—to be the jewel in the crown of their
mission.

But since they are "in the world," prayer has a slightly different place
in the life of this congregation than it does in contemplative orders. The
postulants are taught that prayer is not simply the act of kneeling in
church or meditating on the glories of Christ but is also manifest in the
way they go about their daily activities. They must learn to incorporate
prayer in each act of the day, from bathing an elderly person in a nursing home to feeding the hungry to singing songs with orphaned children
to mopping the dormitory floor. To be able to do this, we learned, they
must have a solid foundation in the spiritual aspects of prayer. But more
than this, the *quality* of their prayer must be particularly rich so that
they will be able to carry this connection with God into situations not
normally considered conducive to such feelings. Prayer is one of the
central topics in the process of formation and is the subject of its own
course of instruction (taught by Mother Veronica) that lasts the entire
ten months of the postulancy. The key to this training is to teach the

initiates how to reorient their interior lives so that their daily activities
are infused with new meanings.

The Work of Prayer

Today we had a special prayer in the classroom. Mother Veronica
had arranged the chairs in circle, with a lit candle sitting on a stool
in center. The topic was Lent and conversion. Although it was
already mid-morning, we started with "Vocal Prayer" from the
Formulary, as in the early morning prayer, and read some selected
biblical cites on sin and conversion. The last passage we read was
about the lowering of the paralytic down to Jesus through the roof.
Mother Veronica stressed that the key to the story is that the four
men carrying the paralytic had faith. We don't know if the paralytic
had faith or not, and it really doesn't matter. It was enough for those
carrying him to have faith. Mother Veronica asked for some
thoughts on this passage.

"Jesus is always pardoning us," said Marta. "When we ask for
pardon, he's already forgiven us. Sometimes we lack humanity—we
want to do everything perfectly, and we feel badly if we screw up.
But this is a stain on an *image* we have—we must realize that Jesus
is always pardoning us."

"I think the paralytic represents us when we're paralyzed by
weakness or inaction," said Iris. "I have problems with this, with
being lazy."

"The story encourages us to persevere," added Carmen. "If we
can't get to God through one door, we should try to get to Him
another way, like through the ceiling."

Mother Veronica returned to the example of the paralytic. "It's
easy to say, 'I pardon your sins' because no one knows for sure if
they've been pardoned or not," she said. "But it's *harder* to say,
'Get up and walk.'"

"But Jesus always combined His words with his acts. He gave
people visual things to show that He could do what He claimed he
could," said Ruth. "Then they would convert to Him."

"*Exactly,*" said Mother Veronica. "We should be, ourselves,
converting *every day.* It's a continuous process."

Excerpted from field notes, March 22, 1995

The style of prayer in the congregation follows mostly the teachings of
St. Ignatius of Loyola, St. Augustine, and, of course, Father Muro. The
postulants are instructed that prayer is necessary to be saved, most of all
for those who have the use of intellect and reason. Scripture, we learned,
teaches the necessity of prayer, as do the fathers and doctors of the

church. St. John Tristosomo, for example, wrote that "[i]t is absolutely impossible to live and die virtuously without the aid of prayer." St. Alfonso Maria de Ligorio, founder of the Redemptoristas, declared that "[h]e who prays is saved. He who does not pray is condemned." And Father Muro affirmed this: "Prayer and more prayer, that is my strength." (*Meditations*).

Today, the sisters continue in this vein, despite the many changes the congregation has seen since its founding in 1885. As was the case with most religious orders, many sisters left the congregation after Vatican II because, as Mother Veronica observed one day in class, they "couldn't adjust to the changes." "The new way called for a more outward focus, but many took this to the extreme and left for good," she said. "And there was a drastic decline in vocations. Why? Because we were missing prayer, missing testimony." Mother Veronica related to the group that things had been much stricter, much more serious, when she was a postulant and novice. "Now things are 'more comfortable,'" she said, "but we Siervas have never lost the *spirit* of prayer and sacrifice." Even so, some of the older nuns who came to the congregation before the changes continue to kneel or prostrate themselves in prayer, even though these rules have since been relaxed. "They already have their bodies dominated," Mother Veronica explained to the postulants. "That's a very hard thing to change."

But ultimately, Mother Veronica observed—despite the emphasis on the postulants' correct physical performance of rituals and tasks during the first few months—prayer is not about what position your body is in. Rather, she clarified, "the heart of prayer is a consciousness of who you're with, who you're talking to." Mother Wilhelmina, the vicaress general, agreed, stressing in a lecture to the postulants that prayer infuses every aspect of a sister's life, regardless of the external trappings of worship. "Living without prayer is like trying to live without breathing," she explained to us. "Even when we're asleep we breathe. It's the same with prayer. It's the respiration of the soul."

This "respiration of the soul," although ideally an unconscious, automatic, continual state of communication with God, is, nevertheless, made conscious through particular acts the sisters perform throughout the day. These activities are set apart from the daily routine and are seen as precious pockets of silence, opportunities for conscious reflection and meditation, and a nurturing of the treasured—and always developing—relationship with God. These daily times of prayer include rising in the morning, the morning meditation, individual prayer, the Liturgy of the Hours,[1] Mass and Communion, Adoration, the particular exam, and the recitation of the rosary. There are also some important weekly and monthly celebrations. For example, the congregation holds a Holy Hour every Tuesday from 9:00 to 10:00 P.M. And on the twenty-eight day of every month, to mark the anniversary of the day they entered the convent, the postulants hold a special Nocturnal Holy Hour from 1:00 to 2:00 A.M. to give thanks for their vocations. The postulants wake up for this vocational prayer hour and then go back to bed for the few short hours left before morning. The congregation also observes other celebrations particular to different times of the year, such as the Stations of the Cross, performed every Friday during Lent.

"Prayer means to exalt one's spirit with good thoughts about the Lord," Mother Veronica instructed us in class. "Think about this as if you were thinking about a boyfriend," she suggested, eliciting giggles from the postulants. "It's like when you have a boyfriend and you're going to have a date with him. This is how you should think about the Lord. Think to yourself that you're going to enter His house, and He's there waiting for you and you're going to talk intimately with Him." Proper prayer, Mother Veronica told us, also means that you keep from falling asleep in the chapel—always a problem.

But prayer is not all about angels and cherubim. There will be times, Mother Veronica said, when the postulants will experience a "dryness" (*sequedad*), when they will feel that the Lord is not with them and will feel nothing in prayer. "When this happens, there is an absence of the comfort that the soul usually feels in the spiritual life," she said. This can be a very great test of one's faith. "But you must remember that *you* are to blame for this," Mother Veronica continued. "It is produced by *your* infidelity. The will of God has become weak within you and you have to reinforce it." Indeed, the postulants learn that true reconciliation with God can come only through a detailed critique of their relationship with Him in all domains, that a genuine connection with God is predicated on a stark and relentless self-evaluation.

---

1. The full Liturgy of the Hours consists of the Invitatory (opening prayer), Lauds (morning prayer), Terce, Sext, None (prayers at midmorning, midday, and midafternoon), Vespers (evening prayer), Compline (night prayer) and Matins or Vigilis (office of readings, traditionally performed in the middle of the night; in the reforms of the Second Vatican Counsel, however, this requirement was modified to allow the office of readings to be performed at any time convenient to the practitioner). Contemplative orders are expected to observe all Liturgical Hours. Apostolic orders like the Siervas generally dispense with Terce, Sext, and None. The practice of Adoration among the Siervas is a particular version of Matins.

"When you feel that God is missing, it's because you've been unfaithful and you need more discipline," Mother Catherine told us one day in moral theology class. The postulants are taught that weakness in other areas of one's life will creep into prayer, making the soul yearn for a contact with God that it can't achieve. Discipline in all areas, then, is essential, and the quality of one's prayer serves as a sort of barometer for the quality of one's spiritual relationship with God. "The most magnificent thing about prayer is that you must leave your self behind and think, 'What is the will of God?' " explained Mother Veronica. "We must realize our faults and work at repairing our relationship with God with the help of the illumination of the Holy Spirit." The secret of prayer, the postulants are taught, is in the union of humans with God, the reorientation of our vision of the world so that it comes to coincide with that of the Lord. This enables us to truly become His servants in the world. One of the central tasks of formation, then, is the incorporation of the internal attitude of prayer into the daily fabric of life, with the purpose of reorienting one's perspective from the mundane to the divine. If one does this, the sisters believe, the corresponding attitude of *entrega*—submission to the will of God—will become manifest.

In my conversations with Mother Veronica about the aims of the first year of formation, engagement in prayer was predictably a central theme. When the postulants first come to the convent, she told me, many tend to think of the prayer experience as an intimate, private communication between the soul and God—a common view. And while this is not wrong, Mother Veronica explained, the postulants must learn to cultivate a different sort of experience of prayer that is simultaneously private *and* communal. Prayer clearly involves the self but, when done correctly, implicates the community not just of the Siervas but of all humans. Ultimately, Mother Veronica clarified, sin and grace are a matter of the state not of any particular soul but of humankind in general. "We all together constitute the mystical body of Christ," she explained. "If a woman is called to the religious life and dedicates herself to serving Christ, then issues of her individual soul become simultaneously issues of humanity, and vice versa." Accordingly, prayer is never simply a personal act but involves an articulation of the tripartite relationship among the self, the world, and God. The idea, then, is that if initiates truly engage the daily tasks of formation, they will carry this attitude with them in all their activities, and their understandings of the world around them will be transformed.

It is here, perhaps ironically, that the issue of *surrender* is essential. The postulants were constantly reminded that, no matter how "good" they were, no matter how carefully they followed all the rules or performed all their duties with the proper attitude, no matter how fully they committed themselves to prayer and service, this did not constitute a repair of the broken relationship with God made so painfully clear to them by their self-critique. Their actions and intentions were an important part of the process, to be sure. But, they were told, the rupture with God caused by their years of infidelity and lack of faith could not be mended by their will alone. This could come only from God, whose ways were mysterious and ultimately unknowable.

Bringing Prayer to Practice

On our bimonthly trip to the orthodontist today, Magda told me
that she's been having a lot of trouble in prayer, that she doesn't feel
the presence of God, and it was really starting to worry her. She said
she spoke to the congregation's priest, and both of them agreed that
it had to do with Magda's overattachment to Sister Teresita. The
priest gave her the task of, for that day, driving all thoughts of Sister
Teresita out of her mind during prayer and concentrating only on
communicating with God. Magda told me she was able to do this
and felt "*bien lindo, bien lindo.*" She said she'd been working on
this and it has really made a difference when she's been able to do it.

Excerpted from field notes, January 26, 1995

The postulants all had some sort of relationship with God before entering the congregation. Some told me they had always felt close to God. Some had gone through painful periods of doubt and disbelief and were just beginning to make their way back to their faith. Others told me they had never really thought about the issue of faith in God before something "happened" to them and they felt the call. But regardless of the relationship with God they came in with, all of the postulants told me in exit interviews that their relationship with God and their spiritual lives had undergone massive transformation since they had entered the convent. They uniformly correlated this with learning how to pray correctly, learning how to adopt a certain communicative stance vis-à-vis God to better hear what He was saying to them: learning to embody the spirit of *entrega*, to surrender themselves to the will of God.

The evidence for this shift in perspective was subtle but discernible and could best be seen in how postulants came to personalize prayer and integrate it into what they had previously considered "separate" domains. As the year wore on, the postulants began to import prayer and the attitude of *entrega*—of deliberately turning anything and everything over to the service of God—into activities they had previously treated as "secular." By late January, for example, I started to see some halting attempts by the postulants to say certain vocal prayers on their own, away from the chapel (for example, when breaking into groups to do school work). The postulants were often embarrassed and nervous in these attempts (giggling and turning red), and the attempts were often bungled. They would say as much of a prayer as they could remember and then either stop there or make up something for the end that "sounded good."

By the end of March, the postulants were asking for more prayer time. It became commonplace that, when Mother Veronica announced it was time for their half-hour of Adoration, Rosita (or someone else) would say, "An *hour* of Adoration, Mother!" "Two hours!" Marta (or someone else) would chime in. Also by this time (late March), the postulants began taking more initiative in individualizing prayer. Pipa began doing a second Novena of Trust during Adoration. Rosita, Marta, and Carmen invoked the Holy Spirit before beginning work on their class assignments in the afternoon. Many also showed an increased devotion in prayer. Many more of the postulants knelt during the morning prayer and Adoration instead of sitting comfortably, as they had done previously. When I asked them about this, the response was immediate and enthusiastic. "Oh, yes!" exclaimed Dulce. "I feel so much closer to God than before." "Me, too," agreed Surella. "It's not so much that you have to learn how to *talk* to God, but you have to learn how to *listen* to Him." "That's where the rewards come," Celeste added. "When you learn to really *listen* to God, that's when you become united with Him."

This facet of the larger project of formation is meant to teach the sisters how to achieve and maintain the proper internal, as well as external, attitudes of spirituality they will need in their lives as Siervas. A complete surrender of the self to God—without, however, relinquishing responsibility for the management of one's own soul—is considered to be of utmost importance in the congregation, particularly because the Siervas are a working order and must be in daily contact with "the world." The sisters, as "contemplatives in action," must learn to embody in even—and perhaps especially—the most mundane actions the spirit of *entrega*. Making a bed or cleaning the bathroom, for example, must come to mean something very different for the Siervas (who should cultivate them as acts of prayer and expressions of humility) than they do, say, for a maid at a Holiday Inn or a housewife or a candy striper at a hospital. On the surface, the behaviors are the same. But the Sierva must learn to transform these regular daily activities into a special category of action offered up with "intentions" that reference another plane of significance.

MISSIONIZING THE SELF: CONVERTING PERFORMANCE, PERFORMING CONVERSION

The postulants get their first real taste of recasting mundane action as prayer in April, when they go off on missions. This is the postulants' first extended contact with outsiders since entering the convent, and they are sent out into the countryside in groups of two or three to educate and lead people during Holy Week and Easter, the most important liturgical time of the entire year. (I was assigned to the group including Marta, Rosita, Magda, and Mother Veronica.) Significantly, they go off on the missions at one of the most vulnerable points in their formation process, when they have recognized the depth of the gulf separating them from God, as well as their own impotence in traversing it.

Preparations for the missions began a month before departure. Mother Veronica instituted a special class on the liturgy of Easter so that the postulants would be well prepared to answer any questions that might arise. In recreation, she began to read to the postulants from Catholic missionary accounts, written either by Father Muro himself or by others who had worked in the poor areas of Mexico. She educated them about the hardships to expect "in the field"—very little food, restricted access to restrooms and bathing facilities, their attention always in demand, the responsibility they would have for spiritual instruction. The postulants (particularly Abby and Ruth) who had been on missions before shared their own experiences with the group. The class received almost daily visits from professed nuns, who shared their personal mission stories. For mealtimes, special readings were selected that extolled the vital importance of missionizing and the eternal dangers to those who—out of ignorance or irreverence—did not practice the faith. By the time the postulants began packing their things to leave for the mission week, the atmosphere in the group had reached a fever pitch of both excitement and anxiety.

The day to leave finally came. That morning, the sisters held a special ceremony in the chapel for the postulants, led by Mother Anabel.

All the other sisters were there—junior sisters, third probations, and professed sisters alike. Sister Matilde, one of the eldest in the Central House, spoke to the group about the importance of going on missions and what a beautiful, transformative experience it can be. She began to cry as she spoke, mourning that she could no longer go on missions, and wishing the postulants well. At the end of the ceremony, each postulant was called to the front of the chapel by name and was given a small wooden crucifix to wear during the missions (I was given one too). The postulants could barely contain their excitement—skipping, giggling, chattering—as they filed out of the chapel and went to the front of the convent to await their rides to "el campo."

The daily schedule during mission week, at least for the group I was with, consisted of a morning prayer service, workshops for the children after breakfast, home visits to houses in the pueblo, a midday service, lectures for the adults in the afternoon, more home visits, and an evening prayer vigil. In addition, the postulants and Mother Veronica continued to recite the primary Offices of the Liturgy (Invitatory, Lauds, Vespers, Compline) and to perform their examinations of conscience. The postulants rotated responsibility for the children's workshops and the adult lectures, with Mother Veronica often—but not always—in supervisory attendance. Special ceremonies were planned, according to Catholic liturgy, for Thursday (commemorating Jesus' washing of the apostle's feet), Friday (the draping of the chapel in black or purple cloth and the "crucifixion" of a life-sized image of Christ), Saturday evening (a solemn, candlelit Mass), and 12:01 Sunday morning (a huge, raucous celebration of the resurrection). In all (save the Mass, celebrated by a visiting priest), Mother Veronica and the postulants played highly visible, leading roles.

Being thrust out into the world at precisely the point in their formation where they had become aware of both their internal despair and their ultimate impotence to relieve it seemed to have a powerful effect on these women. A conversation I had with Magda one day toward the end of the missions is illustrative. It was late afternoon on the Friday of Holy Week. We had spent the morning in a nearby village, with the postulants leading the people in a commemoration of the Via Cruces, the stations of the cross. Around midday, the villagers had enacted the crucifixion of Christ by "nailing" a life-sized statue of Him to a cross and then later taking it down and placing it in a glass coffin. As Magda and I were talking about this, she confided to me that she had wept almost uncontrollably as they took the body of Christ down from the cross.

She said, "I thought about the things I said to the people in the Via Cruces this morning. Ay, Señor [Lord]! I should be an example to these people, and look at my life!" After a moment's pause, she added that when she had started the Via Cruces that morning, she had been very nervous, very unsure. "This morning I didn't even want to recite Lauds!" she said. "I was in a miserable state. And I thought, how am *I* supposed to lead these people, when I can't even pray on my own?" But, Magda told me, when she got to the tenth station, which is the actual crucifixion of Christ, she felt she should say more than was printed on the sheets she was using as a guide. "So I prayed, 'Oh God, please put words in my mouth, because I'm a child in these things, and I don't know what to say.' And then I just started talking. And the Lord *did* put words in my mouth. The people just stared at me, and I thought, 'Who's speaking?' because it wasn't me. The people expect so much from you as a nun. They see you as a sort of god. And praise be to God that He spoke through me."

Later that evening, Magda shared this story with Mother Veronica, Marta, and Rosita. "Ah, yes, *hija,* now you see," said Mother Veronica, smiling. "When you begin to offer everything you do up to God, even the most trivial, that's when you truly become His instrument. Our commitment is not just about sitting in the chapel and enjoying the beautiful feelings of prayer. It's about loving God in *everything* we do during the day. As you become more able to do this, God will work through you."

Magda's experience seemed, in many ways, to be a common one among the postulants. At the end of the missions, we all arrived back in the Central House, the postulants greeting each other with huge bear hugs and tears of joy. The third probation sisters played musical instruments and sang, and the professed sisters had prepared a welcome home feast. And the topic of conversation throughout the evening was the "experiences" they had all had on the missions, the point at which they truly felt they had become instruments of God. Mina, for example, told us about how she helped a young mother see the vital importance of baptizing a baby and how she felt that God had worked through her to save the baby's soul. Evelyn spoke of comforting a dying man, of helping him to reconnect with God through prayer before passing on. Carlota talked about the joy she got from working with the children, recognizing that their unquestioning trust in her meant she could truly make a difference in their lives. And Ruth spoke of the influence of the Seventh Day Adventists in the village she worked in and how she felt she was on the "front line" of God's army. Eavesdropping on the postulants' conversations, the older nuns nodded their heads and gave each other knowing looks, as if to affirm that the missions had, indeed, been a success.

Of course, one might speculate that the postulants produced the sorts of accounts they felt were expected of them. They had, indeed, heard "mission tales" for weeks before they left and had clearly anticipated some kind of intense experience in the field. But be this as it may, the kinds of stories and experiences the postulants related upon their return, and the detail and emotion with which they were delivered, convinced me that many of these women did indeed feel themselves to be significantly changed by the process.

The postulants went on missions, then, during a very vulnerable time in their training, the point at which, perhaps, they felt the least confident or qualified. But by being placed in positions of authority, by being held up as models of religious excellence, and by acting "as if"—*as if* they were confident, *as if* they knew what they were doing, *as if* they were "real" nuns—they found that something happened. The people responded to them. They found a new sense of assurance within themselves. They were able to do things—lead prayers, give catechism, comfort the suffering—they didn't know they were capable of. They began to see themselves, and each other, in a different light. They had left the convent at the time when they felt the most pitiful, and they returned, at least provisionally, as "experts."

SUBMISSION TO THE WILL OF GOD: THE POWER OF SURRENDER

The postulants and the other sisters talked about this as an experience of "conversion." It may seem odd to talk about the conversion of women who have already left home and family to join a religious order. But we have to understand what the sisters meant by this. Conversion in this sense is not a formal change of religious affiliation (though this can, of course, be the case) but an intense, personal, radical transformation of orientation to the world and to God. It is the opening up of a new awareness, a sense of finally "getting it," of seeing things in a new light, "with God's eyes," as the sisters described it. The notion of conversion for the sisters, then, contains an element of rupture, of breaking off from the old life (burdened by the values of the temporal world) and forging a new life in a new arena, with the values of the spiritual always at the forefront. When this happens, there is a sense of viewing the old life with a mixture of sentimentality and pity, and one's old self is talked about as if it had been a child who did cute but stupid things. There is, then, both a *severing*—a rejection of the old (temporal/false) self and an embracing of the new (eternal/true) self—and at the same an *active reintegration* of these two experiences of self within a larger "timeless" narrative of vocation. In other words, there is first a rejection and then a reincorporation of the old self and its dispositions within a new self-framework. This re-collecting of self-experiences into a coherent narrative of self is the subject of the next chapter.

CHAPTER 10

Re/Collection

The Temporal Contours of the Self

By May, the postulants began to talk as if they had experienced a sense of integration. They seemed to talk with a new sense of purpose and cohesion about their experiences with God, their daily activities, and their hopes for continuing in their training. Upon returning from the missions, the postulants took turns recounting their "vocations" to the group under the mentorship of their mistress. And it was here—in the explicit discursive ordering of experience—that I observed the elaboration of temporality to become the focal point of the postulants' training.

THE IMMEDIACY OF ETERNITY: TIME AND TRANSFORMATION IN THE CONVENT

One of the most striking things about life in a Roman Catholic convent is that every second counts. Not in the ways most of us are used to: rushing from meeting to meeting, trying to meet grant and conference deadlines, struggling to balance career and family. In our hyper-rush culture, we have learned to guard our time closely. It is, after all, *our* time—it belongs to us. We get indignant if someone wastes it or imposes on it without our consent because once our time has been wasted, it

This chapter was previously published as "The Immediacy of Eternity: Time and Transformation in a Roman Catholic Convent," *Religion* 33 (2003): 201–19. Reprinted with permission from Elsevier.

can't be recouped. It is a limited, expendable recourse. Our time is a commodity, and the less we have of it—the more it is in demand—the more it is worth.

Time in the convent is conceptualized somewhat differently. Time isn't money for the sisters, but it *is* precious. It is precious precisely because it does *not* belong to us, but to God. Indeed, extracting oneself from the "worldly" temporal plane and relinquishing the false sense of time ownership is one of the first (and often one of the hardest) tasks young women must master when they enter the nunnery. They must come to understand that this illusory perception of time significantly hinders the experience of God, since it privileges human management of time and agency over the divine orchestration of human existence. The ideal in the nunnery, then, is what Spinoza characterizes as living "under the aspect of eternity"([1677] 1910, bk. 5, prop. 29N)—that is, experiencing time in its genuine, eternal fullness rather than as filtered through human distinctions.

In this chapter, I will consider how coming to inhabit a new phenomenology of time functions as a key element in the religious training of the postulants. Specifically, I suggest that learning to navigate two temporal frames—to *read the self* across both contexts simultaneously—helps to effect a change in subjectivity for these women as they progress through their first level of religious formation. The new nuns learn to construct an understanding of their selves as continuous across different temporal spheres, alongside (and, perhaps, in spite of) certain experiences of discontinuity that are purposefully imposed by the nunnery. For example, the experience of rupture or discontinuity a girl experiences when she first leaves home and comes to live in the convent is acknowledged and validated as personally painful, but it is then quickly reframed as parallel to the experience Mary must have had when she left her family to marry Joseph. The newcomer learns that God has chosen her, just as He chose Mary, for a special purpose. Her feeling of disjuncture, then, is recast as simply the growing pains of recognizing her true calling, which God has set out for her since the beginning of time.

Gradually, this continual naming of such experiences of rupture and discontinuity and their reframing as spiritually and temporally continuous with God's plan for her persuade the new nun to move toward an alternate experience of self. She learns how to navigate between temporal realities and, with increasing skill, to use this process instrumentally to achieve a change in the subjective experience of the self. Thus a fundamental part of the formation process is learning how to negotiate these tensions between continuity and discontinuity and developing an experience of self that embraces both. Coming to inhabit a new phenomenology of time helps the postulants to integrate and personalize the various elements of religious formation they encounter over the course of the first year.

RELIGIOUS VOCATION AS A STORY OF THE SELF

To understand how this works, we need to look at the experience of religious vocation (the call to the religious life) not just as a spiritual or psychological event but as a *story of the self*—a "narrative identity " in Ricoeur's (1992) sense of the term—a cohesive account of the self that follows a particular trajectory and is intelligible only in retrospect. Narrative identity in this sense is not necessarily a consciously devised presentation of self, though this may sometimes be the case. Rather, Ricoeur suggests that it is a function of trying to make sense of two radically different experiences of self—the diverse experiences we have of ourselves at different points in our lives ("selfhood") and the sense that there is some essential kernel of self that can be traced through these various permutations ("sameness"). He argues that our subjective sense of who we are is continually produced and reproduced through a dialectical relationship between these modes of experience. What narrative identity does is provide an arena for the integration of these different temporal modes of self-experience in a way that has meaning in a particular context. For Ricoeur, this story of the self is primarily an explanatory exercise for making sense of "how did I get here" (wherever "here" is for the narrator) that reflects multiple layers of experience and interpretation. As the "here" changes, the story, too, is altered to accommodate the new direction. Such a narrative implicitly appeals to a certain kind of temporal organization. Time is understood to unfold along a linear trajectory, with the present firmly ensconced between the past (known) and the future (imagined).

But in the convent, we see something a little different. Newcomers are guided in how to tell a new story of themselves—to construct a particular type of linear, narrative identity—that resituates all life experience, past, present, *and future*, within a temporal framework that favors the *circularity* of time and draws meaning from it. The essential elements of one's human life story are worked into a larger narrative with a different temporal frame of reference. This new temporal frame is both timeless and cyclical—it enfolds the notions of both eternity (time and existence have no beginning and no end) and the shaping of time according to certain meaningful patterns, which find expression in various religious beliefs and observances. Just as Moses led the Jews out of bondage in Egypt and into the Promised Land, for example, it is believed that Jesus leads the faithful out of the bondage of sin and into eternal life. The lambs' blood on the Jews' doorpost caused the Angel of Death to pass over their homes, just as the blood of Jesus—the Lamb of God—protects His followers from sin and therefore from death. Sinful, disobedient, carnal Eve brought about the fall of humankind, but this fall is repaired by the obedience and chastity of Mary, a woman who herself is free of original sin. There is, then, a cycling and overlapping through time, with repeated and varied enactments of key themes such as bondage and freedom, sin and redemption.

These cross-temporal correlates—and many, many others—are woven into the celebrations that make up the liturgical year, which begins with the Annunciation to Mary, continues through Jesus' birth at Christmas, and culminates with His crucifixion and resurrection at Easter. The entire year is structured to parallel the life, death, and resurrection of Jesus, which themselves are understood to parallel the creation, the fall, and the redemption of humankind. The rhythm of convent life is modeled on this cycle on various levels, with the days of the month, the progression of the week, and even the hours of the day organized to replicate this pattern. Within this temporal frame a postulant learns to understand her vocation and her decisions to enter the nunnery not simply as one young woman's desire to unite with Jesus but as part of an awesome, divine plan of salvation.

So how might this happen? Most of the postulants were initially unsure if they had really been called by God. They anxiously looked for any sign—no matter how small—that their vocation was genuine. The postulants learned that it is possible to have a genuine vocation and not know it or to believe falsely that one has been called to the religious life when this is not the case. They tended to view religious vocation as something they did or did not have, and it was not clear to them how to tell the difference. They were wary of their own senses of calling and relied on outside validation from their superiors as to whether their experiences were "real." As Carlota (a nineteen-year-old postulant) told me, "I just wanted someone to tell me, 'Yes, you have a vocation,' or, 'No you don't.' But it's not that easy. No one can tell you for sure if you have a vocation or not. This is between you and Christ."

One way the postulants begin to critically engage their motivations for joining the convent is by learning new ways of thinking about themselves as flesh-and-blood actors within the material world, while at the same time continually (re)interpreting their embodied experience as evidencing important things about their spiritual state. They must come to situate and reinterpret their mundane daily activities within both "worldly" (linear) time and "sacred" (eternal, cyclical) time and to attach meaning to their actions that bridges the two domains.

THE RITUALIZATION OF EVERYDAY LIFE

The crux here seems to be the development of an alternate experience of daily practice as ritual activity, or what we might call a dual movement with regard to action, time, and experience. Specifically, daily life in the convent becomes an arena for negotiating these temporal frames by simultaneously regulating the sisters' every waking and sleeping moment and highlighting the illusory nature of these temporal distinctions.

We can understand this more clearly if we think of the convent as a ritual space, in Bell's (1992) sense of the term, which operates with its own rules and generates its own ritual activities and meanings. The protective and isolative nature of the convent creates a bounded realm of sacred experience where daily life becomes alive with the presence of the otherworldly. For the sisters, the power of God is palpable and infuses every aspect of their lives. The sisters are never "outside" ritual, in the anthropological sense of the term. They feel that they are (or at least should be) constantly communicating with the divine in a powerful and direct way, whether in the chapel praying or doing the laundry. In this way, everyday activities take on new meanings. Washing the floor, for example, is no longer simply utilitarian—it is a tribute to God and a test of one's vocation. Peeling vegetables and preparing meals is not merely a duty but a manifestation of humility and enlightened servility. Studying for courses is an act of gratitude to God for one's intellect. Bathing is a reminder of one's pledged purity of both body and spirit. Eating reminds one of the frailty of the flesh and the eternal nourishment of the soul to be had in heaven.

Thus the postulants are guided in how to experience their every action, no matter how small, as an articulation of their spiritual relationship with God and as an opportunity for them to feel His presence and follow His will. Whereas in the outside world the drudgeries and chores involved in keeping things running are often seen as distractions or burdens that draw us away from "quality time" or "down time," these tasks become for the nuns a means of experiencing God on a deeply intimate level. As Amelia (a twenty-one-year-old postulant) told me, "I used to hate to do chores when I lived at home. I'd do them if I had to, but I resented it because they got in the way. I wanted to go hang out with my friends or do something fun. But we learn here that washing the pots and pans and things can be a way of praying, a way of loving God. It's still not exactly what I'd call 'fun,' but if you offer your work up to God, it's a way of being with Him and showing Him how much you love Him. It can actually be a beautiful experience." Recasting daily activities as drawing their significance from a sacred temporal reference (as well as a mundane one) allows the sisters to engage them as tools in their personal and spiritual transformation. Learning how to analyze their inclinations and actions along these lines—and to internalize this interpretation as the word of God—is the primary skill the postulants must master during that first year.

VOCATION NARRATIVES:
READING THE FUTURE IN THE PAST

But this altered relationship to in-the-world action isn't limited to the confines of the nunnery, or even to the here and now. After all, the present, as William James characterizes it, is "specious"—it contains part of the past as well as part of the future. Our "selves" involve judgments about past events and experiences as articulated through actions and emotions in our present and given meaning through our imaginings of what our future selves will be like. The postulants learn not only how to monitor their present behaviors and inclinations but also how to project these interpretations into the past. And it is here that the question of temporality most explicitly leans on the subjective experience of self.

The postulants are taught that, if they really do have a vocation to the religious life, it is because God chose them, specifically, for this path before they were born. In fact, they are told, God selected them to be His brides since the dawn of creation and wants them to fulfill this vocation regardless of their weaknesses, faults, and personal histories.

If a woman believes she has been called to Christ from the beginning of time, this means that, whether she realized it or not, each thing that she has done or experienced since her birth occurred in the context of that calling. Whether she realized it or not, God had chosen her to become His bride and was gently guiding her toward this path. And whether she realized it or not, God was communicating with her—and she with Him—even as she went about her daily business. It didn't matter if her family wasn't religious or if she didn't start going to church until she was thirteen. It didn't matter that she went through a rebellious stage and would sneak out of the house to meet her boyfriend. It didn't matter that she had planned to go to veterinary school and spent her afternoons at the vet hospital instead of at catechism. The postulants learn that spiritual communion with God not only is possible but can be pervasive in our daily lives if we cultivate it. "There are so many things in my life I didn't give any importance to," Carmen told me, "but now I can see that it was the Lord trying to get my attention. Good thing for me the Lord is patient!"

In their first year in the convent, then, the postulants are guided in reconceptualizing their whole lives as a series of events indicating a divinely directed transformation, a progressive unfolding of self in a particular image. This self is eternal, yet embodied in the here-and-now. It has been singled out by God for special grace, but it risks eternal damnation by virtue of its incarnation in human flesh. It is an agent in the world and is endowed with free will, yet it is constantly guided and persuaded by God in ways beyond its awareness.

To see how these issues play out, let us look closely at narratives related to me by three of the postulants, describing their understandings of "the call" and their own processes in answering it. These accounts are transcribed from private, taped conversations toward the end of the research.

Abby, Age Nineteen

My vocation emerged when I was four years old. Yes, four years old. I didn't do much about it at the time, of course. I do remember playing nun with my friends, tying a towel around my head like a veil. But I did all the normal things—I played, went to school, got into trouble. When I was in middle school I joined a group called the Youth Missionary League. They're dedicated to going on missions, where you go outside of the country and missionize. Everything about the group is dedicated to missions. But for young people. And, well, that's how I started to get a little more involved in religious things, because of this group. I was enamored with the idea of working on missions—I really think it's so important, working with the poor.

Eventually, I went on my first mission. We don't start off going to far-away places like Africa. Eventually, you can get there. But we start closer to home. There are so many people right here in the state of Puebla that need help! So I started out in *el campo* here in Puebla. And ay, no! It's amazingly beautiful because the people are so simple. But they are *so poor,* so poor—materially as well as spiritually. And you say to yourself, "And me, having everything!" Because I didn't lack anything— the love and care of my parents, everything. I had everything. And I thought, "Ay, no, my God! I have to do something, no?" But I didn't realize that God was asking something of me. No, at this point it was nothing more than "Ay! I have to do something! I have to do something!" But I had no idea what.

So I started to go on more missions, I traveled a lot, went out of the region. I met young people from all over Mexico. And I kept liking it more and more. And I got to know priests and some foreigners who came from Peru and missionaries who came from all over and told us their experiences as missionaries and everything. Ah! I loved it!

And eventually I said to myself, "Well, it's time to do something, no?" But I was very, very afraid. So I thought, "Ay, no, no, no. How?" I thought, if God is asking me to do something, then yes! But I didn't know *where* or *when* or anything. So I decided, "Well, I'm going to start to investigate my possibilities. I'm going to start to look for what I want to do."

So I started to look. I went to retreats, I got to know various congregations. I got to know people called *laicos comprometidos*—laypeople who take vows similar to ours but who live wholly in the world. And I evaluated it all. I would say to myself, "This one is good, this one no, no *way* on that one." And I did this for a long time, for almost two years. During this time, I continued with my normal life. I kept going out with my boyfriend and everything. But I kept this other side private, knowing I was looking for something more.

Finally, one day I said, "Enough! I've had enough!" Even with everything I had I wasn't satisfied. Not anymore! Something was missing. *Something.* But something *spiritual,* something very, very profound. Not something superficial. And this is when I went to a conference in Monterrey. And it was *beautiful,* beautiful, because it is there that my vocation started to become clear to me. And I said, "That's it. The religious life. That is where God wants me. And I want to give myself to Him completely. Okay."

So then I began to investigate. Sometimes I would think, "A nun? What am I thinking?" But it's true—I kept coming back to the feeling that *yes*, there was something, something telling me that I was to become a nun. I was surprised because I had always envisioned being a missionary. But there was something not quite complete about that for me. I didn't quite find what I was looking for. But when I *did* find it, I thought, "Well, here it is! *Here* it is! Absolutely, positively, here it is."

And, well, I met the Siervas. My parents' house is close to the novitiate, and my little brothers and sisters go to the Siervas' preschool. But all that is relatively new, so I hadn't spent much time there myself. But I started to visit, and before I knew it I was going by almost every day, staying and talking with the sisters. Finally, I decided to attend the vocational retreats, and it was there that I decided it was time to enter. I thought about entering with the Sisters of Guadalupe, but in the end, it was the Siervas that felt right to me.

And thanks be to God that I'm here! I entered the postulancy. It hurts so much to let go of everything outside. Yes, it hurts. But it is something that goes away eventually. It's that you're full of the things of the world, and you have to let them go. But when you come to the religious life, all of this starts to leave you, leave you, leave you. You scrub everything out, and then new things come, like grace, like the love of God. It's when you feel *universal* love that you know. And when you realize that you've been filled with it, you say, "Ay! No, no no, no! It can't be!" But it is. You can't believe it because it's so beautiful because you are so happy! And outside you can be happy—but only in *parts*. You're kind of halfway happy. You feel happy and you live in the moment, but inside, no. Here in the convent you know what true happiness is, you give everything to others, and you think, "I'm exhausted, but I'm happy! And the more I give, the more I receive! And in the end, I'm going to receive the ultimate prize—eternal life!" Well, anyway, this is what happened to me. I would say to myself, "I exist because of the love of God. Everything I do is for the love of God."

Yes, I'm here inside a convent, and perhaps I should think, "No! I'm incarcerated!" But it's something, I don't know. People on the outside view it differently. They think, "How can you stand being incarcerated?" I'm not incarcerated! I feel *free. Free.* Absolutely free. There are so many things I've let go of, worldly things that were weighing me down. And now I feel so *light,* as we say. Free.

Celeste, Age Nineteen

My vocation—well, I feel it began when I was small, when I was very young. More than anything, when I was young I dreamed of becoming a priest and of giving Mass [laughs]. I told my parents I wanted to be a nun, and finally, when I was nine years old, my parents sent me to stay at Father Muro's school. It was hard because I was only nine years old, and the other girls there were fifteen, sixteen. I was bored and I missed my mom a lot. But I really was curious about what the sisters did—there was something about it that kept calling my attention. When I was at school I missed my mom. But when I was home, I would miss the sisters and the school and couldn't wait to go back.

This was the first stage of my vocation—first wanting to be a priest, and then at the school. But at this age, one doesn't understand, no? As I got older, into middle school, I began to help at the retreats—youth retreats, seminary retreats, retreats for all the congregations in the city. And I became even more curious. I really liked the atmosphere, everyone laughing, everyone treating each other with friendship.

So it was in middle school that I started to look more seriously, trying to discover if I was really meant for the religious life or not. I knew I liked it a lot. I felt very satisfied in the retreats, and it was never the same leaving a retreat and returning to the world, to school, sports—the things I did on the outside that didn't fill me up, didn't satisfy me. And I realize this, that each time I went to the retreats, I felt full, complete.

I spoke with Mother Josephine, the vocations director, about this and told her I thought I might want to enter the religious life. She was supportive but told me I was much too young to decide yet, that I should take at least three years, finish school, and then see where God wanted me. I was disappointed, but she was right.

Something else happened on that particular retreat that changed things. When I was little, I suffered two rape attempts. This really influenced how I thought about things. At the time, I didn't know how to think about what had happened. During that retreat, one of my friends told me that something similar had happened to her. Because it had happened to me, too, I was able to tell her, "Don't worry—I've overcome it, you can, too." But in truth, remembering what had happened to me hurt a lot—it uncovered something in me, and afterwards I didn't want to have anything to do with nuns or vocation or anything. No thank you. I decided it wasn't for me.

When I returned to school, it was very difficult, no? Because I had decided I didn't want that life. I closed myself off to it. I stopped going to Mass, I didn't like going to school. But I did keep going to retreats. I think even then something inside me knew that I would come back to God.

Anyway, I finished middle school, went on to high school. And all the while, I felt this kind of disequilibrium, as if I was trying to figure out who I was and what I wanted to do with my life. I guess this is normal at this age—we all try to figure out our personalities. And not just whether we are aggressive or sensitive. I started to feel drawn again to the religious life. But still, those two rape attempts affected me. As I got more involved in religious things, my spiritual director pointed out to me that maybe I was looking for some sort of compensation, some kind of affective compensation in the religious life for what had happened to me. So I started questioning myself all over again. What if it was true? If that's what was motivating me, she said, then I shouldn't enter the religious life.

So I threw myself into sports. Sports get out all the negative energy, you know? I played a lot of sports, and I spent a lot of time writing and reading, trying to figure out what I really wanted and why. I got interested in psychology and philosophy and threw myself into my studies. I did this until my last year of high school, and then I had to decide if I was going to have a career or what I was going to choose to do.

But, then, I had my boyfriend, and he could always support me [laughs]. My boyfriend was very important to me because it was a way for me to test myself, to see if I really was looking for compensation for what had happened to me, if I really could redo my life, so to speak. Because after something like that happens to you, you feel like dirt, and you don't even know sometimes if you're really alive or not. That's how I felt. So for me, having my boyfriend was very important. And I was very upfront with him. I told him, "I want to be a nun." I don't think he believed me, but he accompanied me on retreats.

At school, I had a spiritual director and went to confession every week. I also had an academic advisor (the psychology teacher). We received Communion every day, and this was very helpful to me. And through all of this, I always felt—I had this *inquietud* here inside, no? And I still felt that the Lord was calling me. I felt it more strongly every day.

I went to more and more retreats. I broke up with my boyfriend. But Mother Josephine thought I should wait longer. I was impatient, so I went and joined another congregation. I felt the call so strongly, you know? And I wanted to turn myself over completely to God. So I entered with the Dominicans. My parents didn't approve at all. I was there for a week. Just a week. I was miserable. I couldn't eat. I couldn't sleep. I got sick. I remember crying and crying, thinking that I just couldn't stay in that congregation. The sisters were so kind to me, but I knew it wasn't right.

But I still felt that the Lord was really calling me. So I went back *again* to Mother Josephine, and I told her, "I feel that the Lord is calling me." "Fine, come back to the retreats," she told me. So I went through the vocational retreats again. I went to visit one of the Siervas' houses in Huajuapan. Mother Josephine thought this would be a good way to see if I really wanted to enter.

I loved the experience in Huajuapan, and when I returned I wanted to give myself to the Lord more than ever. Not so much for the work itself, but to really *give* myself to the Lord.

Oh, the day I entered the congregation I was so happy!! Ayyyyy! For me it was—well, all of us were so excited! And in here, I really began to see how I feel about things. You truly surrender yourself to God, and I love it. The postulancy has been a really beautiful experience for me. The only thing you carry with you is the call. You renounce yourself, join with your sisters. So many things you used to think were important just don't matter anymore. Outside, in the world, you limit yourself. But not anymore. And what's more, you know what you're committing to here, no? So if sometimes you feel discouraged, you can think, "Well, the Lord is with me. What do I have to fear?" And here you continue to clarify your vocation because here you realize that you can be a contemplative in action, right?

And you become aware of your miseries. It's as if the Lord is saying to you, "Do not worry, I am with you, be at peace." For example, here you know that every act you do is an act for the love of God. And I love this. Because every step you take, every word you say is something very special—everything you do is out of love for God. And if you forget something, this is because you're lacking love. For example, if I forget to chop the fruit for lunch, this is a lack of love. So everything must be done for the love of God.

But as I was saying, the rape attempts in my childhood marked my life, and so even today I wonder, "Am I doing this as a compensation?" I'm happy here—who wouldn't be happy being close to the Lord in a place like this? It is beautiful, beautiful. But you start to wonder, "Is this really where God wants me?" Not just whether it's where *I* want to be but if it's where *God* wants me to be. You have to make yourself completely available to God—what the Lord wants, I want. It's like what Mother Veronica told us, "I don't want the outcome to be more or less or better than what He wants." So one should be docile, try to see everything with eyes of faith.

So this is how I've come to think about everything that's happened to me. And it's helped me a lot. You remember that Father Muro says that to live with the poor it is first necessary to *become like* the poor? Well, because of what I've been through I can help young girls that have had similar experiences. And who better to help someone who's traumatized than someone who has been through trauma herself, like me? How can you understand their experience unless you've been through it yourself? But coming through a trauma is one thing. Coming through it and being able to help someone else is a different thing altogether. I think the religious life is helping me know how to do this.

Each vocation is very particular. The Lord takes hold of each of us in a special way. Frankly, this whole experience in the convent has fascinated me. Everything just fills me up. It is a beautiful, beautiful thing to abandon yourself into the hands of God.

Amelia, Age Twenty-Two

Well, my vocation began when I was very young. Ever since I can remember, since I had the use of reason, I used to tell my aunts that I wanted to stay with them—they were cloistered nuns. So whenever we would go visit them, I would always tell them that I wanted to stay with them, that I didn't want to leave. Well, they would laugh and tell me that I just had to grow up and then I could go there.

That's how it was. In my childhood it was always that way. I received my first Communion. I was so excited! My aunt made my little dress for my first Communion. It was so pretty. She made my dress for my *quinceañera,* also.

But when I got to be fifteen years old, I—well, actually, it was from when I was about twelve years old, I no longer wanted to enter a congregation, that is, to be a nun. I hung out at school and with my friends (I usually played with boys rather than girls). And that's how I spent my time. The funny thing is that whenever my friends would make me angry or something, I would tell them that I was going to enter a convent. I would always tell them this as a way of getting out of a problem or out of anger or something.

I remember that on one occasion we were playing, and they left. They were gone for an hour, and I was waiting for them. They didn't come. So I got very angry, and I went home. Later they came to see me in my house. And they said to me, "Why didn't you wait for us?" and I said, "I waited for you, but then I came home." "But why?" they asked. And I said, "Because I shouldn't spend too much time outside and away from home, because *I'm going to enter a convent!*" I don't know why I said that—it just came out. It wasn't something I had been thinking about or anything. But since then was when I feel that—how can I explain it?—it was during this time that I started to say this a lot, that I was going to enter a convent. So from that point on I felt that, how should I put it? After I had gone something like four years without mentioning the convent, I started talking about it again. It was during this time that I started to say a lot that I was going to enter a convent. And since then the idea never left me. Always, in different situations, this idea would come to me. It was constant.

So I went to high school. I didn't like it. I left. But always with this idea that I would someday become a nun. But, how should I put it? It was as if I hadn't yet assimilated it, or rather, like there was something inside that said, "You are going to be a nun, you have to be a nun, you can be a nun." But I would say, "No, I don't want to." It's difficult to explain because it's a feeling that moves you, a kind of an inclination, but at the same time you yourself refuse it, reject it. It's like—it's like your spirit, no? Your spirit calls you one way—let's say, to perfection. It wants you to attend to this. But you, you say no, because it requires sacrifices, it will be too hard. In other words, renunciation. So with the simple word "nun," I said, "no, no!"

I was out of school for three years. And then some musicians came to town and asked me, "Don't you think you might want to study music?" And I did. So they took me to see Father Bruno (the headmaster of the high school), and I went back to school so I could study music.

For the next three years I went on missions with the school, and I liked it more and more. I talked to the director about becoming a nun, but he said he thought I was more excited about the music than about the religious aspect of the missions. So on that third mission, he didn't let me play any music at all but made me stay in the chapel the whole time. I hated it.

I finished school. I didn't like being at home and started to look for a band to play with. And then—who knows what got into me—I went to talk with a priest who was about to be ordained. And I told him *every-thing*—all my *inquietudes,* what had been happening, how I had experienced my vocation. And he told me, "Well, look. I don't know many congregations. But of the few I know, and from what you've told me, I think you'd fit well with the Siervas." He gave me their address and told me to go talk to Mother Josephine.

But I didn't go see her. He gave me the address in December, and it wasn't until the following Easter that I thought about it again. Easter was coming and I knew I didn't want to just stay home. So I decided I would go somewhere, but I didn't know where to go. That's when I dug out the address of Mother Josephine—I figured she would know of somewhere to go. I expected her to be big and fat, at least sixty years old or so. To me, all nuns were like that.

The curious thing is that I arrived at the central office of the diocese— that was the address the father had given me. But when I got there, well, I'm a little timid, so when the secretary said Mother Josephine wasn't there, I didn't tell her whether I was going to wait or leave. I just kind of sat in a chair. When she realized I was still there, it had been four hours! I was waiting there four hours to see this Mother Josephine. "I'll call Mother Josephine right now," the secretary told me, and she did. She told her that there was a girl who had been waiting to see her for four hours. Mother Josephine told her to put me in a taxi and send me to the Central House right away. I arrived at the Central House and met Mother Josephine. She was nothing like what I had expected. We talked for a long time, and she told me I should attend the vocational retreats.

After this I started attending the aspirant retreats. I spent some time at one of the congregation's houses. I was trying to decide what to do. I couldn't decide if I wanted to enter the convent or enroll in the university. I talked to Mother Josephine. "Look, it's your decision," she told me. "Enter the congregation or enter the university. But if you enter the university, you should stay until you've finished. Understand? No dropping out early." It was interesting, though. Because as soon as she said, "Choose the congregation or your career," I thought, "*The congrega-tion!*"

This was at the beginning of August. I went home and told my mom what I wanted to do. "Are you sure?" she asked. "Yes!" I told her. So I got all my papers together quickly. I think I was the last one to turn in my application letter. And then one day they called me on the phone. I answered and Mother Josephine said, "Amelia, guess what." "What, Mother?" I asked. And she said, "They accepted you." And I just stood there for a minute. "What?" I asked. And she said, "Yes! They've accepted you into the congregation!" And I started to laugh. I couldn't believe it. "Now what do I do?" I thought. I didn't have any of the clothes I needed, nothing. But I got my things together, and I entered.

When I entered the congregation, I thought, "Well, let's see what happens." I had only been here two weeks when Mother Veronica wheeled out the piano and I played it. She told me she thought I should continue studying music, and I was thrilled. I always thought that when I became a nun I would have to say goodbye to music, goodbye to every-thing. But now that I'm here, the congregation teaches us that the Lord works through us in all sorts of ways and that music is one way He works through me. So for me this is something, how shall I say it? A very nice surprise. Because bit by bit—there are so many things that I experienced before and now that I'm here—there are so many surprises that come, that now I see that this is my place. This is my place! And not before, not later, but right here in this moment.

There are so many things. Our charism is that of reparation, and our patron saints here are the same ones that were mine outside! There are so many coincidences! I have always had a special devotion to Saint Joseph and to the Sacred Heart and to the Virgin. And they have all that here as well. There are so many things that it's a little bit spooky. And you're not doing anything—it just happens. Sometimes you feel like a boat, drifting here and there, almost turning over in the storm. But from somewhere outside, the Lord guides you, saying, "Over here, come this way." And everything that happens to you helps to reaffirm this. To be more generous in your *entrega* and everything. And although we're not always perfect, we always try to get there, no?

In recounting their vocations, Abby, Celeste, and Amelia go back through their lives, giving significance to things in ways they themselves admit they hadn't before (Amelia wanting to stay with her aunts in the convent, Abby playing nun, Celeste playing priest). They resituate these elements within a larger trajectory, a story that takes "the call" as some-thing that existed throughout their lives, whether or not they were con-sciously aware of it. They talk about their vocations as the gradual realization of their true place in the world. This realization did not come in a flash of insight, though (as in Celeste's case) it was sometimes punctuated by specific, identifiable events. Rather, the recognition of vocation was for these women more a gradual accumulation of feelings, with lots of fits and starts and doubts along the way. Throughout this process, the constant motivating force they all describe is the deeply felt sense that something wasn't right, that something crucial and fundamental was missing in their lives. Each of these women sought out alternative ways to be happy (Abby with her boyfriend, Amelia with her music, Celeste with sports). But despite a superficial satisfaction, they all describe an eventual realization that the void they felt was filled only through their spirituality—and not just any spirituality but an all-embracing, all-engulfing sense of intimacy with God.

Over time, and in different ways, each of these women came to understand their feelings of emptiness in the "outside world" as the call to enter to religious life. But more than this, they came to understand this call as directing them to the Siervas in particular. In separate conversations, Abby, Celeste, and Amelia (along with many of the other postulants) told me that they had originally planned to enter another order—the Dominicans, the Franciscans, the Paulinas. Some of them actually spent time in other congregations before leaving and seeking out the Siervas. All talked about the focus on cultural integrity and social justice—the reclamation of women and the affirmation of Mexican values—as being key things about the congregation that appealed to them, though most of the postulants did not become truly acquainted with this dimension of the congregation's teachings until after they entered. Like the sense of vocation, then, the postulants learned to read these political commitments back through their lives, giving new meanings to their experiences as specifically preparing them for the life of a Sierva.

Celeste's story is, perhaps, the most explicit in terms of the reinterpretation of past experiences through an altered framework in the "recollecting" of vocation. She talks about the trauma she suffered as a child, a victim of two separate rape attempts by different individuals. She acknowledges—both in this particular narrative and in many other conversations we had about these events—that they shook her to the core. She told me that she lost faith in God for a long time after the second attack. "I thought, 'How could there be a God who lets things like this happen?' And I know I'm not the only one—it happens to girls all the time. I just couldn't imagine a God who would permit that." It is perhaps striking, then, that by the end of her first year in the convent, Celeste had come to see her traumatic experiences as, ironically, one of the ways God has worked through her. She does not in any sense believe God "wanted" her to be traumatized or that it was necessarily part of His plan for her that she be raped. Rather, she told me, she feels now that He did *permit* the attacks to take place. Not to punish her for some kind of personal failing (as she sometimes thought in the past), but, as she explained it to me, because He knew she had the strength and the character to "handle it," to transform her experiences into something that would help others.

She sees her calling to the Siervas, in particular, as relating to this in a specific way. "Father Muro talked about the exploitation and abuse of women," she told me one day as we walked in the convent garden. "He believed that this comes from a devaluing of women, from not valuing women for the special qualities that they have *as women* in this world—the care, the tenderness, the *entrega* we give to others. He believed strongly in the *regeneration* of women, of helping women to know their own worth so that they can perform the roles God assigned to them. I think what I went through gave me a special kind of understanding about what he meant."

We can see, then, how the postulants learn to incorporate into their daily experience a new story of who they are and what their purpose is that reorders and restructures their understandings of their own personal histories, while at the same time situating these new understandings within a temporal frame that is different (yet not wholly separable) from that on the "outside." They learn to tell new stories of their lives that, rather than simply recounting facts, move back and forth between temporal frames—between "worldly" and "eternal" domains of reference—overlying them, drawing correspondences and parallels. This shift in self-interpretation serves as the foundation for their subsequent religious training by teaching them to experience their own bodies—in working, praying, eating, studying, playing, cleaning—as the domain of negotiation between temporal worlds.

REARTICULATING SELF AND SOUL: INTEGRATING MODES OF BEING

I suggest that the experience of navigating two temporal frames in the convent leads to fundamental changes in the three key areas. First, the postulants learn to recognize the existence of two temporal systems—one that constructs time as a personal possession and one that recognizes time as belonging only to God—and to see the former as illusory and the latter as genuine. Second, they become increasingly adept at navigating these two arenas by reframing daily practice as ritual acts. In this way, the worldly notion of time as a limited commodity that can be wasted or maximized loses its hold, and the distinction between mundane and sacred time (ideally) falls away. And third, the postulants project this recasting of mundane activities back over the life course and reinterpret past events and experiences as articulations of their vocation. This then permits them to construct coherent narratives of their lives that validate their decisions to enter the convent as inevitable.

Successful formation, then, relies on resituating the story of self within this new temporal reference—not only in the way Ricoeur suggests, where the narrative identity mediates between immediate and continuous experiences of self, but in a way that rests on an particular understanding of time, action, and agency in a context in which, for the sisters, there *is* an ultimate truth.

CHAPTER 11

Changing the Subject

Transformations

The seven components of religious formation I observed in the convent—Brokenness, Belonging, Containment, Regimentation, Self-Critique, Surrender, and Re/collection—work together to slowly and subtly
shift a young woman's understanding and experience of herself and the
world around her. My argument has been that this proceeds through a
reframing of bodily experiences as coded articulations of spiritual and
moral states, with the embodied self becoming a particular avenue of
"knowing." I propose that religious formation for the Siervas is a model
of the self and its transformation that arranges elements of selfhood in
relation to each other and to the material body and facilitates a guided
"working through," within a particular system of meaning, of the metaphysical problematics involved. But how might we understand the persuasiveness of this model for the postulants themselves? How does it
elicit the kind of intense commitment required? How do these young
women internalize the congregation's program?

INSIDE OUT/OUTSIDE IN

Following the two dominant perspectives on subjectivity that I outlined
in chapter 1 (the "seat of being" and "illusion of interiority" approaches), one could try to understand subjective transformation in the
convent from either of two directions. The specific history of this order
links religious motivations to political and economic issues and

advocates a particular kind of femininity as an antidote to the evils of modernization. One might argue, then, that the convent, as a total institution, demands production of a certain kind of subjectivity in its "inmates" that is currently valued due to larger cultural pressures regarding globalization and social change.

Following this line of reasoning, the first stage in the process—Brokenness—might be understood as creating in these women the desire to engage in certain subjectifying practices that speak to these political and social concerns—that make them, in effect, willing and eager replicators of existing structures of power (Asad 1993; Foucault 1977, [1986] 1988). In the stage I call Belonging, we could say that, by becoming part of an elite, selective group with its own codes of conduct, rituals, and modes of dress, the postulants become convinced that their participation in these practices is, indeed, a privilege open to only a few, thereby redoubling their commitment to the program. The process of Containment, we might argue, works to define an imagined inner space that can be known, controlled, and molded (Butler [1990] 1999, 1993). Regimentation of the body in this view might constitute the habituation of the body to the specific practices of convent, over time instilling "proper" feelings and dispositions (Bourdieu 1990). Self-Critique, we might suggest, ensures an inward-looking process of confession and reform—an internalization of the structures of power so that one becomes one's own warden, so to speak (Foucault [1986] 1988). We could interpret the stage I call Surrender as persuading these women to make the ultimate capitulation, wresting out of the last vestiges of self and completely submitting to systems of regulation. And we could understand the guided telling of their life stories as a learned justification for their self-subjection. Each of these elements is communicated to the postulants through the language, symbols, and theology of the Catholic Church. It would not seem unreasonable to suggest, then, that once the postulants have subjected themselves to the congregation's program, the institution works to produce in them a particular set of self-understandings that reinforce the ideology of the church.

But not all young Mexican women join the convent, and only a small portion of those who do join this particular order. And, as I mentioned before, people leave. Some are successful and some aren't. Some are happy, some are bitter, others are indifferent or resigned, and still others are intensely fulfilled. Relying solely on this sort of top-down approach to understanding the persuasiveness of the convent program of formation, then, seems incomplete, as it doesn't allow for considering the differing ways individual people might engage the rules and regulations to which they are submitting themselves, how they might feel about the process, what kinds of personal or emotional issues might become activated, and so forth. And perhaps most importantly, it discourages us from taking seriously the deep passions and emotions the postulants themselves expressed about the experience.

Another way to approach the material is from the other side—with the starting point being the individual rather than the institution—asking: What kinds of women elect this process? What individual psychological needs are met by the convent that they can't get on the outside? As we've seen, there are indeed some interesting features about the women who chose this order (most notably, that of feeling characteristically "different" from other girls their age in terms of gender identity). And we have seen that, by the end of the process, these young women seem to come to an integrated understanding of their lives that "makes sense" of these previously troubling feelings within a new interpretive framework. From this perspective, the convent might offer these women a program of self-discovery that enables them to work through certain personal conflicts within the context of their religious training.

If we were to pursue this line of thought, we might understand the stage I call Brokenness as expressing the phenomenology of psychic distress. As a young woman seeks various ways of assuaging this feeling, she encounters a religious language that seems not only to take her distress as genuine but to reframe it as something exquisitely special—the call of God. We might likewise think about the stage I term Belonging as enabling such a young woman to bond with others in ways that may have been difficult for her in other circumstances. In the convent, she is accepted as she is, faults and all, while at the same time learning tools and motivations for radical self-improvement. By learning strategies of containment, this young woman might begin to experience a new way of ordering the world that encourages her to view her inner self as "true" and "real" and the outside world, where she felt so uncomfortable, as misguided and ultimately illusory. We might also imagine that regimenting the body could help her to feel an increasing sense of control over her situation as she works in concrete, tangible ways to align her will with that of God. Through self-critique, such a young woman might encounter a technique and a language for expressing her own self-hatred and doubt, as well as her own strong desire for wholeness. In the stage I call Surrender, she might achieve a powerful sense of release in admitting her own powerlessness in controlling the specifics of her life, in turning herself over to the care of a loving paternal God. And through renarrating her life in light of this new relationship with God, she might come to a degree of resolution or closure regarding her past difficulties.

But although the quest for spiritual connection with Christ in the convent is highly personal, it is not completely idiosyncratic. As we have seen, the process of religious formation is believed to adhere to certain fundamental rules. There are clearly articulated goals and objectives (dominating the passions and eradicating selfishness, for example) and accepted methods for achieving them (such as written self-monitoring and the use of penitences). Indeed, the *experience* of the call itself is believed to follow a rather predictable developmental path . And, for the sisters, however personalized the experience of religious vocation may be, it is nevertheless an experience of something they believe to be objectively *real,* something that is a manifestation of the laws governing the universe and all of human experience—God's plan for the salvation of the world. As the material extension of Christ's kingdom on earth, the church represents the correct interpretation of these universal truths and their structuring into religious practices. Though the experience of religious vocation is individual, it is an experience that is articulated and interpreted in and through existing institutional forms of meaning and representation. The subjective experience of vocation cannot be separated from the larger context within which vocation itself is conceptualized. Reading the persuasiveness of the formation process for new entrants as a wholly individual matter, then—like focusing solely on the institutional structuring of experience—is partial and inadequate.

To understand what happens in the convent—what claims these women in a fundamental way—we need to integrate these two domains of experience within a framework that takes both the cultural/institutional (top-down) and the individual/subjective (bottom-up) components of the process seriously, while at the same time thinking of them as being in continuous, dynamic interaction (rather than existing in static patterns of relationship). In thinking through this material, I have found the literature on the mechanisms of change in psychodynamic psychotherapy—specifically the self psychological and intersubjectivity schools—to be a promising starting point.[1]

COMING OUT OF THE PSYCHOANALYTIC CLOSET

In a class I teach called "Gender, Culture, and Madness," one of my main objectives is to open my students up to considering—just considering— that psychoanalytic theory might have something to offer for thinking about questions of gender and subjectivity. This is, I have found, a challenging task. To my students, most of whom were born in the late 1980s, *psychoanalysis* means "Freud," which means "misogyny," which means they don't want any part of it. The feminist critiques of Freud have been heard loud and clear by these students, and as deserved as such critiques may be, they have had the unfortunate effect of painting all things psychoanalytic with the same brush—and in an ugly puke green.

One of the first things I emphasize to my students is that psychoanalysis, as a theoretical paradigm and as a clinical practice, is far from homogeneous. Even during Freud's own lifetime there were disagreements about such fundamental founding concepts as the unconscious, the Oedipus complex, and the "nature" of femininity, leading to the emergence of different camps or theoretical offshoots of classical Freudian theory, like object relations theory (which, in turn, has produced many iterations of its own). In the sixty years since Freud's death, such cultural transformations as the sexual revolution, the civil rights movement, second-wave feminism, and the gay rights movement have profoundly shaped psychoanalytic thought and practice. Other elements, including the globalizing effects of the Internet and digital media, advances in biomedicine and neuroscience, and radical changes in the American health care system, have continually challenged psychoanalytically oriented scholars and clinicians to question their assumptions, revise their theories, expand their understandings of the human psyche,

---

1. I have chosen to focus on psychodynamic models of change (versus, for example, cognitive or behavior modification approaches) because, as I will detail throughout this chapter, attending to internal psychic processes *as well as* external manifestations of internal states is important for enabling us to think about what is going on in the convent. While cognitive and behavioral issues are of great importance in this process, I believe they can be adequately addressed within a psychodynamic framework. The reverse however, is rarely true, as cognitive/behavioral approaches generally tend to eschew any focused attention on subjective internal processes beyond the processes of information.

and rethink their approaches to clinical practice. Though there undoubtedly remains a "classical" (i.e., strictly Freudian) contingent within psychoanalysis, there are today dozens of psychoanalytic subfields, each with its own take on, for example, the workings of the unconscious, the structure of the self, the development of desire, and the origin of psychopathologies.

Under the broad heading of "psychoanalysis," then, one finds scholars and clinicians who can be identified (and often self-identify) as classical Freudians, neo-Freudians, Kleinians, Kohutians, relationalists, or intersubjectivists, just to name a few. What makes all these different approaches psychoanalytic is that they share the following three basic principles: (1) all assert the influence of unconscious forces on human feelings and behavior, (2) all conceptualize an idea of the qualities of motivating unconscious elements, and (3) all develop a treatment approach that follows the logic of their understanding of the unconscious. From this, we can say that the main issues that *distinguish* one psychoanalytic school of thought from another are (1) how the structure of psychic experience is conceptualized (as composed of id, ego, and superego; internalized object representations; selfobject constructs; or intersubjective processes, for example), (2) what the principal functions of psychic activity are understood to be (e.g., the repression of unacceptable desires, the struggle for autonomy, the drive for self-cohesion, the desire for intimacy and connection), and (3) the model of analytic treatment proposed.

One of the central problematics around which these various schools of psychoanalytic thought engage is the question of how, precisely, psychoanalysis "works." What is it about the therapist-patient relationship that produces change? How, in the words of Kohut, Goldberg, and Stepansky (1984), does analysis cure? This question of the mechanism of change in psychoanalysis, though certainly not new, was thrust into the center of psychoanalytic scholarship in the early 1970s with publication of Kohut's *The Analysis of the Self* (1971). In this book, Kohut (borrowing heavily from, and then expanding upon, Winnicott) challenged many of the fundamental assumptions of Freudian psychoanalysis regarding psychic development, psychopathology, and the role of the analyst in the therapeutic relationship. He proposed an alternative model of psychological development that, in turn, called for a new theory of how analysis works. Kohut's "psychology of the self" or "self psychology" has become, like object relations theory before it, a significant school of psychoanalytic thought within which various theoretical and methodological perspectives have emerged. I have found in the various schools of self psychology the tools I believe to be the most helpful in thinking through the material I gathered in the convent.

Before turning to the specifics of Kohut's model and how I have found it useful in approaching the process of religious formation in the convent, it is important to stress that the question of what constitutes a therapeutic relationship and the processes by which that relationship can facilitate profound and lasting change in its participants reaches well beyond psychoanalytic theory or practice per se. When Kohut and others ask how analysis cures, what they are really asking is how "selves" are made and unmade and the degree to which individuals can have a hand in this process. To use more contemporary theoretical parlance, the question of how psychoanalysis cures is precisely the question of how "subjectivity" comes into being through social interaction within particular, meaningful relationships. It assumes a fluidity and flexibility of the subject whereby the subject and her world may be slowly and subtly remade. And it requires an understanding of this fluid, changeable subject as historically *embodied,* in social relations, in structures of power, in interstices of desire, in a sexed, physical body. The question of how analysis cures is, at heart, a question of how to theorize an embodied, dynamic, social subject.

VIRTUAL SELVES AND THE ROLE OF EMPATHY: KOHUT'S SELF PSYCHOLOGY

In 1971 Kohut published *The Analysis of the Self,* now commonly recognized as the first major text in a new psychoanalytic movement called self psychology. In fact, the appellation *self psychology* covers a wide range of theories, including Kohut's psychology of the self, Lichtenberg's (1991) motivational systems theory, Stolorow's (1995) intersubjectivity theory, Bacal's (1994) relational self psychology, and Shane, Shane, and Gales's (1997) nonlinear developmental systems self psychology. What all of these approaches share—what makes them "self psychological"— is an understanding of psychological development as a *social process* that is dependent on an empathic environment within which the emerging self finds sustenance in the form of healthy interpersonal attachments.

Kohut departed from earlier psychoanalytic models in arguing that an unattuned early environment (rather than unresolved unconscious conflicts) arrests the development of the self and gives rise to psychiatric symptoms. In developing his notion of the importance of *empathy*, Kohut argued that experiencing empathic attunement with others in the form of idealizing, mirroring, and twinship/alter ego relationships is a fundamental human need—so fundamental, in fact, that it drives the emergence of the self.

Kohut (1977) maintained that in the initial stages of infancy the baby does not yet distinguish between "self" and "other" but experiences a blending of the two. He describes this as a prepsychological stage characterized by bodily needs and feelings of tension but without any kind of conscious awareness. What is central for Kohut, though, is that the infant is treated *as though it were a self* by its parents, caregivers, and others in the environment. The infant's environment responds to it as a "virtual self" (Summers 1994: 249) and thus provides the guiding principles for the process of self formation.[2] Elements (usually people) in the child's environment that become in this way fundamental to the establishment and maintenance of the self are termed *selfobjects* in Kohut's model.

The infant's virtual self can be generated (or not) and responded to (or not) by individuals in her environment in many ways that profoundly influence her development of self. Crucial to the appropriate fostering of the child's nascent self in Kohut's model is the notion of *empathic attunement*, through which caretakers selectively respond to different elements of the child's innate potentialities and different expressions of the child's selfobject needs. As the caretakers recognize and respond to different elements, the child's inclinations, desires, behaviors, and emotions are progressively channeled into a core, nuclear self.

Depending on the quality of the empathy (or lack thereof) in the caretaking environment, Kohut argued, different kinds of "virtual selves" will be recognized and responded to, and different kinds of core psychic structures will be laid down. If the parents respond to the child "as if" she is precious and smart and lovable (so that the child's selfobject needs are validated and met), this will facilitate the channeling of the parts of the child that elicited this response into lasting psychic

---

2. This is reminiscent of the Lacanian "mirror," whereby a child begins to perceive himself as bounded and singular through awareness of how he is perceived as such from the outside (Lacan, 1949, 1953). Unlike Kohut, however, Lacan understands the mirror process to be an alienating experience, rather than one facilitating connection and attunement (see Hamburg 1991). Other authors who have engaged the mirror dynamic include Haglund (1996), Pines (1984), Muller (1982), Laplanche and Pontalis (1973), Lemche (1998), and Lieberman (2000).

structures. Likewise, if the parents respond to the child as if she is an annoyance, an imposition, or an object of disdain (that is, her selfobject needs are denied and left unmet), this, too, will become part of her core psychological composition. At the same time as the parents are responding to the virtual self they have generated for the child, the child in turn expresses her selfobject needs for idealization (my dad is the best!), mirroring (tell me how you see me), and twinship (I'm a chip off the old block). In this way, the needs of the parents and the needs of the child are constantly in dynamic interaction as the child's developing self unfolds.

Kohut stressed that no family environment, no matter how wonderful, can meet all of a child's selfobject needs perfectly all of the time. There are, Kohut says, inevitable disruptions. People in the child's life cannot respond empathically (with just enough—but not too much—attunement and involvement) all the time. Most disruptions are minor and of little consequence in the long run. If, however, the child's needs for empathic attunement are repeatedly rejected or overrun, or if the rejection or denial of these needs is particularly virulent, the child experiences trauma. Kohut understands trauma, then, as a psychoeconomic issue resting on the intensity of the affect involved rather than on the simple content of the event. When trauma occurs, selfobject needs remain "archaic" in the sense of having fundamental significance for the experience and functioning of the self.[3]

The Transforming Work of Analysis

Following from this formulation, Kohut's understanding of the therapeutic process involves remobilizing the client's archaic selfobject needs within the therapy relationship. The core feature of Kohut's idea of "working through" in the analytic process is what he calls "optimal frustration," a term that has been hotly debated in post-Kohutian self psychological theory (e.g., Bacal 1985, 1998; Lindon 1994; Shane and Shane 1996; Fosshage 1997; Terman 1998; MacIsaac 1996).

The job of the therapist in Kohut's model is to be as empathically attuned to the patient as possible: that is, to try to align herself

---

3. Kohut maintained that we continue to have selfobject needs throughout our lives—we never completely stop needing recognition and approval and affirmation of our worth. The difference, however, is that the healthy individual may be enhanced or strengthened by selfobject relationships, whereas the traumatized individual actually *needs* the selfobjects to experience him- or herself as a whole person.

emotionally and experientially with the patient so as to understand from the patient's perspective what he feels and what he needs, and in what degree of intensity. The therapist then endeavors to be available to the client in this capacity, with the hope that she can provide a healthy selfobject function for him.[4]

Inevitably, however, things happen in the therapeutic relationship that will disrupt the selfobject transferences. Just like the parental figures in childhood, the therapist cannot possibly be 100 percent empathically attuned 100 percent of the time, no matter how hard she may try. Even if she could manage this, mundane demands of life can cause disruptions in the therapeutic relationship (the therapist goes on vacation, she is sick, she has to change the appointment time) that can be *experienced* by the client as an empathic break. These "frustrations," Kohut maintains, are part and parcel of all human relationships and cannot be completely avoided. In this, the therapeutic relationship is no different from any other. What *is* different about the therapeutic relationship, however, is what happens *after* the frustration—the loss of empathic connection—has occurred.

We will remember that Kohut locates the derailment of the self in the traumatic frustration of selfobject needs in childhood. In contrast to this, the therapeutic relationship enables the analyst and client to repair the breach by recognizing, containing, and interpreting the disruption in the relationship in ways that restore the client's feeling of being genuinely seen and acknowledged by the therapist, thereby reestablishing the empathic bond. The disrupted bond between client and therapist creates for the client a fragmented state, which in turn creates the opportunity for working through. Working through reestablishes the bond between the client and analyst, restoring the feeling of wholeness for the client. It is this feature—the reforging of the empathic connection through a working through of the empathic break—that makes the frustration in the therapeutic relationship "optimal" rather than "traumatic." Whether a frustration is optimal can be determined only in retrospect, depending on whether the empathic bond is successfully

---

4. According to Kohut, one cannot *choose* to become a selfobject for someone else. By definition, a selfobject is experienced as part of the self and provides self functions that the self cannot. The therapist can make herself available to the client by being empathically attuned to him, but she cannot dictate when or how he might engage her as a selfobject.

restored. Over time, Kohut proposed, these inevitable empathic breaks, coupled with processes of working through and the reestablishment of the empathic connection, enable the client to internalize a nontraumatic experience of his selfobject needs (a dynamic that Kohut, Goldberg, and Stepansky [1984] call "transmuting internalizations"), allowing him to relinquish the archaic versions of these needs and restoring the self to a healthy developmental path.

To summarize Kohut's model in somewhat less psychological parlance, we can say that he understands the development of the self to be an interpersonal, intersubjective process. In and through the responses of important people in a child's environment—they ways they act toward her "as if" she is a certain kind of self—the child is able to understand *herself* as existing in the world in particular ways. Sometimes this involves incorporating what others reflect back to her as part of her own understanding of herself (Daddy always tells me I'm spoiled, so I guess I must be). At other times, this involves the acute experience of a disconnect between the virtual self and the experienced self (Mom thinks I'm the sweetest boy in the world, but I know I'm not).

This disconnect, in my reading of Kohut, can lead in one of three directions. Either (1) the parent becomes more empathically attuned to the child's experienced self and begins to reflect back a virtual self that is more consistent with the child's experience (the parent more accurately recognizes the child); (2) the child desires to *become* the sort of self the parent acts *as if* he is, so he endeavors to bring his experienced self in line with the virtual self (the child struggles to make himself recognizable to the parent, or rather to make himself into the virtual self whom the parent already sees); or (3) a negotiation ensues in which both parent and child work to alter their perceptions and their experiences, gradually moving toward a place where both can genuinely recognize—and be recognized *by*—the other.

Because the child needs the responses of others to reflect back to her who she is *in their perceptions of her* (her virtual self), these people provide a fundamental function in the constitution and maintenance of her self. In a healthy, empathic environment, continual reflection back to the child of *who she is* that is more or less consistent with *who she experiences herself to be* enables her, over time, to develop a sense of self that is less crucially dependent on others for this confirmation. In an unempathic environment—one in which the reflection is nonexistent or systematically inconsistent with her own experiences—the child is unable to develop a cohesive sense of self and remains stuck in the process of seeking confirmation of her existence in the reflections of others.[5]

Rethinking the Mechanisms of Change: Post-Kohutian Formations

In the thirty years since Kohut first elaborated his understanding of self-object needs and the role of the therapist in the restoration of the self to a healthy trajectory of development, a number of theorists have grappled with his model of psychoanalytic transformation. Some (like Lindon 1994) have questioned the necessity of "frustration" in the analytic relationship, preferring instead to talk about "optimal provision." Bacal (1998), Terman (1998), and others (e.g., Teicholz 1996; Doctors 1996) advocate instead an analytic attitude of "optimal responsiveness," which can entail both frustration and provision. Shane and Shane (1996) recommend that the analyst practice "optimal restraint" in his emotional responsiveness to the client. And Fosshage (1997) proposes the idea of "facilitating responsiveness" as the appropriate therapeutic technique. The concern in all these works is how to best manage the therapeutic relationship in order to facilitate the mobilization of deeply held selfobject needs.

Others have concerned themselves not so much with the question of frustration or provision as with the question of psychological structure itself. The debate here is whether, through psychoanalytic psychotherapy, a new "primary" (i.e., core, foundational) psychological structure is laid down (e.g., Stern's [1985] RIGs), or whether, as Kohut, Goldberg, and Stepansky (1984) argued, submerged or atrophied existing structures are strengthened and reconfigured into "compensatory structures," which can come to function as fundamental elements of the self. Here, I find Tolpin's (1997) understanding of structure as "enduring function" to be particularly useful. If we rethink structure not as a specific, inert, construction (something that can "broken," "missing," or "intact") but as a sort of mechanism through which psychic processes

---

5. This is not to say that Kohut places a primacy on independence or that he views dependence on others as somehow indicative of pathology. Far from it. In talking about *selfobjects,* Kohut is exploring one particular category of interpersonal relationships that have fundamental consequences for the development of the self and the ability to interact in healthy ways with others. In suggesting that selfobject needs can lead to psychic difficulties, then, Kohut is saying, not that needing selfobjects is in and of itself somehow bad, but that *early, unmet* selfobject needs can inhibit the client's full participation in the interpersonal, relational domain.

are ordered and given meaning, this would suggest that the work of analysis involves not so much generating new psychic elements as creatively regrouping existing strengths into new configurations. From this angle, we can think of analysis as, effectively, both remobilizing old structures and creating new ones (the newly orchestrated configurations that provide enduring functions), with the work of the analyst being facilitation of the client's ability to marshal existing resources in new ways.[6] I believe this to be the primary transformational element of religious formation in the convent.

Gender and the Body in Psychoanalytic Theories of Change

Oddly, given the traditional psychoanalytic concern with gender, sexuality, and desire, these current theoretical debates about the mechanisms of psychoanalytic transformations have been largely silent on questions of gender and the body. Although much attention has been given in some recent psychoanalytic works to reconsidering the development of gendered selves (e.g., Alpert 1986; Flax 1990; Chodorow 1991; Lax 1997; van Mens-Verhulst, Schreurs, and Woertman 1993) and newly envisioning processes of gendering within post–drive theory psychoanalytic perspectives on the body (e.g., Grosz 1994; Meissner 1998; Dimen 1996; Lieberman 2000) and the way gender informs the therapeutic relationship (Dimen 2002; Lukton 1992; Guarton 1996; Thomas 2003; Tholfsen 2000; Gould 1995; Marcus 1993; Kulish and Mayman 1993; Menaker 1995), the contemporary literature dealing with questions of *how analysis cures* and the literature grappling with *how gendered subjects come into being* tend not to engage with each other in any significant, sustained way. This is somewhat surprising, given that models of how analysis works are necessarily contingent upon models of the psyche and its vicissitudes. Nevertheless, theoretical explorations into how the psyche is formed and shaped in relation to the gendered body and clinical questions of how analysis transforms that psyche have remained remarkably distinct in the psychoanalytic literature.

If it seems reasonable to propose, as I have suggested, that models of psychological change are necessarily also models of psychological

6. Still others have questioned Kohut's understanding of "the self" (e.g., Stolorow, Brandchaft, and Atwood 1988; Goldberg 1990), arguing for a radically intersubjective notion of self that, in turn, alters the way both the therapeutic relationship and the client's experiential transformations in analysis are understood.

structures and dynamics—that is, that models of change are also models of the "self"—then it follows that what constitutes that model of the self will profoundly influence how the mechanism of change is theorized. The problem is that the understanding of the "self" upon which such theories of change are predicated—whether or not this contingency is explicitly acknowledged—is an abstracted, disembodied, degendered one.

Here we begin to run up against some difficulties. De Lauretis (1987) observes that theories of the self that claim to be gender-neutral *are not* and *cannot* be so. There is no such thing as "a" self. Selves are always embodied and therefore always gendered (and classed, raced, historicized, etc.). This makes abstract notions of the self particularly dangerous: although they may appear to counter (or at least avoid) traditional gender assumptions, they may instead inadvertently reinscribe them in more covert ways. And if processes of gendering are, as psychoanalytic theories of all stripes have maintained, some of the most fundamental self processes (processes through which selves come into being), then this lack of engagement with questions of gender and the body in the theories of psychoanalytic change reveals a significant problem in the current literature.

In other words, though processes of gendered subjectification and processes of transformations within the psychoanalytic encounter have both come to the forefront of psychoanalytic thought in the past few decades, the specific relationships between the two have been significantly undertheorized. If the self is always already gendered, always already embodied, then is not the "restoration of the self" in the analytic encounter necessarily a gendered, embodied process? And must we not then actively engage with the ways in which remaking the self is always, at least to some extent, remaking the gendered, embodied self? These kinds of questions have not yet been adequately engaged.

The notable exception to this is, perhaps, Benjamin's work on gender and intersubjectivity (1988, 1995, 1998).[7] Benjamin outlines the ways in which the very existence of our own subjectivity is fundamentally dependent on our relationship with others who are similar to, yet distinct from, us. She traces this dynamic back to the mother-child relationship, which she understands to be predicated on the child's perception of the mother as an independent locus of agency. In this, she

7. Though see also Lukton (1992).

departs significantly from more traditional psychoanalytic theories of development that tend to theorize the mother as an object for the child and nothing else (that is, not a subject in her own right). Benjamin stresses that, for a child to grow and develop a sense of his self as distinct from the rest of his surroundings, he needs the specific responses of his mother (and others) as an independent center of awareness and action. From the earliest stages of psychological development, we are fundamentally dependent on the difference of the other—the other's existence as a separate locus of experience—because we need the other to see and respond to us in order to confirm our existence. If there is no other, then there is no one outside me to see me, which means I do not exist.

Ideally, Benjamin argues, a person becomes able to be fully self-absorbed or fully receptive to the other: that is, she is able to be alone *or* to be with an other without experiencing either as a threat to her self's integrity. When a negative cycle of recognition is established, however, a person feels that aloneness is possible only by obliterating the other or that attunement is possible only by surrendering to the other.

In important ways, then, Benjamin's view of the emergence of the self is very similar to Kohut's. Both insist on the need for interpersonal engagement and "reflecting back" in order for the self to develop, and both locate the genesis of psychiatric difficulties in the breakdown of this process. But whereas Kohut maintains that this interpersonal dynamic necessitates the taking of the other as a selfobject, Benjamin (in line with the two-person models of the intersubjectivists) insists on a more complex understanding of this process. We certainly *can* take others as objects, Benjamin notes. But psychological health is to be found in recognizing and staying within the tension of understanding the other *as a subject*. This tension is what Benjamin calls *mutual recognition*.

The tension of mutual recognition, Benjamin argues, inevitably breaks down. Following Hegel's analysis of the master-slave relationship, Benjamin explores the ways in which the breakdown of mutual recognition comes about, returning the self to a more archaic binary formulation of subject-object, which she proposes underpins relationships of domination. It is the work of psychoanalysis, she suggests, to facilitate the reestablishment of the client's capacity for mutual recognition, an ability to withstand the tension of mutuality without experiencing it as an existential threat to the self.

Gender enters this situation in a number of ways, most specifically in the development of the capacity for recognition of the other in the first place. Benjamin explores the cultural mandates stylizing motherhood as the surrender of any claims to an independent subjectivity and argues that this inhibits the child's ability to recognize others as subjects. This can go one of two ways, Benjamin says. In the desperate quest to find the other, the child may push and push against the limits he encounters in the hopes of provoking a definitive response, a confirmation of the other's existence and, as a result, of his own. In other cases, the child may experience the other's subjectivity as so overwhelming that her only possibility for meeting and being seen by the other is to surrender completely, to allow herself to be, in effect, absorbed by the other. Benjamin suggests that these two responses to the fundamental human need for recognition are highly gendered, with boys (generally) learning that asserting the self is the path to recognition and girls (perhaps following their mother's example) learning that, in order to be seen, they must transform themselves into what the other needs. In this sense, we might read Benjamin as arguing that the struggle of subjectivity is an inherently gendered process, involving the continued cycling of the child's need to recognize and be recognized by the other, the experience of mutual recognition, and the breakdown of this bond in the context of gendered relationships of power.

I find Benjamin's work to be both insightful and creative. I particularly appreciate her personal intellectual stance of resisting complementarities (structures involving an either/or option where the two sides are both conceptually opposed to and dependent upon the other, such as self/other, subject/object, patient/analyst) and pushing readers to remain within the tensions of these seemingly paradoxical relationships. And I have found her thinking on issues of recognition to be extraordinarily helpful in thinking through how transformation proceeds in the convent. But while Benjamin's work is centrally concerned with questions of gender, and she persuasively outlines the ways in which gendered development of the subject inflects the capacity (or lack thereof) for mutual recognition, she does not explicitly tackle the psychoanalytic process as one of remaking the gendered subject. This may be implicit in her analysis (she does write, for example, about the role of the analyst as "Angel" or recognizing other and the differences in this dynamic if the analyst is perceived as paternal or maternal), but she does not explore the specific ways that change in psychoanalytic psychotherapy is itself a gendered process. In this regard, her work, though useful in many ways, does not address the problem I outlined above: namely, theorizing change in conjunction with theorizing the gendered subject within the psychoanalytic process.

This may be due, in part, to the nature of the data upon which Benjamin's and most other theories of both psychoanalytic change and psychological processes of gendering are developed—material gathered in clinical interactions. Whether or not a theorist draws on his or her own clinical data in the formulation of a theory, the analytic interaction is acknowledged in psychoanalytic circles as the legitimate domain in which relevant theory-building information is gathered and other kinds of meanings (e.g., transference and countertransference issues) are generated. But the analytic relationship is, by nature, highly artificial and contrived. Appointment times are set, fees are paid. The explicit purpose for both people to even be engaging in the interaction is to heal a struggling "self." Generally speaking, a client's body remains inert (sitting or lying down), freeing his mind to more freely interact with that of the therapist (or the client's imagination of the therapist's mind). Thus the analytic situation facilitates a highly stylized and abstracted presentation of, and interaction among, "selves." In doing so, it also encourages (and perhaps even requires) the transposition of visceral, sensual, embodied experiences of the client (and the therapist) into verbal language, reinforcing the conceptual and experiential distance between the body and the self (Lieberman 2000). It is not, then, entirely inconsistent with the analytic approach that theories of change within the clinical interaction largely ignore questions of gender and the body or that psychoanalytic theories of gendering have had little to say about the mechanisms of analytic transformation. The two have largely been held to be separate domains of the discipline.

Rethinking the Process of Transformation

My own approach to understanding what happens in the convent (how the convent program "heals" its subjects) attempts to bring together these two domains—the mechanisms of psychoanalytic transformation and the intersubjective processes of gendering—by understanding this process as a project of regendering the embodied subject. In building this model, I draw on the following: (1) self psychological understandings of the role of empathic response to the "virtual self" in subjective development, (2) an understanding of the "work" of analysis as the consolidation of psychic structure as enduring function, and (3) Benjamin's formulation of the dynamics of recognition.

I follow Kohut in understanding the development of the self to be a process in which people in the child's environment respond to her "as if" she were a certain kind of self, a response that shapes (but does not determine) her subjective orientation to the world. As the child expresses more and more of her emerging self, her parents' empathic attunement should enable them to reframe this "virtual self," bringing it more in line (selectively) with the child's self-presentation. In turn, the child learns which elements of her self are acceptable and which are not. There is a struggle for recognition (in Benjamin's terms) on both sides: the parents (ideally) struggle to recognize and respond empathically to the child's unique potentialities, and the child struggles to make herself recognizable to her parents. It is a constant negotiation between the virtual self through which the parents view and respond to the child and the experiential self with which the child meets and experiences the world. Ideally, this negotiation eventually leads both sides to a comfortable middle ground in which parental perceptions and the child's subjective experience are more or less consistent with one another. This enables the child to develop a sense of authenticity and confidence in her own experiences of the world.

Along the way, however, these two elements (the virtual self and the experiential self) will sometimes come into conflict. I again follow Kohut in understanding such disruptions or misrecognitions to be part of "normal" development. When such misrecognitions are profound or sustained, however, the child can experience what I will call a *traumatic misrecognition*, whereby her very existence comes to be in doubt. Traumatic misrecognition, in other words, generates an existential crisis for the child.

I suggest that the work of the therapeutic relationship involves the therapist's *empathic recognition of a new virtual self in response to the client's particular needs* and the client's gradual incorporation of this new virtual self. This is a process of negotiation. It is by no means a wholesale acceptance by the client of what the therapist chooses to reflect back to her, nor is it an uncritical endorsement by the therapist of what the client presents. There is no singular "healthy self" to which all clients should be molded. The virtual self-in-process is exactly that—a process that unfolds within the particular dynamics of the therapeutic relationship involved and that is continually undergoing revision from both sides. Successful therapy, in my view, is contingent on the client's coming to "claim" the new virtual self in a fundamental way in terms of how she understands herself to exist as a self in the world, in relation to other selves.

In my understanding, this always involves an altered relationship to the body. I agree with Merleau-Ponty (1962, 1963, 1964) that in and through our bodies we experience who we are and encounter other embodied "selves," who in turn encounter us through their own bodies. I also follow Meissner (1998) in understanding the involvement of both the analyst and the client in the therapeutic process as inherently bodily. I propose that the body (its sensations, desires, discomforts, symptoms) can serve as a sort of barometer of the degree of correspondence between the virtual self (reflected in the therapist's empathic attunement) and the experiential self. When something "feels wrong" in therapy, or when somatic symptoms or unhealthy behaviors emerge or intensify, this is an indication of a misalignment of the virtual and experiential selves, a *mis*recognition (in Benjamin's terms) between the therapist and the client (what Kohut would call an empathic break). Reading Benjamin and Kohut through Merleau-Ponty and Meissner, then, I suggest that physical sensations (a knot in the stomach, an ache in the chest, the quickening of the heart, a sense of release) often evoked as a result of therapeutic work are not simply somatizations of somehow more "authentic" (abstract) emotions; rather, they are fundamental components in the client's embodied transformation and should hold a central place in the therapeutic process.

I maintain that because the self is always embodied it is also always gendered. Like the experiential self, the virtual self—the "as if" self the therapist reflects back to the client—will always be a gendered self, whether or not these gendered aspects are centrally highlighted in the process of therapy. Indeed, the degree to which the question of gendering makes its way into the manifest discourse of the therapeutic situation will differ, depending on what brought the client into therapy, the particular style and concerns of the therapist, the level of trust developed, and the like. Nevertheless, I suggest that it is always a factor in the process. In some cases the gendered dimensions of the experiential and virtual selves will take center stage. When this happens, I propose that questions of gender can come to organize other elements of the transformational process.[8]

8. Consider, for example, Dora's experience with Freud. For an excellent collection of essays considering different gendered aspects of this case, see Bernheimer and Kahane (1985).

My model of the therapeutic process, then, is as follows. The client comes to the therapist in some kind of psychic distress. Before any therapeutic work can be done, the client and therapist must first forge a solid, trusting relationship based on the therapist's sustained, empathic attunement to the client's needs. Such a relationship enables the client to focus her attention, to become more aware of her own psychological processes and emotions. Specifically, it helps the client to more clearly see the "self" with which she meets and interacts with the world. Often this clarity comes in response to the therapeutic relationship—either the client feels empathically validated, or she feels misrecognized by the therapist. In the early stages of the therapy, the therapist does not interpret or challenge the client's understandings but provides a containing function, allowing the client, as it were, to "try on" different ways of being and discover how it feels to "sit with" these different self forms. As the therapeutic relationship develops, the therapist slowly begins to respond selectively (but still empathically) to the client's enactments of these different ways of being, guiding her toward particular expressions that the client may or may not recognize as consistent with her own experiences.

The real work of the therapy comes, however, in the therapist's inevitable misrecognition of the client and the subsequent working through of this empathic break. Here the client experiences a sort of existential crisis that can involve such emotional responses as rage (How dare you not see me!), pain (I'm not worth seeing), guilt (I should have made myself more visible), or desperation (Please, please see me!). The client may respond to this misrecognition in one of the three ways I described above: (1) she may reject the therapist's construction outright, requiring the therapist to bring his interpretations more in line with her present experience; (2) she may struggle to inhabit the self the therapist reflects back to her, in order to make herself recognizable to him; or (3) she and the therapist may work together toward a new place, both edging closer to the other. This is a dialectical process in which such ruptures and repairs happen again and again, but with a directional movement toward mutual recognition. Figure 5 illustrates this process graphically.

Over time, with repeated misrecognitions and reaffirmations, the process of misrecognition becomes less traumatic, and the client develops enduring strategies for *self*-recognition. In other words, as the client becomes increasingly skilled at determining the fit (or not) of the

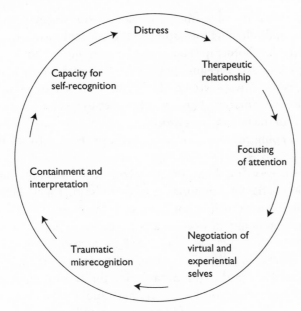

FIGURE 5. The therapeutic process

therapeutic virtual self with her experiential self, the contours of her self become more clearly articulated.

THE PSYCHODYNAMICS OF RELIGIOUS FORMATION

This is also, with some important modifications, what happens in the convent. I suggest that the crux of subjective transformation for the nuns is a dynamic of misrecognition and recognition similar to what I have described above, but with a twist. In psychotherapy, the primary onus is on the therapist to adequately recognize the client, thereby helping her, over time, to develop the capacity for self-recognition. In the convent, something slightly different happens. There, the onus is on the *new nun* to *adequately recognize God* and to *make herself recognizable to Him* in a particular way. The goal, then, is not so much self-recognition in the psychodynamic sense as learning to *see oneself through God's eyes*—that is, recognizing oneself by seeing oneself as a reflection of the glory of God.

Despite this difference, the processes of transformation in psychotherapy and religious formation in the convent have many parallels.[9] Like the psychotherapy client, a girl comes into the convent with a sense of restlessness, a feeling that her life is somehow off track, that something is definitively wrong. She begins a process of introspection and self-discovery that she hopes will lead her to greater calm and contentment. And she initiates this process by seeking out others who know what she is going through and have, perhaps, been through it themselves.

One of the very first things the postulants learn when they enter the congregation is the vital importance of establishing strong bonds with the community, with their cohort, and with the mistress of postulants. Within this community of women, a new nun begins a process of identification with others who are "like her," a provisional recognition of herself as reflected in others. The postulants learn to think of each other and the other nuns in the convent as going through the same process, experiencing the same kinds of fears and doubts and desires. They become progressively more able to empathically identify with one another and to appreciate others' empathic attunement to them. As they continue their training, these relationships will bear the weight of their self-explorations. At the same time, this process is closely monitored and mirrored back to the postulants by the mistress of postulants (and, to a lesser degree, by the other older nuns) through such techniques as direct critique or praise, gentle guidance, group exercises, private consultation, didactic instruction, and, when necessary, the imposition of penitences. To ensure that this mirroring is consistent and appropriate and that it works to facilitate rather than hinder the process, the postulants are prohibited from forming close ties with (i.e., seeking recognition from) women in other levels of formation.

The selective structuring of different interior/exterior positionings within the convent (convent/world; postulant/professed sister; soul/body) helps the new nun to delineate a split within her self—between her false (temporal) self and her true (eternal) soul—and to problematize the relationship between them. Here, the convent program begins to present to the new nun a "virtual self"—it treats her *as if* she were part of the sacred world inside the convent, *as if* she were

---

9. Notable contemporary works on the psychological dimensions of religious experience and spiritual transformation include Jones (1996), Meissner (1987, 1999), and Rector (1996, 2000, 2001).

already a Sierva. In doing so, it also highlights the disjunctions between this virtual self and the new nun's own experiential self. We can think of this process as generating different *vectors of recognition,* shaping the domains within which different selves may be seen and affirmed, as well as those iterations of self that are disavowed or excluded.

Importantly, however, the distinction between the virtual self and the experiential self is *not* congruent with the distinction between the temporal and eternal selves, although the postulants themselves often make this misassociation in the beginning. The postulants learn over time that the virtual self—the "as if" self—is more complex than this and involves a recalibration of temporal (bodied) and nonbodied experiences rather than a collapsing of one into the other.

As a postulant becomes more regimented in her daily practice, she becomes increasingly adept at sensing how her temporal, bodied experience both reveals and affects the state of her nonbodied soul. At the same time, she learns that the management of this relationship is a central factor in the process of transformation itself—it is the way she makes herself "visible" to God as His bride. She begins to become attuned to her bodily sensations in a new way and to interpret them as communications from God that affirm her successes or signal her failures and guide her toward the appropriate path. In this sense, her body becomes the portal of recognition, the instrument through which she experiences *God* experiencing *her.*

As she becomes more attuned to these dynamics, the new nun (with some coaxing by the older sisters) eventually confronts the notion that, despite what she may have believed, she has, in fact, never actually *known* God in any significant sense and, consequently, has never adequately made herself *known to Him* in her fullest potential. Since God is a perfect being, the responsibility for this radical, traumatic misrecognition rests with the woman herself. In the drive to remedy this situation, to affirm God's presence and to make herself known to Him, she may redouble her efforts through mastering daily routines or exceeding the regular demands of prayer. But this, the sisters teach, is yet another misrecognition of who God is and what He wants. In fact, the harder a new nun tries to insist on a new bond with God, the more elusive it becomes.

The sisters maintain that this break with God can be remedied, but only through the most radical affirmation of God's being: complete surrender of the self to God. This does not mean that the self disappears; rather, it means that one learns to read the self *through* God. In genuinely recognizing God for the first time, the new nun comes to finally recognize herself, to see herself with God's eyes.

This new understanding of self and God is then reframed through the recounting of vocation narratives, where the postulants learn to speak in a language of recognition and misrecognition in the telling of their stories. Here the virtual self and the experiential self become integrated as a postulant learns to understand her life as the progressive unfolding of a mutual recognition between herself and God, played out through a developing relationship between her temporal (bodied) self and eternal (nonbodied) soul. Figure 6 illustrates these parallels between the processes of psychotherapy and religious formation in the convent.

The process of religious formation is far from over after the first year—indeed, it is just beginning. As the postulants progress in their training, they will confront these same issues again and again. They will struggle with periods of disillusionment, difficulties in prayer, weaknesses of the flesh. In some ways, as Mother Miriam explained it to me, the postulants are like alcoholics who have become sober for the first time. "But it certainly won't be the *last* time they have to struggle through this," she said. "Just like the alcoholic, we all relapse. It's part of being human. The point is to keep working, to keep trying to find God, even through the difficult times. *Especially* through the difficult times. This is how we become sanctified."

REGENDERING IN THE CONVENT

I argued above that theories of psychological change are also theories of embodied selves, which means they are also theories of *gendered* selves. I have also suggested that, in some cases, gender can become foregrounded in the transformational process as an organizing frame through which other elements of the process are understood. This is what happens in the convent. The postulants explicitly assert that the process of religious formation is about (re)learning gender, coming to inhabit a particular kind of femininity that does not fit comfortably in the outside world.

New Women for a New Millennium

The past twenty years have seen dramatic changes in gender relations in Mexico, with more women than ever attaining high levels of education, working in the formal sector, and participating in political

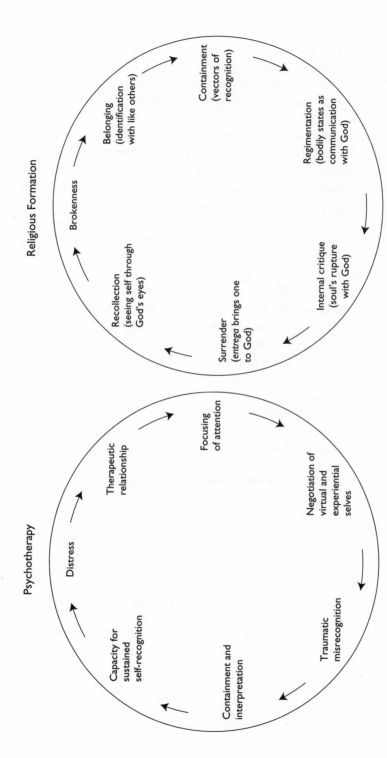

Psychotherapy

Distress

Therapeutic relationship

Focusing of attention

Negotiation of virtual and experiential selves

Traumatic misrecognition

Containment and interpretation

Capacity for sustained self-recognition

Religious Formation

Brokenness

Belonging (identification with like others)

Containment (vectors of recognition)

Regimentation (bodily states as communication with God)

Internal critique (soul's rupture with God)

Surrender (*entrega* brings one to God)

Recollection (seeing self through God's eyes)

FIGURE 6. The therapeutic process and the dynamics of religious formation

movements.[10] At the same time, birth rates have dropped, shaking up the traditional linkage between womanhood and motherhood. The postulants, all of whom came of age during this transition in gender roles, talked frequently about these changes, noting how different things were for them than for their mothers and grandmothers at their age.

Each of the postulants had dramatic stories to tell that she had heard from female relatives who had run away from home to avoid undesirable marriages or had been beaten by their husbands for studying or wanting to work outside the home. Uniformly, the postulants talked about how thankful they were that things had changed, that they would not be married off without their consent, that they could instead go to school and pursue a career (although many also had stories to tell of their own experiences with violent and possessive boyfriends, overprotective fathers, and sexually harassing teachers).

But they also all talked about something else—the fine line women had to walk between being strong and independent and being "feminist," a word that had particular meaning for them. A "feminist," in their view, was, as the mother general put it, "a woman who wants to be just like a man." When I asked the postulants individually in interviews to tell me about feminism, Carlota put it to me this way: "Feminism is an extreme. And it's an illusion. It tells women that, in order to be good and valuable, they have to be like men. They have to dress like men, work like men, act like men. It takes away their femininity. It makes them egotistical and individualistic. They don't want to be affectionate anymore, so they get cold and reserved. And it's the family who suffer. No. Feminism isn't really feminism at all. It's the masculinization of women." Surella gave a similar answer. "I don't agree with feminism," she told me.

> These days you see many women who want to be like men, but when women try to be like men, they only hurt themselves. Many women today have their careers and all that. And that's fine. Women should want to improve themselves. But look, at no time should a woman stop being the *ama de casa* (housewife), being a mother, caring for her children, her husband. . . . No. . . . It's great for a woman to get ahead, to better herself, no? But never, never, should she want to be equal to a man. She should stay in her place.

10. For more on the changing situation of women in Mexico in the past few decades and its antecedents, see Gutmann (1996), Lamas (1997), Bedolla Miranda (1989), Lau Jaiven (1987), Macías (1982), and Nuñez Vera et al. (1995).

At this point I asked Surella if she thought we should go back to more "traditional" relationships between women and men. "No, no," she said quickly.

> I don't agree with the idea that women should be submissive to men, the idea of machismo and all that, where the man tells the woman, "Don't move from here." No. I think both women and men should have their freedom, but always conserving their identities—the man as head of the house, the woman as mother and *ama de casa*. . . . I feel that the fact that today women are getting involved in politics and things, they're neglecting their homes—and these kinds of women don't give the affection they should to their children and their families. And if in the family, in the children, is the future of Mexico, of the country, where will we be, you know?

Surella's comments are representative of the sentiments each of the postulants expressed to me in our interviews.

The postulants often talked about this tension between being a traditional woman and a modern feminist in terms of national and cultural differences, referencing a larger popular political debate regarding the crumbling of traditional Mexican values under the pressures of U.S. cultural imperialism. In this discourse, which explicitly compares the current situation in Mexico to that of the prerevolutionary period, the United States is seen as socially cold, terrifyingly violent, religiously depraved, and morally ill. The core cause of this is seen to be the breakdown of the family, resulting directly from the women's liberation movement—or, as the nuns would put it, "women trying to be men." Mexico's emulation of the United States in terms of economic and social policy, and the pervasive infatuation with American culture, threaten what many in Mexico see as the core of their national identity as they race along the path of modernization, sparking a profound ambivalence about these changes.

This gendered articulation of the cultural tension between "American modernity" and "Mexican tradition" was central to the way the postulants talked about their vocations and their life choices as young Mexican women. As Pipa expressed it to me,

> If *la mujer* applied herself to what's assigned to her, there wouldn't be so many problems here in Mexico. This "liberation of *la mujer*" has so many consequences! If women try to be like men—have careers and everything—everything breaks down and falls apart. Women should be *women*, and leave men to be men. . . . *La mujer* should be what she's *supposed* to be—*ama de casa*, caretaker of the family. If she did, maybe we'd be able to stand up to the U.S. and say, "No! *This* is what we believe! *These* are our values!" and Mexico wouldn't have so many problems.

This might seem to be an unusual statement coming from a woman who herself has decided to leave her home and give up the possibility of having children in pursuit of what might be viewed as professional goals. And this tension says something compelling about the double bind these women are experiencing. Most of the postulants are smart, capable, active women who want more from life than a constant string of pregnancies, an alcoholic and abusive husband, and a career in home-making—several described their images of marriage to me in almost these exact words. But going to the university and pursuing a career in medicine, for example, makes them guilty participants in the decline of Catholic and family values that are seen to be so important in distinguishing Mexico from the corrupt United States and in some capacity diminishes the degree to which they are fulfilling their roles as women as they understand them.

In interviews toward the end of my stay, I asked each of the postulants how she thought they, as Siervas, could mediate these positions. "Well, for example," Surella told me,

> we may be in a situation where there's a girl who has become sexually active, promiscuous. It's up to us to help her, to help her see that she doesn't have to be that way, that she has more value than that. . . . I think that since the moment in which the Lord has chosen us, He has chosen us for something specific. We can, with this faith He's giving us, do so much—so much!—as nuns and, more than anything, as His chosen brides. I think our prayers, our supplications, our sacrifices, our *entrega* really do reach Him. And I believe that this can change the mentality of the young people who are falling into all these vices.

Clara gave a similar answer. "Our testimony, more than anything, is what counts, no?" she told me one day in an interview.

> Because our vows—our vows have already begun, no? Poverty contradicts power, and many times out there in the world people search relentlessly for power, and they crush whoever is in their way. They kill you. . . . So our testimony comes through poverty, including poverty of the habit. Outside, everyone is preoccupied with style, and if you're not in style people look at you strangely. I mean, when you hang out with a clique, you have to dress like them, right? But here, well, we live in poverty with the habit, no? And as they say, if you don't change or if you only have one to wear, you won't even notice, no? And then there's chastity. This is love, but it is really *true* love, because out there in the world, it's nothing more than giving in to passion and pleasure, no? So chastity counteracts pleasure. And we as a unit—it's important that our love be universal. We don't attach ourselves to a few people and that's it, as in a family. Rather, we want to embrace more people. You see, if you get

married, you just have your husband and your children, and you care
for and worry about them before others. But here, no. Here, you care
for others and for yourself, and in caring for others you take care of
yourself. And you start to think more that way—universally. And obedience, also, because outside we all want to kill ourselves and fight against
each other. If you don't obey, rivalries start, power struggles and all that.
But here, we practice humility, right? We start to see that—we present
ourselves in a position of humility and in this humility we can separate
ourselves from what we want, which can sometimes be to put ourselves
in God's place. If we put man first and then God and then the world [in
terms of our priorities], when the ideal arrangement is first God, then
man, and then the world, then we are trying to occupy the place of God.
So in professing humility we are putting ourselves in the place designed
for us, as creatures and children of God, and not trying to be gods just
because that's what we want.

Each of the postulants expressed similar sentiments about how she
understood the social and political import of her decision to enter the
convent: that, as a nun, she saw herself as actively countering the foreign pressures of modernity (as she understood it) that undermined the
moral and cultural base of her nation. The notion of modernity that
emerged from my many discussions with these women incorporated
themes such as technological advance, individualism, the valuing of
career over family, egotism, greed, materialism, abuse of power, manipulation, wealth, and, most prominently, feminism.

But these were not ideas the postulants merely absorbed to evaluate
how to run their lives in the future. Particularly striking to me was the
way in which, toward the end of my stay with them, many of the postulants used these ideas to reevaluate events and circumstances in their
lives before coming to the convent, sometimes representing them completely differently than they had a few months prior. Often, they would
come to see things in their childhoods in a new light and as evidence for
their vocations—not just their vocations in a general sense but their
calling to *this specific congregation.* Again and again in our interviews,
I was told stories about how, looking back, the postulants could now
understand why they never really "fit in" as women, why they always
felt there was something different about them.

Amelia's story provides a striking, but not unusual, example. "I was
the only girl in my family," she told me.

I had four brothers. So I didn't really have any girls to play with. But it
was fine. I mean, I don't think I really thought about it. But the result
was that I liked to play boy games and do the things boys do. Playing in

the dirt, building things, all that. And since I was about seven years old, when I started dressing myself, I wouldn't wear a skirt for anything! Always pants. Never skirts. I kept my hair short, I didn't wear makeup, even when I got older. It just didn't appeal to me. Sometimes the other girls in school would make fun of me, and that was hard. But I was the way I was, no? So now it's kind of funny that here in the congregation we can *only* wear skirts! [laughs] But at the same time, it makes me think about what I was like back then. I think part of me knew that being a woman wasn't only about looking pretty and doing girly kinds of things. Even then, I think I had a sense that women need to move beyond that, to get involved, to make the world a better place. That's why I was so interested in Father Muro's teachings. I think that's why I ended up joining the Siervas instead of another congregation.

But again, the postulants did not understand their coming to the Siervas simply as a means of easing some internal tensions they might have had about being women in a time of rapid cultural change, although this was certainly a prominent part of how they talked about their experiences. The idea that a woman would enter the religious life solely to attend to personal psychological needs was specifically addressed in our classes on vocation, and the postulants were told time and time again that if this is why they had entered the convent, they would never last. There must, they were told, be a commitment to something larger than oneself.

For the postulants, I found that this commitment frequently took on nationalist overtones, echoing the teachings of their founder. "Mexico was once a great culture," Rosita told me one day as we were chatting in the library. "We're still a great culture. We have amazing traditions and a richness that's really rare. But we're losing it. We're letting it slip away. We're so enamored with everything that comes from the United States that we're losing our sense of who we are. It's not just the women, of course. It's everyone—the men, the teenagers, everyone. But if we want to keep our culture alive, if we want to keep Mexico a Catholic country, with its eyes set firmly on God, we have to start with the families, which means we have to start with the women." Thea, who was sitting nearby working on an embroidery piece, agreed. "Yes. It's not that we can *blame* the women for what's happening to Mexico. But as our founder said, the women are the heart of the family, so they are the heart of the society. If you want to make a society more *santa* [holy], you have to work to make the women more *santas*. That's when you'll begin to see change."

This conversation was typical of dozens I had with the postulants and with older sisters in the congregation during my eighteen months with the order. Generally, these sorts of discussions would arise when we were talking about a news story or some other political event. Typically, there would be commentary on how unjust and irreligious the world was becoming, followed by affirmations of the importance of Father Muro's vision for contemporary Mexico and the world more generally. "Of course, we're not just focused on Mexico," Carmen explained to me during our study period one day, when I observed that the congregation's mission seemed to have a nationalistic flavor.

> What kind of nuns would we be if we only cared about our own country? But you have to start where you are, no? And Mexico is in a kind of interesting situation. Economically, we're growing. Politically, we're growing. We have to deal with the United States, who wants to tell us how to think, what to eat, what to wear, how to run our country. It's a tough situation. So if we start with Mexico and show the world what can be done, then hopefully people will recognize the power of God's blessings. Maybe that's why God chose Father Muro to found the congregation here in Mexico.

"It's like what Father Muro said about women," Celeste offered, chewing on the eraser of her pencil, a bad habit of hers she could never quite seem to break. "He tells us that we don't just have to choose between the old way and the new way. We don't have to be subservient, not studying, making tortillas all day. But we don't have to be like men either. It's the same with Mexico. We don't have to go back to the old days when everyone wore sandals and sombreros and drank tequila and rode on donkeys. But we don't have to be just like the United States, either." As the sisters told me in different ways at different times, Mexico does not have to be *either* backward and traditional *or* modern and materialistic. Mexico needs to find its own "third way." The "regeneration" of women and the reviving of Catholicism, I learned, are seen by the sisters as essential for finding this third way of being a good, moral, *and* successful nation in the modern world.

But this linkage of gender, religion, and nationalism is not idiosyncratic to these postulants or even this religious order. The sisters are not simply huddled away behind the convent walls inventing connections and discussing these issues among themselves. The conversations going on in the congregation are part of a larger dialogue that has been churning for centuries, a dialogue about what it means to be Mexican. Life in the convent and life "outside" are not isolated from one another but are engaged in a dynamic interchange. Particularly, the practices inside the convent draw their meanings from things in the outside world because they are understood to be the opposite of what people do "out there." The daily activities of the religious life in this congregation articulate the sisters' particular understandings of—and provide them with a language of resistance to—modernity.

JESUS IN OUR WOMBS

From my experiences with these young women, I believe that the decision to enter the convent can become a means of dealing with the anxiety of entering uncharted territory in terms of women's roles. This is complicated. On the one hand, becoming a nun can be read as a "feminist" move, allowing a woman to work, obtain an education, or have a career without being encumbered by a husband and children. Entering the convent, for all its rules and restrictions, definitely provides women with more freedom than they would find in the outside world and was often described to me this way by the postulants as part of their motivation for entering the congregation.

But it is not that clear-cut. At the pre–religious life retreat I attended in December of 1994, I found that a large number of women thinking about joining a convent were on the brink of completing their academic degrees and becoming professionals (one as a lawyer, one as a dentist, another as a computer technician, etc.). Many were really struggling with this. One woman told me, "I don't want to drop out of the university when I'm so close to finally receiving my degree, but if God is calling me, what can I do? I *have* to answer." Entering the convent, then, may be a way to get around the conflicts of—or manipulate the classification of—being a "modern woman" and all the unsavory consequences this is seen to carry.

In practical terms, becoming a nun involves a transformational process that persuades these women to adopt new understandings of their own womanhood. They learn to interpret the internal distress of *inquietud* as a call to a more "authentic" femininity. In the convent, they learn to substitute the community mothers for their own, orienting to an alternate model of productive (vs. reproductive) femininity. Through strategies of enclosure they develop an altered notion of domestic space and the phenomenology of containment, such that their own bodies become infused with sacred potential. In a May retreat on the Virgin Mary, for example, one month before they were to enter the novitiate, Mother Veronica observed to the group that the ten months of the postulancy were like the ten months of pregnancy—that the postulants were, in a very real spiritual sense, gestating Jesus in their own wombs. Through the praxis of the religious life, postulants learn how to become dutiful housewives for God. The suffering of in-depth internal critique comes, they learn, from shedding worldly notions of value for what they *do*—a masculine perspective in the sisters' eyes—and focusing instead on what they *are*—women offering themselves up to God. They learn that this surrender and sacrifice is a particularly feminine disposition, requiring both an effacement of self and a genuineness of being that are devalued in the male-dominated world outside. As women, they are taught, they already possess this potentiality and need only break free of the bonds of modern life long enough for their true feminine essence to find a voice. Finally, they learn to integrate their new experiences of "authentic" femininity within an altered developmental story of their lives and to go out into the world as shining examples of how God's grace can be transformative for even the most miserable among us. In the next section I consider how this configuring of femininity in the postulants' religious formation articulates with compelling social issues outside the convent walls.

PART THREE

Articulations

CHAPTER 12

Mexican Modernities

Mexico has changed a lot in my lifetime. I'm old, you know!
[laughs]. For me, Mexico is still evolving as a country. It's still in the
process of becoming a true and accepted democracy because we've
had so many years of revolutions. Now, for example, the party that
is in power, the PRI . . . well, we here perceive many defects in the
party and see it as a species of dictatorship. But people who come,
for example, from Central America or South America tell us, "We'd
love to have a PRI where we come from, because we go from coup
to coup and from revolution to revolution, with guerrilla warfare
and everything. At least your Mexican government is stable."

So I think that Mexico is a society that is continually changing,
continually maturing. I've lived through various different stages of
this process, from the time of the furious persecution that created so
many martyrs in the time of Calles, and later the religious persecution
in general, then the particular persecution of the Catholic schools—
Catholic education was forbidden, so they closed all the schools—I
lived though all that. Afterwards, there was a kind of peaceful tolerance. The church ignored the state and the state ignored the church.
And everyone went about their own business, and it was more or less
comfortable because people just lived their own lives.

Then now, finally, this last president [Salinas de Gotari] decided to
forge an official relationship with the church, since Mexico already
figured very prominently in the principal countries of the world. And
it didn't look good to not have relations with the church when even
the smallest countries seek to build relationships with the church. And
since Mexico is 90-something percent Catholic, well, it wasn't good.
All governments have deficiencies and make mistakes, but I think this
was a very good decision because up until now the religious factions
here haven't had their own political rights. Their power was all
hidden, you know? Before, I couldn't teach religion in the church. But
now, I can make my school completely Catholic and I can teach the
religion that I profess. So for me, these are very, very positive changes.

Interview with Mother Wilhelmina, April 4, 1994

In the last chapter, I proposed a model for understanding religious
formation for the postulants as a process in which they come to experience
new subject positions through a gradual regendering within a context of

highly particularized dynamics of recognition. The postulants, however, learn to recognize themselves not only as newly authentic women but also, specifically, as newly authentic Mexican women living in a time of rapid social, economic, and political change. In other words, the work of religious formation for the Siervas is not just about personal transformation. It is also about the deliberate linking of this personal journey with urgent social concerns, an engagement with larger dynamics of political recognition (Taylor 1995; Honneth 1997) in Mexico itself as well as in the global arena. In this way, learning to be a good Sierva can also become a political act. This politico-nationalist aspect of the Siervas' religious mission not only is rooted in the order's own history but has gained renewed relevance (and taken on new meanings) in recent years as Mexico has been thrust into the geopolitical dynamics of globalization.

PUEBLA DE LOS ÁNGELES: LIVING ON THE BRINK

It is no coincidence, the sisters tell me, that their founder decided to move the Central House of the congregation—the order's world headquarters—to the city of Puebla shortly before his death in 1904. The Siervas boast that they were the first congregation of active-life sisters to become established in the city (which serves as the capital to the state of the same name), and they assert that their mission is in many ways tied to both the history and the contemporary social and religious circumstances that give this city its distinctive character.

From its founding in the sixteenth century, Puebla has been a conservative city, both politically and religiously. According to legend, in 1531 a vision came to Friar Toribio de Benavente in a remarkable dream. He saw a legion of angels hovering over a lush green valley surrounded by five volcanoes. As he looked on, they unrolled a map of the central area of New Spain and showed him where the valley was to be found. The angels did not speak. But Friar Toribio de Benavente knew what they were telling him: to build a city on that spot.

Originally, this city was conceived of as a sort of experiment. In establishing earlier cities, the Spanish had relied heavily on the indigenous peoples to provide them with labor and services to keep the cities up and running. The idea behind this city, though, was that it was to be a purely Spanish city, built by Spanish hands and fed on crops grown by Spanish farmers. After receiving permission to build the city on April 16, 1531, Friar Toribio de Benavente recruited sixteen thousand men from the surrounding areas as builders. In honor of the vision he had received, the city would be named Puebla de los Ángeles, City of Angels.

The name of Puebla is synonymous in Mexican lore with some of the most glorious—and troubling—pages in the nation's history. Historically, Puebla has been unfalteringly conservative in its politics. During the War of Independence, for example, Puebla sided with the Spanish and defended the crown. But in 1847, the conservative core of the city met a fierce challenge. The United States invaded Mexico and occupied the city of Puebla, forcing the government of the state to flee to other cities. In the following years, the state of Puebla became a haven for many liberalist movements that advocated the secularization of church property and the closing of convents. But the old core of the city—the traditional families who had been there for generations—remained very Catholic and very conservative and were persecuted and discriminated against for their beliefs, values, and politics for decades.

The French intervention in the mid-nineteenth century, however, roused the conservative factions in Puebla, who saw the invasion as the inevitable outcome of the nation's liberalist policies. The call to defend the city's traditional values animated the *poblanos*—so much so that, as the French troops neared the city, the locals took up arms to fight them. When the French attacked the city of Puebla at the forts of Loreto and Guadalupe on the outskirts of town, they met fierce resistance, which exploded into a bloody battle. On May 5, 1862, General Zarragoza led the hodgepodge Mexican troops (mostly untrained *campesinos* and laborers) to victory, defeating the (supposedly) invincible French army. This catapulted Zarragoza into the history books, where he was named the patron of the city and of the nation. To this day, the battle of the *cinco de mayo* is celebrated throughout Mexico—and beyond—as a reminder that strong faith and unwavering nationalism can surmount even the most insurmountable odds.

During the regime of Porfirio Díaz (the period in which the congregation was founded), industrialization increased in many parts of the country. One of the most important industrial centers to emerge during this period was that of Puebla, whose textile industry grew, by the end of the nineteenth century, to be the most important in the republic. This rapid development brought a dramatic increase to the population of the state and of the city. While beneficial for the overall economic situation of the region, the growth threw into relief the economic inequalities of the urban populations, and tensions began to rise. Puebla, still a conservative stronghold, became the headquarters of a number of revolutionary groups working to overthrow the liberal Díaz.

On November 18, 1910, these tensions finally erupted. The police laid siege to the house of the Aquiles Serdán family in the city of Puebla on the charge that the brothers of the family had instigated antiestablishment protests. The brothers denied the charges and refused to surrender to the authorities. Federal troops were brought in to help the police. In the end, the soldiers and police penetrated the house and killed the brothers Serdán. This incident is believed to have been the turning point of the resistance to the Díaz regime, initiating the revolution that would bring dramatic political, social, and economic transformation of Mexico.

Today, Puebla boasts close to four million residents in its metropolitan area. The city rests in a central valley surrounded by the highest volcanoes in the country and is strategically located, both geographically and economically, between Mexico City and the important port of Veracrúz, making Puebla the intermediate point of the transoceanic route that connects the Gulf of Mexico to the Pacific Ocean. The state of Puebla also shares borders with the states of Oaxaca, Morelos, Mexico, and Tlaxcala, making it one of the most important industrial, business, cultural, and financial centers in all of Mexico. As such, Puebla is often held up by the national government as a jewel in the crown of modernization.

But at the same time, Puebla remains a key hub of conservative social and religious values. Despite the liberal challenges launched at the city over the years, Puebla has remained steadfastly Catholic—a dramatic contrast to cosmopolitan Mexico City, a mere two hours' drive to the north. So loyal was the city to the values of Catholicism that the 1978 World Conference of Bishops was held in the city, and the pope himself visited. The documents from this conference (known as "The Conference of Puebla") are hailed as important by church scholars for upholding the resolutions of Vatican II, particularly on the issue of the advocacy for human rights in underdeveloped areas.

Puebla's tradition of religious conservatism has been challenged by recent growth and industrialization. Many *poblanos* I talked to cited the disastrous Mexico City earthquake in 1985 as a key turning point for the city. In the aftermath of the tremors, thousands of Mexico City residents rushed into Puebla, breaking up enclaves of concentrated Catholic, colonial power in the city and "sending the city to the devil," as many *poblanos* described it to me. The city's population almost doubled between 1985 and 1995, and the cobbled old colonial streets and poor infrastructure were unable to cope with this explosion. In 1991 the city instituted the Angelopolis Project, an ambitious project of modernization and urban development aimed at widening highways, bringing potable water to all parts of the city, improving electricity and phone service, and generally improving the living conditions of city residents. As part of this massive development plan, old houses are being torn down and old thoroughfares rerouted. The city is spilling over its borders, with new housing developments and condominium complexes springing up on what used to be cow pastures. In the interior of the city, restored colonial buildings now house, among other things, a Kentucky Fried Chicken, a McDonald's, and an Eckard's. The shiny new mall in the center of town displays architectural models of the projected changes Angelopolis will bring to the city.

In the face of all this change, tensions between the liberal and conservative political factions have once again heated up. One concrete example can be seen in the 1995 campaign and election for the mayorship of the city. As in the rest of Mexico, the American-friendly PRI traditionally held control of the city, despite conservatives' accusations of electoral fraud and corruption. The PRI had long considered control of Puebla to be particularly vital because of the region's importance as an industrial and cultural center. But in November 1995 a vigorous campaign and monumental election put the conservative, Catholic-supported PAN party in the mayorship of the city, defeating the carefully groomed PRI candidate. Manuel Bartlett, the governor of the state of Puebla and a PRI member, reacted with unrestrained anger to the PAN victory, vowing to obstruct all attempts by the PAN to institute their conservative agenda.

Some *poblanos* I talked to told me they viewed the election of the PAN as an indication that the tide was turning, that days of greater freedom and democracy were ahead, and that the country might finally be wresting its honor from the corrupt clutches of the PRI. Others, however, said that they saw the PAN's victory as completely disastrous, taking the city a step back in time. For example, Rena, a professional single mother with whom I lived for several months, told me that she thought the victory of the PAN represented a regressive backlash that would keep Mexico in the Dark Ages both socially and economically.

In the midst of all this, Puebla maintains a strong and tightly knit Catholic community that tends to represent itself as the beleaguered but determined moral core of this old city, guardians of the true heart and identity of Mexico as it was meant to be. Puebla is, for example, a favorite location for Catholic retreats, religious conferences and lectures, and religious celebrations, and it remains a center of Catholic spirituality.

In short, Puebla is a city divided. Avenida Juárez, one of the main corridors of the city, is lined with flashy discos, cellular phone shops, and glitzy restaurants serving American-style hamburgers and bland versions of *chalupas* and *taquitos,* while just steps to the north, in the old neighborhood of La Paz, traditional Catholic families scramble to get together the tuition to send their children to private Catholic schools and universities, where they will, at least while they are within the schoolyard, be somewhat protected from the influences of consumerism, materialism, and moral decay.

Many of today's *poblanos* told me they felt once again besieged from the outside, that their integrity—and perhaps their very existence—as a people was being actively threatened, and that they had to fight, despite the odds and whatever the cost. As Rosa, a thirty-four-year-old married mother of one, told me, "We have to hold our community together. If we don't, it will disintegrate right before our eyes. You can already see it at the edges of our community. Slowly but surely, we're being eroded away." But this time the challenge is, perhaps, even greater. The enemy, as Ariana, a college student at the local university explained it to me, was not charging at the walls of the city's defenses with cannons and guns ablazing. "This time," she said, "the enemy is much more subtle and insidious because it has targeted Mexico's most vulnerable and most treasured citizens—its children." As what were perceived to be foreign values entered the minds of Mexico's youth through the media, music, and the public education system, many *poblanos* openly admitted that they were on the brink of panic. But, many told me, they had to maintain the faith that, after the dust settled, their destiny—as patriotic Mexicans and as good Catholics—would be realized.

It seems reasonable to propose, then, that at least in some ways Puebla may articulate struggles precipitated by the processes of development and cultural change in the Third World in general and Mexico in particular. The tensions revealed in the way *poblanos* talk about their city seem to speak to larger national concerns about how to mediate between the old and the new. In short, while Puebla may not be representative of Mexico in the strict sense of the term, the changes going on there speak to the difficulties of finding what we might call a Mexican-style modernity.[1]

COMING OF AGE IN A TIME OF TRANSITION

When I began my research in 1994, the postulants were between the ages of seventeen and thirty, meaning that they were born between 1964 and 1977. They were all, then, coming of age during this time of transformation. Many of the postulants independently referred to the changes in the city when telling me how they learned they might have a vocation. Most commonly, they talked about hearing their parents and other adults lament, as indicative of a larger moral and cultural crisis, the changes in the city and the erosion of the city's Catholic foundation as evangelical groups such as the Jehovah's Witnesses moved into town. Many of the postulants told me they remembered that some of their relatives had begun looking more self-consciously to the church and to church-related organizations as the city's population grew and as old communities were fractured. Many of the postulants said that as traffic congestion, pollution, crime, and violence in the schools had escalated, they had found solace in participating in church activities and youth groups. "It was a way for me to remind myself what really mattered," Evelyn told me. "It's so easy to lose sight of that these days."

It seems, then, that the experiences of religious vocation of the young postulants I worked with were not only intimately personal dimensions of faith but expressions of nationalist concerns in a time of rapid cultural change within the context of the congregation's particular historical and theological development. Specifically, the sisters understand the particular practices of convent life in this order to both reference and evaluate a whole host of understandings, relationships, connections, and meanings relevant to Mexican nationalism. To do so, they must engage larger discussions of these issues as they are played out in the media (newspapers, television shows, advertisements, soap operas, magazines, etc.), in academic writings, and in common discourse. And, as with the dynamics of recognition explored in chapter 11, the postulants learn to discern, with increasing clarity, the mismatch between the

1. For an excellent collection of anthropological perspectives on the possibilities of multiple modernities, see Knauft (2002). Other significant recent works on this topic include Gaonkar (2001), Saunders (2002), and Hodgson (2001).

congregation's and the outside world's understandings of Mexicanness, as well as their own positioning in relation to these often conflicting perspectives. They learn to recognize themselves as authentically "Mexican" in a process parallel to (and indeed inseparable from) that of recognizing themselves as women called to God.

The language the sisters most often use for articulating these relationships between gender, religion, and Mexicanness in a world gone awry is the language of modernity. The associations brought to bear on these discussions, both within the convent and without, are firmly rooted in the emergence of the Mexican nation. Indeed, this coupling of religious and nationalist concerns has a long history in Mexico, reaching back at least to the time of the Conquest. I learned from the sisters, as well as from academic sources, that historically themes not only of religion but also of race and gender (albeit in different permutations and elaborations) have been central to the common understandings in Mexico of what it means to be Mexican. Specifically, the condition of *mestizaje* (being of mixed Indian and European blood), the gendering of Mexico as a female repeatedly raped by conquest and cultural expansionism by Europe and the United States (represented in the Mexican nationalist cry "Hijos de la chingada!" [Sons of the raped woman!]), and the linkage of Catholicism to the nationalist cause through the symbol of the inviolate Virgin of Guadalupe have been core themes. As I learned more about these and other historical notions of Mexicanness, I began to recognize the complexity of the political, religious, and social issues the postulants were invoking when they spoke of their vocations in nationalist terms.

GENDERED NATIONALISMS

Many of the issues raised by the postulants' nationalist expressions of their religious vocations accord with recent scholarly literature on postcolonial nationalisms (see, for example, Hodgson 2001; Saunders 2002; Dhruvarajan and Vickers 2002). The emotional and moral force of discourses of nationalism and cultural identity, particularly in postcolonial areas, has received much attention in recent scholarship. Specifically, the centrality of one's national affiliation to one's larger sense of identity—of who one is in the world—has been emphasized. Anderson (1983: 16, 14), for example, observes that "in the modern world everyone can, should, will 'have' a nationality, as he or she 'has' a gender."

Perhaps because nationality is experienced as such a fundamental aspect of one's being, gender and sexuality are frequently invoked, in Mexico as well as elsewhere, as metaphorical representations of nationalist concerns.[2] Specifically, much of the scholarship on nationalism suggests that relationships of power are often injected with this symbolism, with the aggressor characterized as male and the conquered as female. "One need only recall the title of a book that sold like hotcakes during the recent Gulf War—*The Rape of Kuwait*—to appreciate how deeply ingrained has been the depiction of the homeland as a female body whose violation by foreigners requires its citizens and allies to rush to her defense," Parker writes in the introduction to *Nationalisms and Sexualities* (1992: 6). But more than this, such constructions reference larger cultural concerns regarding femininity, sexuality, and the social positioning of women. "This trope of the nation-as-woman," the author goes on, "of course depends for its representational efficacy on a particular image of woman as chaste, dutiful, daughterly or maternal" (6).[3]

To understand how debates about modernity frame understandings of femininity and Mexicanness both within the convent and outside, we must examine these concepts against the backdrop of Mexican national history. First I consider how, as the nation moved from independence to revolution and embarked on the radical project of modernization, race, religion, and gender were variously articulated as central to constructions of Mexicanness. I then highlight some of the dominant themes that seem to have gained prominence in discussions of Mexican nationalism and cultural identity in the past twenty years.

Before moving on, I want to be clear that I am not arguing that these constructions of Mexicanness were or are "true" in the sense of representing real flesh-and-blood individuals in any direct way, although they undoubtedly have some tangible point of reference. Rather, much as Gergen (1991) conceptualized modernity, I take representations of "national character" to be stories a nation tells itself about itself.

2. Central texts on the issue of nationalism and identity (collective as well as individual) include Anderson (1983), Bhabha (1990), Hobsbawm (1990), and Hobsbawm and Ranger (1983).
3. For more on the interstices of nationality and constructions of gender and sexuality, see Doane and Hodges (1987), Jayawardena (1986), Luhrmann (1996), Mosse (1985), Nájera Ramírez (1993), and Yuval-Davis, Anthias, and Campling (1989), among others.

And the story one tells oneself about oneself (whether that "self" is a nation, a religious group, an individual, or something else) takes its meaning from the context in and through which it emerges. The story, then, always has a particular agenda, a *point*, a context to which it is referring and responding. This is the aspect of characterizations of Mexicanness that interests me here.[4]

BIRTHING PAINS

Oh beautiful Guadalupe
Sacred and beloved Virgin
You must not let the gringos
Consume the blood of your children
Mexican Corrida, 1916

Bastard children of a violent rape. This would seem an unlikely foundation for a national identity, but it is an identity most Mexicans claim as their own, evincing indignation—if not exactly pride—at their nation's painful birth. For over three centuries, Mexico (or New Spain, as it was then called) suffered the oppression and exploitation of the Spanish colonialist regime. The Spanish were cruel to the indigenous peoples of the country, reserving the pleasures and luxuries of colonial life for the *criollos* (Spanish families who had settled in the New World) and the *peninsulares* (Spanish diplomats and dignitaries sent over to preside over the governing of New Spain), as the Indians starved in the countryside or worked as servants or slaves in the rambling colonial mansions.

Despite this separation, Spanish men intermarried more or less freely with indigenous women (although the "freedom" of the women to reject such intentions is, of course, questionable), and a fourth racial category soon appeared on the scene—the *mestizos,* born of mixed Spanish and indigenous heritage. In the eyes of many Mexicans, the Spanish conquest corrupted the innocence of their land, the innocence of their women, and the purity of their race.

---

4. This will be a necessarily superficial treatment of these issues. For a more complete discussion of the political history of Mexico in the nineteenth and twentieth centuries, I direct the reader to some of the many excellent works that have appeared on the academic scene in recent years, most notably Anna (1998), Archer (2003), Eisenhower (2000), Frazier (1998), Krauze (1998), Lomnitz-Adler (1992), Ridley (2001), Rugeley (2001), Van Young (2001), Vanderwood (1998), and Wasserman (2000).

The conditions for independence in Mexico were seeded by happenings in Europe and the United States. The American Revolution and its independence from Britain in 1776 and the French Revolution and the ratification of the new French Constitution in 1793 sent an unequivocal message of hope to groups all over the world struggling against imperialist domination. These successful campaigns were founded on a set of new philosophies emerging from Europe, proclaiming a new way of thinking about society, human nature, and the relationship of the people to their government. The works of radical thinkers (e.g., Rousseau, Montesquieu, Diderot, Voltaire) advocating the governing of nations by the people were traded and debated covertly among intellectual groups in New Spain, and slowly but surely a revolutionary sentiment began to take hold.

Just after dawn on September 16, 1810, Miguel Hidalgo y Costilla, the parish priest of the small Indian town of Dolores, ascended to the pulpit and gave the call to arms—the *grito* that is still given each year by the president of Mexico to commemorate the beginning of the War of Independence. *"Hijos de la chingada!"* (Children of the raped woman) was the Mexican rallying cry to fight the Spanish and to claim independence. Fury and humiliation at what the Spanish had done to Mother Mexico—violating her and abusing her as a scoundrel would rape and abuse a whore—fueled the fighters, six hundred thousand of whom would lose their lives before it was over. The dark-skinned Virgin of Guadalupe, who had first appeared to the Indian Juan Diego on the hill of Tepeyac in 1531, became the symbol of the Independence movement—the pure and inviolate counterpart of the raped and disparaged Mexico. Under her banner the troops charged forward to death and glory, Guadalupe's virginity and divinity reminding them of what their beloved Mexico had suffered at the hands of the cruel Spanish aggressors (Lafaye 1987).

After ten long and bloody years of fighting, Mexico freed itself from Spanish colonization and domination, only to find itself ripped apart by internal struggles. The economy was in ruins, the power vacuum left by the defeated Spanish regime was exploited through the feverish plotting and political scheming of the Catholic Church, and the Indians and *mestizos,* no longer under the nominal protection of the Spanish crown, fell prey to unprecedented exploitation and abuses perpetrated by the *latifundios,* the large landowners.

NATIONAL IDENTITY IN THE INTERWAR YEARS

The post-Independence period was crucial for the development of the social construct of Mexicanness.[5] On the political front, the very idea of a "nation" or a "national identity" was still relatively new on the world stage, and it was certainly new in Mexico, with its political factions and competing loyalties. Leaders rose up only to be assassinated or forced into exile, and political wrangling consumed the country and threatened to pull the nation apart.

By 1850 two principal factions had emerged, often referred to as the liberals and the conservatives. The liberals tended to be middle-class urban intellectuals and professionals. They argued that the new Mexican nation should be directly modeled on France and the United States and that all ties to Spanish, Indian, and Catholic models of society and government should be vehemently rejected. They favored a constitutional regime inspired by the secular rationalist philosophies of the French and American Revolutions, while at the same time maintaining an undisguised anticlerical sentiment and a distinct mistrust of the power of the Roman Catholic Church in political and social affairs.

The conservatives, on the other hand—who both supported and were supported by the landed, military, and church hierarchies—strongly defended the social tenets of Roman Catholicism, which they believed to be the "true face of the Mexican people." They applauded the natural humanist principles that led to the overthrow of the Spanish and the establishment of a society based upon the people's right to liberty, but they strongly objected to the "liberal" interpretation of this stance, which led, in their view, to a militant philosophy of liberty and progress wholly divorced form the norms of the past. Fearing that the liberals would unleash anarchic individualism, the conservatives appealed to Europe for the installation of a dictatorship. This was granted in the form of the Austrian archduke Maximilian, who became the Emperor of Mexico and ruled from 1864 to 1867. But Maximilian faced bitter opposition from Mexican liberals. Following the withdrawal of French troops from Mexico in 1866, he was unable to maintain power. He was soon captured and shot, propelling the country again into chaos.

5. For key works on postcolonial Mexican nationalism, see Gómez-Quiñones (1992), Mallon (1995), and Rodriguez (1997).

Far from mere theoretical differences, the ideological divisions between the liberal and conservative factions provoked a series of bloody confrontations, throwing the country again and again into turmoil. Revolution followed revolution as leader after leader was assassinated or deposed. Tensions between the conservatives and the liberals continued to heighten as the young nation sought in vain to find its center. By the mid–nineteenth century, the country had been independent for over thirty years, but it was in absolute chaos.

As Franco (1989) notes, the reconfiguration of power dynamics during this period fostered the emergence of a new domain of discourse in the press and in coffeehouses that would become crucial in defining a post-Independence Mexican national identity. The Mexican "nation" at this point did not exist, Franco contends, but was conjured into existence by writers who lovingly dedicated their odes to their homeland "as a creature new born out of the murky obscurantism of the colony" (79). Writers such as Fernández de Lizardi, Ignacio M. Altamirano, and Martínez de Castro crafted novels and other works about their beloved Mexico during this period, exploring what it "meant" to be Mexican.

Faced with political turmoil and instability, the participants in the discussions of Mexicanness tended to invoke the one thing that seemed to bind the country together—the problematic of race. It was during this period that the condition of the *mestizo* came to symbolize the new nation. Mexico was neither Spanish nor Indian, this view held, but literally a mixture of the two—a unique creation. The Mexicans were a new race, *hijos de la chingada,* born from a loving motherland that had been abused, shamed, and torn apart in the process.

One possible appeal of this classification of *mestizo* is that it in many ways seemed to articulate the colonial experience in all its manifestations and contradictions. The coffee color of the *mestizo*'s skin—darker than that of a *güero* (a white person) but lighter than that of an Indian—can be read as literally embodying the domination, oppression, and shame of the Conquest, as well as the victory, glory, and triumph of the War of Independence. The condition of *mestizaje,* in the eyes of many Mexicans, enfolded this ambivalence and celebrated it (cf. Basave Benitez, 1992).

During the late 1800s, the sublime paradox of the *mestizo* gradually came to symbolize the paradox of the new nation itself. And somehow, it seemed, the condition of *mestizaje* helped unify the nation, to give the Mexican people a sense of uniqueness, something that set them apart from all peoples who had come before. They were *mestizo*—they were Mexican.[6]

With independence won, Maximilian ousted, and their political dominance apparently secure, the liberal intelligentsia set about an ambitious project of homogenization and modernization, a project aimed at "cleaning up" Mexican society. Mexico was to become, as Franco (1989: 79) puts it, "a society dressed in European clothes and generally scrubbed and tidied up." Although Mexico could never become a "white" society, the plan was for the "wild Indians of the north and the descendants of the black slaves [to be] eventually . . . symbolically whitened through education, through the influence of the press and civilizing literature" (79). Mexico was to be remade, to become, like America and the European countries on whose political and social philosophies it had modeled its fight for independence, a shining example of the triumph of the modern nation over religious tradition and social backwardness.

In the wake of these challenges the Catholic Church was demonized and open season was proclaimed. Religion and faith were rejected in favor of science, enlightenment, and progress. Churches, monasteries, convents, and schools were closed, and their land was seized and used for more appropriate endeavors dedicated to logic, reason, and the public good (one of the Siervas' convents, for example, was converted into a public health clinic).

But the liberal project of homogenization and modernization encountered unexpected resistance from almost all sides. The liberal humanist orientation of the mostly upper-class urban intelligentsia was incongruent with the beliefs and experience of much of the populace. The tug-of-war between the liberals and the conservatives continued, and the stakes were exceedingly high—the future of the Mexican nation and the understanding of what it meant to be a Mexican were seen to hang in the balance. Conflicts erupted again into armed confrontations, disagreements led to the drawing of battle lines and the spilling of yet more blood.

Against the backdrop of these tensions, the humiliating loss of over half of Mexico's territory to the United States in 1848 gave the competing factions in the troubled nation something they desperately needed: a common enemy. During this period the United States, prized as

6. For more on the centrality of *mestizaje* to the formation of an official Mexican national identity, see Basave Benitez (1992) and Reyes (1992). For the interstices of race and gender in constructions of *mestizaje* and Mexicanness, see Anzaldúla (1987).

Mexico's model of democratic and economic development, became at the same time the official nemesis of Mexico as a nation, and the establishment of Mexico's economic, political, and cultural independence from the greedy, bossy, covetous United States became a rallying point that offered the country some sense of unity and cohesion. This juxtaposition of admiration and emulation of the United States with a growing anti-American sentiment provided the context within which Mexico's internal political struggles began to take more definitive shape.[7]

THE UNITED STATES AND MEXICAN NATIONALISM

Although xenophobia with respect to all foreign nationals skyrocketed during the late 1800s, by far the most prolonged and pronounced xenophobia was directed against the North Americans. Many Mexicans viewed the expansion of American industry into Mexico and the slow but steady takeover of the Mexican economy by American entrepreneurs as part of a conspiracy to take over the country. Anti-American sentiment ran at fever pitch by the early 1900s as fears spread that the United States might take advantage of Mexico's civil unrest to seize the rest of its land.

Hatred of Americans was not particular to any one class or geographic region in Mexico. American Consul Samuel E. Magill at Guadalajara reported to the Secretary of State that "the anti-American sentiment is almost universal among the rich and poor alike," adding that "at the national celebration commemorating Hidalgo's Grito de Dolores (the call that started the War of Independence), Mexican mobs paraded through the streets yelling 'Death to the Americans!' " (quoted in Turner 1968: 209). Another striking example comes from Anna Sherwood, the American proprietress of a hotel in Manzanillo. She reported to the consul in April 1912 that the Mexican railroad employees who had boarded a train with her intimidated her constantly and persisted in "speaking ill" of Americans. She became particularly nervous when

7. For more on the influence of the United States in the shaping of Mexican cultural nationalism, both during the revolution and more recently, see Bagley and Aguayo Quezada (1993), Calero (1916), Chavezmontes (1988), Creel (1926), Cue Canovas (1970), de la Garza and Velasco (1997), Eisenhower (1993), Fernández MacGregor (1960), Gilly (1994a, 1994b) González Souza (1994) Hall and Coerver (1988), Hart (1987), Harvey (1993), Langley (1991), Schulz (1997), Selby (1978), Trueba (1994), Vásquez and García y Griego (1983), and Weintraub (1990).

they threatened to shoot her at the first sign of U.S. intervention in Mexican affairs and to seize the American consul, tie weights to his feet, and throw him off the wharf (Milton B. Kirk to Henry Lane Wilson, May 1, 1912, cited in Turner 1968: 210–11). This anti-Americanism permeated even the most isolated regions of Mexico and was directly linked to the hostility felt toward the liberal government. Not surprisingly, many Americans fled Mexico during this time.

For their part, the Mexican leaders tried to walk a fine line. They wanted to maintain as much American support as possible without alienating the Mexican nationalists. But then the lynching and burning of a young Mexican man named Rodríguez at the hands of an American mob in Rock Springs, Texas, turned the tide, and the nation was galvanized against the Americans as the embodiment of evil, injustice, and greed. The Mexican periodical *El Diario del Hogar*, in a commentary typical of the period, called the people of the United States "giants of the dollar, pygmies of culture, and barbarous whites of the North" (quoted in Turner 1968: 216). The Americans lashed back, accusing the Mexicans of being "jealous" of American success and the fact that Americans had come to control key sectors of the Mexican economy. This position had a decisive effect on Mexican popular opinion. "By bringing this underlying Mexican jealousy and antagonism toward Americans to the surface," writes Turner (1968: 218), "the Rodríguez burning prompted Mexicans to perceive the later events between 1910 and 1917 in an anti-American and nationalistic manner." The United States and all things associated with the American way of life became targeted "enemies of Mexican values."

Indianism became an important symbol for expressing anti-Americanism during this period. Mexicans began to view their Indian heritage in a new way, and Cuauhtémoc came to replace Cortés as the symbolic progenitor of the Mexican people. A passion for indigenous dances, songs, dress, art, and moral codes gripped the nation, and great pride was taken in a heritage that before had represented only shame and defeat. The dark skin and "primitive" ways of the Indian were juxtaposed with the white skin and slick "modern" ways of the Americans.

In the same way, the Catholic Church came to symbolize the "non-American" and a direct repudiation of the Protestant ethic that formed the foundation of the hated capitalist expansionism. The profession of a common faith, furthermore, gave a cohesion and a divine sanction to the Mexican cause and articulated a populist opposition to American aims. Father José Cantú Corro (1924: 33–35, 53–54) synthesized this position when he proclaimed that the Mexican race was particularly powerful because it was made up of both Indian and Spanish strains and could therefore lay claim to "the spirit of El Cid and of Cuauhté-moc." "Mexico must not be for foreigners; no, a thousand times no. . . . Mexico, idolized Motherland, nest of affections, mansion of happiness, noble Republic; Mexico, my Motherland, let the Saxons never assault your soil, nor implant their false religion, nor tarnish your flag." Not surprisingly, the Virgin of Guadalupe—the dark-skinned maternal pro-tector of Mexican soil and national honor—once again came to the forefront during this period as a symbol of Mexican nationalism and resistance to American domination.

MODERNIZATION AND THE "MEXICAN NATION"

When Porfirio Díaz came to power in 1876 he offered the troubled nation something it hadn't seen in decades: stability. He found a coun-try weakened by long years of social and political turmoil and charac-terized by a pervasive malaise. Realizing that some sort of mediation between the liberal and conservative factions was necessary, Díaz relaxed the enforcement of the 1857 laws against the church and adopted an attitude of relative tolerance. One important outgrowth of these upheavals and the relaxing of sanctions against the Catholic Church was the birth of dozens of new religious communities of both men and women, aimed specifically at responding to the many sociore-ligious problems produced by decades of war, civil unrest, and the insti-tutionalization of the "liberal" agenda. One of these communities was the Siervas.

After sixty-six years of bloody war and confrontation, Díaz brought to the country a long period of peace. But he also brought much more. The thirty-five years of his rule witnessed the radical transformation of Mexican society. The passage of Mexico from a predominantly rural to a mostly urban-centered country during his tenure was facilitated by the building of massive railroads—between the years of 1877 and 1910 alone the railroad system expanded from 287 miles to 12,000 miles. Highways and telecommunications links were established and radical changes in education and business legislation dramatically transformed the nature of social life in Mexico, dragging it slowly but surely out of the depths of disorganization and fragmentation.

Díaz, encouraged by the eagerness of foreign banks and investors (attracted by the appearance of Mexican stability coupled with an economy that had nowhere to go but up), decided to open Mexican markets to foreign entrepreneurs after nearly sixty years of protectionism following the War of Independence. The country was quickly overrun by Yankee prospectors looking for cheap materials and even cheaper labor. American industries, poised to exploit Mexico's mining, agriculture, and human resources, sprang up across the country, and Díaz eventually had to encourage investment by France and Britain to counterbalance growing U.S. control of the economy. Foreigners were getting so rich off the Mexican economy, in fact, that it became a common saying that "Mexico is the mother of foreigners and the stepmother to Mexicans."

During this period the ephemeral notion of the "Mexican nation" began to assume a more tangible form. The railways and telegraph lines that spanned the country and connected the provinces began to give the nation a sense of cohesion. Mexico City was turned into a "showcase of modernization" (Franco 1989: 80), with the style of grand new architectural projects in the capital modeled on the classical structures of European and American cities. Broad boulevards, museums, banks, statues, and universities were built. The commissioning of a monument depicting the defeated Aztec prince Cuauhtémoc was, perhaps, the final statement, the sign that the door had finally been closed on the Mexican past.

But there was a dark side to all this glorious "progress." The press was censored, and all criticism of the government was stifled and kept from public view. Díaz created a federal force of *rurales* trained in the *ley fuga*—the law stating that fleeing prisoners can be shot—as a method of "keeping the peace" in the countryside (Riding [1984] 1985). The Porfirian "peace" was, for those not in the cities at any rate, generally achieved through terror and bloodshed.

Worse than this were the economic inequities. José Limanatour, Díaz's finance minister, eagerly applied the new "scientific" theories coming out of the United States and Europe to the Mexican economy, taking the system to unprecedented extremes of injustice. While Mexico City and the other major urban centers flourished, very little trickled down to the miners and farmers who formed the backbone of the Mexican labor force, many of whom continued to subsist in squalor on the traditional peasant diet of tortillas and beans. "Some 3,000 families owned half the country and lived in Mexican haciendas," writes Riding (1985: 40), "while millions of Indians and *mestizo* peasants were virtual serfs, tied either by their debts to the local store or by unpaid back wages which they still hoped to receive." Almost half of the nation's population of thirteen million were Indians living (subsisting) in traditional communities whose lands were being quickly stolen from them and sold primarily to foreign industries and investors looking to turn a quick profit.

This exclusion of the Indians and *mestizos* from the project of modernization was, Franco (1989: 80) argues, no accident—it was fundamental to the project itself. "The dark faces and the native dress," she writes, "the non-European customs and languages of recent immigrants to the city, were mute witnesses to the real stratification within the nation. The economic development of Porfírian Mexico depended on the 'backwardness' of sectors of the population, while its very idiosyncrasy as a nation made those same indigenous and mestizo masses symbolically central." While the nation was pushing rapid modernization, the "heart" of Mexican national identity—the very embodiment of what it meant to be Mexican—continued to be symbolized by the underdeveloped, the backward, the excluded, the *mestizo* peasant.

This is an interesting juxtaposition. Mexico was an emerging nation modeling itself on Europe and the United States, but its core, its soul, what made Mexico *Mexico* in the eyes of many Mexican people, consisted of those very elements that ran directly counter to the polished, light-skinned refinement of nineteenth-century Europe and America. Bonfíl Batalla (1990) describes this situation as the divergence of two Mexicos—the "imaginary" Mexico modeled on the blueprint of European and American modernity and the "profound" Mexico—the "real" or "true" core of Mexican civilization.

In 1910 the simmering tensions caused by the radical social and economic disparities between the landed and peasant classes finally boiled over, launching the country into full-fledged civil war. The explicit goal of the revolution was to affect a redistribution of land so that farmers could hold their own property and labor for their own sustenance, rather than being permanently under the thumb of the rich landowners for whom they worked as, essentially, indentured servants. But the revolution was not solely about material or economic change. For many, it was also (and perhaps primarily) a war of values, a battle between the ideals of capitalist exploitation driven by loyalty to foreign powers and the ideals of humanitarianism driven by loyalty to Mexico's own people who labored in the soil of their beloved homeland. Indeed, long after its end in 1917, the revolution has remained a symbol of this clash of values, with writers, politicians, journalists, satirists, and intellectuals evoking "the spirit of the revolution" as shorthand for the enduring tensions between the drive for "progress" and the need for maintaining cultural integrity.

GENDER AND THE MEXICAN STATE

The Indian, *mestizo*, and religious factions were not the only groups marginalized by the project of modernization and implicated in the development of Mexican national identity during the late nineteenth century. As in many parts of the world, modernization in Mexico was experienced as a "masculine" project, and women were, on the timeline of "progress," an anachronism.[8] Tending to remain stubbornly loyal to the Catholic Church and—in the middle and upper classes, at least— leading lives concentrated on the labors of the home and the luxuries of colonial life, women were seen as an unexploited resource, and a campaign to mobilize them was launched.

The need to redefine the position of women in society soon became a consuming goal of the liberal intelligentsia. Generally speaking, the idea was that if women were properly educated and "trained," they could give much-needed stability, nurturing, and care to the "new man" needed for the "new Mexico." A stable, loving, peaceful home, the reasoning went, would produce a stable, loving, peaceful nation, and a woman well conditioned in the demands of work, home, and patriotic service would foster these characteristics in her children, the nation's future. A project of teaching women how to be properly domestic and feminine was set into motion, an ideological mission supported by such paraphernalia as special calendars adopting religious calendar divisions for secular purposes and including things such as short stories, poetry, fashion tips, and romantic vignettes (Franco 1989: 90).[9]

Franco (1989: 81) identifies two aspects of this recodification of gender that deserve special attention: the isolation of a domestic sphere, with the expulsion from this sphere of any "low elements," and the displacement of the religious onto the national, which served to make purity (national, familial, and otherwise) the responsibility of women. If women were to remain in the home, a new understanding of a woman's

8. For an introduction to these issues, see Felski (1995) and Marshall (1994).
9. These calendars have made a comeback in recent years, offering, among other things, marriage advice, recipes, and tips on using the rhythm method.

role in the family had to be fashioned—one that would both legitimize the modern state and facilitate the reproduction of the bourgeois family ethos. On November 17, 1914, for example, President Obregón (1917: 227) exclaimed, in a manifesto against Pancho Villa, "Mothers, wives and daughters!: Kneel before the Altar of the Motherland and bring to the ear of your sons, husbands and fathers the sacred call of Duty, and cursed be those who, forgetting every principle of honor, place themselves in the hands of treason to stab the Motherland!" Women, it was argued, had to be properly "civilized" and shaped so they could fulfill their destiny (Franco 1989: 90).[10]

The key point here is that the intelligentsia argued, not against the subordination of women to men, but against the subordination of women to the church. The fear of the intelligentsia was that church influence would extend to the next generation of children through their mothers, an influence that they sought to counter through an aggressive education campaign stressing patriotism, the work ethic, and a belief in progress.

But this "education of women," it seemed, was going to be a challenge. Women's "lazy habits" (Hale 1978) permitted by generations of colonial and ecclesiastical rule had to be unlearned. Women who had previously farmed their children out to wet nurses and nannies were encouraged to "mother" them in an unprecedented hands-on fashion, to take personal responsibility for their children's intellectual and social development.[11] The spotlight was turned to women as the guardians of Mexico's future.

Women, then—and especially the *performance* of certain elements of femininity—became the battleground of the liberal and conservative factions in the shaping of Mexican national identity, and a woman's maternity and her carefully defined role in the home became the focus of their efforts. Gender, a nationalistic trope since the days of Guadalupe, assumed new importance during this period. Mexican women were not simply homemakers and mothers; in their wombs and in their homes

---

10. This idea of "civilizing women" to make them "proper" and "acceptable" continues to be very powerful in Mexico today. It is a recurrent theme, for example, on several popular Mexican soap operas, including *María la del Barrio* and *Acapulco, Cuerpo y Alma*. Both of these shows employ a Pygmalion-type theme in which the uncultured, uneducated, but stunningly beautiful girl from the *pueblo* is enculturated into "proper" society (learning how to speak, walk, dress, talk, and use the proper silverware in the proper order), usually to win the affections of the son of the manor.

11. For more detailed discussions on the situation of women in Mexico during this period, see Arrom (1985), Herrick (1957), and Mendleson (1978).

they nurtured and shaped the future of the Mexican nation. They would literally bring forth the "new" Mexican nation from their bodies and suckle it at their breasts.[12]

As the revolution of 1910–17 exploded, many aspects of Mexican society were transformed, including notions of gender. Women were active participants in the war: many left their homes, fought in armies, followed the troops, and nursed the sick. Women's emancipation became a central political concern during the seven years of fighting, emerging into a full-fledged feminist movement after the war ended in 1917. As the political crucible cooled, women demanded more recognition within the realm of political debate and participated actively in the postrevolutionary political congresses that would set the tone for the nation.

But whereas the prerevolutionary liberal agenda had focused on isolating women from the public sphere in a drive to "purify" and "nationalize" domestic femininity, the revolutionary period was characterized by the breakdown of these invisible walls of confinement and the integration of women into the public arena: "Unless we elevate women," wrote General Salvador Alvarado (1918: 45), "it will be impossible for us to construct a motherland."

Despite the advances made through women's active participation in the war, however, women were not accepted easily into the nationalist narrative. As Franco (1989: 102) notes, "[T]he Revolution with its promise of social transformation encouraged a Messianic spirit that transformed mere human beings into supermen and constituted a discourse that associated virility with social transformation in a way that marginalized women at the very moment when they were, supposedly, liberated." This model of nationalism, then, posited an understanding of patriotism and Mexican national character that was unequivocally male. Thus, Franco argues, "women were often at the forefront of rebellions against capitalist modernization" (100) as a means of resisting their marginalization. I will return to this issue below.

POSTREVOLUTIONARY MEXICO: MASCULINITY
AND THE IDEA OF "NATIONAL CHARACTER"

As Mexico pulled itself back together after the long revolution and the war-weary nation struggled to maintain its balance, the need for a

---

12. This new interest in motherhood as patriotic duty was made evident during this time in a proliferation of articles on the subject in the newly founded *Diario de México*.

unifying sense of Mexicanness that could embrace the country's economic, racial, ethnic, and political diversity became more urgent (Becker
1995). Between 1910 and 1940 a new generation of literati emerged to
steer the Mexican nation toward its new identity. Mexican philosophers,
anthropologists, psychologists, poets, playwrights, essayists, and sociolo-
gists all contributed to the formation of this new national consciousness.

But these writers did not extol "modernity" and "progress" as did
the generation of revolutionary writers before them. They did not cele-
brate the grand march of Mexican society toward a shining future.
Rather, they turned their gaze inward. If a new Mexican nation was to
be formed on an industrial-modernist base, they had to start at the
beginning. What did it mean to be Mexican? The concern was not so
much with the trajectory of Mexico as a nation as with what constituted the "essence" of Mexicanness. This introspective therapeutic exercise, characterized by deep, angst-filled soul searching, explored both
the damage Mexico's troubled history might have inflicted on the "character" of the Mexicans as a people and, perhaps more urgently, aspects
of their national character that seemed to invite defeat and turmoil. But
the question considered most important was whether it was possible to
discern a core complex of attitudes and behaviors that made Mexicans
different from Americans.

The quest for this notion of Mexicanness, argues Mexican sociolo-
gist Roger Bartra (1992), was legitimated by the invention of a paradise
lost—a mystical, magical Mexican past where everything was beautiful
and peaceful and right with the world. The invocation of a utopianized
past at this stage is not in itself surprising, Bartra suggests. The incon-
sistencies and contradictions inherent in the capitalist system invariably
lead to the positing of a lost primitive innocence. People tend to reach
to the past for comfort, inventing a paradise that not only becomes the
object of much guilt and anxiety (for its loss) but also opens a space of
resistance to the established order (17–18).

But nostalgia for a lost paradise assumed a particular form in Mexico
in the 1940s, 1950s, and 1960s. "After the Revolution," writes Bartra
(1992: 124), "the Mexican nationalists, orphans of native bourgeois
traditions, had only the peasants and the proletariat as sources of inspiration." During the revolution, as we have seen, the image of the
Indian—the "native"—came to represent an ideal of Mexicanness that
was outside the scope of Porfirian dialogues of progress and gentrifica-
tion. But in the postrevolutionary period this archetype of Mexicanness
was replaced by a new stereotype with which the cultured classes could,

to a certain extent, identify: the violent revolutionary Mexican, emotional and festive, urban and aggressive (Bartra 1992: 90). This core transformation was articulated in the image of the docile peasant—the *pelado*—who rose up as the revolutionary *Zapatista,* the forces of progress turning him into a new man: the proletarian, hero of the modern age (90).

But the glorification of the *pelado*-turned-proletarian posed a problem for the intellectuals and political leaders of the nation. It was too close for comfort to the Porfirian reification of positivist models of efficiency and modernity, the very ideology *against* which the revolution had been launched. As industrialization and modernization proceeded in Mexico, "an ideological dissection had to be performed in order to extract some features of popular culture for elevation to the category of national ideology" (Bartra 1992: 90): characteristics that were no longer useful were simply discarded, and a new Mexican prototype emerged from the ruins of the old.

Mexico at this time found itself in an extremely difficult position, as the interests of groups calling for land reforms and respect for indigenous traditions came into direct conflict with those of factions advocating modernization and progress according to an American model of development, despite the realization that adoption of this model was likely to develop Mexico (or "traditional" Mexico, at any rate) right out of existence. The result, suggests Bartra (1992, 19–20), was the invention of a national character that naturalized dependency, immaturity, and incompetence:

> The wound is still open which the revolutionary shrapnel of modern society, guided by the symbols of future and progress, inflicted on the rural, indigenous past. Through this wound the political culture wheezes; and in the name of pain for the shattered past it devises a profile of contemporary man that corresponds, point by point, with the myth of paradise subverted. Thus, the Mexicans resulting from the immense tragedy begun with the Conquest and ending with the Revolution are imaginary and mythical inhabitants of a violated limbo. Backwardness and underdevelopment have come to be seen as manifestations of a perennial static infancy that has lost its primitive innocence.

The myth of paradise subverted and of hopeless ineptness and dependency in the modern world came to dominate the cultural scene, becoming "the inexhaustible spring at which Mexican culture quenches its thirst" (Bartra 1992: 20) and the defining feature of Mexican national identity in this period.

While one must always be skeptical of generalizations about things as complicated as identities—national or otherwise—it is possible to comment on dominant discourses about certain identities, whether or not they directly reflect individual experience. With this in mind, we might say that the key to the trope of the *pelado* is that he articulated the clash of the traditional and the modern. The image of the *pelado* reflected the profound identity crises within the Mexican nation itself— a sense of alienation from the traditional but an extreme discomfort with the modern and a strong resistance to assimilation. The *pelado*, then, was a liminal creature, wavering somewhere between the past and the future.

The giants of Mexican literature and scholarship contributed actively and decisively to this construction, producing, through their work, a particular portrait of the Mexican people. Beginning in the twenties, thirties, and forties with writers such as Jose Vasconcelos, Antonio Caso, and Alfonso Reyes, and continuing up through the fifties and sixties with the works of Octavio Paz, Carlos Fuentes, Samuel Ramos, and Leopoldo Zea, a portrait of "the Mexicans" emerged that depicted them as "archaic souls whose tragic relationship with the modern age obliges them to reproduce their primitivism permanently" (Bartra 1992: 20). Immortalized in Diego Rivera's brilliantly colored murals, this "primitiveness" grew out of what was considered the core of the Mexican psyche, a unique psychological complex that established the Mexican as fundamentally different from the "modern man" of the industrialized West.

The interesting thing, as Bartra highlights, is that this understanding of Mexicanness—embodied in the *pelado*—was generated in dialogue with both U.S. perceptions of Mexico and Mexican perceptions of the United States and closely resembles the pejorative image disseminated by the United States during the postrevolutionary period. By Bartra's interpretation, this construction of Mexicanness, far from being a stance of resistance against the United States, was actually a *product of* the hegemonic influence of American industrial culture. It was, he argues, an historical invention that reproduced and legitimized a certain subjectivity that served certain political ends. A largely passive and uninquisitive constituency highly invested in the *patrón* system, for example, was much more likely than an educated and informed one to permit a ruling party to persist undefeated in the presidency for over sixty years as its leaders embezzled hundreds of millions of dollars. And Mexicans conditioned to see themselves as naturally ingenuous, passive, lazy, tradition oriented, and resistant to change were more likely to confine themselves to manufacturing and labor markets while inviting the United States to expand its industrial superiority.

As we can see from this discussion of the *pelado,* despite the important efforts of the revolutionary feminists the problem of Mexican identity continued to be constructed as one of *male* identity, leaving women marginalized as "the territory over which the quest for (male) national identity passed" (Franco 1989: 131). An emblematic construction of this configuration is the legend of La Malinche (Doña Marina), an indigenous woman who was given to Hernan Cortés by a Tabascan tribe. La Malinche became Cortés's mistress, bore him a *mestizo* child, and served as his translator and interpreter in his dealings with the indigenous peoples. She has been described as the most hated women in the Americas because it is believed that if it were not for her treachery—her betrayal of her people in her service of Cortés—the Conquest would never have taken place. She is seen as a traitor to her race, the disgrace of her people. When Mexico became an independent nation and the problem of national identity surfaced, Doña Marina, transformed into La Malinche, "came to symbolize the humiliation—the rape of the indigenous people and the act of treachery that would lead to their oppression" (Franco 1989: 131).

Octavio Paz, in his famous discourse on Mexican national character *The Labyrinth of Solitude* (1961), immortalized the betrayal of La Malinche as the fundamental trauma and the heart of the experience of Mexicanness, arguing that the Mexican male subject had been constituted as a result of this violent rejection by a shameful and disgraced mother (Franco 1989: 131): "Doña Marina has become a figure that represents those Indian women who were fascinated, raped, or seduced by the Spaniards, and, just as the child cannot forgive the mother who leaves him to go in search of his father, the Mexican people cannot forgive the treason of La Malinche. She incarnates the open, the raped [*lo chingado*], in opposition to our stoic, impassive and closed Indians" (Paz 1961: 86). The result, Franco (1989: 131) argues, is that "the problem of national identity was thus presented primarily as a problem of *male* identity, and it was male authors who debated its defects and psychoanalyzed the nation." Gutmann (1996: 241) agrees, observing that historically "the fate of machismo as an archetype of masculinity has always been closely tied to Mexican cultural nationalism" so that "the macho became 'the Mexican.'" In short, he notes, "'being *mexicano*' has been a male Mexican project. . . . In all versions, Mexican masculinity has been at the heart of defining a Mexican nation in terms of both its past and its future." Women, then, were in a tricky position during this period. To be nationalist—indeed, to be properly Mexican—was to subscribe to a distinctly male model of experience and action.

THE RETURN OF THE REVOLUTION

Many of these tensions have taken on new significance and urgency as Mexico faces the challenges of globalization. Thrust into the dizzying games of international politics, the nation teeters between the "under-developed backwardness" of the Third World and the "industrialized sophistication" of the First World, and the clash of these cultures has been thrown into painful relief as never before. The situation is complicated by Mexico's ambivalent and tenuous relationship with the United States and Mexico's continual struggle to maintain its autonomy and sovereignty in the face of the United States' hegemonic ambitions. As Mexico is drawn further and further into the model of Western indus-trial development, the central conflict seems to be whether, how, and to what degree Mexico should model its project of modernization on the United States, and with what consequences for its sense of cultural integrity. Thus concerns about Mexicanness have once again assumed center stage as the country struggles to make sense of its past and plot a course for the future.

Contemporary debates over cultural authenticity and the potential for developing a Mexican modernity are grounded in everyday struggles and conditions of inequality. It has been widely proclaimed in recent years that Mexico, despite the efforts of its leaders, is currently experi-encing a repetition of many of the social conditions it saw during the time of Porfirio Díaz, just before the Revolution of 1910 (Riding 1985; Stavenhagen 1990). Coca Cola, McDonald's, Kentucky Fried Chicken, Domino's, Cheetos and Doritos, Colgate, Ford, Woolworth's, Sears, Sam's Club, Tide, Kellogg's, Madonna, the Red Hot Chili Peppers—American products and celebrities are everywhere and seem to be almost uniformly preferred over Mexican ones.[13] The passion for things American has reinforced and legitimated governmental policies strongly favoring foreign investment and ignoring the needs of the indigenous

---

13. "American products are just better than Mexican ones," Lucia, a Mexican col-lege student, told me. "I don't know why. You Americans are just more industrious, I guess. So I look for things with English on the label, even if I don't know exactly what it says" (interview, October 17, 1995).

landowners, with the result of replicating many of the social ills that eventually brought the country to bloody and destructive revolution in 1910. This has been exacerbated by the financial crises of 1976, 1982, and 1994–95, which forced Mexico to accept enormous amounts of monetary aid from the United States and to subject itself more than ever before to America's explicit manipulating and directing of Mexico's internal economic and political affairs (Barry and Belejack 1992; López Flores 1988).

But many contemporary political writers stress that Mexico today, in contrast to the late 1800s, faces special challenges as American culture is pumped directly into Mexican homes and into lives of Mexican children via the electronic media (García Canclini 2001; Mosqueda Pulgarín 1988; Lozano 1991). The threat today, many contend, is not so much an industrial invasion as a cultural invasion, a campaign to "Americanize" Mexicans and transform them into proper consumers of American products and images (cf. Ritzer 1996; Gruzinski 2001).

Material goods are not the only avenue for this enculturation. Mexican television is saturated with sitcoms and movies imported from the United States and dubbed in Spanish, and those that are Mexican in origin showcase blonde, blue-eyed, light-skinned women as the unattainable objects of desire, the embodiment of what is "cool" and "modern" and "beautiful." *Baywatch, Beverly Hills 90210, Married . . . with Children,* and *The Simpsons* were among the most popular imported shows during my fieldwork, transmitting a worldview that diverged dramatically from traditional Mexican cultural and family values and causing alarm in many circles (Esteinou Madrid 1980; Lozano 1991; Xaltín Rivera 1988). Movies, television, radio, and magazines all communicate the "chicness" and "modernity" of American people, places, things, and lifestyles and aim to foster a new sense of individualism that, many contend, is in its very nature founded upon the rejection of traditional Mexican values (López Flores 1988; Mosqueda Pulgarín 1988).

Issues of cultural integrity and national identity, then, have again come to the forefront of Mexican national discourse. There has been an explosion of writing on the topic of Mexico's uncertain future, with works sporting names that seem to speak to a growing tension about Mexico's identity as a nation on the global stage. A selection of these works includes titles such as *Vocation and Style of Mexico: Fundamentals of Mexicanness* (Basave Fernández del Valle 1990), *Mexico, towards the 21st Century: Vision of a Generation* (Escobedo Delgado

1988), *Mexico Madness: Manifesto for a Disenchanted Generation* (Garcia Aguilar and Miskowiec 2001), *The Spiral without End: Political Essay about Contemporary Mexico* (Flores Olea 1994), *Mexico at the Threshold of the Millennium* (Colegio de México 1990), *The Profile of the Mexican: Bases for Forging a New Mexico* (Matute Vidal and Matute Ruíz de Vázquez 1992), *Profound Mexico: Reclaiming a Civilization* (Bonfil Batalla 1990), *Exits from the Labyrinth: Culture and Ideology in the Mexican National Space* (Lomnitz-Adler 1992), *Toward the New Millennium: Studies on Messianism, National Identity, and Socialism* (Martínez González 1986), *Wounded Pride: Mexico–United States in the Hour of Globalization* (González Souza 1994), *Rethinking the Nation: Borders, Ethnicities, and Sovereignty* (Arizpe and de Gortari Krauss 1990), *Culture and National Identity* (Blancarte 1994), *Chiapas, 1994: The Enemies of Modernity* (Arriola 1994), *Mexico: Obstacles for Modernity* (Parra Orozco 1992), *The Great Changes of Our Time: The International Situation, Latin America and Mexico* (Arbatov 1992), *Consumers and Citizens: Globalization and Multicultural Conflicts* (Garcia Canclini 2001), and *Wounds That Don't Heal* (Chavezmontes 1988). Despite their different foci, the central problematic in each of these works seems to be how to develop and pursue a "Mexican modernity" without eviscerating what Bonfil Batalla (1990) calls the "deep Mexico" in the process.

GENDER AND THE ANTIMODERNIST CRITIQUE

The maternal element of the Indian was overlain by the masculine
Spanish element. The humid and smooth contact of the
autochthonous world . . . by the rude, emphatic, paternal Spaniard.
    Basave Fernández del Valle, *Vocation and Style of Mexico*

Gender has again emerged as a central idiom through which these struggles over cultural integrity are articulated. Franco has argued that the archetype of Mexicanness that arose in the postrevolutionary period was modeled on an unequivocally male schema for being in and experiencing the world and that women were pushed to the margins, coming to represent "the space of loss and of all that lies outside the male games of rivalry and revenge" (Franco 1989: 131). During this time, she argues, femininity was relegated to the sidelines as the antithesis of patriotic sentiment founded on the traditional Mexican nationalist myth. It became a "space off," the domain outside the discourse from which a new critique might be launched.

Of course, the question of whether anything can truly be "outside" a complicated cultural system of meaning such as gender is highly questionable. But what is important here is the increasingly dominant theme in both academic writing and popular portrayals of Mexican cultural identity that "revived" constructions of femininity and motherhood are the new secret weapon in the war against the encroachment of American culture and U.S.-style modernity. In response to the challenge of modernization and globalization, the traditional conservative agenda advocating the expulsion of foreigners and the modeling of the country on the tenants of Roman Catholicism has reemerged, but with a twist. A Mexican national identity founded on a blend of femininity, nationalism, and religion is taking shape, a discourse of "rediscovering" and "reclaiming" Mexican culture, its religion and its traditional values, through the reclamation of its women.

This emerging notion of Mexicanness is far from monolithic or coherent. To my knowledge there is no widespread, coordinated national movement with these themes as the cornerstone of a clearly articulated agenda. But one does not have to look hard or far to find this blending of gender and religion in emergent representations of Mexican nationalism. It is hard to miss. It is everywhere, both in its explicit articulations (such as the annual Nuestra Belleza [Miss Mexico] pageant, television ads, and soap operas) and in what might be called its expression-in-relief, the invoking of *opposites* of these representations to convey certain messages (for example, many commercials use English and generalized representations of the United States and other symbols of "modernity" to appeal to a certain kind of clientele and to sell "modern" products from blue jeans to cellular phones). When I began to notice the prominence of these themes in the media and in casual discussions with my Mexican friends, I started to pay closer attention. I watched Mexican television, making notes on commercials, sitcoms, soap operas, and news programs that spoke to these issues. I read newspapers, news magazines, and popular magazines, clipped political cartoons and advertisements and articles. I interviewed my neighbors, my friends, taxi drivers, waitresses, shoeshine boys, and my colleagues. Gradually, I was able to piece together what I believe to be an accurate sense of this emergent representation of Mexicanness.

Generally speaking, this discourse does not call for a return to the rural paradise of *el campo* (the country) or for the elevation of a feminist agenda (as in the period following the revolution); rather, it calls for reformulation and application of traditional Catholic/Mexican values (the two are often conflated in this discourse) to the unique problems facing a rapidly developing nation. Unlike some of the projects of the first half of the twentieth century, the idealized form of this utopian/traditional culture has not been merely resurrected from the dusty pages of Mexican history. Instead, in an unprecedented way, it has been explicitly and consciously defined *against* the United States as the symbol of "modernity," a modernity that finds embodiment in specific cultural institutions explicitly coded as male. The two most visible of these "breeders of modernity" are Protestantism and the American feminist movement.

The threats of these forces are generally seen as inseparable and as leading to the same inevitable end—disaster. Mexican national identity and the concept of the "essence" of Mexicanness have always contained both a strong gender component (Hijos de la Chingada, the Virgin of Guadalupe, etc.)[14] and an explicit anti-Protestant sentiment, but in the past twenty to twenty-five years these have moved to the center of an emergent religio-nationalist articulation of Mexicanness. Although this discourse is modeled on national projects of the past, the strategic use of these representations banks on the symbolic capital of these images, not in the Mexican context alone, but in the global arena.

REGENDERING THE MEXICAN SUBJECT

Voices of the past resound in the wounded body of Mexico. The seas softly girdle the waist of this body as if to mitigate its pain. A patient pain, without sign of anguish, with apparent placidity. . . . Artistic Mexico. Intuitive Mexico. Humanized and humanizing Mexico. . . . Through our race the spirit will always speak. The vocation of Mexico is realizing itself in every one of us, the Mexicans, and in the whole of our collective style of life. The business of fidelity to our way of being is a beautiful risk. And the future belongs to those who assume their destiny and know how to wait.

Basave Fernández del Valle, *Vocation and Style of Mexico*

In a juxtaposition reminiscent of colonial days, much contemporary nationalistic discourse in Mexico bemoans the surrender of Mexican

---

14. We will remember, though, that, despite these central images of femaleness, the point of reference for the nationalist subjectivity has always been distinctly male, as constructed in and through the (male) Mexican's relationship with these powerful symbols of femaleness.

national integrity to a particular aggressor—the United States—who has for years economically and culturally "raped" it. Mexico is once again *la chingada*. But here we see something very interesting. Whereas previous interpretations held up the Mexican people as the (male) *sons* of the raped woman, the current discourse advocates adopting the identity of the raped mother *herself*: the "femininity" of *la chingada* has become the banner of resistance to American masculinist expansion. In an insurgent "matriotism" (*matriotismo*)[15] developed to counter the "patriotism" of years past (Bartra 1993), femininity is invoked to represent the purity, pristine beauty, and Third World vulnerability and innocence of Mexico and is associated with rich natural resources, life-giving sun, and rich soil—treasures to be protected from the lecherous aims of the "masculinizing" modernization project of the United States. "The country, like a woman, is tender, sweet," writes Basave Fernández del Valle (1990: 32). Vulnerable, innocent, suffering in silence, the Virgin becomes a symbol of the righteousness of the Mexican condition, her inviolate body representing the incorruptible core of the Mexican identity besieged by the United States.

Femininity, associated with nature and the countryside, is also frequently used as a symbol for the poor of Mexico's barrios in this emergent discourse. Victimized by the system, chewed up and spit out by the machine of capitalist development, the poor are the abused, the mistreated, the workers who, like a dedicated mother, toil day and night doing the "dirty work" so that the great glittering "modern" Mexico can survive and flourish. The poor are associated in this discourse with the soil, the clean air of the countryside, the crops and the animals that feed the rest of the nation. They are construed as simple folk who lead the simple life, guided by the principles of religion and the family. At the end of the day, it is the poor who constitute the "essence" of Mother Mexico, as they nestle into her bosom on the floors of their huts to sleep.

---

15. *Matria* (whose root implies "motherhood") is a term used to describe the small, rural villages of Mexico, distinguishing them from the (masculine) *patria* of its bustling industrial centers and cities. This is an interesting distinction, since *patria* also means "nation" and is the linguistic root of *patriotismo* or patriotism, the heart of nationalistic pride. The suggestion is that somehow these rural areas are "feminine" and lie outside of the traditional political construction of what constitutes the "male" (industrial, modern) Mexican nation.

RELIGION AND ANTICAPITALISM

Catholicism, traditionally associated with women and femininity in Mexico, has become a particularly powerful symbol in this model, representing not only the sanctity of the family and tradition and respect for life but the last bastion of morality and honor in the face of a powerful Protestant ethic that underpins capitalist development and implicitly prescribes the breakup of the home and the deification of the dollar. Protestantism is generally associated with materialism and the shameless pursuit of material wealth, whereas Catholicism, like femininity, is associated with the poor, the downtrodden, the oppressed.

This association of Catholicism and the poor has been institutionalized and radicalized through the remarkable success of the liberation theology movement in Mexico, particularly in the southern regions, where the indigenous populations have been the most ignored and mistreated by the government. Liberation theology is a "theology from the underside" (Torres and Fabella 1978): a theology of the oppressed proclaiming that Christ meant Christianity to be about emancipating the poor from the shackles of imperialism, injustice, and hegemony. Religion, then, is translated into a voice of protest against the workings of the capitalist system, which, through the power plays and explicit meddling of the United States in the Mexican economy, continues to oppress and exploit the poor of Mexico. The association between femininity, Catholicism, and the rural poor, then, is paralleled in this understanding by the association between masculinity, Protestantism, and the urban rich, with "American" religion providing the legitimating ethic behind the destructive "raping" of Mexico by aggressively expanding American industrial development.

In the more explicitly religious articulations of this emergent national project, this dichotomy of a Catholic, feminine Mexico versus a Protestant, masculine United States once again references the realm of femininity and motherhood. The key point of disagreement between the Catholics and the Protestants (according to this particular take on the issues) is that Protestants refuse to accept the perpetual virginity of Mary. Other theological differences are completely effaced by the assertion that the Protestants are wrong simply because "*no creen en la Virgin*"—they don't believe in the Virgin. The Protestants, as many of my Catholic Mexican friends explained it to me, reject Mary's divinity and salvific purity just as the liberal secularists did after the War of

Independence. The coincidence, according to the Catholics I spoke with, is not accidental. And not only the Virgin but the essence of femininity and motherhood is under attack.

TRIANGULATING GENDER, NATION, AND RELIGION
IN THE MEXICAN NATIONAL SPACE

What brought the issues of gender and religion to the political forefront after almost a century of relative unconcern? Perhaps the most important aspect of the resurrection of gender as a nationalist trope and the reorientation of the nationalist character from a male to a female model was the rise of the second wave of feminism in the United States beginning in the 1970s, which many Mexicans interpreted as a devilish and frightful embodiment of "U.S. subjectivity"—the inevitable outcome of a society founded on a masculinist/Protestant value base. Not content to erase the importance of the Virgin, it seemed to some, Protestantism and the masculinist ethos underlying Western industrial-technical society would ultimately "masculinize" Western women, creating automatons who would breed amoral, unethical, violent children and raise them to be slaves to the liberal capitalist state (see, for example, Belmar 1995).

Religion again became a focal point for nationalist fervor beginning in the late 1970s, as the Mexican countryside was flooded with Evangelical and other Protestant missionary groups bent on converting the masses. This saturation of the Mexican pueblos with Protestant groups has been (and continues to be) interpreted by many Mexicans as an obvious and deliberate plot by the United States to undermine the morality of the Mexican people and weaken resistance to capitalist development. In response, Catholicism has become a trope of righteous resistance to U.S. imperialism and, by extension, the conversion of Mexico into a "modern" culture.

Bonfíl Batalla (1990) suggests that the use of religious tropes in nationalist projects is a particularly powerful weapon for Third World countries wishing to preserve their cultural identity in the wake of globalization and to proclaim their independence from Western hegemony and that the success of such movements in other parts of the world should serve as a model for Mexican nationalists. "In the face of Kentucky Fried Chicken in Peking," he writes, "we should think about the Islamic Revolution, which occurred, contrary to all prediction, in what was the most Westernized country of the Middle East: Iran." The significance of this, he stresses, is that "it triumphed against the most powerful army in the Third World and . . . it is not possible to deny that it appealed, in order to mobilize a people, to the contents of a civilization different from the West." To write off the use of religion as merely "retrograde" or "anachronistic," he claims, is to dangerously underestimate its mobilizing force in the sociopolitical arena (106).

THE RESPONSE: A CRUSADE OF WOMEN

As these interpretations of cultural changes and their threats to Mexican national and cultural integrity have gained prominence, the response has been dramatic. In a move reminiscent of the liberal campaign to "mobilize" and "educate" women following the War of Independence, a no-holds-barred campaign has been launched to "reclaim" Mexico's women from the clutches of liberal, modernist control and, by extension, to reclaim Mexico. Once again the domain of motherhood and femininity has been targeted as the focus of nationalistic struggle, and the responsibility for the future of the nation has been laid on the shoulders of Mexico's young women. One television ad, for example, shows a Mexican mother struggling with her crying, nagging children. "Ay! These children! I just can't take it anymore!" she yells, exasperated. The camera pulls back to show her throwing herself into a chair, exhausted. She looks up as a European-looking man in a nice suit enters and begins a speech to the camera—"It's the responsibility of a mother to form good citizens for Mexico's future," he says. As he continues, the mother continues to look at him, his exaltation of her role making her glow with pride and respect. "She [indicating the mother] is Mexico. Our mother is Mexico. And this means commitment (compromiso)!" The mother jumps up and firmly shakes the man's hand, saying the word compromiso in time with him. "Mexico, you'll be proud of me!" she says into the camera, eyes glowing with the important charge given her. This ad was part of a larger campaign that used images of the "real" Mexico combined with messages about cultural unity and national pride.

In the 1995 Miss Mexico pageant, the notion of woman as the articulation of Mexican pride was made explicit. The announcer began by thanking the participants: "Thank you to all the participants for showing us that the Mexican woman has her feet on the ground and her eyes on the future." As the contestants were introduced, each one came out in a version of the traditional dress of the region—"The traditional costumes speak to us of their pride at being women—Mexican women. . . . The culture and tradition of Mexico are revealed in its women."

Far from being the product of extremist fringe groups or fanatic fundamentalists operating outside the mainstream, then, this discourse has made its way into the commercial and popular presses and is rapidly gaining ground. While the movement is by no means uniform or tightly organized, its ideology is omnipresent, and various facets of this discourse are expressed everywhere, in varying degrees of coherency and completeness. One particularly colorful, though not unusual, example is José Luis Belmar's 1995 work *Women . . . Root of All Evil? The Conspiracy of the Feminists against Women.*

Belmar (1995), a Mexican intellectual, journalist, and author, articulates this perspective in a particularly vivid way. He warns women not to be fooled by feminist claims, arguing that "women's liberation has done nothing but hurt women, making them work two jobs instead of one: forty hours a week in the office and then more in the home attending to their children" (37). "Women have been hurt by their own feminist movement," he adds, and they should run the other way fast.

But the danger goes much deeper, he claims; it strikes at the future of Mexican society. If women don't get their act together, Mexico is doomed. He illustrates this through a discussion of the Adam and Eve story, emphasizing the punishment Adam received for listening to his wife: "Eve is the one who, from the beginning, should have obeyed the voice of Adam and not the reverse. God created Adam to rule and Eve to obey. In punishment, Eve was condemned to suffer pain in pregnancy [and] God reminded Eve that it would be her husband who would be in charge of her and not the reverse" (12–13).

The feminist "conspiracy," which celebrates Eve's (and other women's) "disobedience," is occasioning, just as in the expulsion from Eden, the disintegration of Mexican society, leading to unemployment, hunger, drug abuse, alcoholism, pornography, and prostitution. Belmar calls to men to rise up, to take back control, to put an end to the "stupid war of the sexes that has been initiated in the United States by feminists like Gloria Steinem (*Revolution from Within*), Naomi Wolf (*The Beauty Myth*), Ann Landers, who has become, through her syndicated newspaper column, the heart of feminism, Carolyn Heilburn, Marilyn French (*The War against Women*), and others" (43). The feminist "plot" has entered Mexico from the United States and, he argues, is working its slow evil in Mexican society.

The problem, Belmar claims, is that Mexico has forgotten how to value its women for being *women*. "Why . . . do thousands of 'feminists' insist on looking like men?" he asks. "Why do they wear pants and shorts? . . . Why have many adopted men's suits, wearing them with shirts and ties?" (49). The answer, he suggests, is that women have been conditioned by American feminists to think that to be worth anything they have to become like men. "Here we return to what I consider to be the origin of many of the evils that pain the world today: women's liberation" (90).

But worse than bringing about women's own destruction, the "feminist plot" is literally destroying Mexico's children, the nation's future. "Did you know that more than twenty newborn babies are assassinated every month in the United States? And that this tendency is being imitated in other developed countries?" he writes. "And do you think that it is the fathers of those babies who are committing these assassinations? No! It is the 'little mothers' (['little'] because they are young and because they value little) that kill their babies and later throw them in the trash. . . . Long live women's liberation!" (63–64). The children of feminists—if they survive—are bound for disaster because their feminist mothers tend to be "young women who have always done what they wanted to because they have had no one in the home to show them the correct road or put a stop to their misconduct and licentiousness. In other words, young women of the new wave of feminism . . . love luxury, are capricious, disrespect authority, talk back to their parents, cross their legs, and tyrannize their teachers" (64). These modern women try to raise their children by "remote control" (37), and the result is a nation of miscreants, a nation of immorality and corruption.

The antidote, Belmar claims, is to be found in Mexico's traditional values. The virtues of femininity, he argues, must once again take center stage in Mexican society, as in "times past." "It is my desire that, in the name of equality, women return to being the ideal feminine companion and stop acting like the arch-enemy of men" (104). Men must help women to this end by asserting their authority and "rescuing" their women from the evil of American feminism.

The striking thing about this gendered religio-nationalist discourse and the way it is expressed in Belmar's work (among others) is it that it trades upon what are perceived to be the "essential" natures of two things normally held to be outside the domain of modernization and industrialization and indeed antagonistic to it—religion and femininity.

Faith, tenderness, unconditional love, "humanness," moral righteousness, disdain for oppression, the glorification of poverty—this discourse
purports to open a new space for the critique of globalization as experienced in Mexico through the launching of a national project from the
margins of Western capitalist development.

FATHER MURO AND MEXICAN MODERNITIES

Against this backdrop the political dimensions of Father Muro's vision
of the Siervas as prototypes of Mexican femininity (and therefore of
Mexico herself) are thrown into relief. Father Muro intended the Siervas
to serve, through their example, as a grounding force, helping to keep
the most vulnerable segments of Mexico's population from falling prey
to capitalist ideologies and their social trappings. In this way, Father
Muro understood his Siervas as helping Mexico remain true to what
was in his view its God-given essence.

Given the current pervasive cultural discourse, the gendered articulations of nationalism as a religious duty within the congregation do not
seem quite so strange. In fact, there are some striking similarities
between this emerging nationalist discourse and Father Muro's own
theological vision. Specifically, the linkages between femininity, tradition, and religion on the one hand and masculinity, modernity, and secularization on the other—central to Father Muro's perspective and the
impetus for his founding of the congregation—have become prominent
in Mexico, enjoying increasing popularity in the past two decades.

What is interesting where the postulants are concerned, though, is
the way in which these larger debates interface with the century-old philosophy of the congregation's founder to provide what seems to be a
treasured bit of flexibility—a carved-out space for maneuvering
between discourses and representations—for some young women grappling with what it means to be a Mexican woman in a time of rapid cultural change. For these women, I suggest that the convent seems to offer
an alternative to the oppositional representations of gender, tradition,
modernity, and power in dominant discourses of Mexican cultural and
national identity and at the same time persuades them to experience this
as personally and psychologically compelling in the context of their
own lives.

CHAPTER 13

Bodies and Selves

Theorizing Embodiment

I began this book with a problematic: Does a theory of the self require a theory of the body? If so, why? How might the systematic theorizing of an *embodied self* alter our current understandings of subjectivity and social processes? And what might the material I gathered in the convent contribute to this discussion?

I argued that theorizing on these issues has largely tended to collapse one side of the body/self dichotomy into the other, analytically producing either a disembodied self or a de-selfed body. Alternatively, I suggested, there has been a tendency to transpose the body/self distinction into the terms of "culture" versus "individual," without significantly disrupting the conceptual bases for such attributions. I argued that a significant part of the problem with these theoretical formulations stems from a need for more focused and intensive engagement with real people in real situations. I observed that some anthropologists have recently taken the problem of embodiment as a central theoretical project and have engaged in the sorts of investigations that lend themselves to the development of new theoretical understandings of embodiment. I framed the present ethnography as a specific contribution to this emerging literature, as an account of the systematic and deliberate reshaping of bodily experience of self over time and within a particular moral and religious framework. Here I want to return to these theoretical concerns and to offer a provisional theory of embodiment.

THE DUAL CATHEXIS OF THE BODY

I take embodiment to be a process of dual cathexis of the body. On the one hand, we use our bodies to communicate—to ourselves and to others—our inner states and desires. The body becomes a source of material and symbolic power for concretizing and representing experiences that feel private. Through the body, inner processes become visible. In the act of self-mutilation, for example, some psychiatric patients state that through feeling physical pain and seeing actual blood their psychic distress can find some grounding and become less overwhelming. By cutting, these individuals can see and touch and feel material evidence of their inner distress. In similar ways, we continually invest our bodies with enormous amounts of psychic energy—we cathect our bodies as a physical manifestation of our "selves," whatever we take that experience of self to be.

I understand the body to be the material grounding of experience, which cannot be abstracted from the visceral, lived aspect of physicality. At the same time, however, I acknowledge that the body is inscribed by structures of power in the Foucauldian sense. I agree with Probyn (1993) and Butler (1993, [1990] 1999) that the body cannot be taken as an ontological source of "truth" because its very material (flesh, bones, muscle, organs, skin) is infused with cultural values and meanings that are often beyond our immediate domain of experience but that nevertheless shape that experience. We cannot simply make our bodies—or what we *do* with our bodies—mean whatever we want them to mean. Bodily practices are subject to the logic of the context in which they emerge, and they often carry multiple—and sometimes conflicting—meanings. In the case of anorexia nervosa, for example, I have explored the ways in which the overdetermination of "thinness" as both an aesthetic and a practice leads young women into a double bind in which their anorexic behaviors simultaneously accomplish and undo the self-project they pursue (Lester 1997). In other words, the body is cathected from the "outside" as well as from the "inside," and because these cathexes are overdetermined and alterable, the experience of "embodiment" is a process through which these domains interact.

Subjectivity, then, as I understand it, is the current experience of this interaction of dual cathexis. The self, in my formulation, is the cohering of a sense of continuity across diverse subjectivities over time within the same person. In this sense, I rely largely on Ricoeur's (1992) distinctions between the immediate experience of being in the world and the reflective construction of a narrative of continuity of that being.

This model rests on a particular understanding of human agency. Just as I believe it is possible to talk about the self without reifying it as a nonbodied, nongendered, nonhistoricized entity, I believe it is possible to formulate a notion of agency that does not necessitate a reliance on the concepts of free will or the autonomous agent. My understanding of agency is one of generativity or the creative orchestration of cultural elements. Here I am building on Obeyesekere's ([1981] 1984: 44) understanding of personal symbols as "cultural symbols whose primary significance and meaning lie in the personal life and experiences of individuals." In this way, he argues, personal symbols involve a process of dual symbolic communication: with the larger cultural system from which the outward form of the symbol and its accepted public meanings are drawn and with the individual's own experiential world and the specific personal meanings she associates with the symbol. Personal symbols, then, have both personal and interpersonal meaning and carry deep motivational significance. The manipulation of these symbols, therefore, can transform meaning and experience on multiple levels.

While I agree with Obeyesekere that cultural symbols may assume powerful personal meaning in this way (though I take issue with his appeal to a universalized notion of the unconscious as generating, cross-culturally, particular kinds of symbolic meanings), I propose broadening this understanding to include the ways in which different cultural elements are brought into relationship with one another and how these relational configurations become both personally and interpersonally significant. It is in the orchestration of culturally available meanings—bringing them together, reversing them, arranging them in new and unconventional associations—that I believe agency is located.

In the case of anorexia, for example, cultural understandings about thinness, control, and power are brought into a certain kind of relationship and assume powerful personal motivational force for individual people. While the associations among these elements are available to all members of our culture (see Bordo 1993), not everyone becomes anorexic. Some young people link these cultural associations with their own particular personal experiences in ways that give the associations deeper meanings for them, so much so that they can come to feel as if the associations are an integral part of their beings.[1] At the same time, however, they cannot freely choose what being thin will mean. Indeed,

---

1. For a particularly powerful personal account of these issues, see Hornbacher (1998).

because of the contradictory meanings of thinness in our culture (such as, for example, simultaneously strength *and* weakness, nonsexual *and* eroticized), many anorexic women become caught in a process I have written about elsewhere as a paradox of liberation (Lester 1995). While agency may be manifested in the selective or creative bringing together of different cultural elements, this does not mean that we exercise this agency in a way that is free of culture (see, for example, Hollan 1994). We are still constrained by the cultural meanings associated with various symbolic forms, even when we attempt to subvert them by pairing them in unconventional ways (cf. Hopkins 1994; Lindon et al. 1982).

A successful theory of embodiment, therefore, must contend with (1) the dual cathexis of the body as both a material representation of inner experience and a domain for the (re)production of structures of power; (2) the subjective experience of the interaction of these domains within a particular cultural and historical context; (3) the structuring, over time, of a coherent narrative that selectively rearticulates these subjectivities within a developmental framework; and (4) an understanding of a generative agency that involves the manipulation of cultural meanings but that is not free of those meanings. Such a theory should engage embodiment not simply as a state of being but as an ongoing process of transformation and meaning making. I have taken this approach in thinking through what I observed in the convent and what the postulants themselves told me of their experiences.

RELIGIOUS FORMATION AS A
TECHNOLOGY OF EMBODIMENT

We can understand the process of formation in the convent as what I call a *technology of embodiment*. Each of the seven stages of formation uses the body in a different way, and each is understood to be crucial in creating a bride of Christ. These stages are arranged in contingent relationship to one another—the tasks of one stage must be mastered before one can effectively proceed to the next. Whether one has truly mastered a stage is not always immediately apparent, but a failure to do so eventually comes to light—indeed, as I mentioned, people did drop out of the program. But if all goes well, as they progress through the seven stages of transformation newcomers to the order approach an altered phenomenology of embodiment that fundamentally shifts their experience of self. In naming their feelings of brokenness, they learn to identify their discomforts in the outside world as a call to a radical rejection of temporal understandings of self. Through living and working side by side with other women, they learn new methods of perception and imagination that tie them to a community of others whom they come to recognize as significantly similar to themselves in God's eyes. Through the management of the physical body they develop a heightened sensitivity to interiorization as a process of bounding sacred potential. They become experts in the practices of the religious life, so that the body becomes routinized to "appropriate" performances. They learn to "read" what their bodies tell them about the state of their souls and to harness the desires of the body for radical transformation. By physically placing themselves in the service of authority, they come to inhabit bodily the ideal of *entrega*. And they learn to retell and reinterpret the stories of their fleshy selves—their struggles and temptations, difficulties and triumphs—as reflections of their changing relationship with God. In this way, new entrants achieve a bodily transformation of self that draws its meaning from a particular cultural and moral universe.

EMBODIED CONTRADICTIONS

The postulants I worked with came of age during a time of a radical transformation of expectations in gender roles. This challenging of traditional gender norms is invested with a kind of heightened cultural meaning in Mexico right now, becoming a symbolic language for articulating larger political and social issues. As a result, these young women are faced with a dilemma—what kind of woman they become carries with it a whole host of implications and signifies that they have bought into a certain kind of worldview. As individuals in a cultural system, they cannot independently decide which values will be attached to which markers of femininity. So these women—particularly those who are significantly uncomfortable with available cultural models of femininity—often find themselves having to choose the lesser of two or more evils while sitting uneasily with the result.

At the same time, each of these young women looked for, and found, strategies to resolve their conflicts. To what degree these strategies actually "work" for the individuals involved is debatable. But what I observed in the convent illustrates how complicated and sophisticated this project can be. It also demonstrates how cultural understandings— about, for example, feminism and nationalism—that may seem on the surface to be only tangentially related to the issues at hand (such as religious vocation and the salvation of the soul) can assume center stage in this process.

These understandings become compelling for these young women in very real, very personal ways. Celeste explained it to me like this: "We don't change our names anymore when we join the congregation. But if we did, you know what name I'd choose? My name would be Jerusalem. Jerusalem was a city so full of sin and degradation, she had fallen into such chaos and had lost her way. And then Christ was born and he redeemed her. And that's what he's done for me." It seems that some women in the convent, at least, do come to recognize themselves, reflected in the eyes of God.

Appendix

The definitions (with some minor editing and clarification) and prayers in this section are taken from the Catechism of the Catholic Church *(U.S. Catholic Conference 2000) and the* Catholic Encyclopedia *(Broderick and Broderick 1990).*

GLOSSARY OF CATHOLIC TERMS

BAPTISM: Baptism is one of the seven sacraments of the Christian Church; frequently called the "first sacrament," the "door of the sacraments," and the "door of the church." Usually performed on infants, the contemporary rite of baptism in the Catholic Church involves the applying holy water to the infant's forehead in the shape of a cross (or sprinkling the baby's head with holy water) while saying, "I baptize thee (or This person is baptized) in the name of the Father and of the Son and of the Holy Ghost." In administering this sacrament it is absolutely necessary to use the word *baptize* or its equivalent—otherwise the ceremony is invalid. Through baptism, the recipient is thought to be incorporated into the mystical body of Christ and to experience the remission of all sin (including original sin) accompanied by an infusion of the three graces of faith, hope, and charity. At the same time, baptism is believed to imprint a special character on the soul, forever binding the recipient to the obligations of the faith. Baptism is believed to be necessary for salvation because it opens the way for receiving the other sacraments. The practice of baptism emerged out of earlier Jewish traditions, most notably that of circumcision, through which Jewish males are entered into the Jews' covenant with God.

FEAST DAYS: The annual cycle of liturgical celebrations commemorating the mysteries of Jesus' life. Feast days commemorating Mary and the saints are also celebrated.

GENUFLECTION: A reverence made by bending the knee, especially to express adoration of the Eucharist.

IMMACULATE CONCEPTION: The dogma, proclaimed in Christian tradition and defined in 1854, that from the first moment of her conception, Mary—by the grace of God and by virtue of the merits of Jesus Christ—was preserved immune from original sin.

LENT: The liturgical season of forty days that begins with Ash Wednesday and ends with the celebration of the paschal mystery (Easter Triduum). Lent is the primary penitential season in the church's liturgical year, reflecting the forty days Jesus spent in the desert in fasting and prayer.

LITURGY OF THE HOURS: Also known as the "Divine Office," the Liturgy of the Hours is a compendium of prayers to be recited at fixed hours of the day or night by priests, monks, nuns, clerics, and any others who may feel compelled by virtue of their vocations. The Liturgy of the Hours is composed of certain prayers from the breviary. The Roman breviary, which with rare exceptions (certain religious orders, the Ambrosian and Mozarabic Rites, etc.) is currently used throughout the Latin church, is divided into four parts according to the seasons of the year: (Winter, Spring, Summer, and Autumn) and is constructed of the following elements: (a) the Psalter; (b) the Proper of the Season; (c) the Proper of the Saints; (d) the Common; (e) certain special offices. Liturgically, the day is divided into hours founded on the ancient Roman divisions of the day, of three hours apiece—Prime, Terce, Sext, None, and Vespers, and the night is divided into Vigils, Matins, and Lauds. Matins itself is subdivided into three nocturns, to correspond with the three watches of the night: nine o'clock at night, midnight, and three o'clock in the morning. The office of Lauds is supposed to be recited at dawn. The day offices correspond more or less to the following hours: Prime to 6 A.M., Terce to 9 A.M., Sext to midday, None to 3 P.M., Vespers to 6 P.M. At the hour for each office, prayers are recited that correspond to that office for that time of year.

MASS: The Mass (also called "the Lord's Supper" or the "Celebration of the Eucharist") is the complex of prayers and ceremonies that make up the service of the Eucharist in the Latin rites. The Catholic Mass is understood to be a commemoration of the events at the Last Supper, where Jesus reportedly gave bread and wine to his apostles, telling them, "This is my body. This is my blood. Do this in remembrance of me." The Catholic Mass is centered on the notion of transubstantiation of the Eucharist—the belief that the wafer the priest elevates on the altar during the mass *literally becomes* the body and blood of Christ (vs. being a symbolic representation of Christ's sacrifice). In accepting the Eucharist (the consecrated Host) into their own mouths in the act of Communion, the faithful understand themselves to be in contact with the very substance of Christ.

PENTECOST: The fiftieth day at the end of the seven weeks following Passover (Easter in the Christian dispensation). According to Church teaching, at the first Pentecost after the resurrection and ascension of Jesus the Holy Spirit was manifested, fulfilling the paschal mystery of Christ according to his promise. Annually the church celebrates the memory of the Pentecost event as the beginning of the new "age of the church," when Christ lives and acts in and with his church.

ROSARY: The rosary is a sequence of prayers said in meditation upon the various "mysteries" associated with the life of the Virgin Mary and her relationship with her son. These entail:

The Joyful Mysteries (recited Mondays, Thursdays, Sundays from Advent to Lent): The Annunciation; Visitation of Mary; the Nativity; the Presentation of Baby Jesus in the Temple; the Finding of Young Jesus Preaching in the Temple

The Sorrowful Mysteries (recited Tuesdays, Fridays, Sundays from Lent to Easter): Agony in the Garden; Scourging at the Pillar; Crowning with Thorns; Carrying of the Cross; Crucifixion and Death of Jesus

Glorious Mysteries (recited Wednesdays, Saturdays, Sundays from Easter to Advent): The Resurrection; the Ascension; Descent of the Holy Spirit (Pentecost); Assumption of the Blessed Virgin Mary; the Crowning of Mary

The recitation of the rosary begins with the Apostles' Creed and then an Our Father, Three Hail Mary's for an increase in the virtues of Faith, Hope, and Charity (love), and a Glory Be (see below). Depending on the day, the first decade of the rosary is begun by saying an Our Father. While meditating on the first mystery (Ex: The Resurrection of Christ), practitioners say ten Hail Mary's and a Glory Be. At the end of each decade some people will say the Fatima Prayer (see below). One then moves on to the second decade of the rosary and repeats the steps by saying one Our Father, ten Hail Mary's, and one Glory Be. After the final recitation, one ends the rosary by saying the Hail Holy Queen. The rosary is recited daily by the faithful and is often invoked in times of grief or need.

SACRAMENT: A sacrament, broadly defined, is an external sign of something sacred. *The Catechism of the Catholic Church* defines a sacrament as "an efficacious sign of grace, instituted by Christ and entrusted to the Church, by which divine life is dispensed to us through the work of the Holy Spirit" (U.S. Catholic Conference 2000: 774, 1131). The seven major sacraments of the Catholic Church are baptism, confirmation, reconciliation (also called confession or penance), matrimony, ordination (also called holy orders), sacrament of the sick (also called extreme unction or last rites), and the Eucharist (also called Mass).

SACRAMENTALS: Sacred signs that bear a certain resemblance to the sacraments and by means of which spiritual effects are signified and obtained through the prayers of the church.

SIGN OF THE CROSS: A sign in the form of a cross made by the Christian as a prayer honoring the Trinity, "in the name of the Father and of the Son and of the Holy Spirit" (U.S. Catholic Conference, 2000: 2157, cf. 786). In Mexico, when making the sign of the cross upon one's own body, one uses the right hand and the procedure is thus: "In the name of the Father [touch the forehead], and of the Son [touch the chest] and of the Holy Spirit [touch first the left shoulder, then the right]." This is followed by kissing the thumb of the right hand.

STATIONS OF THE CROSS: Also called Way of the Cross, Via Cruces, and Via Dolorosa, a series of pictures or tableaux representing certain scenes in the passion of Christ, each corresponding to a particular incident, or the special form of devotion connected with such representations. The Stations of the Cross figure prominently in religious observance during the period of Lent leading up to Easter, as the faithful say special prayers while meditating on each station. They are as follows:

1. Christ condemned to death
2. The cross is laid upon him
3. His first fall
4. He meets His Blessed Mother
5. Simon of Cyrene is made to bear the cross
6. Christ's face is wiped by Veronica
7. His second fall
8. He meets the women of Jerusalem
9. His third fall
10. He is stripped of His garments
11. His crucifixion
12. His death on the cross
13. His body is taken down from the cross
14. His body is laid in the tomb

TRINITY: The mystery of one God in three Persons: Father, Son, and Holy Spirit. Belief in the revealed truth of the Holy Trinity is at the core of Catholic faith as expressed in the creed. The mystery of the Trinity in itself is held to be inaccessible to the human mind and is the object of faith only because it was revealed by Jesus.

SELECTED CENTRAL PRAYERS

The Apostles' Creed (Profession of the Catholic Faith)

We believe in God, the Father, the Almighty, I believe in Jesus Christ, his only Son, our Lord He was conceived by the power of the Holy Spirit and born of the Virgin Mary. He suffered under Pontius Pilate, was crucified, died, and was buried. He descended to the dead. On the third day he rose again. He ascended into heaven, and is seated at the right hand of the Father. He will come again to judge the living and the dead. I believe in the Holy Spirit, the Holy Catholic Church, the communion of saints, the forgiveness of sins, the resurrection of the body, and life everlasting. Amen.

Fatima Prayer

O My Jesus, forgive us our sins, save us from the fires of hell and lead all souls to heaven, especially those who are in most need of Thy mercy.

Glory Be

Glory be to the Father, and to the Son, and to the Holy Spirit, as it was in the beginning, is now, and ever shall be, world without end. Amen.

Hail Mary (Ave Maria)

Hail Mary, full of grace, the Lord is with Thee. Blessed are thou among women, and blessed is the fruit of thy womb, Jesus. Holy Mary, Mother of God, pray for us sinners now and at the hour of our death. Amen.

Hail Holy Queen

Hail Holy Queen! Mother of mercy, hail, our life, our sweetness, and our hope. To Thee do we cry, poor banished children of Eve. To Thee do we send up our sighs, mourning and weeping in this valley of tears. Turn then, O most gracious Advocate, Thine eyes of mercy towards us. And after this our exile show unto us the blessed fruit of thy womb, Jesus. O clement, O loving, O sweet Virgin Mary.

Nicean Creed

We believe in one God, the Father, the Almighty, maker of heaven and earth, of all that is seen and unseen. We believe in one Lord, Jesus Christ, the only Son of God, eternally begotten of the Father, God from God, Light from Light, true God from true God, begotten, not made, one in Being with the Father, Through him all things were made. For us men and for our salvation he came down from heaven: by the power of the Holy Spirit he was born of the Virgin Mary and became man. For our sake he was crucified under Pontius Pilate; he suffered, died, and was buried. On the third day he rose again in fulfillment of the Scriptures; he ascended into heaven and is seated at the right hand of the Father, He will come again in glory to judge the living and the dead, and his kingdom will have no end. We believe in the Holy Spirit, the Lord, the giver of life, who proceeds from the Father and the Son. With the Father and the Son he is worshipped and glorified. He has spoken through the Prophets. We believe in one holy catholic and apostolic Church. We acknowledge one baptism for the forgiveness of sins. We look for the resurrection of the dead and the life of the world to come. Amen.

Our Father

Our Father, Who art in heaven, hallowed be thy name. Thy kingdom come, thy will be done on earth as it is in heaven. Give us this day our daily bread and forgive us our trespasses as we forgive those who trespass against us, and lead us not into temptation but deliver us from evil. Amen.

References

Alpert, Judith L., ed. 1986. *Psychoanalysis and Women: Contemporary Reappraisals.* Hillsdale, NJ: Analytic Press.

Alvarado, Salvador. 1918. *Mi actuación revolucionaria en el estado de Yucatán.* México, D.F: C. Bouret.

Anderson, Benedict. 1983. *Imagined Communities: Reflections on the Origin and Spread of Nationalism.* London: Verso.

Anna, Timothy E. 1998. *Forging Mexico: 1821–1835.* Lincoln: University of Nebraska Press.

Anzaldúa, Gloria. 1987. *Borderlands: The New Mestiza.* San Francisco: Spinsters/Aunt Lute.

Appadurai, Arjun. 1996. *Modernity at Large: Cultural Dimensions of Globalization.* Minneapolis: University of Minnesota Press.

Arbatov, G. A. 1992. *Los grandes cambios de nuestro tiempo: La situación internacional, América Latina y México.* México, D.F.: Universidad Nacional Autónoma de México.

Archer, Christon I. 2003. *The Birth of Modern Mexico, 1780–1824.* Wilmington, DE: Scholarly Resources.

Arizpe, Lourdes, and Ludka de Gortari Krauss. 1990. *Repensar la nación: Frontera, étnias y soberanía.* México, D.F.: Centro de Investigaciones y Estudios Superiores en Antropología Social.

Arriola, Carlos. 1994. *Chiapas, 1994: Enemigos de la modernidad.* México, D.F.: Miguel Angel Porrúa.

Arrom, Sylvia Marina. 1985. *The Women of Mexico City, 1790–1857.* Stanford, CA: Stanford University Press.

Asad, Talal. 1993. *Genealogies of Religion: Disciplines and Reasons of Power in Christianity and Islam.* Baltimore: Johns Hopkins University Press.

Augustine of Hippo. 2002. "On the Ascension of the Lord." In *Sermons to the People: Advent, Christmas, New Year's, Epiphany*, edited and translated by Henry William Griffen. South Lancaster, MA: Image Publications.

Bacal, Howard A. 1985. "Optimal Responsiveness and the Therapeutic Project." In *Progress in Self Psychology*, edited by Arnold Goldberg, 202–27. New York: Guilford Press.

———. 1994. "The Selfobject Relationship in Psychoanalytic Treatment." In *A Decade of Progress*, edited by Arnold Goldberg, 21–30. Hillsdale, NJ: Analytic Press.

———. 1998. "Is Empathic Attunement the Only Optimal Response?" In *Optimal Responsiveness: How Therapists Heal Their Patients*, edited by Howard A. Bacal, 289–301. Northvale, NJ: Jason Aronson.

Bagley, Bruce Michael, and Sergio Aguayo Quezada, eds. 1993. *Mexico: In Search of Security*. New Brunswick, NJ: Transaction Publishers.

Barry, Tom, and Barbara Belejack. 1992. *Mexico: A Country Guide*. Albuquerque, NM: Inter-Hemispheric Education Resource Center.

Bartra, Roger. 1992. *The Cage of Melancholy: Identity and Metamorphosis in the Mexican Character*. Translated by Christopher J. Hall. New Brunswick, NJ: Rutgers University Press.

———. 1993. *Oficio mexicano*. México, D.F.: Grijalbo.

———. 1994. *Wild Men in the Looking Glass: The Mythic Origins of European Otherness*. Translated by Carl T. Berrisford. Ann Arbor: University of Michigan Press.

Basave Benitez, Agustin. 1992. *México mestizo: Analisis del nacionalismo mexicano en torno a la mestizofília de Andrés Molina Enriquez*. México, D.F.: Fondo de Cultural Económica.

Basave Fernandez del Valle, A. 1990. *Vocación y estilo de México: Fundamentos de la mexicanidad*. México, D.F.: Editorial Limusa.

Bateson, Gregory. 1999. *Steps to an Ecology of Mind: Collected Essays in Anthropology, Psychiatry, Evolution and Epistemology*. Chicago: University of Chicago Press.

Becker, Marjorie. 1995. *Setting the Virgin on Fire: Lázaro Cárdenas, Michoacán Peasants, and the Redemption of the Revolution*. Berkeley: University of California Press.

Bedolla Miranda, Patricia. 1989. *Estudios de genéro y feminismo*. México, D.F.: Universidad Nacional Autónima de México.

Beduhn, Jason. 2002. *The Manichaean Body: In Discipline and Ritual*. Baltimore: Johns Hopkins University Press.

Bell, Catherine. 1992. *Ritual Theory, Ritual Practice*. New York: Oxford University Press.

Bell, Rudolph. 1985. *Holy Anorexia*. Chicago: University of Chicago Press.

Belmar, José Luis. 1995. *La mujer—Raiz de todos los males? Complot feminista contra la mujer*. México: D.F.: Edamex.

Benjamin, Jessica. 1988. *The Bonds of Love: Psychoanalysis, Feminism, and the Problem of Domination*. New York: Pantheon.

———. 1995. *Like Subjects, Love Objects: Essays on Recognition and Sexual Difference*. New Haven, CT: Yale University Press.

———. 1998. *Shadow of the Other: Intersubjectivity and Gender in Psychoanalysis.* New York: Routledge.

Bernheimer, Charles, and Claire Kahane. 1985. In *Dora's Case: Freud—Hysteria—Feminism.* New York: Columbia University Press.

Bhabha, Homi K. 1990. *Nation and Narration.* New York: Routledge.

Blackwood, Evelyn, and Saskia Wieringa. 1999. *Female Desires: Same-Sex Relations and Transgender Practices across Cultures.* New York: Columbia University Press.

Blancarte, Roberto. 1994. *Cultura e identidad nacional.* México: Consejo Nacional para la Cultura y las Artes: Fondo de Cultura Económica.

Bloch, Maurice. 1992. *Prey into Hunter: The Politics of Religious Experience.* New York: Cambridge University Press.

Boddy, Janice. 1989. *Wombs and Alien Spirits: Women, Men and the Zar Cult in Northern Sudan.* Madison: University of Wisconsin Press.

Bonfíl Batalla, Guillermo. 1990. *México profundo: Una civilización negada.* México, D.F.: Consejo Nacional para la Cultura y las Artes.

Bordo, Susan. 1993. *Unbearable Weight: Feminism, Western Culture, and the Body.* Berkeley: University of California Press.

———. 1999. *Feminist Interpretations of Rene Descartes.* University Park: Pennsylvania State University Press.

Bourdieu, Pierre. 1990. *The Logic of Practice.* Stanford, CA: Stanford University Press.

———. 1995. *Outline of a Theory of Practice.* New York: Cambridge University Press.

———. 1998. *Practical Reason: On the Theory of Action.* Stanford, CA: Stanford University Press.

Broderick, Robert C., and Virginia Broderick. 1990. *The Catholic Encyclopedia.* Rev. ed. Nashville, TN: Thomas Nelson.

Burck, Charlotte, and Bebe Speed, eds. 1995. *Gender, Power, and Relationships.* New York: Routledge.

Burkitt, Ian. 1999. *Bodies of Thought: Embodiment, Identity, Modernity.* Thousand Oaks, CA: Sage Publications.

Butler, Judith. [1990] 1999. *Gender Trouble: Feminism and the Subversion of Identity.* New York: Routledge.

———. 1993. *Bodies That Matter: On the Discursive Limits of "Sex."* New York: Routledge.

Bynum, Carolyn Walker. 1987. *Holy Feast, Holy Fast: The Religious Significance of Food to Medieval Women.* Berkeley: University of California Press.

Calero, Manuel. 1916. *The Mexican Policy of President Woodrow Wilson as It Appears to a Mexican.* New York: Press of Smith and Thomson.

Cantú Corro, José. 1924. *Patria y raza: Discurso pronunciado por su autór en la "Fiesta de la Raza," celebrada en Huajuápam de León (Oajaca) en el 12 de Octubre 1919.* México: Escuela Tipográfica Salesiana.

Caplan, Paula J. 1993. *The Myth of Women's Masochism.* 2nd ed. Buffalo: University of Toronto Press.

Chavezmontes, Julio. 1988. *Heridas que no cierran.* México: Grijalbo.

Chesler, Phyllis. [1972] 1997. *Women and Madness*. New York: Four Walls Eight Windows.

Chodorow, Nancy. [1989] 1999. *The Reproduction of Mothering: Psychoanalysis and the Sociology of Gender*. 2nd ed. Berkeley: University of California Press.

———. 1991. *Feminism and Psychoanalytic Theory*. New Haven, CT: Yale University Press.

———. 1999. *The Power of Feelings: Personal Meaning in Psychoanalysis, Gender, and Culture*. New Haven, CT: Yale University Press.

Cole, Jennifer. 2001. *Forget Colonialism? Sacrifice and the Art of Memory in Madagascar*. Berkeley: University of California Press.

Colegio de México. 1990. *México en el umbral del milenio*. México, D.F.: Colegio de México.

Comaroff, Jean. 1985. *Body of Power, Spirit of Resistance: The Culture and History of a South African People*. Chicago: University of Chicago Press.

Comaroff, Jean, and John Comaroff. 1993. *Modernity and Its Malcontents: Ritual and Power in Postcolonial Africa*. Chicago: University of Chicago Press.

Crapanzano, Vincent. 1986. *Tuhami: Portrait of a Moroccan*. Chicago: University of Chicago Press.

Creel, George. 1926. *The People Next Door: An Interpretive History of Mexico and the Mexicans*. New York: John Day.

Csordas, Thomas J. 1994a. *Embodiment and Experience: The Existential Ground of Culture and Self*. Cambridge Studies in Medical Anthropology 2. New York: Cambridge University Press.

———. 1994b. *The Sacred Self: A Cultural Phenomenology of Charismatic Healing*. Berkeley: University of California Press.

Cue Canovas, Agustín. 1970. *Los Estados Unidos y el México olvidado*. México, D.F.: B. Costa-Amic.

Curb, Rosemary, and Nancy Manahan. 1985. *Lesbian Nuns: Breaking Silence*. Tallahassee, FL: Naiad Press.

de la Garza, Rodolfo, and Jesús Velasco, eds. 1997. *Bridging the Border: Transforming Mexico-U.S. Relations*. Lanham, MD: Rowman and Littlefield.

De Lauretis, Theresa. 1987. *Technologies of Gender: Essays on Theory, Film, and Fiction*. Bloomington: University of Indiana Press.

Desjarlais, Robert R. 1992. *Body and Emotion: The Aesthetics of Illness and Healing in the Nepal Himalayas*. Philadelphia: University of Pennsylvania Press.

———. 2003. *Sensory Biographies: Lives and Deaths among Nepal's Yolmo Buddhists*. Berkeley: University of California Press.

Dhruvarajan, Vanaja, and Jill Vickers, eds. 2002. *Gender, Race, and Nation: A Global Perspective*. Toronto: University of Toronto Press.

Dimen, Muriel. 1996. "Discussion of Symposium, 'The Relational Construction of the Body.'" *Gender and Psychoanalysis* 1(13): 385–401.

———. 2002. "Deconstructing Difference: Gender, Splitting, and Transitional Space." In *Gender in Psychoanalytic Space: Between Clinic and Culture*, edited by Muriel Dimen and Virginia Goldner, 41–61. New York: Other Press.

Dinnerstein, Dorothy. 1976. *The Mermaid and the Minotaur: Sexual Arrangements and Human Malaise.* New York: Harper and Row.

Doane, Janice L., and Devon L. Hodges. 1987. *Nostalgia and Sexual Difference: The Resistance to Contemporary Feminism.* New York: Methuen.

Doctors, Shelley R. 1996. "Notes on the Contribution of the Analyst's Self-Awareness to Optimal Responsiveness." In *Basic Ideas Reconsidered,* edited by Arnold Goldberg, 55–63. Progress in Self Psychology 12. Mahwah, NJ: Lawrence Erlbaum Associates.

Douglas, Mary. [1966] 1984. *Purity and Danger: An Analysis of the Concepts of Pollution and Taboo.* London: Ark.

Downey, Gary Lee, and Joseph Dumit, eds. 1997. *Cyborgs and Citadels: Anthropological Interventions in Emerging Sciences and Technologies.* Santa Fe, NM: School of American Research Press.

Durante Espinoza, María de Jesús. 2001. *Frontera y diplomacía: Los relaciones México-Estados Unidos durante el Porfiato.* México: Secretaría de Relaciones Exteriores.

Eisenhower, John S. D. 1993. *Intervention! The United States and the Mexican Revolution, 1913–1917.* New York: W. W. Norton.

———. 2000. *So Far from God: The U.S. War with Mexico, 1846–1848.* Norman: University of Oklahoma Press.

Escobedo Delgado, Juan Francisco, ed. 1988. *México, hacía el siglo XXI: Visión de una generación.* México, D.F.: Seminario de Estudios Nacionales.

Esteinou Madrid, Javier. 1980. *Apartos de comunicación de masas, estado, y puntas de hegemonía.* México, D.F.: Universidad Autónoma Metropolitana.

Fanon, Frantz. [1963] 1968. *The Wretched of the Earth.* New York: Grove Press.

———. 1967. *Black Skin, White Masks.* New York: Grove Press.

Felski, Rita. 1995. *The Gender of Modernity.* Cambridge, MA: Harvard University Press.

Fernández MacGregor, Genaro. 1960. *En la Era de la Mala Vecindad.* México, D.F.: Ediciones Botas.

Ferree, Myra Marx, Judith Lorber, and Beth B. Hess, eds. 1999. *Revisioning Gender.* Thousand Oaks, CA: Sage.

Figert, Anne E. 1996. *Women and the Ownership of PMS: The Structuring of Psychiatric Disorder.* New York: Aldine de Gruyter.

Fineman, Martha, and Isabel Karpin. 1995. *Mothers in Law: Feminist Theory and the Legal Regulation of Motherhood.* New York: Columbia University Press.

Flax, Jane. 1990. *Thinking Fragments: Psychoanalysis, Feminism, and Postmodernism in the Contemporary West.* Berkeley: University of California Press.

Flores Olea, Víctor. 1994. *La espiral sin fin: Ensayo político sobre México actual.* México, D.F.: Editorial Joaquín Mortiz.

Fosshage, James L. 1997. "Listening/Experiencing Perspectives and the Quest for a Facilitating Responsiveness." In *Conversations in Self Psychology,* edited by Arnold Goldberg, 33–55. Progress in Self Psychology 13. Hillsdale, NJ: Analytic Press.

Foucault, Michel. [1972] 1982. *The Archaeology of Knowledge.* New York: Pantheon.

——. 1973. *The Birth of the Clinic: An Archaeology of Medical Perception.* New York: Pantheon Books.

——. 1977. *Discipline and Punish: The Birth of the Prison.* Translated by Alan Sheridan. New York: Pantheon.

——. 1979. *The History of Sexuality.* Vol. 1. *An Introduction.* Translated by Robert Hurley. London: Allen Lane.

——. [1985] 1986. *The History of Sexuality.* Vol. 2. *The Use of Pleasure.* Translated by Robert Hurley. New York: Vintage Books.

——. [1986] 1988. *The History of Sexuality.* Vol. 3. *The Care of the Self.* Translated by Robert Hurley. New York: Vintage Books.

Foy, Felician A., and Rose M. Avato, eds. 1986–94. *Catholic Almanac.* Huntington, IN: Our Sunday Visitor.

Franco, Jean. 1989. *Plotting Women: Gender and Representation in Mexico.* New York: Columbia University Press.

Frazier, Donald S., ed. 1998. *The United States and Mexico at War: Nineteenth-Century Expansionism and Conflict.* New York: Macmillan.

Gaonkar, Dilip Parameshwar, ed. 2001. *Alter/Native Modernities.* Durham, NC: Duke University Press.

García Aguilar, Eduardo, and Jay Miskowiec. 2001. *Mexico Madness: Manifesto for a Disenchanted Generation.* Minneapolis: Aliform Publishing.

García Canclini, Néstor. 2001. *Consumers and Citizens: Globalization and Multicultural Conflicts.* Minneapolis: University of Minnesota Press.

Gergen, Kenneth J. 1991. *The Saturated Self: Dilemmas of Identity in Contemporary Life.* New York: Basic Books.

Gilly, Adolfo. 1994a. *El Cardenismo, una utopia Méxicana.* México, D.F: Cal y Arena.

——. 1994b. *La revolución interrumpida.* México: Ediciones Era.

Ginsberg, Faye, and Rayna Rapp, eds. 1995. *Conceiving the New World Order: The Global Politics of Reproduction.* Berkeley: University of California Press.

Glucklich, Ariel. 2001. *Sacred Pain: Hurting the Body for the Sake of the Soul.* New York: Oxford University Press.

Goffman, Erving. 1961. *Asylums.* New York: Anchor.

Goldberg, Arnold. 1990. *The Prisonhouse of Psychoanalysis.* Hillsdale, NJ: Analytic Press.

Gomez-Quiñones, Juan. 1992. *Mexican Nationalist Formation: Political Discourse, Policy and Dissidence.* Encino, CA: Floricanto Press.

Gonzalez Díaz, F. 1988. "Juventúd y modernización." In *México, hacía el siglo XXI: Visión de una generación,* edited by J.F. Escobedo Delgado, 117–22. México, D.F.: Seminario de Estudios Nacionales

González Souza, Luis. 1994. *Soberanía herida: México–Estados Unidos en la hora de la globalización.* México, D.F.: Editorial Nuestro Tiempo.

Gould, Carol C. [1983] 1984. *Beyond Domination: New Perspectives on Women and Philosophy.* Totowa, NJ: Rowman and Allanheld.

Gould, Edith. 1995. "Seduced and Abandoned: Special Transference-Counter-transference and Gender Themes When Women Analysts Treat Male Patients." *Psychoanalysis and Psychotherapy* 12(1): 60–76.

Green, Gill, and Elisa J. Sobo. 2000. *The Endangered Self: Managing the Social Risk of HIV.* New York: Routledge.

Grosz, Elizabeth A. 1994. *Volatile Bodies: Towards a Corporeal Feminism.* Bloomington: Indiana University Press.

Gruzinski, Serge. 2001. *Images at War: Mexico from Columbus to Blade Runner (1492–2019).* Translated by Heather MacLean. Durham, NC: Duke University Press.

Guarton, Gladys Branly. 1996. "Masculinity, Femininity and Change in Psychoanalysis." *Journal of the American Academy of Psychoanalysis* 24(4): 691–708.

Guerra Castellanos, G. 1988. México-Estados Unidos: Los retos de fin de siglo. In *México, hacía el siglo XXI: Visión de una generación,* edited by J. F. Escobedo Delgado, 45–49. México, D.F.: Seminario de Estudios Nacionales.

Gutmann, Matthew. 1996. *The Meanings of Macho: Being a Man in Mexico City.* Berkeley: University of California Press.

Haglund, Pamela E. 1996. " 'A Clear and Equal Glass': Reflections on the Metaphor of the Mirror." *Psychoanalytic Psychology* 13(2): 225–45.

Hale, Charles A. 1978. *El liberalismo en México en la época de Mora: 1821–1853.* México: Siglo Veintiuno.

Hall, Edward T. 1990. *The Hidden Dimension.* New York: Anchor Books/Doubleday.

Hall, Linda B., and Don M. Coerver. 1988. *Revolution on the Border: The United States and Mexico, 1910–1920.* Albuquerque: University of New Mexico Press.

Hamburg, Paul. 1991. "Interpretation and Empathy: Reading Lacan with Kohut." *International Journal of Psychoanalysis* 72(2): 347–61.

Hanigsberg, Julia E., and Sara Ruddick, eds. 1999. *Mother Troubles: Rethinking Contemporary Maternal Dilemmas.* Boston: Beacon Press.

Hart, John M. 1987. *Revolutionary Mexico: The Coming and Process of the Mexican Revolution.* Berkeley: University of California Press.

Harvey, Neil, ed. 1993. *Mexico: Dilemmas of Transition.* New York: Institute of Latin American Studies, University of London and British Academic Press.

Herdt, Gilbert H. 1997. *Same Sex, Different Cultures: Exploring Gay and Lesbian Lives.* Boulder, CO: Westview Press.

———. 1999. *Sambia Sexual Culture: Essays from the Field.* Chicago: University of Chicago Press.

Herrick, J. 1957. "Periodicals for Women in Mexico during the Nineteenth Century." *Americas* 14(2): 135–44.

Hobsbawm, E. J. 1990. *Nations and Nationalisms since 1780: Programme, Myth, Reality.* New York: Cambridge University Press.

Hobsbawm, E. J., and T. O. Ranger. 1983. *The Invention of Tradition.* New York: Columbia University Press.

Hodgson, Dorothy, ed. 2001. *Gendered Modernities: Ethnographic Perspectives.* New York: Palgrave.

Hollan, Douglas. 1994. "Suffering and the Work of Culture: A Case of Magical Poisoning in Toraja." *American Ethnologist* 21(1): 74–87.

Hollywood, Amy. 2002. *Sensible Ecstasy: Mysticism, Sexual Difference and the Demands of History.* Chicago: University of Chicago Press.

Honneth, Axel. 1997. *The Struggle for Recognition: The Moral Grammar of Social Conflicts.* Cambridge, MA: Polity Press.

hooks, bell. 1981. *Ain't I a Woman: Black Women and Feminism.* Boston: South End Press.

———. 2000. *Where We Stand: Class Matters.* New York: Routledge.

Hopkins, Patrick D. 1994. "Rethinking Sadomasochism: Feminism, Interpretation, Simulation." *Hypatia* 9(1): 116–41.

Hornbacher, Marya. 1998. *Wasted: A Memoir of Anorexia and Bulimia.* New York: Harper Collins Publishers.

Hsu, Francis L. K. 1983. *Rugged Individualism Reconsidered: Essays in Psychological Anthropology.* Knoxville: University of Tennessee Press.

Hughes, Judith M. 1999. *Freudian Analysts/Feminist Issues.* New Haven, CT: Yale University Press.

Instituto Nacional de Estadística, Geografía e Informática. 2000. *Estados Unidos mexicanos: XII censo general de población y vivienda.* Mexico: Mexico.

Irigaray, Luce. 1985a. *Speculum of the Other Woman.* Translated by Gillian C. Gill. Ithaca, NY: Cornell University Press.

———. 1985b. *This Sex Which Is Not One.* Translated by Catherine Porter. Ithaca, NY: Cornell University Press.

Jaggar, Alison M., and Susan Bordo, eds. 1989. *Gender/Body/Knowledge: Feminist Reconstructions of Being and Knowing.* New Brunswick, NJ: Rutgers University Press.

Jayawardena, Kumari. 1986. *Feminism and Nationalism in the Third World.* Totowa, NJ: Zed Books.

Jones, James W. 1996. *Religion and Psychology in Transition: Psychoanalysis, Feminism, and Theology.* New Haven, CT: Yale University Press.

Kaplan, E. Ann, and Susan Merrill Squier. 1999. *Playing Dolly: Technocultural Formulations, Fantasies, and Fictions of Assisted Reproduction.* New Brunswick, NJ: Rutgers University Press.

Kleinman, Arthur. 1988. *The Illness Narratives: Suffering and Healing in the Human Condition.* New York: Basic Books.

Kleinman, Arthur, and Veena Das. 1997. *Social Suffering.* Berkeley: University of California Press.

Kleinman, Arthur, and Byron J. Good. 1985. *Culture and Depression: Studies in the Anthropology and Cross-Cultural Psychiatry of Affect and Disorder.* Berkeley: University of California Press.

Knauft, Bruce M., ed. 2002. *Critically Modern: Alternatives, Alterities, Anthropologies.* Bloomington: Indiana University Press.

Kohut, Heinz. 1971. *The Analysis of the Self: A Systematic Approach to the Psychoanalytic Treatment of Narcissistic Personality Disorders.* New York: International Universities Press.

———. 1977. *The Restoration of the Self.* New York: International Universities Press.

Kohut, Heinz, Arnold Goldberg, and Paul E. Stepansky. 1984. *How Does Analysis Cure?* Chicago: University of Chicago Press.

Komesaroff, Paul A. 1995. *Troubled Bodies: Critical Perspectives on Postmodernism, Medical Ethics, and the Body.* Durham, NC: Duke University Press.

Krauze, Enrique. 1998. *Mexico, Biography of Power: A History of Modern Mexico, 1810–1996.* Translated by Hank Heifetz. New York: Perennial.

Kristeva, Julia. 1982. *Powers of Horror: An Essay on Abjection.* New York: Columbia University Press.

Kulish, Nancy, and Martin Mayman. 1993. "Gender-Linked Determinants of Transference and Countertransference in Psychoanalytic Psychotherapy." *Psychoanalytic Inquiry* 13(2): 285–305.

Lacan, Jacques. 1949. "The Mirror Stage, Source of I-Function, as Shown by Psycho-Analytic Experience." *International Journal of Psychoanalysis* 30:203.

———. 1953. "Some Reflections on the Ego." *International Journal of Psychoanalysis* 34: 11–17.

Lafaye, Jacques. 1987. *Quetzalcóatl and Guadalupe: The Formation of Mexican National Consciousness, 1531–1813.* Chicago: University of Chicago Press.

Lamas, Marta. 1997. "The Feminist Movement and the Development of Political Discourse on Voluntary Motherhood in Mexico." *Reproductive Health Matters* 10: 58–67.

Langley, Lester D. 1991. *Mexico and the United States: The Fragile Relationship.* Boston: Twayne Publishers.

Laplanche, J., and J. B. Pontalis. 1973. *The Language of Psycho-Analysis.* Translated by Donald Nicholson-Smith. Oxford: W. W. Norton.

Lau Jaiven, Ana. 1987. *La nueva ola del feminismo en México: Conciencia y acción de lucha de las mujeres.* México, D.F.: Fascículos Planeta

Lax, Ruth F. 1997. *Becoming and Being a Woman.* Northvale, NJ: Jason Aronson.

Lemche, Erwin. 1998. "The Development of the Body Image in the First Three Years of Life." *Psychoanalysis and Contemporary Thought* 21(2): 155–275.

Lester, Rebecca J. 1995. "Embodied Voices: Women's Food Asceticism and the Negotiation of Identity." *Ethos* 23(2): 187–222.

———. 1997. "The (Dis)Embodied Self in Anorexia Nervosa." *Social Science and Medicine* 44(4): 479–90.

———. 1999. "Let Go and Let God: Religion and the Politics of Surrender in Overeaters Anonymous." In *Interpreting Weight: The Social Management of Fatness and Thinness,* edited by Jeffery Sobal and Donna Maurer, 139–64. New York: Aldine de Gruyter.

———. 2003. "The Immediacy of Eternity: Time and Transformation in a Roman Catholic Convent." *Religion* 33 (2003): 201–19.

Lichtenberg, Joseph D. 1991. "A Theory of Motivational-Functional Systems as Psychic Structures." In *The Concept of Structure in Psychoanalysis,* edited by Theodore Shapiro, 57–72. Madison, CT: International Universities Press.

Lieberman, Janice. 2000. *Body Talk: Looking and Being Looked at in Psychotherapy.* Northvale, NJ: Jason Aronson.

Lindenbaum, Shirley, and Margaret M. Lock, eds. 1993. *Knowledge, Power and Practice: The Anthropology of Medicine and Everyday Life.* Berkeley: University of California Press.

Lindon, John A. 1994. Gratification and Provision in Psychoanalysis: Should We Get Rid of "the Rule of Abstinence"? *Psychoanalytic Dialogues* 4(4): 549–82.

Lindon, Robin Ruth, Darlene R. Pagano, Diana E. H. Russell, and Susan Leigh Star, eds. 1982. *Against Sadomasochism: A Radical Feminist Analysis.* San Francisco: Frog in the Well.

Lomnitz-Adler, Claudio. 1992. *Exits from the Labyrinth: Culture and Ideology in the Mexican National Space.* Berkeley: University of California Press.

———. 2001. *Deep Mexico, Silent Mexico: An Anthropology of Nationalism.* Minneapolis: University of Minnesota Press.

López Flores, B. 1988. "La política exterior de México." In *México, hacía el siglo XXI: Visión de una generación,* edited by J. F. Escobedo Delgado, 38–44. México, D.F.: Seminario de Estudios Nacionales.

Lozano, José Carlos. 1991. *Prensa, radiodifusión, e identidad cultura en la frontera norte.* Tijuana, Baja California: Colegio de la Frontera Norte.

Lucy, John Arthur. 1992. *Language and Diversity and Thought: A Reformulation of the Linguistic Relativity Hypothesis.* New York: Cambridge University Press.

Luhrmann, T. M. 1989. *Persuasions of the Witch's Craft: Ritual Magic in Contemporary England.* Cambridge, MA: Harvard University Press.

———. 1996. *The Good Parsi: The Fate of a Colonial Elite in a Postcolonial Society.* Cambridge, MA: Harvard University Press.

Lukton, Rosemary. 1992. "Gender as an Element in the Intersubjective Field: The Female Therapist and the Male Patient." *Clinical Social Work Journal* 20(2): 153–67.

Lutz, Catherine. 1988. *Unnatural Emotions: Everyday Sentiments on a Micronesian Atoll and Their Challenge to Western Theory.* Chicago: University of Chicago Press.

Macías, Anna. 1982. *Against All Odds: The Feminist Movement in Mexico to 1940.* Westport, CT: Greenwood Press.

MacIsaac, David S. 1996. "Optimal Frustration: An Endangered Concept." In *Basic Ideas Reconsidered,* edited by Arnold Goldberg, 3–16. Progress in Self Psychology 12. Mahwah, NJ: Lawrence Erlbaum Associates.

Mahmood, Saba. 2001. "Feminist Theory, Embodiment, and the Docile Agent: Some Reflections on the Egyptian Islamic Revival." *Cultural Anthropology* 16(2): 202–36.

Mallon, Florencia E. 1995. *Peasant and Nation: The Making of Postcolonial Mexico and Peru.* Berkeley: University of California Press.

Mansfield, Nick. 2000. *Subjectivity: Theories of the Self from Freud to Haraway.* New York: New York University Press.

Marcus, Barbara F. 1993. "Vicissitudes of Gender Identity in the Female Therapist/Male Patient Dyad." *Psychoanalytic Inquiry* 13(2): 258–69.

Marshall, Barbara L. 1994. *Engendering Modernity: Feminism, Social Theory, and Social Change.* Boston: Northeastern University Press.

Martin, Emily. [1987] 2001. *The Woman in the Body: A Cultural Analysis of Reproduction.* Boston: Beacon Press.

———. 1992. "The End of the Body?" *American Ethnologist* 19(1): 121–40.

———. 1994. *Flexible Bodies: Tracking Immunity in American Culture from the Days of Polio to the Age of AIDS.* Boston: Beacon Press.

Martínez González, Humberto. 1986. *Hacía el nuevo milenio: Estudios sobre mesianismo, identidad nacional y socialismo.* México, D.F.: Universidad Autónoma Metropolitana.

Mattingly, Cheryl. 1998. *Healing Dramas and Clinical Plots: The Narrative Structure of Experience.* New York: Cambridge University Press.

Matute Vidal, Julián, and María Isabel Matute Ruíz de Vázquez. 1992. *El perfíl del Mexicano: Bases para forjar una nuevo México.* México, D.F.: Edamex.

Meissner, W. W. 1987. *Life and Faith: Psychological Perspectives on Religious Experience.* Washington, DC: Georgetown University Press.

———. 1998. "The Self and the Body: IV. The Body on the Couch." *Psychoanalysis and Contemporary Thought* 21(2): 277–300.

———. 1999. *To the Greater Glory: A Psychological Study of Ignatian Spirituality.* Milwaukee, WI: Marquette University Press.

Menaker, Esther. 1995. *The Freedom to Inquire: Self Psychological Perspectives on Women's Issues, Masochism, and the Therapeutic Relationship.* Northvale, NJ: Jason Aronson.

Mendelson, J. S. R. 1978. "The Feminine Press: The View of Women in the Colonial Journals of Spanish America, 1790–1810." In *Latin American Women: Historical Perspectives,* edited by Asunción Lavrín, 198–218. Westport, CT: Greenwood Press.

Merleau-Ponty, Maurice. 1962. *Phenomenology of Perception.* New York: Humanities Press.

———. 1963. *The Structure of Behavior.* Boston: Beacon Press.

———. 1964. *The Primacy of Perception, and Other Essays on Phenomenological Psychology, the Philosophy of Art, History, and Politics.* Evanston, IL: Northwestern University Press.

Mitchell, David A., and Sharon L. Snyder, eds. 1997. *The Body and Physical Difference: Discourses of Disability.* Ann Arbor: University of Michigan Press.

Mitchell, Juliet. [1974] 2000. *Psychoanalysis and Feminism: A Radical Reassessment of Freudian Psychoanalysis.* New York: Basic Books.

Moraga, Cherrie, and Gloria Anzaldua, eds. 1983. *This Bridge Called My Back: Writings of Radical Women of Color.* New York: Kitchen Table, Women of Color Press.

Mosqueda Pulgarín, M. 1988. "Los medios de communicación y las nuevas formas culturales." In *México, hacía el siglo XXI: visión de una generación,* edited by J. F. Escobedo Delgado, 123–33. México, D.F.: Seminario de Estudios Nacionales.

Mosse, George. 1985. *Nationalism and Sexuality: Respectability and Abnormal Sexuality in Modern Europe.* New York: H. Fertig.

Muller, John P. 1982. "Ego and Subject in Lacan." *Psychoanalytic Review* 69(2): 234–40.

Nájera Ramírez, Olga. 1993. *Engendering Nationalism: Identity, Discourse, and the Mexican Charro.* Santa Cruz: Chicano/Latino Research Center, University of California, Santa Cruz.

Natter, Wolfgang, Theodore R. Schatzki, and John Paul Jones, eds. 1995. *Objectivity and Its Other.* New York: Guilford Press.

Nuñez Vera, Miriam Aidé, María Arcelia González Butrón, and Cecilia Fernández Zayas. 1995. *Estudios de género en Michoacán: Lo feminino y lo masculino en perspectiva.* Morelia, Michoacán: Universidad Autónomo de Chapingo.

Obeyesekere, Gananath. [1981] 1984. *Medusa's Hair: An Essay on Personal Symbols and Religious Experience.* Chicago: University of Chicago Press.

Obregón, Alvaro. 1917. *Ocho mil kilómetros en campaña: Relación de las acciones de armas, efectuadas en más de veinte estados de la república durante un periodo de cuatros años, por el E. General Alvaro Obregón, y descritas por el mismo.* México, D.F.: C. Bouret.

Office of Church Statistics. 1984–94. *Statistical Yearbook of the Church.* Vatican City: Vatican Press.

Omari-Tunkara, Mikelle Smith. 2003. *Manipulating the Sacred: Yoruba Art, Ritual, and Resistance in Brazilian Candomblé.* Detroit, MI: Wayne State University Press.

Ortner, Sherry. 1996. *Making Gender: The Politics and Erotics of Culture.* Boston: Beacon Press.

Ortner, Sherry, and Harriet Whitehead. 1982. *Sexual Meanings: The Cultural Construction of Gender and Sexuality.* New York: Cambridge University Press.

Parker, Andrew, ed. 1992. *Nationalisms and Sexualities.* New York: Routledge.

Parker, Richard G., Regina Maria Barbosa, and Peter Aggleton. 2000. *Framing the Sexual Subject: The Politics of Gender, Sexuality, and Power.* Berkeley: University of California Press.

Parra Orozco, Miguel Angel. 1992. *México: Los nudos de la modernidad.* El Paso: Center for Inter-American and Border Studies.

Paz, Octavio. 1961. *The Labyrinth of Solitude: Life and Thought in Mexico.* Translated by Lysander Kemp. London : A. Lane Penguin Press.

Pines, Malcom. 1984. "Reflections on Mirroring." *International Review of Psychoanalysis* 11(1): 27–42.

Probyn, Elspeth. 1993. *Sexing the Self: Gendered Positions in Cultural Studies.* New York: Routledge.

Rector, Lallene. 1996. "The Function of Early Selfobject Experiences in Gendered Representations of God." In *Basic Ideas Reconsidered,* edited by Arnold Goldberg, 249–68. Progress in Self Psychology 12. Mahwah, NJ: Lawrence Erlbaum Associates.

———. 2000. "Developmental Aspects of the Twinship Selfobject Need and Religious Experience." In *How Responsive Should We Be?* edited by Arnold Goldberg, 257–75. Progress in Self Psychology 16. Hillsdale, NJ: Analytic Press.

———. 2001. "Mystical Experience as an Expression of the Idealizing Selfobject Need." In *The Narcissistic Patient Revisited,* edited by Arnold Goldberg, 179–95. Progress in Self Psychology 17. Hillsdale, NJ: Analytic Press.

Reyes, Govea. 1992. *El mestizo, la nación y el nacionalismo mexicano.* Chihuahua: Gobierno del Estado de Chihuahua.

Ricoeur, Paul. 1992. *Oneself as Another.* Translated by Kathleen Blamey. Chicago: University of Chicago Press.

Riding, Alan. [1984] 1985. *Distant Neighbors: A Portrait of the Mexicans.* New York: Knopf.

Ridley, Jasper. 2001. *Maximillian and Juárez.* London: Phoenix Press.

Ritzer, George. 1996. *The McDonaldization of Society: An Investigation into the Changing Character of Contemporary Social Life.* Thousand Oaks, CA: Pine Forge Press.

Rodriguez, Jaime E., ed. 1997. *The Origins of Mexican National Politics, 1808–1847.* Wilmington, DE: SR Books.

Romanucci-Ross, Lola, Daniel E. Moerman, and Laurence R. Tancredi. 1997. *The Anthropology of Medicine: From Culture to Method.* 3rd ed. New York: Bergen and Garvey.

Rugeley, Terry. 2001. *Of Wonders and Wise Men: Religion and Popular Cultures in Southeast Mexico, 1800–1876.* Austin: University of Texas Press.

Saunders, Kriemild, ed. 2002. *Feminist Post-Development Thought: Rethinking Modernity, Post-Colonialism, and Representation.* London: Zed.

Scheper-Hughes, Nancy, and Margaret Lock. 1987. "Mindful Body: A Prolegomenon to Future Work in Medical Anthropology." *Medical Anthropology Quarterly* 1(1): 6–41.

Schulz, Donald E. 1997. *Between a Rock and a Hard Place: The United States, Mexico, and the Agony of National Security.* Carlisle Barracks, PA: Strategic Studies Institute, U.S. Army War College.

Selby, John Millin. 1978. *The Eagle and the Serpent: The Spanish and American Invasions of Mexico: 1519–1846.* London: Hamilton.

Shane, Morton, and Estelle Shane. 1996. "Self Psychology in Search of the Optimal: A Consideration of Optimal Responsiveness; Optimal Provision; Optimal Gratification; and Optimal Restraint in the Clinical Situation." In *Basic Ideas Reconsidered,* edited by Arnold Goldberg, 37–54. Progress in Self Psychology 12. Mahwah, NJ: Lawrence Erlbaum Associates.

Shane, Morton, Estelle Shane, and Mary Gales. 1997. *Intimate Attachments: Towards a New Self Psychology.* New York: Guilford Press.

Smith, Joseph H., and Afaf M. Mahfouz, eds. 1994. *Psychoanalysis, Feminism, and the Future of Gender.* Baltimore: Johns Hopkins University Press.

Spinoza, Baruch. [1677] 1910. *Ethics.* In *Spinoza's Ethics and "De intellectus emendatione,"* translated by A. Boyle. New York : E. P. Dutton.

Spivak, Gayatri Chakravorty. 1987. *In Other Worlds: Essays in Cultural Politics.* New York: Methuen.

———. 1999. *A Critique of Postcolonial Reason: Toward a History of the Vanishing Present.* Cambridge, MA: Harvard University Press.

Spivak, Gayatri Chakravorty, and Sarah Harasym, eds. 1990. *The Post-Colonial Critic: Interviews, Strategies, Dialogues.* New York: Routledge.

Stavenhagen, Rodolfo. 1990. "El semenario 2010." In *México en el umbral del milénio*, edited by Centro de Estudios Sociológicos, 475–98. México, D.F.: El Colegio de México.

Stein, Howard F., and Margaret A. Stein. 1990. *American Medicine as Culture*. Boulder: Westview Press.

Stern, Daniel N. 1985. *The Interpersonal World of the Infant: A View from Psychoanalysis and Developmental Psychology*. New York: Basic Books.

Stoller, Robert J. 1985. *Presentations of Gender*. New Haven, CT: Yale University Press.

Stolorow, Robert D. 1995. "An Intersubjective View of Self Psychology." *Psychoanalytic Dialogues* 5(3): 393–99.

Stolorow, Robert D., Bernard Brandchaft, and George E. Atwood. 1988. *Psychoanalytic Treatment: An Intersubjective Approach*. Hillsdale, NJ: Analytic Press.

Summers, Frank. 1994. *Object Relations Theories and Psychopathology: A Comprehensive Text*. Hillsdale, NJ: Analytic Press.

Taylor, Charles. 1995. *Philosophical Arguments*. Cambridge, MA: Harvard University Press.

Teicholz, Judith Guss. 1996. "Optimal Responsiveness: Its Role in Psychic Growth and Change." In *Understanding Therapeutic Action: Psychodynamic Concepts of Cure*, edited by Lawrence E. Lifson, 139–61. Hillsdale, NJ: Analytic Press.

Terman, David M. 1998. "Optimal Responsiveness and a New View of Structuralization." In *Optimal Responsiveness: How Therapists Heal Their Patients*, edited by Howard A. Bacal, 59–74. Northvale, NJ: Jason Aronson.

Tholfsen, Barbara. 2000. "Cross-Gendered Longings and the Demand for Categorization: Enacting Gender within the Transference-Countertransference Relationship." *Journal of Gay and Lesbian Psychotherapy* 4(2): 27–46.

Thomas, Gordon. 1986. *Desire and Denial: Celibacy and the Church*. Boston: Little Brown.

Thomas, Simon D.R. 2003. "Talking Man to Man: Transference-Countertransference Difficulties in the Male Same-Gender Analytic Dyad." *British Journal of Psychotherapy* 19(3): 335–47.

Thompson, Becky W. 1994. *A Hunger So Wide and So Deep: American Women Speak Out on Eating Problems*. Minneapolis: University of Minnesota Press.

Tolpin, Marian. 1997. "Compensatory Structures: Paths to the Restoration of the Self." In *Conversations in Self Psychology*, edited by Arnold Goldberg, 3–19. Progress in Self Psychology 13. Hillsdale, NJ: Analytic Press.

Torres, Sergio, and Virginia Fabella. 1978. *Emergent Gospel: Theology from the Underside of History*. Maryknoll, NY: Orbis Books.

Treichler, Paula A., Lisa Cartwright, and Constance Penley, eds. 1998. *The Visible Woman: Imaging Technologies, Gender, and Science*. New York: New York University Press.

Trueba, Alfonso. 1994. *Conquista y colonización*. México, D.F.: Editorial Jus.

Turner, Frederick C. 1968. *The Dynamic of Mexican Nationalism*. Chapel Hill: University of North Carolina Press.

Turner, Victor W. 1995. *The Ritual Process: Structure and Anti-Structure.* New York: Aldine de Gruyter.

U.S. Catholic Conference. 2000. *Catechism of the Catholic Church: Revised in Accordance with the Official Latin Text Promulgated by Pope John Paul II.* 2nd ed. Vatican City: Libreria Editrice Vaticana.

Ussher, Jane M. 1992. *Women's Madness: Misogyny or Mental Illness?* Amherst: University of Massachusetts Press.

Vanderwood, Paul J. 1998. *The Power of God against the Guns of Government: Religious Upheaval in Mexico at the Turn of the Nineteenth Century.* Palo Alto, CA: Stanford University Press.

Van Gennep, Arnold. 1961. *The Rites of Passage.* Chicago: University of Chicago Press.

Van Mens-Verhulst, Janneke, Karlein Schreurs, and Liesbeth Woertman, eds. 1993. *Daughtering and Mothering: Female Subjectivity Reconsidered.* Florence, KY: Taylor and Francis.

Van Young, Eric. 2001. *The Other Rebellion: Popular Violence, Ideology, and the Mexican Struggle for Independence, 1810–1821.* Palo Alto, CA: Stanford University Press.

Vásquez, Carlos, and Manuel García y Griego, eds. 1983. *Mexican-U.S. Relations: Conflict and Convergence.* Los Angeles: UCLA Chicano Studies Research Center Publications and UCLA Latin American Center Publications.

Walters, Kerry S. 1994. *Re-Thinking Reason: New Perspectives in Critical Thinking.* Albany: State University of New York Press.

Wasserman, Mark. 2000. *Everyday Life and Politics in Nineteenth Century Mexico: Men, Women, and War.* Albuquerque: University of New Mexico Press.

Weil, Simone. 1952. *The Need for Roots.* Translated by Arthur Willis. New York: Putnam.

Weintraub, Sidney. 1990. *A Marriage of Convenience: Relations between Mexico and the United States.* New York: Oxford University Press.

Wierzbicka, Anna. 1999. *Emotions across Languages and Cultures: Diversity and Universals.* New York: Cambridge University Press.

Williams, Drid. 1975. "The Brides of Christ." In *Perceiving Women,* edited by Shirley Ardener, 105–26. New York: John Wiley.

Xaltín Rivera, M. 1988. La televisión comercial y el desarollo de México. In *México, hacía el siglo XXI: Visión de una generación,* edited by J. F. Escobedo Delgado, 134–37. México, D.F.: Seminario de Estudios Nacionales.

Yuval-Davis, Nira, Floya Anthias, and Jo Campling, eds. 1989. *Woman— Nation—State.* New York: St. Martin's Press.

Index

Note: Italicized page numbers indicate figures.

Abby (postulant): age of, 9; on betrayal
    of God, 186; on broken feeling, 96;
    on group dynamics, 126; on habit
    and veil, 147; on humility, 78; on
    mission, 205; vocation narrative of,
    216–18
abortion, 13, 34
accountability, personal, 86, 192
Adam (biblical), 84–85, 300
Adoration, 175, 201, 204
aesthetics of embodiment concept, 36
age, 9, 11, 119, 142
agency: concept of, 305–6; in *entrega*,
    82; performative childishness and,
    113; renegotiation of, 18
Alfonso Maria de Ligorio, Saint, 200
Alicia (postulant), 9, 61, 167
Alma (postulant), 124–25
Altamirano, Ignacio M., 277
Alvarado, General Salvador, 286
Amelia (postulant): age of, 9; on call
    from God, 97, 98, 109; on daily
    tasks, 215; on God's presence, 138;
    on group dynamics, 126–27; on
    Magda and Teresita, 138; on peni-
    tence, 190; recreation project of,
    173; team-building activities and,
    123–24; vocation narrative of,
    222–25, 257–58
Americanization. *See* United States
Anabel, Mother: on family, 50–51;
    humility of, 79; meetings with, 48,

49–50; missions and, 205; on morti-
    fication, 191; research of, 60; tasks
    of, 107
Anderson, Benedict, 272
Angelopolis Project, 269
anthropology: on boundaries, 132–34;
    concern with body in, 46–47. *See
    also* fieldwork
Apostles' Creed, 312
Appadurai, Arjun, 133
appetite. *See* desires; food and eating
Aquiles Serdán family, 268
architecture: communal areas,
    137–38; dining room, 166–67;
    floor plans, *135, 140, 143*; levels
    of formation reflected in, 138–39,
    141; main gates, 134, *136*; personal
    space and privacy, 141–42; poverty
    and, 71–72; semipublic areas,
    136–37
Asad, Talal, 22, 36
aspirants: description of, 66–67; retreats
    for, 190, 224; stage of, 14, *15*
Augustine, Saint, 35, 157, 199
authenticity: political and feminine, 5,
    260–61; quest for, 80; recognition
    of, 87, 273

Bacal, Howard, 235, 240
baptism, 207, 309
Bartlett, Manuel, 269
Bartra, Roger, 287–89

331

Basave Fernández del Valle, A., 293, 295, 296
Baywatch (television show), 292
Bell, Catherine, 214
Bell, Rudolph, 24
Belmar, José Luis, 300–302
Belonging: to cohort group, 122–27; commonalities as basis for, 119–20; concept of, 16, 17; to congregation as whole, 121–22; as enabling bond with others, 231; integration of women into cohesive unit and, 111–19; mutual support in, 131; as privilege, 230; in psychodynamic model, 250; role of mistress of postulants in, 127–30
Benavente, Friar Toribio de, 266
Benjamin, Jessica: on dynamics of recognition, 246, 247; on gender and intersubjectivity, 21, 242–45
Beverly Hills 90210 (television show), 63, 292
birth control, 34
Boddy, Janice, 46–47
bodily experiences: of medieval ascetic nuns, 33–34; prayers as, 179. *See also* embodiment
body: as barometer of correspondence between selves, 247; Catholic concern with, 34–36; chastity and, 73–74; communication with God through, 174; contradictory constructions of self joined in, 16; as domain of negotiation, 5; as ground for production of self, 41; mindfulness of, 154, 179; as portal of recognition, 251; in psychoanalytic theories, 241–45; as regulator/stabilizer/moderator of interior, 154; soul's relationship with, 35–36, 165, 176, 178–79; theorizing of, 37, 43–44, 303–8; "thinking," 47. *See also* body management; Containment; embodiment
body management: chastity in, 157–58; concept of, 17–18, 150; food and eating in, 154–57; gaze in, 150–52; personal hygiene in, 163–65; physical comportment in, 153–54; posture in, 174–76; in rhythm of daily life, 162–63; speech/silence in, 152–53; tensions in, 90–91
Bonfíl Batalla, Guillermo, 283, 293, 298
Bordo, Susan, 4
boundaries: containment of, 150–58; gates as, 134, 136; between levels of formation, 139, 141; in managing

distractions of world, 159–60; mediation of, 17–18; theorizing of, 132–34; transitional spaces between, 137; uniform as marker of, 146–50
Bourdieu, Pierre, 42, 47
boyfriends, 220
Brokenness: acknowledgment and articulation of, 95–98; as betrayal of God, 185–86; as call to authentic femininity, 260–61; concept of, 16, 17; in cultural context, 230; deepening awareness of, 102–3; interpretation of, 109–10, 112; naming of, 98–99, 102; as psychic distress, 231; in psychodynamic model, 250; reevaluation of, 257–58; reflections on, 180; vocation narratives on, 217, 220, 224, 226
Burkitt, Ian, 47
Butler, Judith, 42–43, 304
Bynum, Carolyn Walker, 24

calendars, 284
call from God. *See* religious vocation
Cantú Corro, Father José, 281
capitalism, 54, 55, 56, 297–98. *See also* United States
Carlota (postulant): age of, 9; appetite of, 167; on examinations of conscience, 185, 192; on feminism, 254; on mission, 207; penitence of, 189–90; personal items of, 144; on religious vocation, 110, 213; on scrutiny, 152
Carmelita, Mother, 8
Carmen (postulant): age of, 9; appearance of, 125; clique of, 117, 124–25; on discipline, 178–79; on Jesus and the paralytic, 199; on liberalism, 63; personal items of, 142, 144; on prayer, 204; on religious vocation, 216; on shoes, 147; on tradition and modernity, 259
Caso, Antonio, 289
Castro, Martínez, 277
Catherine, Mother, 65–66, 76, 202
Catherine of Siena, 24, 33
cathexis, 41, 112, 304–6
Catholicism and Catholic Church: as bastion against Protestantism, 297–98; body as concern in, 34–36; celebrations of, 201, 213; decline of, 55; doctrines of, 98, 101; Judaism and, 28; language concerns in, 176; liberal intelligentsia's fear of, 285; nationalist cause linked to, 272; organization of time in, 15; persecution of, 265, 278; in

post-Independence Mexico, 276; Puebla as stronghold of, 24, 268, 269–70; as real expression of God, 232; religious formation as localized articulation of, 65; as repudiation of U.S., 280–81; revival of, 259–60, 281, 294–95

Celeste (postulant): age of, 9; appearance of, 125; background of, 96; clique of, 117, 124–25; examination of conscience and, 182; on humility, 77, 80; on name, 308; on prayer, 177–78, 204; recreation project of, 173; on tradition and modernity, 259; on veils, 148; vocation narrative of, 219–22, 226–27; working with, 170

celibacy, 35. See also chastity

Central House: authority structure of, 75; description of, 48–49; location of, 266; third probation retreat in, 68

change. See psychological development

chapel and tabernacle, 137–38

Chapter of Faults, 175

charism: call from God and, 91; definition of, 103; reparation as, 197, 225

charismatic healing practices, 47

charity, 181, 194

chastity: concerns about, 103; custody of eyes in, 151; rationale for, 35; as technique of enclosure, 157–58; vows of, 73–74

children: education of, 58–59; foreign values as influence on, 270, 301; mirroring as experienced by, 236n2; mothers' influence on, 57–58, 63; others as perceived by, 242–44; parental response to, 236–37; self-object needs of, 237–40; shelter for, 56

chocolate, 142, 155

Chodorow, Nancy, 39–40

cinco de mayo battle, 267

Clara (postulant): age of, 9; on family and call from God, 98; family of, 125; on Siervas' role, 256–57; in silence exercise, 153

Clare of Assisi, 33

Clarissa, Mother, 75, 117

colonialist attitudes, 126, 274–75

conflict and confrontation, 115, 133

consumerism, 55, 270. See also materialism and greed

Containment: body management in, 150–58; concept of, 16, 17; delimitation of space in, 134–46; inner

space defined in, 159, 230; managing distractions of world in, 159–60; in psychodynamic model, 250–51; theorizing of, 132–34; uniform as, 146–50; as way of ordering world, 231

convent philosophy: broader concerns in, 6; political subjectivity in, 12–13; on separation by levels of formation, 139, 141. See also religious formation

convents: active-life vs. cloistered, 2, 36, 74, 80, 168n1, 198; classificatory position vs. actual identification in, 112; control of physical body in, 90–91, 161–62; depth of relationships in, 118; factors in selecting, 104; fieldwork in, 24–29; inside/outside distinctions of, 17; as material and social spaces, 134; regendering in, 252–60; rhythm of life in, 213; as ritual space, 214; as special crucibles, 33; time in, 210–12. See also architecture; daily practices

conversion experience, 208–9

Cortés, Hernan, 290

crosses, wearing of, 148

Csordas, Thomas J., 47

Cuauhtémoc, 280, 281, 282

cultural change: coming of age in period of, 271–72; congregation's history in context of, 52; discourse on, 25, 291–93; gendered articulation of, 6, 255–56; Puebla as example of, 270–71

cultural practices: boundaries in, 133; femininity in context of, 62–63; interiority produced via, 41; repetition of, 42

custody of the eyes concept, 150–52

daily practices: as articulation of modernity, 260; body management in, 90–91; of chastity, 74; examinations of conscience in, 183; experiential and virtual selves joined in, 21; of humility, 77–80; at mealtimes, 166–68; as mechanism for religious formation, 6; Muro's message as central in, 61–64; of obedience, 76, 82; occupations in, 169–71; physicality of, 36; of poverty, 70–73; prayer in, 198–201, 204–5; of purity, 80–81; recreation in, 171–73; religious vocation's implications for, 19–20; rhythm of, 1–2, 26, 162–63; ritualization of, 214–15;

daily practices *(continued)*
 separated by levels of formation, 139,
 141; silence in, 153; team-building
 activities in, 123–24; as technologies
 for cultivating subjectivity, 12; transformation evidenced in, 90
De Lauretis, Theresa, 45, 242
desires: custody of eyes in, 151; food and
 eating as, 154–57; reshaping of,
 150, 188; respect toward body vs.,
 165; sex as, 157–58
Desjarlais, Robert R., 47
Diario de México, 286n12
Díaz, Porfirio: economic inequities under,
 282–83; industrialization under,
 267–68; modernization under, 53,
 55, 281–82; resistance to, 268
Diego, Juan, 275
discipline: in institutions, 36; by mistress
 of postulants, 128; past forms of,
 190–91; prayer and, 202; relationship to God linked to, 178–79
dispositions: of *entrega*, 81–82; of humility, 77–80; as pillar of religious formation, 70, 76, 89; posture linked
 to, 175–76; of purity, 80–81
divine motherhood concept, 58
divinity: chastity as emulation of, 73
Douglas, Mary, 133
Dulce (postulant), 9, 96, 204

earthquake (1985), 268
eating disorders, 23–25, 304, 305–6. *See
 also* food and eating
economy, 282–83, 292
education: in female domesticity, 284–85;
 foreign values in, 270, 301; Muro's
 views of, 56–59; of postulants, 10, 11
embodiment: aesthetics of, 36; as always
 gendered, 6, 242, 247; approach to,
 23; components of, 5, 235; in
 encounters with others, 247; of personal space, 145–46; reorientation
 of, 20, 70, 83–84, 179; soul revealed
 and affected by, 251; source and
 object of cultural meaning in, 46–47;
 technology of, 65, 306–7; theorizing
 of, 44–46, 303–8. *See also* body;
 gender; race; self
embroidery, 172
emotions: investment of, in group identity, 112–14; phenomenology of, 38;
 reflective stance toward, 121
empathic attunement: concept of,
 236–37, 239–40; failure of
 (empathic break), 247–48; among

postulants, 250; in regendering of
 embodied subject, 246
empathy: with Jesus and with
 humankind, 195–97; in psychological development, 235–37; of sisters
 for postulants, 121–22
Enlightenment, 37–38, 275, 278
entrega: concept of, 18, 193–94; disposition of, 81–82; empathic identification in, 195–97; inhabiting ideal of,
 20; practices of piety as encouragement of, 174; in prayer and worship,
 198–205
environment: in analysis, 237–40; in
 childhood, 235–37
eternity: immediacy of, 210–12
Eve (biblical), 76, 84–85, 300
Evelyn (postulant): age of, 9; on entering
 convent, 112; on mission, 207; on
 penitence, 190; on prayer, 177; on
 religious vocation, 13–14, 271; on
 veils, 149
examinations of conscience: concept of,
 181–83; in mission week, 206;
 points of, 184–85; prayer in, 201;
 righting wrongs found in, 186–92
experiential self: parental response to,
 239–40; use of term, 21; virtual self
 in conflict with, 246

faith: politics of, 11–14
family: of aspirants, 66–67; breaking
 news to, 104, 107; contributions to
 convent from, 71–72; environment
 of, 235–40; fights and beatings in,
 116–17; Mexican customs for, 11,
 112, 114; in Mexico vs. U.S.,
 255–56; of novices, 67; of postulants, 10, 11, 119–20; postulants'
 leaving of, 108–9, 112–13, 211;
 response to religious vocation, 98;
 sisters as, 50–51; woman's role in,
 57–58, 63, 254–55, 258, 284–86
Fatima Prayer, 312
feast days, 309
female domesticity: emphasis on,
 284–86; traditional models of, 11,
 57–58, 62–63, 63, 254–55, 258
femininity: authentic, politically engaged
 form of, 5, 260–61; Catholicism and
 poor linked to, 296–97; chastity
 and, 73–74; conflicting models of, 4;
 marginalized in national identity,
 293; Mary as model of, 109;
 reclaiming of, 56–61; revived constructions of, 64, 294–95, 298–99,

299–302; Siervas' views of, 12–13, 230; spiritual model of, 5; traditional and modern styles of, 11, 62–63; uneasiness with expectations of, 120. See also *entrega*

feminist movement and theory: becoming nun in context of, 260; critique of, 63, 254–55, 300–302; on embodiment, 44–46; on Freud, 233; on gender and self, 38–40; second wave of, 298; U.S. linked to, 295

fieldwork: advantages of, 46; approach to, 23–29; permission for, 48–51

food and eating: management of, 156–57; regimentation of, 165–68; as temptation, 154–56

Fosshage, James L., 240

Foucault, Michel: on body discipline, 36; on material creation of space, 134; on power, 42, 302; on sexuality, 40–41; on subjectivities, 22

France: Mexico invaded by, 267; as model, 275, 276

Francis of Assisi, 168n1

Franco, Jean: on gender, 284–85; on indigenous people, 278, 283; on Marina (La Malinche), 290; on Mexicanness, 293; on power, 277; on revolution, 286

fraternity, 74

free will: dilemma of, 84, 109–10; humility and, 77; surrendering of, 74–76; in vocation, 7. See also God: submission to will of

Freud, Sigmund, 233

Fuentes, Carlos, 289

Gales, Mary, 235

gates, 134, 136

gaze, 150–52

gender: approach to, 23; centrality of, 6; Muro on, 56–61; psychoanalytic perspective on, 233, 241–45; regulatory practices of, 42–43; religiosity and national identity triangulated with, 64, 294–95, 298–99; religious formation as (re)learning, 252–60; technologies of, 45; theorizing of, 38–40; as trope in national identity, 273, 284–86, 293–95. See also gendering/regendering; sexuality

gendering/regendering: in convent, 252–60; in Mexican context, 295–96; model of, 245–49; of nationalism, 272–74, 302

General Council, 50, 75, 105–6

genuflection, 309

Gergen, Kenneth J., 273–74

globalization, 291–93, 298–99

Glory Be (prayer), 175, 313

God: actions as articulating relationship with, 214–15; body as avenue of communication with, 174; brokenness as evidence of betrayal of, 185–86; feeling distant from, 185, 192, 201–2; feeling presence of, 138; healing relationships with, 193–94, 195–97; plan of, 84; pronouns for, 2n2; reorientation to, 18, 208–9; self and soul in relation to, 82–83, 84, 131; self and world in relation to, 71, 83, 202; submission to will of, 86–87, 109–10, 202–5, 208–9; time as belonging to, 211

Goffman, Erving, 22, 134

Goldberg, Arnold, 240

Gotari, Salinas de, 265

grace, 202

group identity, 112–14

Gutmann, Matthew, 290–91

habitus concept, 42

Hail Holy Queen (prayer), 313

Hail Mary (prayer), 313

hair styles, 147

Hall, Edward T., 134

Haydee (postulant), 9, 145, 167

health/illness, 38–39, 47

Hegel, G. W. F., 243

hermana formadora (formation sister). See mistress of postulants

Hidalgo y Costilla, Miguel, 275

"holy anorexia," 24

Holy Hour, 62, 201

Holy Spirit, 163

Holy Week, 205–8

homosexuality, 118

honesty, 185

humankind: empathy with, 195–97; repairing relationship to God of, 195–97; in state of grace and sin, 202. See also men; poor; woman/women

humility: disposition of, 77–80; *entrega* as exercise in, 197; lack of, 181; about personal hygiene needs, 164; posture as expression of, 175; practices of piety as encouragement of, 174; purity as foundation of, 80–81; uniform as sign of, 146, 148; work as expression of, 170

hygiene, personal, 163–65

identity: centrality of national affiliation
to, 272; group, 112–14; narrative,
212; as normative ideal, 42–43.
See also national identity; self;
subjectivity
Ignatius of Loyola, Saint, 199
illusion of interiority perspective, 40–44
Immaculate Conception, 310
Indianism, 280. *See also* indigenous people
indigenous people: homogenization plan
for, 278; ignored, 291–92; marginalization of, 284; poverty of, 282–83;
Spanish cruelties to, 274–75; as
symbol, 280
individualism: traditional values vs.,
292–93
individuality: body management and,
90–91; embrace of, 8
industrialization, 267–68
institutional settings: body discipline and
management in, 36, 90–91; subject
formation in, 22–23. *See also*
convents
interiority and interior space: body as
regulator/stabilizer/moderator of,
154; as illusion, 40–44; privileging
of, 17; production of, 20, 159;
tension of exteriority with, 179
intersubjectivity: concept of, 21–23;
gender and, 242–45
Iranian Revolution, 298–99
Iris (postulant), 9, 60–61, 196, 199

James, William, 215
Jehovah's Witnesses, 271
Jesus Christ: as empathic, 121; empathy
with, 195–97; humility of, 77; incu-
bation of, 102; listening of, 175;
liturgical year based on, 213; as
model, 182; novices as sweethearts
of, 68; paralytic and, 199; pronouns
for, 2n2; role in salvation, 81; on
serving Him, 168–69; suffering body
of, 34; as Word, 176
"Jesus in their wombs": use of phrase, 5,
261
Jew: doing fieldwork as, 28–29
John Paul II (pope), 60
John Tristosomo, Saint, 200
Josephine, Mother: advice from, 219,
220, 221, 224; Magda chastised by,
187; in Marta's dream, 96–97; on
sexuality, 157–58; tasks of, 66–67,
106, 107, 123, 225
Judaism: Catholicism and, 28
Julian of Norwich, 33
junior sisters, 15, 68, 138

knowledge, 19–20, 47
Kohut, Heinz: Benjamin compared with,
243; on empathic break, 247; on
intersubjectivity, 21; on optimal
frustration, 237; on psychological
structure, 240; on self psychology,
234, 235–37

Lacan, Jacques, 236n2
language, 43, 176, 272. *See also* speech
lay sisters, 79, 169
Lent, 156, 310
Leona, Sister, 131
liberalism: Catholicism feared by, 285;
modernity as project of, 278; Muro's
critique of, 54–55; postulants' cri-
tique of, 63
liberation theology movement, 297
liberty, 13. *See also* free will
Lichtenberg, Joseph D., 235
"Life Project" worksheet, 103, 104
life stories, 18, 212. *See also* Re/collection
Limanatour, José, 282
Linette, Sister, 76
Lion King, The (film), 151
Liturgy of the Hours, 201, 310
Lizardi, Fernández de, 277
Luhrmann, T. M., 4
Luís, Father, 101, 102
Luisa (kitchen help), 49
lynching, 280

Magda (postulant): age of, 9; background of, 96; on being a woman,
63; brother's wedding and, 126–27,
128; characteristics of, 115–17; on
entering convent, 67, 106, 108–9;
on fraternity, 186–88; on mission,
206–7; on mistress of postulants,
129; personal items of, 142; on
pleasing Jesus, 111; on prayer, 203;
rule breaking by, 130; on Ruth's
weight, 156; on scrutiny, 152;
silence and, 153, 167; team-building
activities and, 124; Teresita's
relationship with, 117–18, 138,
141, 142, 167, 186–88, 203; vocational crisis of, 117–19; working
with, 169
Magill, Samuel E., 279
Margarita, Sister, 19–20
Marguerite, Sister, 60
Maria, Mother, 121, 165
Marina (La Malinche), 290–91
marriage: lack of interest in, 120; of postulants' parents, 125; religious life
compared with, 182–83

Married . . . with Children (television show), 292

Marta (postulant): age of, 9; appearance of, 125, 147; on broken feeling, 95; clique of, 117, 124–25; examination of conscience and, 181–82; humility and, 77, 80, 181; on Jesus and the paralytic, 199; on prayer, 204; questions of, 62; recreation project of, 173; on religious vocation, 6–7, 91, 96–97, 198; team-building activities and, 123–24

Martha (biblical), 169

Martita, Mother, 101–2

martyrs, 196

Mary, Virgin: chastity as emulation of, 73; as model, 101–2, 109, 160; obedience of, 76; perpetual virginity of, 34, 297–98; postulants' parallels to, 211; purity of, 81; as symbol of Mexican condition, 296; as Virgin of Guadalupe, 272, 274, 275, 281; work of, 169

Mary Margaret, Sister, 100

masculinity and masculinization: of modernity, 12, 294, 295, 296, 297; of mothers, 56; in national identity, 290–91; of U.S. women, 298

Mass: definition of, 310; for entering postulants, 108, 121; hymn singing in, 177; language of, 176; posture in, 175; prayer in, 201; vocation narratives on, 220

materialism and greed: Americanization via, 292; Catholicism as bastion against, 297–98; critique of, 55; as influence, 270; vows of poverty in context of, 72

Matilde, Sister, 206

matria: use of term, 296n15

maturation process, 113. *See also* psychological development

Maximilian (emperor), 276, 278

media: Americanization via, 292; censorship of, 282; "civilizing women" theme of, 285n10; controlling access to, 151; false perception of liberty in, 13; femininity and motherhood emphasized in, 299–302; foreign values in, 270; gender and religion in, 294; liberalism of, 63; violence in, 62

medieval ascetic nuns, 24, 33–35

Meissner, W. W., 247

men: Belmar's charge to, 301–2; chastity of, 73, 74; rehumanization of, 57; sisters' behavior around, 158. *See also* masculinity and masculinization

Merleau-Ponty, Maurice, 47, 247

mestizos and *mestizaje* condition: emergence of, 274; exploitation of, 275; marginalization of, 284; poverty of, 282–83; as symbol, 277–78, 281, 283; as theme, 272

metaphysical problematics: concept of, 83–84; dilemma of free will as, 84; personal accountability as, 86; physicality as, 85–86; as pillar of religious formation, 70, 82–84, 89; rearticulation of self and soul as, 87–88; sin of humanity as, 84–85; submission to will of God as, 86–87; of temporal world, 85

Mexico: anti-Americanism in, 279–80; as Catholic and feminine, 297–98; economic and social reforms in, 53–55; economy of, 282–83, 292; family customs in, 11, 112, 114; as female, 272–74; foreign investment in, 291–92; gender relations in, 252, 254, 284–86; land redistribution in, 283–84; *matria* and *patria* in, 296n15; national history of, 274–79; paradise lost myth of, 287–88; skin color in, 125–26; social and political crises in, 2; "third way" for, 64, 259–60; U.S. invasion of, 267, 278–79. *See also* cultural change; modernity and modernization; national identity; nationalism; sociopolitical context

Mexico City: earthquake in, 268; modernization in, 282

Mina (postulant), 9, 177, 207

Miriam, Mother, 8, 252

mirroring: child's experience of, 236n2; concept of, 20–22; idiosyncrasies of, 23; by mistress of postulants, 250

Misioneras, 114

missions of postulants: description of, 205–8; as experience of conversion, 208–9; vocation narratives on, 217, 223

Miss Mexico pageant, 294, 299–300

mistress of postulants: mirroring by, 250; obedience to, 163; role of, described, 127–30; scrutiny of, 151–52; self-critique and, 180. *See also* Veronica, Mother

modernity and modernization: ambivalence about, 255–56; congregation's history in context of, 52; critique of, 54–56, 293–95; daily activities as articulation of, 260; dehumanizing effects of, 56; discourse on, 25, 291–93;

modernity and modernization *(continued)*
    examples of, 269, 270–71; feminin-
    ity as antidote to, 57, 230; as
    foreign, masculine, evil, 12, 294,
    295, 296, 297; language of, 272; as
    liberal project, 278; "Mexican
    nation" and, 281–84; personal and
    political concerns about, 11–12;
    postulants' notion of, 257; reforms
    geared toward, 53–55; regendering
    in dialogue with, 6; woman's role
    and, 284–86
modesty, 149, 164. *See also* uniforms
morality: boundaries in, 133
mortification, 188, 190–91, 192
mother general, 50, 75
mothers and motherhood: as central to
    family, 57–58, 63; child's perception
    of, 242–44; emphasis on, 284–86;
    masculinization of, 56; as patriotic
    duty, 286; rape of, 296; revived con-
    structions of, 294–95, 299–302
mother superior, 78
Muro y Cuesta, Father Juan Miguel de:
    background of, 53; canonization of,
    60; as founder of congregation, 51,
    52; on humility, 79; interpreting
    message of, 61–64; on lay sisters,
    169; on mistress of postulants, 127,
    128; as model, 194; on moderniza-
    tion, 54, 302; on poverty, 71; on
    prayer, 199, 200; prayers to, 60–61;
    on reparation, 195; vocation of,
    55–56; on women, 56–59, 227, 259;
    on working with poor, 165, 222
mutual recognition: applied to regender-
    ing of embodied subject, 246–49,
    249; concept of, 243; failure of, 17,
    246; gender in, 244; national
    context of, 266; religious formation
    in context of, 249–52, 253
Myrna, Mother, 139

narrative identity concept, 212. *See also*
    Re/collection
national identity: congregation's history
    in context of, 52; crises in, 289;
    dependency in, 288–89; discourse
    on, 25, 259–60, 292–93; femininity
    and motherhood emphasized in,
    62–63, 299–302; foundation for,
    274–75; gender as trope in, 273,
    284–86, 293–95; as male, 286; mas-
    culinity in, 290–91; *mestizo* as
    symbol of, 277–78, 281, 283;
    nationalism, gender, and religiosity
    triangulated in, 64, 294–95, 298–99;

post-Independence development of,
    276–79; quest for, 286–88; religious
    vocation linked to, 258–59; U.S.
    culture as threat to, 255–56
nationalism: discourse on, 295–96;
    gender and religiosity triangulated
    with, 64, 294–95, 298–99; gender-
    ing of, 272–74, 302; religious voca-
    tion in context of, 271–72;
    solidification of, 282; xenophobia
    in, 279–80
necklaces, 148
Nicean Creed, 313
Nietzsche, Friedrich, 40
nightstands, 142, 144–45
Novena of Trust, 177
novices: applications for advancement to,
    128–29, 168; description of, 67–68;
    group dynamics of, 126–27; habits
    and veils of, 148, 149; living quar-
    ters of, 145; requirements of, 172;
    stage of, 15
nunnery. *See* convents
nuns: in charge of gate/door, 136; contin-
    uing formation of, 69; examinations
    of conscience of, 182, 183; medieval
    ascetic, 24, 33–35; personal items of,
    72; popular image of, 8, 218; on self
    and soul, 44; as sponsors, 66–67;
    struggles of, 252; ties within, 20;
    vocation narratives on, 222. *See also*
    aspirants; junior sisters; mistress of
    postulants; mother general; mother
    superior; novices; postulants; pro-
    fessed sisters; Siervas; third proba-
    tion sisters

obedience: as component of *entrega*, 194;
    concerns about, 103; humility as
    foundation of, 77, 79; lack of, 76,
    84–85, 181, 300; to mistress of pos-
    tulants, 128, 129; in observing
    silence, 82; rhythm of daily life
    based in, 163; vows of, 74–76
Obeyesekere, Gananath, 305
Obregón (president), 285
occupations. *See* work
Offices of the Hours, 177
Offices of the Liturgy, 206
optimal frustration concept, 237–39
optimal provision concept, 240
optimal responsiveness concept, 240
optimal restraint concept, 240
others: Belonging as enabling bond with,
    231; embodied encounters with,
    247; misrecognition of, 17, 246;
    respect for privacy of, 151;

subjectivity and relationship with,
242–44; trust in, 142, 144
Our Father (prayer), 313

Paco (handyman), 49
PAN (political party), 269
Parker, Andrew, 273
paschal mystery, 34
patria: use of term, 296n15
Pauline (postulant), 9
Paz, Octavio, 289, 290
pelado-turned proletarian concept,
288–91
penitence, 188–90, 192
Pentecost, 310
perfectionism, 78, 115, 197
performative childishness concept, 113
perpetual vows, 68–69
person: theories of, 37–38, 82–83, 84.
See also others; self; subjectivity
personal accountability, 86, 192
personal hygiene, 163–65
personal space and privacy: in dormitory,
141–42; letting go of, 144–45; limits
on, 145–46; respect for others', 151
physicality: bonds of, 178–79; containment of, 150–58; of daily practices,
36, 154, 168–71; as metaphysical
problematic, 85–86; of Second
Coming, 34. *See also* body; desires;
embodiment
piety: practices of, 174–78
Pipa (postulant): age of, 9; on food, 167;
on humility, 77; on mortification,
191; on prayer, 204; on tradition
and modernity, 255–56
political parties, 265, 269
politics, 6, 11–14. *See also* sociopolitical
context
poor: Catholicism linked to, 297; femininity as symbol of, 296; working
with, 165, 222
poststructuralism, 43
postulants: arrival of, 107–9; assurance
of, 208; characteristics of, 2–3,
8–11, 9, 10, 67; coming of age of,
271–72; constant companionship of,
145–46; departure of, 9, 90; dormitory of, 72, 138–39, 141–42; as
embodied contradictions, 307–8;
evaluations of, 128–29; female subjectivity as meaningful to, 60; feminist and Catholic interpretations by,
12–13; fieldwork among, 27–29;
food anxieties of, 155; function of,
149; as housewives for God, 261;
levels of relatedness of, 120; motiva-

tions of, 3–4, 5–6, 214; Muro's
message for, 61–64; as one with and
removed from world, 85; primary
concerns of, 36; radical transformation of, 131; reading of, 52, 61;
scrutiny of, 151–52, 167–68; stage
of, *15*; supplies needed by, 106–7.
See also daily practices; religious formation; religious vocation
poverty: concerns about, 103; daily practice of, 70–73; humility as foundation of, 77; uniform as sign of, 146,
148; vows of, 70–73
practices: of charismatic healing, 47; concepts of, 42; of piety, 174–78; of
poverty, 70–73. *See also* cultural
practices; daily practices; ritual practices and ritualization
prayer: bodily sensations as, 179; at
closing of retreat, 104–5; consciousness in, 200–201; for entering postulants, 107–8, 121; falling asleep in,
162; to Father Muro, 60–61; mealtime, 166; on missions, 205–8;
necessity of, 199–200; posture in,
174–76; as private and communal,
202; quality of, 198–99, 202; reorienting view of, 203–5; for reparation, 195; at rising, 1–2; of secret
friends, 123; solitude in, 145–46;
versions of, 312–13; vocalization of,
176–78
pride, 78
priests, 137, 219
PRI (political party), 265, 269
Probyn, Elspeth, 4, 44, 304
professed sisters: habits and veils of, 148;
living quarters of, 139, 145; on missions, 205–6; ring as symbol of,
68–69; stage of, 15
prostration, 175
Protestantism: Catholicism as bastion
against, 297–98; critique of, 56; hostility toward, 28, 101, 271; opposition to, 280–81; teachings about,
172; U.S. linked to, 295
psychoanalysis: basics of, 234–35;
changes in, 233–34; theories of self
in, 38; transference process in,
39–40; transforming work of,
237–40. *See also* psychological
development; self psychology; therapeutic relationship
psychological development: applied to
regendering of embodied subject,
245–49; gender and body in, 241–45;
mechanisms of, 234–35, 240–41;

psychological development *(continued)*
psychodynamic models of, 233n1;
religious formation in context of,
249–52, 253; as social process,
235–37; structure in, 240–41
Puebla de Los Ángeles: approach to, 4–6;
description of, 48–49; history of,
51–53, 266–71; illiteracy in, 11;
living in, 26–27; mayoral election in,
269; religious activities in, 29; as
stronghold of Catholicism, 24, 268,
269–70; underground culture of, 48;
youth mission in, 217. *See also* Siervas
purity, 80–81, 174

race: discourse on, 277. *See also* indigenous people; *mestizos* and *mestizaje*
condition
Ramos, Samuel, 289
rape: of Marina (La Malinche), 290–91;
political use of term, 273, 274, 275,
296; vocation narrative on, 219,
220, 221–22, 226–27
recognition, 87, 251, 273. *See also*
mutual recognition; traumatic
misrecognition
Re/collection: concept of, 16, 18, 210; as
learned justification, 230; in psychodynamic model, 252; reevaluations
in, 257–58; resolution/closure in,
232; ritualization of daily practices
in, 214–15; temporal concepts and,
210–12; in vocation narratives,
215–27
recreation, 171–73
Regimentation: concept of, 16, 17–18,
161–62; of food and eating, 165–68;
goal of, 178–79; as habituation to
convent practices, 230; of personal
hygiene, 163–65; of practices of
piety, 174–78; as providing sense of
control, 231–32; in psychodynamic
model, 251; in rhythm of daily life,
162–63; of sociability, 171–73; of
work, 168–71
relatedness. *See* Belonging
religiosity: anticapitalism and, 297–98;
gender and national identity triangulated with, 64, 294–95, 298–99
religious formation: approaches to,
229–33; architecture as reflective of,
138–39, 141; concept of, 65; as
courtship, 66, 68, 69; as developmental model of self-transformation,
90–91; dining tables as reflective of,
166–67; dispositions in, 76–82;
domains of, 69–70, 89; elements of,

16–18; "finding way" in, 63–64;
foundation of, 131; getting to business of, 122; goals of, 88, 90; levels
of, 14–16, 15, 66–69; life story as
events leading to, 216; metaphysical
problematics in, 82–88; mission's
role in, 205–8; personal hygiene
and, 164; process of, 4–6, 20–23;
psychodynamic model of, 249–52,
253; as (re)learning gender, 252–60;
as remobilizing old and creating new
structures, 241; as reorientation,
188; rethinking process of, 245–49;
role of mistress of postulants in,
127–30; sociopolitical component
of, 266, 271–72; struggles with,
119; as technology of embodiment,
65, 306–7; tensions of
continuity/discontinuity in, 212;
uncertain outcome of, 7–8; uniform
as reflective of, 146; vows in, 68–76,
103. *See also* Belonging; Brokenness;
Containment; Re/collection; Regimentation; Self-critique; Surrender
religious vocation: age at, 9, 11, 119;
approach to, 6–8; as from beginning
of time, 215; as call and obligation,
4–5, 14; certainty about, 69; concept
of, 65–66; examinations of conscience in discerning, 182–85; experience of, 232–33; femininity's role
in, 13–14; food anxieties and, 155;
fulfillment of, 91–92; identification
of, 100–101; knowledge of, 19–20;
Mary as model of, 101–2, 211; narratives of, 18, 180, 212–27; national
identity linked to, 258–59; persever-
ance in, 104–5; persistence of,
96–97; personal items and, 144–45;
personal nature of, 91; questions
about, 97–98; recreation projects
and, 173; signs of, 17, 95–98, 226;
in sociopolitical context, 256–58,
307–8; uncertainties about, 25,
109–10, 117–19, 213. *See also* vocational retreats
reparation, 195–96, 197, 198, 225
reproduction, 5, 260–61
restaurants, 269, 270
Reyes, Alfonso, 289
Ricoeur, Paul, 212, 304
Riding, Alan, 282–83
ritual practices and ritualization: boundaries in, 133; of daily practices,
214–15; in eating disorders, 23–24;
for entering/leaving chapel, 138; of
healing, 47

Rivera, Diego, 289
Rodríguez murder, 280
romantic period, 38
Rosalita, Mother, 49
Rosary, 176, 177, 201, 311
Rose of Lima, 73
Rosita (postulant): age of, 9; appearance of, 125; characteristics of, 114–15; clique of, 117, 124–25; examination of conscience and, 182, 185; on leaving family, 112–13; on Mexican culture, 258; on penitence, 190; on prayer, 204; recreation project of, 173; on reparation, 196
Ruth (postulant): age of, 9; on humility, 77; on Jesus and the paralytic, 199; on mission, 205, 207–8; recreation project of, 173; weight and appetite of, 156, 167

sacrament and sacramentals, 311
sacrifice, 81–82, 175. See also *entrega*
saints' relics, 34
salvation: femininity as pivotal to, 59, 61; postulant's decision as part of plan of, 213, 232; role of surrender in, 81–82; through suffering, 34
Schindler's List (film), 151
schools, boarding, 58–59
seat of being perspective: description of, 37–40; illusion of interiority compared with, 41, 43–44
Second Coming, 34
secular rationalist philosophy: critique of, 54–56; femininity of antidote to, 57, 59–60
self: body as expression of, 5, 6, 247; contradictory constructions of, 16; disillusionment with, 185, 192; as function of language, 43; gender-neutral theories of, 45, 242; God and soul in relation to, 82–83, 84, 131; God and world in relation to, 71, 83, 202; as illusion of interiority, 40–44; infant treated as, 236; misrecognition of, 17, 246; missionizing of, 205–8; "natural" state of, 44; navigating temporal differences and, 211–12; new way of knowing, 19–20; posture as revealing attitude of, 175–76; preconvent, 8; rearticulation of, 87–88, 225–28; religious formation as model of, 229; religious vocation as story of, 212–14, 212–25; as seat of being, 37–40; selfobject as part of, 238n4; severing and reintegration of, 209; surrender

of, 72–73; tensions between embodied and transcendental, 161–62; theorizing of, 37, 43–44, 242, 303–8. See also embodiment; experiential self; self psychology; subjectivity; virtual self
Self-critique: concept of, 16, 18; as expression of self-hatred and doubt, 232; healing in, 201–2; as internalization of power structures, 230; introduced to postulants, 180–81; mechanism of, 181–85; in psychodynamic model, 251; righting wrongs found in, 186–92; understanding betrayal of God in, 185–86
selfobject needs: concept of, 236–37; difficulties with early, unmet, 240n5; remobilizing of, in analysis, 237–40
self psychology: applied to regendering of embodied subject, 245–49; Benjamin on, 242–45; empathic environment concept in, 235–37; Kohut on, 234, 235–37; optimal frustration concept in, 237–39; rethinking mechanisms of, 240–41
Seventh Day Adventists, 207
sexuality: channeling of, 157–58; as dangerous force, 34–35; as metaphor of nationalist concerns, 273; power structures of, 40–41. See also gender
Shane, Estelle, 235, 240
Shane, Morton, 235, 240
Sherwood, Anna, 279–80
sibling order of postulants, 10, 11
Siervas: charism of, 91, 103, 197, 225; desire to be, 21, 61, 257–58; as devoted to founder, 52, 60–61; duties of, 90; empathy and support from, 121–22; food and, 25; founding of, 51, 52, 281; hierarchy of, 74–75; integration into, 111; mission of, 2, 12, 56, 70, 77, 90, 194, 195, 198, 302; naturalization of decision to join, 112; number of, 61, 194; physical activities of, 36, 154, 168–71; relationships among, 117, 118, 131, 171, 187; requirements for joining, 105–6; revival of interest in, 3; studying history of, 12; use of term, 2; on vocation, 7; vocation narratives on, 218, 226, 227. See also aspirants; junior sisters; mistress of postulants; mother general; mother superior; novices; postulants; professed sisters; third probation sisters

sign of the cross, 311
silence: concept of, 152–53; obedience in, 82, 167; during occupations, 170
simplicity, 80, 194
Simpsons, The (television show), 62, 292
sin: bodily dimensions of, 34–35; disobedience as function of, 76; distance created by, 87; as metaphysical problematic, 84–85; as state of humankind, 202; vanity as, 163, 167; verbalization of, 176
singing, 177
sisters. *See* nuns
Sisters of Guadalupe, 218
skin color, 125–26
soap operas, 285n10, 294
sociability, 171–73
social justice/injustice, 13, 60, 151
social relations, 38–39, 133–34. *See also* Belonging
sociopolitical context: congregation's history in context of, 51–53; regendering in dialogue with, 6; religious formation in, 266, 271–72; religious vocation in, 256–58, 307–8
solidarity: challenges of, 111–19; importance of, 122–24, 131. *See also* Belonging
soul: body's relationship with, 35–36, 165, 176, 178–79; chastity and, 73; clean body as evidence of clean, 163; Foucault on, 41; God and self in relation to, 82–83, 84, 131; nuns' belief in, 44; posture as evidence for attitude of, 175; rearticulation of, 87–88, 225–28; as revealed and affected by embodiment, 251
Spain: as colonial power, 274–75; overthrow of, 276
speech: containment of, 152–53; at mealtimes, 166–68; practices of piety in, 176–78. *See also* language
Spinoza, Baruch, 211
spiritual advisors: designation of, 103–4; recommendations of, 105, 106; response to women's call from God, 97–98
spirituality: as answer to brokenness, 226; proper attitudes toward, 204–5. *See also* religiosity; religious vocation; soul
spiritual poverty concept, 72–73
sponsor nuns, 66–67
Stations of the Cross, 201, 206–7, 312
Stepansky, Paul E., 240
Stolorow, Robert D., 235

story of self: reading future in past of, 215–25; religious vocation as, 212–14; resituation of life trajectory in, 225–27
subjectivity: critique of, 56–61; as dependent on relationship with others, 242–44; as experience of cathexis, 304–6; as female, Mexican, Catholic, 12; in institutional settings, 22–23; in Mexican context, 295–96; processes in, 14, 235, 244; psychoanalytic perspective on, 233; rearticulation/reformation of, 18, 19–20; selfhood and sameness in, 212; theorizing of, 43–44; use of term, 40. *See also* gender; intersubjectivity; religious formation; self
submission: surrender as, 230; to will of God, 86–87, 109–10, 202–5, 208–9
suffering, 34, 194
Surella (postulant): age of, 9; on entering convent, 108; family of, 125; friendships of, 117; on habit and veil, 149–50; personal items of, 142; on prayer, 204; recreation project of, 173; on religious vocation, 97; on reparation, 197; rule breaking by, 130; on Siervas, 105, 256; silence and, 167; team-building activities and, 124; on women's roles, 254–55
Surrender: concept of, 16, 18; empathic identification in, 195–97; as essential, 203, 204–5; missions and, 205–8; power of, 208–9; in prayer and worship, 198–205; in psychodynamic model, 251–52; role in salvation, 81–82; of self, 72–73; sense of release in, 232; as submission to regulation, 230; trust in, 130. *See also entrega*
sweets, 142, 155–56

talents and skills, 77, 78
technologies: for cultivating subjectivity, 12; of embodiment, 65, 306–7; of gender, 45
technologies of enclosure: architecture as, 134–46; body management as, 150–58; as process of interiority, 20, 159; theorizing of, 132–34; uniform as, 146–50
Tere, Mother, 103
Teresa of Ávila, 24, 33
Teresita, Sister: Magda's relationship with, 117–18, 138, 141, 142, 167, 186–88, 203; on penitence, 189

Terman, David M., 240
Thea (postulant): age of, 9; appearance of, 125; on applications for novitiate, 129; clique of, 117; diet of, 154–55, 156–57; examination of conscience and, 181–82; on humility, 77; on religious vocation, 66, 98; on women, 258
therapeutic relationship: gender and body in, 241–45, 247; model of, 248–49, 249; processes in, 234–35; recognition/misrecognition in, 243–44, 246–48; rethinking mechanisms in, 240–41; transforming work of, 237–40
Theresa, Saint, 91
thinking body concept, 47
third probation sisters, 15, 68, 139
time: concepts of, 210–12; cycling and overlapping of, 212–13; daily activities in both worldly and sacred, 214–15; as organized in Catholicism, 15; rearticulation of self and soul in two frames of, 227–28; in vocation narratives, 215–16, 225–27
Tolpin, Marian, 240–41
traditions: femininity, Catholicism, and national identity triangulated in, 64, 294–95, 298–99; individualism vs., 292–93; postulants on, 259; woman's role in, 11, 57–58, 62–63, 63, 254–55, 258, 284–86, 301
transformation of subjectivity. See religious formation
trauma: selfobject needs and, 237
traumatic misrecognition: concept of, 246; responsibility for, 251; in therapeutic model, 248–49, 249
Trinity, 312
trust, 129–30, 131, 142, 144
truth, 38, 77
Turner, Frederick C., 280
Turner, Victor W., 133
twelve-step programs, 127n1

uniforms: color of, 104; as containment, 146–50; marked with embroidery, 172; of novices, 68; of postulants, 2, 67, 108; provision of, 72; as regimentation, 164–65; requirements for, 106–7; as symbol of poverty, 71
United States: appeal of, 13; differentiation from, 287, 295; as economic and political power, 54–55, 291–92; as evil force, 12, 292; feminist plot of, 300–302; as masculine, 12, 294,

295, 296, 297–98; Mexican hatred of, 279–80; Mexico invaded by, 267, 278–79; as model, 275, 276; as Protestant, 297–98; questions about, 62, 173; as threat, 255–56

Van Gennep, Arnold, 133
vanity, 163, 167
Vasconcelos, Jose, 289
vectors of recognition concept, 251
veils, 147–50
Veronica, Mother: advice from, 225; on chastity, 73–74; on examinations of conscience, 181–85; on falling asleep, 162; on getting down to business, 122; on gossip and factionalism, 124; on group dynamics, 8; on humility, 77–80; on Jesus and the paralytic, 199; on "Jesus in their wombs," 261; on martyrs, 196; on men, 158; on missions, 205, 207; on penitence and mortification, 189, 190, 192; on perfectionism, 197; on personal hygiene, 163–64; on poverty, 71, 72–73; on prayer, 175, 200–202, 204; on purity, 80; recreation projects of, 171–73; on religious formation, 69; on religious vocation, 91, 109; on reparation, 195; on separation by levels of formation, 139, 141; on shoes, 147; on silence, 152–53; on suffering, 194; sweets and, 155–56; tasks of, 126–27, 128–29, 144, 151; team-building activities of, 123–24; Teresita and Magda's relationship and, 117; trust of, 130; on uniforms, 148–49; on vanity, 167; on work, 169–71
Virgin of Guadalupe, 272, 274, 275, 281
virtual self: as always gendered, 247; claiming of, in therapy, 246–47; convent program's presentation of, 250–51; parental response to, 236–37, 239–40; use of term, 21
vocation, 7, 14. See also religious vocation
vocational retreats: attendees at, 96; closing ceremony of, 104–5; as deepening awareness of brokenness, 102–3; fees for, 99; Mary as model at, 101–2; materials for, 95, 97–98; orientation interviews at, 100; requirements for participating in, 98–99; selecting congregation in, 103–4; setting of, 99–100; struggles at, 260; vocation narratives on, 218, 219, 220, 221, 224

vocation narratives. *See* Re/collection
vows: of chastity, 73–74; concerns about,
103; of obedience, 74–76; perpetual,
68–69; as pillar of religious formation, 70, 89; of poverty, 70–73

War of Independence, 267, 275, 277, 279
watches, 147
wedding rings, 68–69, 104, 148
Wilhelmina, Mother: on chapel's design,
138; on eating, 165; on Mexican
governments, 265; on postulants,
121; on prayer, 200; on work, 165,
169
Winnicott, D. W., 234
woman/women: anxieties about roles of,
120, 260–61; chastity of, 73, 74;
"civilizing" of, 285; marginalization
of, 290–91, 293; Mary as model of,
101–2; masculinization of, 298;
mission of, 56–61; modern role of,
254–55; nation as, 272–74; regeneration of, 227, 259–60, 294–95,
298–302; "third way" of being, 64,
259–60; traditional role of, 11,
57–58, 62–63, 63, 254–55, 258,
284–86, 301
work: eating in relation to, 165, 168; as
expression of humility, 170; with
poor, 165, 222; regimentation of,
168–71
world: God and self in relation to, 71,
83, 202; as hostile and dangerous,
136; letting go of, 144–45, 218;
managing distractions of, 83,
159–60; prayer in, 198–99; reorientation to, 208–9; as temptation, 186;
transformed relationship to, 85–86
World Conference of Bishops, 268
worship. *See* Mass; prayer

Youth House retreats, 99–100
Youth Missionary League, 216

Zapatista: as symbol, 288
Zar cult, 46–47
Zarragoza, General, 267
Zea, Leopoldo, 289

Compositor: International Typesetting and Composition
Indexer: Margie Towery
Text: 10/13 Sabon
Display: Sabon
Printer and Binder: Maple-Vail Manufacturing Group